HIS EXCELLENCY GEORGE CLINTON

THE MACMILLAN COMPANY
NEW YORK · BOSTON · CHICAGO · DALLAS
ATLANTA · SAN FRANCISCO

MACMILLAN & CO., Limited
LONDON · BOMBAY · CALCUTTA
MELBOURNE

THE MACMILLAN COMPANY
OF CANADA, Limited
TORONTO

GEORGE CLINTON

From a painting by Ezra Ames

HIS EXCELLENCY GEORGE CLINTON

Critic of the Constitution

by

E. WILDER SPAULDING

NEW YORK

THE MACMILLAN COMPANY

1938

PRINTED IN THE UNITED STATES OF AMERICA
NORWOOD PRESS LINOTYPE, INC.
NORWOOD, MASS., U.S.A.

To
J. B. S.

FOREWORD

GEORGE CLINTON was one of the foremost of the prophets and agitators of the American Revolution; he was perhaps the greatest of all the war governors; he was the foremost opponent of the Constitution of 1787; and he was a figure to be reckoned with in virtually every New York gubernatorial contest and in every national election until his death in 1812. The friend and trusted colleague of Washington, the foe of Hamilton and Burr, the rival of Jefferson, the uncle of DeWitt Clinton, and the father-in-law of the notorious Citizen Genêt, he exerted a quiet but amazingly persistent influence upon men and politics in New York and the nation for over forty years.

Yet he has been all but forgotten by the historian. He is the most important individual in American history who has not had a biography. Historians of the Federalist school who have, for better or for worse, dominated the writing of history in America, very naturally disliked Clinton because of his fervid Antifederalism; New England historians have had no love for the New Yorker who so bluntly expressed his unflattering opinions about New England troops and generals and who was so ready to resort to arms to keep Vermont subject to New York; and those who worship at the shrine of Hamilton, who have been legion, have taken pains to ignore Hamilton's greatest New York rival or to damn him with the faintest of praise. Yet Clinton is an immensely significant figure because he does represent the radical republicanism and democratic ferment of his times that Hamilton so distrusted.

Without men of his stamp the American Revolution would have been only a political movement, not a democratic one. And after the states had cut loose from monarchy, he worked to build a true political democracy in America. Other Americans preached the doctrines of the Declaration of Independence only while the war lasted; Clinton never forgot them. He remained a sincere democrat and a fanatical republican in an era when every democrat and every republican was suspected of rank Jacobinism.

Consequently he became a rallying point for the masses who sought complete liberty from England and genuine Republicanism in America. Few men of his generation enjoyed such a following, in war and politics, as did George Clinton. The masses of men admired his rugged, manly qualities, his integrity and his essential democracy. They loved and followed him because of that very simplicity of character—naïveté, perhaps—that has made him seem uninteresting to the historian searching for profundities.

Born in rural New York, the son of an immigrant surveyor and farmer, himself a surveyor, soldier, farmer, country lawyer, land trader and politician, he was of common clay, and men of common clay revered and trusted him. They sent him to the provincial assembly for seven years and to the Continental Congress, applauded when he was made both a state and a Continental brigadier general, elected him seven times governor of New York, chose him to oppose a federal Constitution that they heartily disliked, and made him twice vice president of the United States. They nearly succeeded in making him president. Surely no New Yorker of his entire generation had nearly so great and so devoted a following in his own state as had Clinton. Hamilton's popularity with the rank and file did not begin to approach the governor's. The masses of men suspected Hamilton of leaning toward monarchy, of conspiring to create an autocratic central government that would destroy the states, and of trying to build a governmental system for the benefit of the bankers, merchants, and gentlemen of blue blood. Clinton they knew to be a genuine republican, a foe of centralization in government, and an enemy of banks and of the time-honored alliance between the mercantile and the landholding families.

It has been said that the American character is a strange combination of idealism and materialism, a dualism somewhat like that which John Randolph found in the alliance of John Quincy Adams and Henry Clay and so aptly characterized as the union of Puritan and Blackleg. George Clinton, like so many of his fellows in that formative period of American life, combined the idealistic and the sentimental with the grossly materialistic. On the one side he possessed a refreshing and almost fanatical faith in the future of American institutions and in political democracy, and on the other hand he shared the unlovely enthusiasms of his age for shillings and pence, for speculations in land and, even less fortunately, for practical politics. In his shortcomings as in his virtues, he was, however, no mere "stuffed shirt." He was perhaps only too typical of his age.

Had he possessed Jefferson's eloquence in ink he might have been the first Republican president. But he was no philosopher, except in the homeliest sense of that word, and the Virginian instead of the New Yorker became the standard bearer of the Republican cause. Lacking the power of the pen, Clinton could win to his cause only the men with whom he came into immediate contact. He remained, therefore, a local figure to the end of his life, but a local figure of such importance that he became vice president of the Union and several times a serious candidate for the presidency.

CONTENTS

ILLUSTRATIONS

HIS EXCELLENCY GEORGE CLINTON

CHAPTER I

BLUE BLOOD

GEORGE CLINTON'S NOBLE ANCESTORS

A ROYALIST GREAT-GRANDFATHER

CHARLES CLINTON'S TRAGIC VOYAGE

CHARLES MEETS THE FIRST GOVERNOR GEORGE

HE ADMONISHES HIS SON

A POLITICALLY PROLIFIC FAMILY

WHEN George Clinton became the first governor of the state of New York, a famous contemporary commented that Clinton's family connections did not entitle him to such a distinction. Yet Clinton had noble blood in his veins. He was a direct descendant of Henry the second Earl of Lincoln. His ancestry can be traced back to John of Gaunt, to the famous Lord Henry Percy known as Hotspur, and to most of the Plantagenets. He was also a distant cousin of that other George Clinton, the son of the sixth Earl of Lincoln, who was governor of the province of New York from 1743 to 1753, and of his son, Sir Henry Clinton, the gallant British officer who occupied New York City during some months of the Revolution. Of this ancestry there can be but little doubt.

The Earls of Lincoln were of the English family of Clinton; and the seal of the New York Clintons, which Governor George Clinton used in 1777 as his official seal before the New York state seal was designed, was similar to the arms of the Earls of Lincoln. Not only does the similarity between the two seals show the relationship between the two families, but it also makes it clear that the ancestors of Governor George, who are known to have been in Ireland for several generations before their migration to New York, were in all probability descended from the English Clintons and had migrated to Ireland after the adoption of the Lincoln arms in comparatively recent times.[1] That is, they did not belong to any Irish branch of the family and George Clinton was not an Irishman as so many historians have asserted. This is not to say that he did not, through his mother, have a splendid dash of Celtic blood in his veins, a dash that may have been responsible for some of his most attractive qualities.

There is conclusive evidence of the relationship of Governor George with the Earls of Lincoln. A Sir Henry Clinton, "vulgarly called Fynes," was the first son, by the second wife, of the second Earl of Lincoln. Sir Henry took unto himself a second wife who was "full of divilish and unreformable humors." This couple had two sons of whom William the younger seems to have been that mysterious great-grandfather of Governor George Clinton about whom much has been written but little is known.

This great-grandfather, the key figure in establishing Governor George's family tree, used in 1663 the surname "Fiennes," one of the spellings of "Fynes," a family name acquired by the Clintons through a fifteenth-century marriage long before Good Queen Bess created Edward Clinton Earl of Lincoln. Inasmuch as great-grandfather William used both surnames, Clinton and Fynes, he is in all probability the William Clinton, "son of Sir Henry Clinton, alias Fynes, of Kirkstead Co. Lincoln, Knt, dec'd," who was in 1650 apprenticed for eight years to William Methold, "Skinners Company." [2] Although it has been stated that William was the son of Sir Thomas and the grandson of Edward the first earl, that parentage seems most un-

---

[1] Arthur Pound, *Native Stock* (New York, 1931), 152. In August 1777 the Council of Safety of New York gave Governor Clinton permission to use his personal seal for official purposes. I. N. P. Stokes, *Iconography of Manhattan Island* (6 vols., New York, 1915–28), V, 1054.

[2] The statement regarding the apprenticeship was furnished in 1933 by M. I. Holden, Kirkstead Manse, Woodhall Spa, Lincolnshire, to Dr. Joseph M. Beatty Jr. of Baltimore, a descendant of the sister of the first American Clinton. For the Clinton ancestry see also Dr. Beatty's excellent accounts in the *New York Genealogical and Biographical Record,* LI (1920), 360–61 and LXVI (1935), 330–35; Arthur Collins, *Peerage of England* (7 vols., London, 1768); Cuyler Reynolds, ed., *Genealogies of Southern New York* (New York, 1914), 542. Beatty quotes from the family Bible of George Clinton regarding the Clinton ancestory, *loc. cit.,* LXVI, 331.

likely. Had he been the son of Sir Thomas he would have been an elderly gentleman by 1661 when he was, as a matter of fact, doing active service in the army. It is much more probable that he was the grandson of the second Earl of Lincoln and the son of Sir Henry Clinton who was not married until 1624.

After the period of his apprenticeship, which may have lasted to 1658, William Clinton's career is not easy to trace. Governor George wrote years later in his Bible that Sir William was a Royalist who was forced to leave England to find asylum in Spain; he then went to Scotland where he married an Elizabeth Kennedy, and later to Ireland to settle on his estate, "Glengary." General James Clinton, the brother of Governor George, told a similar story and attributed it to his father. An ingenious descendant of William Clinton, alias Fynes, has pointed out that if Clinton did escape from Cromwell's England to France, he would probably have gone to Spain with the many other Royalist soldiers who deserted France after Cromwell made peace with Louis XIV in 1655. Subsequent to the Restoration, Charles II brought a body of these Royalist troops from Spain to garrison the great fortress of Dunkirk, which was in the hands of the English from 1658 to 1662, and we find that an officer named Fiennes was in the British regiment under Sir Robert Harley which left Dunkirk in December 1661. Two years later a Captain Finnes, alias Clinton, was serving in the Tangier Regiment and in July 1666 Captain William Clinton received a lieutenant's commission in the Holland Regiment.[3] It is entirely possible then, that William, the great-grandfather of Governor George, did in fact escape from Commonwealth England to serve with the exiled Royalists in France and Spain, and that he remained in active service in the army for some years after the Restoration. It does not, however, seem quite fitting that Governor George, New York's first great democratic statesman, should have had a Royalist ancestor.

Why Sir William went to Scotland we do not know. Whether he moved on to Northern Ireland because he had acquired a fondness

---

[3] Beatty, *loc. cit.*, LI, 360–61. Beatty cites Charles Dalton, ed., *The English Army Lists and Commission Registers, 1661–1714* (4 vols., London, 1892), and Richard Cannon, *History of the First or Royal Regiment of Foot* (London, 1847).

for roving, or because an appreciative Stuart king had rewarded his services with an estate there, or whether he found Scotland too much in turmoil politically and religiously to suit him, I have not been able to discover. It seems probable, however, that he died on Irish soil leaving Governor George's grandfather, James, an orphan at the age of two.

Family tradition has it that this James returned to England to claim his patrimonial estates but succeeded only in obtaining a wife, a certain Elizabeth Smith, who was the daughter of an officer of the Commonwealth.[4] He returned to Ireland, took up arms in the cause of William of Orange and, it is said, as a reward for his valiant services in the defense of Enniskillen, acquired an estate in the County of Longford, a county in central Ireland that had been "planted" with English and Scotch settlers by the first Stuarts.[5] Like his father, James was a Presbyterian.

His son Charles, the father of Governor George, was born at Corbay, County Longford, in 1690. It was over thirty years later that this gentleman was married to a young Irish woman named Elizabeth Denniston who was to outlive her husband and to see her son the first governor of an American state. In spite of William Dunlap's acrid pen which wrote over a century later that Charles Clinton "had married below himself an Irish drab,"[6] Elizabeth Denniston seems to have been a woman of wit and ability who could write a charming letter in an age when charm was sadly lacking in family correspondence. If Elizabeth Denniston was indeed of Scotch ancestry, as has been asserted, then her seven children had in their veins blood that was entirely Scotch and English.[7]

[4] Charles A. Clinton's sketch of the Clinton family in A. C. Niven, ed., *The Centennial Memorial: Hundredth Anniversary of the A. R. Presbyterian Church of Little Britain* (New York, 1859), 225.

[5] W. W. Campbell, *Life and Writings of DeWitt Clinton* (New York, 1849); Charles B. Moore, "History of the Clinton Family," *New York Genealogical and Biographical Record*, XII, 198; Dorothie Bobbé, *DeWitt Clinton* (New York, 1933), 4. James Clinton died January 24, 1717–18 and his wife December 5, 1728 according to C. B. Moore, *loc. cit.*

[6] New York Historical Society, *Collections* [1931], "Diary of William Dunlap," 679.

[7] C. B. Moore in *New York Genealogical and Biographical Record*, XIII, 5. Sympathetic sketches of Elizabeth Denniston appear in Bobbé, *op. cit.*, and in Charles A. Clinton, *op. cit.*

Like so many thousands of Scotch-Irish families during the generation that followed the Battle of the Boyne, the Clintons found life in Ireland intolerable. Elder Charles Clinton of the Corbay congregation discovered that the ruling classes had little use for dissenters. English conquerors imposed economic shackles on Irish industry and it is probable that the estate at Corbay did not prosper. There were many other nonconformists in the neighborhood who were willing to try their fortunes in Pennsylvania; so Clinton leased his estate for a long term of years to Lord Granard and with four hundred kindred spirits organized a large party of emigrants, chartered at Dublin a ship called the *George and Anne,* and sailed for America on May 20, 1729. The *George and Anne* was of about ninety tons, approximately half the size of the *Mayflower.*

The voyage was a tragic one. The Clintons took with them their three small children: Catharine who had been born in 1723, James born in 1726, and Mary born less than a year before, in July 1728. Of the three, only Catharine survived the epidemic of measles that broke out soon after the ship left Dublin. Mary and George and over ninety other passengers died before they saw the American coast on October 4! It would seem from his diary that Charles Clinton accepted the gruesome voyage philosophically enough; but tradition has it that, enraged by Captain Rymer's criminal incapacity or duplicity, Clinton schemed to seize the ship but failed to get the support of his fellow passengers. They were finally landed, not at Philadelphia, but at Cape Cod, where they seem to have remained until the following year when they arrived in Ulster County, New York, and settled at Little Britain not far from the west bank of the Hudson.[8]

Thus was founded the American branch of a family that was to give New York a great political dynasty and was probably to give America more place names than any other family has been responsible for.

[8] Charles Clinton's diary of the voyage is printed in *Olde Ulster* (10 vols., Kingston, N.Y., 1905–14), IV, 175–80. A typed copy is in the New York State Library. See also David Hosack, *Memoir of DeWitt Clinton* (New York, 1829), 137–39, extract from the journel of Dr. David Young, a descendant of one of the emigrants; and Charles A. Clinton, *loc. cit.,* 225–26. Little Britain is now in Orange County.

Charles Clinton was in every way an exemplary ancestor. Even the ill-natured Tory historian, Thomas Jones, wrote kindly of him, calling him "open, generous, and hospitable," an honest man and a loyal subject. He was tall and of commanding appearance. His contemporaries were impressed with his polish, his knowledge of literature and the arts, and his facility as a mathematician. Cadwallader Colden, the surveyor-general of the province, employed Clinton as his deputy for the survey of lands in Orange County as early as 1731 and in later years, and seems always to have had the utmost confidence in him. In 1748 Colden sent Charles Clinton to his distant cousin, Governor George Clinton, that "jolly toaper," with a letter recommending the surveyor as "a person I can safely trust who on all occasion has shown the greatest regard for your Excellency and your family as well as for me." The governor in his reply said nothing of family connections, but referred to "Mr. Clinton who I take to be a very good Sort of a Man & coud have wished I had been acquainted with him sooner." [9] The governor showed his good will by offering him the office of sheriff of the City and County of New York "or any other commission" in his power; but Clinton, who was in "good business" and so had no need for assistance from the public treasury, declined.

The governor showed a special interest in his namesake, Charles Clinton's boy George. He named the boy to be clerk of the Court of Common Pleas of Ulster County, the appointment to be consummated at the time of the death of John Crook, the incumbent. Accordingly, George Clinton was to serve as clerk of the county court of Ulster, in person or through his deputy, from 1759 to his death in 1812. One of New York's most outspoken republicans did not object to holding for fifty-three years an office which the royal governor had bestowed upon him.

Like so many of his contemporaries Surveyor Charles Clinton dabbled in land. He saw active service in the French and Indian War, was appointed a justice of the peace, and served from 1769 to his

[9] New York Historical Society, *Collections*, "Cadwallader Colden Papers" (New York, 1918–23), II, 43, 155, 161; IV, 47, 61, 62; VI, 342.

death as first judge of the Ulster Court of Common Pleas.[10] It is said that when he died at Little Britain November 19, 1773, he implored his youngest son George "to stand by the liberties of America." George needed no such admonition.

A generation later the descendants of Charles Clinton were accused of monopolizing the best political offices in the state. Of his seven children only three survived him. Two had died on the fearful voyage to America. Catharine, the eldest, who in 1749 married neighbor James McClaughry, died without children in 1762. The promising young physician Alexander graduated from the College of New Jersey, learned to know music and the broadsword, studied "physic" under a Dr. Peter Middleton at New York, and practiced medicine in Ulster County. He married Mary Kane, but left no children when he died in March 1758, in his twenty-sixth year. His brother Charles, two years his junior, was also a physician, also studied under Dr. Middleton and returned to practice in Little Britain. After his father's death he moved to Hanover, a few miles away. Although he served in 1775 and 1776 on the Hanover and Ulster County committees and in the Provincial Congress which met in May 1775, he was apparently not an ardent patriot. He died, unmarried, in 1791.[11]

Charles Clinton's most prolific son was that substantial old warrior, surveyor, and farmer, Brigadier General James. James seems to have been stolid and unsociable, with a fondness for soldiering but no gift for politics. Born on August 9, 1736, he served in the French and Indian War and returned to make an excellent marriage in 1765 with Mary, the "aimiable, sensible" daughter of Egbert DeWitt—the DeWitts were Dutch and had influence in Ulster. His services during the Revolution won for him a comfortably large niche in history. General James spent most of his long career on or near his father's home at Little Britain. After his marriage and until his

[10] *New York State Library Bulletin*, Number 58, March 1902, "Calendar of Council Minutes 1668–1783," p. 328; E. M. Ruttenber, *History of New Windsor* (Newburgh, N.Y., 1911), 135.

[11] Dr. Joseph Young as quoted in Hosack, *op. cit.*, 139f., describes the children of Charles Clinton, the immigrant. Dr. Charles was born July 20, 1734.

father's death in 1773 he lived at the village of New Windsor and it was probably nearly thirty years later that he built his own home in Little Britain, a house that is still standing. He died on December 22, 1812, a man of means and of lands.

James was the patriarch who was largely responsible for the politically appalling spread of the Clinton family tree. His first son Alexander was for a time secretary to Governor Clinton; his second son Charles became clerk of the United States District Court; DeWitt, the third son, at one time or another held nearly every important political office within the gift of the State; George served in the State assembly and in Congress; Mary the fifth child and Catharine the second both married the politically prominent Judge Ambrose Spencer; and Elizabeth the sixth married William Stuart, the district attorney. By his second wife, Mrs. Mary Little Gray, General James had six children, raising his total to an impressive thirteen. The six children of his younger brother, Governor George, could show no such record of important political marriages. Indeed, General James and his brood were to prove far more useful supporters of George Clinton's political fortunes than were George's own progeny.

CHAPTER II

WAR, LAW, AND THE SEXTANT

CHARLES' YOUNGEST SON IS BORN

THE ULSTER SETTING

GEORGE'S SCHOOLING AND CHURCHING

HE GOES PRIVATEERING

A HEROIC TRADITION BLASTED

GEORGE AND LORD JEFFREY AMHERST

HIS NAVAL VICTORY

HE PREFERS THE LAW

HE SURVEYS THE NEW JERSEY BOUNDARY

GEORGE CLINTON, the youngest child of Charles the immigrant and the subject of this book, was born on July 26, 1739 at the homestead in Little Britain. In 1739 dull, methodical George II had been king of Britain for twelve years; little George Washington had just passed seven; and of George Clinton's great rivals of later years, John Adams was a chubby tot of four, while Jefferson's birth was four years in the future, Burr's seventeen and Hamilton's a full eighteen. The American Revolution was in the cradle.

Little Britain, then in Ulster County and later made a part of Orange County, was a tiny frontier settlement situated southwest of Newburgh and two or three miles west of the Hudson and west of the little village of New Windsor. It was so near to the unsettled Indian country that Charles Clinton is said to have fortified his home for protection against attack—as well he might. Neither reds nor whites had much regard for the distant hand of the law in those primitive days. In the early months of the French and Indian War, for instance, we find Charles Clinton informing the governor that the

Indians had killed a certain Morgan Owen of Ulster County and that the whites had avenged the killing with compound interest by massacring four Indians, three squaws, and two papooses![1] Ulster in 1756 was no peaceful Arcadia. It was a part of the first American frontier.

Although the Clinton family possessed some good meadow land, the country was generally rough and the soil thin and uncongenial to the plow. According to William Smith, the eighteenth century historian of the province, Ulster County was noted more for the fine quality of its millstones than for its other products: flour, beer, and draught horses.[2] It is not surprising that most of the Clintons turned to other occupations to supplement the meagre income that they wrung from their lands.

The sterility of Ulster's agriculture had its compensations, however. The county was not overrun with great manorial estates like those to the east and north which monopolized the finest lands and settled them with a subservient tenantry. There were no haughty patroons. Although a prosperous country gentleman like General James Clinton might have a negro slave or two,[3] and other men of means might rent small holdings of fifty to one hundred acres to their tenants, the Ulster farmers, unlike the patroons of Westchester, Dutchess, and Albany Counties, usually worked their own fields and milled their own flour. They were of many stocks—Scotch-Irish, English, Dutch, Huguenot, and Palatine. A serious, earnest folk, they were "not so gay a people as our neighbors in Boston, and several of the southern colonies."[4] The Anglican Church, which had been established in other less primitive counties of the province, had only a few communicants in Ulster. Such a region was almost certain to be democratic in its politics.

[1] Letter of March 4, 1756, in Historical Society of Pennsylvania.
[2] S. W. Eager, *An Outline History of Orange County* (Newburgh, N.Y., 1846–47), 608; William Smith, *History of the Province of New York to 1762* (2 volumes, New York, 1830), I, 315f.
[3] James Clinton to DeWitt Clinton, November 4, 1793, DeWitt Clinton Letters, Columbia University Library, Col. James McClaughry who married a sister of George Clinton also kept slaves. Ruttenber, *op. cit.*, 128.
[4] William Smith, *op. cit.*, 328; E. M. Ruttenber, *Obstructions to the Navigation of Hudson's River* (Albany, 1860), 110–11.

BIRTHPLACE OF GEORGE CLINTON, LITTLE BRITAIN

George Clinton's birthplace was an unpretentious, story-and-a-half cottage, an eminently proper birthplace for a man of his democratic convictions. It had a large living, eating, and cooking room on the ground floor and one large bedroom under the rafters on the second floor. It was built like so many of the houses in provincial New York, of stone, with board siding on the gable ends and clumsy stone chimneys. As the Clintons prospered, additional rooms and kitchens were added. General James was the last of the Clintons to occupy the old house which was finally demolished later in the nineteenth century.

There were no public schools in the province and were to be none worthy of the name until Governor George Clinton himself should recommend them to his legislature a half century later. George Clinton's early education was therefore entrusted to a young Scotch clergyman named Daniel Thain who had graduated from the University of Aberdeen. It was said by an amiable contemporary of Governor George that "the activity and strength of the intellectual faculties of the young student became very perceptible at an early period, which caused him to be caressed by all his friends." [5] Nevertheless, it was only in his later years that he learned to write correct English and to spell passing well, and he was never an eager reader. We may suspect that he took more readily to mathematics, which was to make him a good surveyor, than to the classics.

Clinton's boyhood association with tutorial clergymen seems to have developed in him no enthusiasm for institutionalized religion, no piety in the orthodox sense. Yet he showed a proper interest in the church. The Clintons had been Presbyterians for three generations and Presbyterianism was very naturally the outstanding creed of the Scotch-Irish district in which George was brought up. It was the Bethlehem Church on the road to New Windsor that the Clintons attended. In 1773, George Clinton, then a leading citizen of the county, was made a Presbyterian trustee for the New Windsor district.[6] The Loyalist Thomas Jones called him a "rigid, true Presbyterian," but

[5] Dr. Joseph Young, loc. cit.
[6] Historical Society of Newburgh Bay and the Highlands, Publication Number III (1896), 9–10. Clinton's daughter Martha was baptized at the New Windsor Presbyterian Church, April 3, 1783. Ibid., p. 27.

we may suspect that the "rigidity" that Jones had in mind was not Clinton's orthodoxy but his dislike for Anglicans—so many of whom were to turn Tory in the Revolution. There is no evidence that he attended church regularly or had any considerable interest in church affairs. Some years after the Revolution his followers in New York City were accused of propagating deism and flouting orthodox Christianity. Probably Clinton's religion, like that of certain even more famous Americans of his era, was in fact deistic and little more. He referred vaguely to "the Supreme Dispenser of all good," to our "becoming gratitude to the great ruler of nations, on whose favor all our happiness depends," and hoped that he might "be able in some Measure to promote the Exercise of virtue and Religion which [he would] always consider as essential to the Existence of Freedom." Apparently "the Existence of Freedom" was the end to be achieved and virtue and religion (he mentioned virtue before religion) only the means. Clinton was brought up in a secular age in a province that had never been deeply touched by the religious currents of the time.[7]

The oft-told tale that George ran away in 1755 at the age of sixteen to go privateering against the French is in all probability only an interesting myth. The French and Indian War did indeed involve the American colonies as early as 1755, but it was not until the summer of 1756 that any considerable number of privateers went out from the port of New York.

George did, however, go privateering when he was eighteen. The newspapers in 1756 and 1757 carried alluring advertisements inviting "Gentlemen, Sailors and others" to ship on "private ships of war." Some of George Clinton's neighbors, such as old Captain Anthony Rutgers, went to sea to attempt to win fortunes at that highly respectable trade which was then recognized as a legitimate part of any war. Lieutenant de Lancey complained that "the Country is

---

[7] Ruttenber, op. cit., 37; Thomas Jones, History of New York during the Revolutionary War (2 vols., New York, 1879), II, 326; George Clinton, Public Papers of . . . (10 vols., New York and Albany, 1899–1914), II, 268; C. Z. Lincoln, ed., Messages from the Governors, Vol. II, 1777–1822 (Albany, 1909), 506, 541. John Wood's "A Full Exposition of the Clintonian Faction" (1802) exposes the deistic tendencies of the Clintonians in New York City.

drained of many able bodied men, by almost a kind of madness to go privateering," and in the first year and a half fifty-nine prizes were brought into New York. The valiant, greedy privateersmen from British ports played havoc with French shipping. A French officer at Quebec lamented that of the thirty-six ships that recently sailed from Bordeaux, twenty-four were missing. "The sea swarms with English privateers, and we have not one."[8] It was on October 4 in the fall of 1757 that young Clinton shipped on the *Defiance,* Captain Francis Koffler, of New York.[9]

During the spring of 1757 Koffler had commanded the privateer *Revenge,* a snow of 14 guns, on a West Indian cruise. His new ship, which carried 16 guns probably 16 pounders and 140 men, was not among the largest, but it was a sizeable vessel if compared with some of the smaller types of privateers, brigantines, and sloops, such as Alexander McDougall's *Tyger* with her 6 guns and a crew of 50 men. The owners petitioned in August 1757, for a commission for the *Defiance* and she was ready to sail the tenth of October.[10] George was then a big-boned, gawky lad of eighteen.

The voyage of the *Defiance,* which was principally in West Indian waters, was a long one, lasting over ten months. Clinton modestly wrote very little of himself in his diary except that on October 29 he was made "Stewarts mate." During the first few weeks the ships which they encountered proved to be too fast for the *Defiance* or turned out to be British or Dutch. Koffler did not hesitate to use the French flag, which Clinton called "the Pope's colors," to attract other vessels, or to speak to them in French.

[8] New York Historical Society *Collections,* 1931, III, 679; *New-York Mercury,* January 9, 1758 and *passim;* letters from de Lancey and M. Doreil in E. B. O'Callaghan, ed., *Documents Relative to the Colonial History of . . . New York,* VII (Albany, 1856), 343, and X (Albany, 1858), 718.

[9] A typed copy of Clinton's diary of part of his voyage, October 4, 1757–January 21, 1758, is in the State Library at Albany. This copy was certified by the Archivist, January 24, 1902, as a correct transcript of the whole of the original. The original was probably burned in the State Library fire. The copy is printed in *New York History,* Jan. 1935, 90–95, with a note by E. W. Spaulding.

[10] List of New York privateers, 1757, in *Historical Magazine,* Second Series, VI, 250; Stokes, *Iconography,* IV, 692, August 2, 1757; Report of New York State Historian, 1897, 508. The voyage of the *Defiance* can be followed in the *New-York Gazette,* October 3, 7, 1757 and *New-York Mercury,* January 2, 9, February 20, March 13, May 29, July 31, August 21, 1758.

Finally, on the first of December after a number of disappointments, the *Defiance* took a French ship, *La Fidelle,* bound from Cape Breton to Cape François and sent her back to New York where the cargo of fish and provisions was sold at auction at the New Wharf. Later in December the *Defiance* rescued the miserable crew of the sloop *Fanny,* bound to St. Kitts, which had lived for 103 days in the hull of the hurricane-swept sloop on flour, fish, and rain water. She passed Nevis and St. Eustatius on December 31, put in at St. Thomas in January, was seen off Haiti in February, and assisted the privateer brig *Duke of Marlborough* and another New York privateer in capturing on May 1 "a large French Dutch ship called the *Clara Magdalena"* which was bound for Amsterdam from Port au Prince with a cargo of sugar, coffee, and indigo. A few weeks later the *Defiance* was seen east of Bermuda and on August 14 she returned to New York. Young Clinton's share of prize money from the two or three captures, one of which had to be divided among the crews of three privateers, could not have brought him much of a return for months of hardship and it is not of record that he went privateering again.[11] Certainly the experience must have toughened the young man and put brawn on his powerful frame. It gave him almost the only glimpse of foreign lands that he was to have in his long career.

Meanwhile George's father was serving in New York against Louis XV. His friend Colden recommended him as a suitable man to survey the Minisink-Rochester frontier and, that accomplished, urged upon Governor Hardy that blockhouses be built as planned by Clinton and that Clinton be given a frontier command. It was upon Colden's recommendation in 1756 that Charles Clinton was appointed lieutenant-colonel of the second regiment of Ulster County.[12] Two years later he was happily transferred from service in the north, which saved him from participation in Abercrombie's bungling repulse before Ticonderoga, and ordered to serve under Colonel Bradstreet on the "secret" expedition to retake Fort Frontenac, on the present site of Kingston, Ontario, from the French. James Clinton was at the time a lieutenant in his father's regiment. Bradstreet's capture of Fort

---

[11] The *Defiance* does not appear to have made any other voyage in 1758.
[12] "Cadwallader Colden Papers," IV, 469; V, 66, 76, 83f., 106f., 254.

Frontenac, a mere skirmish, was, after the fall of Louisburg, the most important victory of the French and Indian War to that time.

Tradition to the contrary notwithstanding, George Clinton did not campaign against Fort Frontenac. The *Defiance* returned to New York only on August 14, 1758; Bradstreet was already at Wood Creek up in the northern forests of the province, and Fort Frontenac fell on August 27. There is nothing to indicate that Clinton had a commission in 1758, and if further proof of his innocence of all connection with the campaign against Fort Frontenac is needed, it may be added that his father left a diary of the expedition in which he makes several references to Captain James but says nothing of George. A father would scarcely have omitted all mention of a son, had that son served for weeks in his own regiment.[18]

In the fall of the next year, 1759, George Clinton fell heir to the not very profitable clerkship of Ulster County that the roistering Governor Clinton had promised him a few years earlier. The position did give him a taste of the law and it made it necessary for him to stay most of the time at the little metropolis of Kingston.[14] He grew restless, however, and in the spring of 1760, just before he reached man's estate, George Clinton was commissioned a lieutenant in his brother's new company.

All of the many accounts which have found their way into print of Clinton's service as a subaltern in his brother's company during the French and Indian War originated, in all probability, with the campaign of 1760 when James and George accompanied forces under Lord Jeffrey Amherst that captured Montreal and so made Canada irrevocably English. That campaign was Lieutenant George Clinton's only experience as a soldier before the outbreak of the Revolution.

James Clinton's company of 104 men, mustered in during April 1760, was an excellent cross-section of colonial Ulster. Three of the soldiers declared themselves to be English, 4 Scotch, 10 German, 36 Irish, 41

---

[18] That George Clinton served in his father's regiment in the Fort Frontenac campaign is stated in the introduction to the *Public Papers of George Clinton*, I, 17, and in numerous other accounts. A copy of Charles Clinton's diary is in the New York State Library.

[14] Charles Clinton to his "Dear Son," October 25, 1759, Historical Society of Pennsylvania.

native New Yorkers, and 10 natives of other colonies. They were farmers, cordwainers, weavers, blacksmiths, coopers, laborers, carpenters, and one a tailor. All were volunteers. Thirty had been enlisted by Lieutenant George Clinton. It was a company of the second New York regiment of provincials commanded by Colonel Isaac Corsa, a veteran of the Niagara expedition of 1759.[15]

Wolfe's great victory at Quebec had come in the previous September. Amherst planned for 1760 a decisive and systematic, but scarcely brilliant campaign that would wipe out the few remaining French garrisons in Canada, especially that at Montreal. While Murray was to come up the river from Quebec, Colonel Haviland was to advance on Montreal from Crown Point, and Amherst himself, with the Clinton brothers in his train, was to conduct the main army against that place by way of Oswego, Lake Ontario and the St. Lawrence River. In May and June Amherst was fretting at the "Sloth of the Colonies in raising their Troops," and sending them to the rendezvous. It was August 10 before he was ready to embark from Oswego with an army of nearly 11,000 men which included 706 Indians, 190 sailors for two armed vessels, 4479 provincial troops and 5586 British regulars. The three New York regiments commanded by Colonels Corsa, Le Roux, and Woodhull consisted altogether of over 1500 men.[16] Charles Clinton had sent his final advice to his sons, congratulating them upon their health, but suggesting that, to prevent fevers in August and September, they make use of an effective emetic.[17]

Accounts of the early career of George Clinton have generally been embellished with the story of a heroic naval engagement "on the northern waters, where with four gun boats, after a severe engagement, he captured a French brig of eighteen guns." Sometimes the story is related as of the campaign against Fort Frontenac and sometimes it is told in connection with the Amherst expedition of 1760. Often brother

[15] New York State Historian, Third Annual Report (Albany, 1897), 515, 536, 542–45. May 6, 1785 Clinton filed a claim for public land for his services as a provincial lieutenant; he withdrew the claim July 19. Calendar of Land Papers 1643–1803 (Albany, 1864), 670, 678.

[16] Amherst's letters to Pitt, Library of Congress Transcripts: Great Britain, Public Record Office, C.O. 5:58 and 59; A. G. Doughty, ed., Historical Journal of the Campaign in North America, 1757–60 by Captain John Knox (3 volumes, Toronto, 1916).

[17] Charles Clinton to James Clinton, July 21, 1760; Historical Society of Pennsylvania.

James is credited with a share in the achievement.[18] The actual engagement seems to have taken place a week after Amherst's army left Oswego in the upper Saint Lawrence near Oswegatchie, and, as a matter of fact, it is more than likely that the New York provincials played a necessary but inglorious part in the encounter.

Of two French vessels that had been hovering about during Amherst's passage down Lake Ontario, one, a brig with ten 12-pounders and 100 men, attempted to enter the Saint Lawrence. As Amherst's two snows had been delayed, he ordered Colonel Williamson to attack the French brig with his five row galleys. One of the galleys carried a howitzer, the others 12-pounders. The calm favored the row galleys and handicapped the French brig which fought bravely for four hours and then struck her colors. She had lost three killed and twelve wounded; in the row galleys a sergeant had been killed and a New York provincial had lost a leg. Observers agreed that the engagement had been gallantly fought; but the glory seems to have gone to the royal artillery, for a contemporary has recorded that the provincials "only rowed." [19] It seems probable, therefore, that Lieutenant Clinton was present only to supervise the oarsmen.

On the same day Amherst took Oswegatchie, now Ogdensburg, and eight days later, on August 25, the small French garrison of Fort Lévis surrendered. Then followed a strenuous voyage down the river in bad weather through fatal rapids where boats and stores were lost and eighty-four men were drowned in one day. Probably the New Yorkers saw more than their share of laborious boat service. Murray, Haviland, and Amherst arrived almost simultaneously before Montreal and Vaudreuil, helpless before the combined forces, signed on November 8, articles of capitulation by which all of New France passed to George II. The young Ulster lieutenant might well be proud of his part in such an event.

Although his brother James served several years longer in the New York forces, George, who never thoroughly enjoyed soldiering, had had enough of the war. Perhaps he realized that the army, in those

[18] *E.g.,* introduction to *Public Papers of George Clinton,* I, 16; *An Address to the People of the American States* (Washington, 1808).
[19] A. G. Doughty, *op. cit.,* II, 552; III, 87; Thomas Mante, *The History of the Late War in North-America* (London, 1772), 303.

days when British gentlemen monopolized the higher ranks, was not the most promising profession for the American-born. He returned home, obtained in December a reappointment as clerk of the Ulster County Court of Common Pleas, and soon went to New York City to read law in the office of William Smith the younger. For the country-bred son of a modest surveyor the months spent in the metropolis of 20,000 souls was a very satisfactory substitute for the college education that he never received. Indeed, three years in an excellent law office in the capital of the province may well have been worth far more to him than the scant Greek and laborious Latin to which he might otherwise have devoted his time.

William Smith the younger was one of the eminent lawyers of his day and, what was perhaps more important in shaping young Clinton's course, an outspoken critic of British policy, governor, and council. He had been educated at Yale, that breeding place of radicals, and he, with William Livingston and John Morin Scott, composed the republican triumvirate that by tongue and pen plagued the royal government of the province. They were Presbyterians and vigorous opponents of Anglican influence. Yet after the outbreak of the Revolution Smith was to declare for the king, exile himself from New York and become Chief Justice of Canada—the "very extraordinary and exceptional conduct of Mr. William Smith," George Clinton called it.[20] When Clinton went to New York Smith was in his early thirties but he had already written in 1757 his famous *History of the Province of New York*. His law office was to become a veritable school of law for promising young New Yorkers including such men as Robert R. Livingston and Gouverneur Morris.

Rural courts, justices, and lawyers in provincial New York were primitive enough. But the supreme court, the mayor's court and the bar in New York City were creditable and even distinguished. In the early sixties Clinton must have met and associated with many young lawyers of the metropolis who were later to distinguish themselves in war and politics. If we may judge from the following outline, found in the Smith papers, the training of candidates for the bar in New York City at that time was a broad one:

[20] Letter of 1780, George Clinton to Thomas Smith, in State Museum, Newburgh.

The sciences necessary for a lawyer are 1. The English, Latin and French Tongues. 2. Writing, Arithmetick, Geometry, Surveying, Merchant's Accounts or Bookkeeping. 3. Geography, Cronology, History. 4. Logick and Rhetorick. 5. Divinity. 6. Law of Nature and Nations. 7. Law of England.[21]

Clinton seems to have done more in these New York years than to witness wills and read "cronology" and divinity; for in May 1763 he wrote to his brother Charles that he kept a clerk. Charles had returned in 1762 from the siege of Havana, Cuba, to serve in the hospital at Elizabethtown before commencing to practice in 1764 in his native county.[22]

Returning to Little Britain the young lawyer "followed his profession with reputation, though not with distinction. He was not supposed to possess considerable talents, but upon the whole, stood fair on the score of probity."[23] This was the grudging admission of an illustrious political opponent of later years, during the heat of a campaign for the governorship. It was scarcely to be expected that a village lawyer in his twenties would greatly distinguish himself, yet he seems to have gained the confidence of his neighbors. On September 12, 1764, he was commissioned attorney-at-law to practice in the mayor's court at Albany and in the inferior courts of common pleas in the various counties, and on August 26, 1765, at the age of twenty-six he commenced a year's service as surrogate of Ulster County.[24]

Meanwhile he had followed in the footsteps of his father in practicing one of the most ancient and honorable of American professions, surveying. For a time he was surveyor of the town of New Windsor. It is, however, as the surveyor of the commons of Bergen, New Jersey, and of the disputed New York–New Jersey boundary that George Clinton the surveyor will be longest remembered. Under a New Jersey law seven commissioners were appointed to have a survey made of

---

[21] Quoted by Julius Goebel Jr., "The Courts and the Law in Colonial New York," in A. C. Flick, *History of the State of New York* (10 vols., New York, 1933–37), III, 36.

[22] Charles Clinton Jr. to George Clinton, October 22, 1762 and George Clinton to Charles Clinton Jr., May 23, 1763, State Museum, Newburgh.

[23] Alexander Hamilton, *Works*, H. C. Lodge, ed. (12 volumes, New York, 1904), I, 539.

[24] In the place of Petrus E. Elmendorf. Alfred B. Street, *Council of Revision* (Albany, 1859), 88.

the Bergen line, a line through rough country that had never been carefully surveyed. Charles Clinton, widely known as a competent surveyor, was one of the commissioners; and so it was that George Clinton and one Jonathan Hampton were appointed to make the actual survey. As Hampton did not serve, Clinton was the active surveyor and was the only one to sign the field book which was completed and signed March 7, 1765. He spent several weeks at the work in March to June, 1764.

It was said over a century later that the survey of 1764, "though intricate, is accurate, exhaustive, and authoritative; while the adjudications of ownership, as therein contained, have never been questioned. On questions of title it has always been held in high estimation,—in fact, final and conclusive." [25] Evidently George had the Clinton faculty for surveying. The surveying episode may also indicate that his law practice was not so extensive during that first year of practice in Ulster as to prevent his leaving Little Britain for three or four months.

Three years later he turned again to the sextant to survey the 4,000 acre tract in Ulster County that was the property of Sir Henry Clinton, son of the provincial governor, George Clinton. When he wrote to Sir Henry to report that he had subdivided the tract, he assured him of his desire to render every service in his power to the son of the man who had given him the clerkship of Ulster.[26] That was just ten years before Sir Henry was to make him a fugitive in his own Hudson Valley.

[25] Charles H. Winfield, *History of the Land Titles in Hudson County, New Jersey* (New York, 1872) reproduces the field book of the survey. George Clinton's notebook containing his notes for the survey is in the New York State Library.
[26] George to Sir Henry Clinton, October 14, 1767, in William L. Clements Library.

CHAPTER III

POLITICS AND A GOOD MARRIAGE

GEORGE CLINTON'S FIRST ASSEMBLY

HE JOINS THE LIVINGSTON PARTY

HE IS RETURNED AGAIN

HE TURNS RADICAL WHIG

CLINTON AND NEW YORK'S WILKES CASE

A DUTCH ALLIANCE

EARLY in February 1768 Sir Henry Moore, Governor of the Province of New York, dissolved the General Assembly that had too often forgotten what Moore thought was its duty to the Crown and the Constitution, and four days later issued writs for the election of a new Assembly. At this election the freeholders of Ulster rejected such candidates of the governor's party as Cadwallader Colden Jr., son of the great lieutenant governor, and chose as their representatives two plebeians who were to become anathema to the governor and his friends. One was a "fiery young radical" of Kingston named Charles DeWitt and the other was DeWitt's good friend, the 28-year-old lawyer, George Clinton.

To represent a rural county in the General Assembly in 1768 was no great distinction. In fact, the successful candidate probably considered himself an unfortunate victim of his neighbors' confidence, doomed to exile from his own farm and law office for several months each year. Yet service in the legislature was exactly what George Clinton needed. It drew him away from the Ulster rustics and compelled him to mingle with the sharper wits and more polished manners that were to be found in New York City. It was an auspicious beginning for his political career.

With the elections of the spring of 1768 the de Lancey party had recaptured control of the Assembly from the Livingston faction. It was a red letter day for the faithful—the fall of Presbyterianism and the triumph of the Episcopalians, as Thomas Jones put it.[1] The returns showed that the strength of the de Lancey group was neatly concentrated in the southern counties—counties that were to be loyal to the Crown up to 1776 and even after. Except for one delegate from New York County, Philip Livingston, the Livingston party captured no seats from constituencies south of Cortlandt Manor. Westchester County and Borough, Richmond County, the Long Island counties, New York County with the exception already noted, all went for the de Lanceys. But north of Westchester and excepting only the County of Dutchess the Livingstons made a clean sweep. To them went Albany, Orange and Ulster Counties, the township of Schenectady, and the three manors of Rensselaerswyck, Cortlandt, and Livingston. It was the defeat of the Hudson River counties by commercial and courtly New York City and its neighbors: Clinton's party had received its first defeat in the better part of a decade, but Clinton's political apprenticeship had begun. He was present when the new Assembly met in the New York city hall on October 27, 1768.

The Clinton who sat in the Assembly of 1768 was no "fiery young radical"; nor was he, as the critical Thomas Jones would have us believe, a mere creature of the governor carefully "secured" by the gift of a license to practice in all the courts of the province.[2] He was an able young man, still in his twenties, whose father had received favors from the royal governor, who had fought under the flag of England, and who had himself accepted favors from the King's governors. It is hardly likely that he was elected as a revolutionary or fire-eater. On the other hand, he was chosen by an obstinate rural county, where the Episcopalians were few and the lesser dissenting sects numerous, where there were few merchants or great land-holding aristocrats of the court party and many independent farmers, and where the unprivileged racial minorities such as the Scotch-Irish and the Germans were to be found in considerable numbers. His colleague, Charles DeWitt, was an out-

[1] *New York*, I, 18.
[2] Jones, *New York*, II, 326–27.

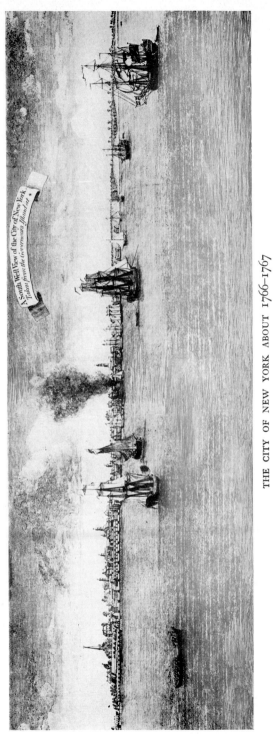

A South West View of the City of New York.
Taken from the Governors Island, Oct. *

THE CITY OF NEW YORK ABOUT 1766-1767

standing Ulsterite, twelve years his senior, who was well known to be opposed to the court party. And Benjamin Myer Brink, author of a series of articles on Clinton that appeared in *Olde Ulster,* states that the war cry of the privileged in the March elections of 1768 had been "No Lawyers and No Presbyterians!" For the lawyers wanted political freedom and the Presbyterians wanted religious freedom.[3] Elected from such a county and in such an election, it is only natural that Clinton should have kept carefully away from the de Lancey party and should after some indecision have become the fiery radical that he was not in March 1768.

He played, however, no great part in his first assembly. To pay his debt of gratitude to his constituents, he introduced a bill for the relief of the poor in Ulster and Orange which provided for the election of overseers of the poor; and the bill became law.[4] He was placed with Philip Schuyler and Ten Broeck on the committee on privileges and elections. The Assembly, however, chose to consider the disputed elections of de Lancey and Jauncey in committee of the whole, thus ignoring Clinton's committee which had probably turned out to be four to three Livingston in character.[5] The young Ulsterite voted almost invariably with that leader of dissent, Philip Schuyler, and with his colleagues DeWitt, Ten Broeck of Rensselaerswyck, Livingston, and Pierre Van Cortlandt. These six were the nucleus of the party of protest.

The dominant de Lanceyites might obtain, as they did, the passage of a resolution providing a grant of £1800 for the supply of the King's troops in the province [6]—a concession that was not much to the liking of the Sons of Liberty and their kind; but they showed themselves to be better defenders of the commercial interests of the province than the governor expected. On November 8 the Assembly formally protested the Townshend duties and ordered that a committee be appointed to draw up a petition to the King, a memorial to the Lords, and a

---

[3] Brink's life of George Clinton runs through volumes IV and V of *Olde Ulster.*

[4] *Assembly Journal,* November 4, December 24, 1768. The *Assembly Journal* has been consulted for the years 1768–75. Citations to it, however, will generally be omitted.

[5] *Assembly Journal,* October 28, November 8, November 18, 1768. Only Schuyler, Clinton, Ten Eyck, and Livingston voted not to refer the disputed seats to the Committee of the Whole.

[6] *Assembly Journal,* November 9, 1768.

remonstrance to the Commons, praying relief from the grievances the colonies were suffering. Evidently the de Lanceyites of 1768 would be loyal to governor and Crown only so long as their trade was not interfered with.

Clinton was present on the last day of 1768 when the Assembly tempted fate by resolving that the General Assembly, like the House of Commons, might petition the Crown; that the powers of the General Assembly might be lawfully abridged only by the Crown; that the Assembly might correspond directly with other colonies or subjects of the Crown; and that a committee should be appointed to correspond during the recess with the colony's agent at the Court of Great Britain.

Here, thought Sir Henry Moore, was treason enough! A colonial assembly claiming for provincials the constitutional rights of Englishmen, including the right of petition, and, most serious of all no doubt, the right to appoint a recess committee to correspond over the head of the King's own governor with authorities in Britain! Perhaps a royal governor could scarcely be expected to accept such resolutions with complete equanimity. He met with the council on January 2 and dissolved the Assembly.

The January elections of 1769, however, returned an Assembly with a majority that was also decidedly de Lanceyite. "Our election is ended," wrote Peter Van Schaack whose politics were hardly open to question, "and the Church triumphant. Messrs. Cruger, Delancey, Walton and Jauncey were the members [for New York County], in spite of all the efforts of the Presbyterian interest combined with some other dissenting sects. This is what the Churchmen call a complete victory;—'tis a lasting monument to the power of the mercantile interest. It is impossible that there ever could be a more decently conducted election, . . ." Van Schaack was greatly pleased at the outcome. The Presbyterians, he declared, believe that they, as a religious body, have everything to fear from the dominance of the Church. But their apprehensions were, he believed, entirely chimerical. Nevertheless, the Presbyterians had made a mighty effort to regain control of the Assembly; for the Episcopal Church, they said, was secure in every other branch.[7] As indeed it was.

[7] Henry C. Van Schaack, *Life of Peter Van Schaack* (New York, 1842), 10–11.

The elections in Ulster County were bitterly contested and they brought with them the regrettable but inevitable alienation of the Colden and Clinton families which had been for so long friends and neighbors.[8] George Clinton and Charles DeWitt were re-elected by a generous majority to take their places with the little junto of Livingston Whigs in the last General Assembly of the province.

The Whig minority was even more hopeless than that of 1768. After the confident majority had effectually disposed in the first weeks of the session of two of the Whig members, Philip Livingston and Lewis Morris, on the ground that they were not *bona fide* residents of their constituencies, the effective strength of the Livingston group was about eight to their opponents' eighteen.[9] The group included DeWitt of Ulster, Ten Eyck of Albany, Woodhull of Suffolk, Minderse of Schenectady Township, Ten Broeck of the Manor of Rensselaerswyck, Pierre Van Cortlandt of the Cortlandt Manor, and the leaders, George Clinton and Philip Schuyler. Had the Assembly of 1769–1775 been less predominantly de Lancey in character, it might well have provided more satisfactory leadership in the campaign against parliamentary aggression and so have obviated the need of setting up extra-legal committees until months after the time when they actually appeared. New York might in such an event have been even slower than she was to arrive at the decision to declare independence.

It is worth noting that in the last colonial Assembly the Whigs captured and held only one seat south of the Cortlandt Manor. It was strikingly the party of the up-country, of the farm, of mixed racial stocks, of religious minorities, and of opposition to the merchants of the seaboard, to the established church, and to parliamentary measures. These northern New York farmers were the stuff of which the Revolution was to be made.

In the sessions of 1769 Clinton felt entirely at home. He was often on his feet, advocating, suggesting, and opposing, or introducing curious little bills for the gratification of the Ulsterites. He had his bill to prevent damage by swine in Orange County and parts of Ulster, his better

---

[8] Carl Becker, "Nominations in Colonial New York," *American Historical Review*, VI, 268n.

[9] *Assembly Journal*, April 12, 20, 1769. Gale of Orange cannot be definitely awarded to either group.

roads bill for Ulster, and his bill for the regulation of the use of spirituous liquors at Ulster vendues. In December and January he supported the ill-fated bill providing for the election of delegates to the assembly by ballot, a bill that was pressed by the "Friends to Liberty." He voted for bills that would relieve the lesser Protestant sects from discrimination of various kinds.[10] He was again a member of the Committee on Privileges and Elections, and again the Assembly ignored the committee by taking upon itself the task of deciding contested elections. The April votes which unseated Livingston and Morris were clear party votes,[11] and Clinton of course voted with the minority.

Clinton was very often in the minority. Perhaps only the pugnacious Schuyler was more consistent in his detestation of everything that emanated from the de Lancey party. It was indeed significant that Philip Schuyler, the first citizen of Albany, a man of wealth and, for that day and age, of culture, should have been one of the two recognized leaders of protest against things as they were. He was a man of ability; he was according to Hamilton superior in ability to George Clinton; and he had wealth, vast estates, and immense influence in his community. But he was one of those who had been neglected by the governor and the de Lanceyites whose political horizon ended well south of Westchester's northern border. And Schuyler, always politically ambitious, fought the privileged group which neglected him. New York's royal governors made a serious blunder in overlooking such a man who might easily have been attached to their cause by a few favors and a little attention. "To him and Governor Clinton," wrote Timothy Dwight, "it was chiefly owing, that this province made an early and decided resistance to those British measures, which terminated in the independence of the colonies." [12]

The Assembly was prorogued late in May and was to meet again in the city hall of New York on November 21. In this interval Governor Moore died, leaving a more remarkable man to act as the King's governor and to worry over the fumings of the mob and the impudence

---

[10] *New-York Journal*, January 4, 1779; *Assembly Journal*, January 9, 24, 25, 1770.
[11] *Assembly Journal*, April 12 and 20, 1769. Woodhull, however, voted against Livingston and Boerum championed Morris.
[12] Timothy Dwight, *Travels in New England and New York* (4 volumes, London, 1823), II, 476.

of the press. This was Cadwallader Colden,[13] the old friend of Charles Clinton. Colden was something of a mathematician, a philosopher, a botanist, and a student of medicine and history—for he was the author of the *History of the Five Nations*. This versatile man held a degree from Edinburgh and had studied at the London School of Medicine. Although born in Ireland of Scotch parents, there was nothing of the democrat about him. In 1720, two years after his arrival in New York from Philadelphia, he became surveyor-general and served valiantly defending the public lands against the land-grabbers of his time. He was for years a councillor and from 1761 to his death at his Long Island farm in 1776, lieutenant governor. Naturally he was closely identified with the court party and naturally Clinton was to oppose in the Assembly virtually every cause that Colden championed. Clinton was, for instance, with the minority that voted in December 1769 against granting £2000 for supplying His Majesty's troops in New York.

This grant of £2000 was the beginning of a drama that added considerably to the patriotic laurels of George Clinton. It gave New York its own "Wilkes case."

Three days after the grant was voted the Assembly received a handbill dated December 16 and signed "A Son of Liberty." It had been distributed in the night and posted throughout the town, but its authorship was a mystery. It was an attack on the Assembly for having betrayed the liberties of the people by voting the £2000 for the supply of the King's troops. The Assembly, according to the "Son of Liberty," made the disgraceful concession to keep itself in power by preventing a dissolution.[14]

A day later the Assembly voted the handbill of the "Son of Liberty" a "false, seditious, and infamous libel." Only Schuyler voted no, and for some inexplicable reason Clinton followed the majority. Soon the Presbyterian James Parker, in whose shop the mischievous "Son of Liberty" handbill had been printed, was questioned, and his statements

[13] See Alice M. Keys, *Cadwallader Colden* (New York, 1906) and the article on Colden by the same author in the *Dictionary of American Biography*.

[14] *Assembly Journal*, Dec. 15, 1769; C. E. Carter, ed., *Correspondence of General Thomas Gage* (New Haven, 1931), I, 248. A handwritten copy of "A Son of Liberty" is in the Library of Congress.

led to the arrest of a radical Scotch-Presbyterian merchant named Alexander McDougall. This leader of the Sons of Liberty was later to be a revolutionary major general of considerable valor and distinction, and, in his more conservative years before his death in 1786, the first president of the New York Society of the Cincinnati and the first president of the Bank of New York.[15] The arrest of such a man on February 7, 1770, caused an immense sensation in the unruly little province.

Having refused bail, although he could well afford it, this American Wilkes was placed in the New Gaol, where he at once became the idol of the mob. In memory of the immortal Number 45 of the "North Briton" of John Wilkes fame, "45" became the charmed number. Forty-five "Virgins of the City" called on him; forty-five friends break-fasted with him; and he was presented with forty-five bottles of Madeira and forty-five pounds of beef. The wave of popular indignation was reminiscent only of Stamp Act days. The dissenting sects especially were enthusiastic for McDougall.[16]

Riots, demonstrations, and attacks on the Liberty Pole followed. But McDougall's release in the early spring brought a hiatus until the meeting of the Assembly on December 11 when George Clinton became involved.

On the second day of the session the General Assembly ordered that Alexander McDougall, still under indictment for libel, be brought before it. Clinton did not vote. Confronting the Assembly McDougall demanded that he be faced with his accusers and informed of the reasons for delaying his trial. De Noyelles, the Huguenot merchant from Orange, demanded in turn that he answer yes or no to the question whether he was "A Son of Liberty." McDougall objected and talked on. Speaker Cruger threatened to commit him for contempt. Clinton then interrupted to suggest that as long as McDougall showed proper

[15] For McDougall and the McDougall case see *Dictionary of American Biography*, XII, 21; Jones, *New York*, I, 25ff.; Isaac Q. Leake, *Life and Times of General John Lamb* (Albany, 1850), 61–73; John Adams, *Works*, C. F. Adams, ed. (10 vols. Boston, 1850–56), II, 345, 347; *Assembly Journal, passim;* W. C. Abbott, *New York in the American Revolution* (New York, 1929), 85f., 92; McDougall's statement in the *New-York Journal*, February 15, 1770, and contemporary newspapers.

[16] Auchmuty to Sir William Johnson, March 5, 1770, *Papers of Sir William Johnson*, VII (Albany, 1931), 309.

respect for the house he might better be allowed to give his reasons for his refusal to give a categorical answer. The speaker yielded, and McDougall explained. He had no counsel and had had no time to prepare a case. Further, he argued that as his case was pending in the civil courts where the Assembly itself was prosecuting him, the Assembly could not at the same time sit as his judge. There were threats from de Noyelles and more demands for the categorical answer. Again Clinton intervened to save McDougall, and, admitting the full power of the House to deal as it chose with the prisoner even to the extent of throwing him out of the window, declared that the public would in the end pass judgment and might well doubt the justice of any summary proceedings. Clinton then moved that the House enquire whether it was indeed a party to the suit against McDougall. Although Clinton urged that the true dignity of the Assembly might be "better supported by justice than by any overstrained authority," the de Lanceyites showed no mercy. The prisoner refused to ask pardon of the house, and he was committed again to the jail. Clinton was one of the five who voted against this action. His defense of McDougall added greatly to his credit with the patriots.

The rest of the McDougall case was anticlimax. The Assembly prevented the sheriff from serving a writ of *habeas corpus* for McDougall's release, but the chief witness was dead, evidence was lacking, and McDougall was finally dismissed. The city was quiet once more.

After the McDougall affair there was for George Clinton no turning back. Indeed, the significance of that affair lay in the fact that the party of prerogative, which had often joined the party of protest in opposition to restrictions on trade, had now broken definitely with the radicals of the Sears, McDougall, Schuyler, Clinton type. The conservative merchants were even ready to break the non-importation agreement of 1768. Henceforth the merchants might occasionally join the protestants, as on the tea issue, but the majority of the de Lanceyite group in the Assembly would stand for law and order and the government of the Crown against the assaults of the republican Sons of Liberty and the mob. It was, thought Thomas Jones, a conflict of the eminently respectable with the riff-raff.

It is perhaps significant that Clinton's rise to legislative prominence

and his frank espousal of the cause of the demos came at approximately
the time of his marriage. For his marriage was an alliance with several
of the outstanding families of Ulster and the middle Hudson Valley.
The marriage license was dated October 28, 1769, but it was not
until February 27, 1770, that he wrote from Kingston to his colleague
Charles DeWitt: "Dr Sir:—Give me leave to inform you, that shortly
after my return from New York, I completed that long talked of
business of getting married [scarcely an enthusiastic observation!], and
now having with my partner, visited my parents 'till when I did not
choose to make it public, I propose myself the pleasure of having
some of my most intimate friends and acquaintances stop and spend
the evening with me on Friday next. . . ." Those invited were
Mr. and Mrs. Wynkoop, Henry Jansen, Henry Sleight, and DeWitt.[17]
Lieutenant Governor Colden had prorogued the legislature on January 27, so releasing the groom-elect who returned to Ulster and on the
evening of Wednesday, February 7, stole away from his friends and
traveled with Anthony Hoffman, a well-to-do young Dutch merchant
and patriot of Kingston, to East Camp across the river in the Livingston
region of Columbia County, twenty miles away. Here the Reverend
Gerhard Daniel Koch of the Reformed Church married Miss Tappen
and Mr. Clinton.[18]

Lawyer Clinton was often at Kingston, the county seat, and it was
there that he wooed Miss Tappen. According to Joseph Young she
possessed "an ingenious, friendly, placid disposition." Born in 1744 she
was about twenty-six when married. Thomas Jones called her a pretty
Dutch maid, yet her profile with its weak chin and tapering nose was
not an impressive one. She was not, during much of her married life,
a healthy woman; and possibly it was because of her poor health that
she was not more given to society and entertaining, a deficiency which
in no way reflected upon her devotion as a wife but was decidedly unfortunate in the wife of a man who was to become governor and vice
president. Nevertheless George Clinton's marriage has often been
called a fortunate one, for Cornelia belonged to an established Dutch

[17] *Olde Ulster*, IV (1908), 183.
[18] According to the photostats of pages of the Clinton family Bible which are in the
George Clinton House at Poughkeepsie, the minister's name was Daniel Gerard Cock.

family of influence. Her father was Peter Tappen, "an eminent, substantial, burgher" of the Kingston corporation. Her younger brother Peter was a physician of note and a dabbler in politics. Her older brother Christopher was a trustee of Kingston and a clerk of the corporation. He was later to sit in the provincial congress and he was a man of property. And through the Tappens, Clinton was to acquire Gilbert Livingston as a brother-in-law. Gilbert was a cousin of the better known Livingstons who was not without influence in Poughkeepsie and in the Livingston Manor country, and that influence was later to win votes for Clinton. There were also the Wynkoops, among the more prominent of the Ulster families, and Cornelia Tappen's mother was Tjaatje Wynkoop. Not the least of the Wynkoops was Dirck, a man of parts and of property, who was later to enjoy the patronage of Governor Clinton's government and to support his illustrious kinsman in politics. Indeed it has been said that the Tappen family was related to the entire town, and that any degree of cousinhood was recognized. Clinton now belonged to a staid Dutch community which was to be loyal to him in many a political battle.[19]

Furthermore, the Tappens and the Wynkoops and their connections were ardent opponents of Crown and parliament and were to become patriots in the Revolution. Benjamin Y. Prime wrote in April from New York to his friend Dr. Peter Tappen: "If I'm not mistaken, I've heard that Mr. Clinton has Marry'd your Sister. If so, I give you joy! He is a *very good* man; but I'm afraid he has been overseen in voting against my Friend McDougal. i.e. in joining in the Vote, that the paper signed *A Son of Liberty,* was a Libel; whoever it might be that wrote it."[20] And Prime asked Tappen to use his influence in the coming elections for the good of the cause. It was perhaps this influence, judiciously applied, that made a radical patriot of Clinton. He was throughout his life easily attracted to popular causes, easily won over to humanitarian ideals. Always Whiggish in sentiment, he was easily converted into a radical patriot.

[19] Jones, *New York,* II, 326; Mercantile Library Association, *New York City during the American Revolution* (New York, 1861), 109 note; Richard Wynkoop, *Wynkoop Genealogy* (3d ed., New York, 1904), 48, 51.
[20] *New York City during the American Revolution* (1861), 52.

For the blood ran warm in the young Ulsterite's veins. His virtual
elopement with Cornelia Tappen would indicate that. Even before
the wedding he was addressing her as "my dearest Girl" and writing
that he would have been more fervent but for the fear that his letters
might be seen. After the marriage he was a more ardent husband than
most—if we may judge by the devotion expressed in his letters. In an
age when men often addressed their wives as "Madam," Cornelia was
his "dearest wife." And although diminishing ardor may have been
responsible for the "dearest wife" becoming "my dear wife" by the
time a year had passed, his letters still betrayed devotion to his wife and
home. In spite of his own distinguished political career, his family
always remained his first and chief interest. Even while he was governor
or vice president he could write charming letters to his children or
grandchildren without a single reference to politics or to his own
importance.

Clinton was now established, at a little over thirty. After his marriage he moved to a farm at New Windsor located on a hillside above
the Hudson and commanding a superb view to the southward of the
rugged Highlands of the Hudson that he was so soon to be called upon
to defend. He apparently enjoyed the process of getting the house
into condition, shopping in New York for paint, sheet iron for the
fire places, "English superfine tiles," paper for the walls, pots and kettles
for the neat kitchen, and chairs, which he had difficulty in finding to
his liking. He had very definite ideas about the color scheme, prefer-
ring cream for the parlor and stone color for the entry and "common
room." [21] We can well imagine the enthusiasm of the young couple
over this delightful little establishment. Unfortunately it was to be
raided by the British during the Revolution and demolished by American vandals during the World War.

Here at the New Windsor farm were born his first two children.
Catharine, born November 5, 1770, was to marry first John Taylor and
then Pierre Van Cortlandt; and Cornelia Tappen, born June 29, 1774,
was to marry a certain French minister known as "Citizen" Genêt. Here
at New Windsor Clinton turned miller as well as farmer, purchasing
wheat to grind in his mill. His flour was to help feed the Revolutionary

[21] Letter of August 1, 1771, to Mrs. Clinton, New York Historical Society.

armies in New York.[22] He seems also to have continued his law practice and, by and large, to have prospered. Possibly the hundred pounds left him by his brother Alexander who died in 1758 was his first nest egg. Certain it is that a short time before his father's death in 1773 George valued his own assets in bonds and notes at £1466, no small sum for that time.[23]

[22] *New York Genealogical and Biographical Record,* XIII, 179; *Public Papers,* I, 367, 371, 373, 445.

[23] Clinton to John Jay, October 8, 1774, ms. letter copied from Iselin Collection by Dr. Frank Monaghan; Gustave Anjou, *Ulster County, New York Probate Records* (2 volumes, New York, 1906), II (will of Alexander Clinton); George Clinton's accounts in Clinton Papers, New York State Library (duplicates, Box 2).

CHAPTER IV

THE RADICAL WHIG

THE New York General Assembly of 1769 was to sit on until it should be forgotten in the hubbub of Lexington, Bunker Hill, and Long Island. During those years Clinton and his little minority occasionally registered their protests, but there is no evidence that the young Ulsterite or any of the other radicals of the Assembly provided any really effective leadership.

At least he seems to have taken his legislative duties seriously enough to have expected others to do likewise. In March 1771, four days after the governor had prorogued the Assembly, he wrote to DeWitt from New Windsor: "Dear Charles:— Don't you think it highly derogatory to the honor power and dignity of the body of the Representatives of the good people of this colony, that a majority of their members should not attend, and a minority attend agreeable to adjournment, adjourn over from day to day for a whole week without being able to do any business, this is the case however and while you think of it *tremble,* you know you are one of the delinquents, and if the Lord had pleased you would have been waited on by that tremendious man the *Searjant-at-arms.* How foolish you would have looked. . . ."[1] Perhaps it was Clinton's conscientiousness where public service was concerned that encouraged his compatriots to call upon him more and more for important trusts that could not be delegated to the careless and the neglectful.

It is unnecessary to follow him vote by vote through the many legislative sessions of December 1770 to March 1773. From time to time he introduced a peanut bill or two, such as the bill to prevent the use of spirituous liquors at vendues in Ulster and Orange. He championed the popular cause, when he maintained in the legislature of 1771 that the Assembly had no right to unseat representatives duly returned by their constituencies.

As the long term of the Assembly wore on, he became widely known as the most radical of the Whig members. He was an even more consistent opponent of the royal governor's measures than his famous colleague, Philip Schuyler. In February 1773, he was one of a minority of three, which did not include Schuyler, to vote against making any grant at all for the support of the King's troops. And on March 5, when some of those who were usually in the de Lancey camp voted with Clinton against increasing the appropriation for the troops, Schuyler favored the increase. In January and February of 1774 only Clinton, Woodhull, and Captain Seaman fought the appropriation. Of course Philip Schuyler was not to turn Tory, but unlike Clinton he was conservative at heart and would never stay long in any company of radicals. He could never quite forget that he was a landed aristocrat who, in Albany at least, belonged to the ruling class.

It was the refusal of the consignees to receive the famous shipments of tea that was responsible for the renewal of agitation in the fall of 1773. The Sons of Liberty were again in the field denouncing and threatening. New committees of correspondence were formed. The

[1] *Olde Ulster*, IV, 215f.

radicals were suspicious of every British move, and even the merchants were aroused. Yet the Committee of Correspondence that the impotent Assembly chose to meet the new crisis was, indeed, not a committee of firebrands, for it contained the ten well-known reactionaries: Cruger, James de Lancey, Jauncey, Walton, Benjamin Seaman, Philipse, Kissam, Rapelje, Boerum, and de Noyelles; Isaac Wilkins and Zebulon Seaman who were middle-of-the-road men, and only one radical, George Clinton. But the very composition of the committee, including as it did so many merchant members, was significant of the renewal of merchant protest against British measures.

After the prorogation of the Assembly on March 19, 1774, Clinton probably returned to New Windsor, leaving New York City which was for over two years to remain the center of agitation and of action. He consequently played no direct part in the rise of the committees which were to dominate politics and to leave the General Assembly a neglected and innocuous body.

It has been said that the rural counties of New York remained decidedly apathetic during the ten years of protest; that the farmers, naturally conservative, made good allies for the merchants. Colden wrote to Dartmouth on July 6 that, "The present Political zeal and frenzy is almost entirely confined to the City of New York. The People in the Counties are in no ways disposed to become active, or to bear any Part in what is proposed by the Citizens." [2] The farmers of Ulster and the other river counties were, however, quietly sympathetic toward the forces that were leading to revolution. Few of them were to become Tories. In the General Assembly of 1769–1775, no member of Clinton's party came from a constituency that bordered on New York County. They came only from the rural regions. But political organization in the country districts was difficult: there were very few public carriers in 1774; roads were wretched and forty miles was a day's travel. Naturally patriot agitation came first from the mechanics, tradesmen, and Sons of Liberty of New York City where it was easier to agitate and organize.

Difficult as it was to meet and arouse public sentiment in the rural

[2] Jones, *New York*, I, 469. *Cf.* A. M. Schlesinger, *The Colonial Merchants and the American Revolution* (New York, 1917), 332.

counties, they were not always inactive. The New York County Committee, ready for any measures short of non-importation, suggested to the counties that produce might be sent to relieve Boston which was now bottled up by the notorious Port Bill. The people of Ulster seized upon the opportunity and many farmers gave two or three bushels each of wheat. George Clinton offered to grind, bolt, and pack without charge all the wheat sent to his mill for the purpose. And the response was evidently a generous one, for a neighbor estimated late in October that the county would probably send four or five hundred barrels of flour to Boston.[3] Evidently Clinton did not forget politics between March 19, 1774, and January 10, 1775, when the Assembly was not in session.

During the first three months of 1775 the party of law and order had its last inning. The tenacious General Assembly, which had been elected in April 1769, met on January 10 and adjourned for the last time on April 3, regretted only by George III. Its adjournment marked the end of the colonial period in New York.

Indeed, no one very much cared whether it met or not.[4] The fire-eaters of course favored approval of the radical measures of the First Continental Congress which had gathered in Philadelphia in September of 1774. But if the Assembly decided to approve, which was unlikely, it would probably proceed to choose a delegation of stand-patters to represent the province—or was it now the state?—in the next Congress. The moderate conservatives of the Schuyler brand had no great love for the Congress and its measures, but they saw that the Assembly, by repudiating the Congress, would play into the hands of the demagogues. The Loyalist members of the Assembly from New York and Westchester only wanted to ignore the Congress. Colden alone seems to have hoped for something from the Assembly: appropriations and just enough assertiveness to prevent the calling of a revolutionary provincial congress.

Clinton and his party would fight for a vote of approval of the Continental Congress and its non-importation proposals, for the ap-

[3] *Newport Mercury*, November 22, 1774, quoted in the *Magazine of American History* (1882), 359.
[4] Carl L. Becker, *The History of Political Parties in the Province of New York, 1760–1776* (Madison, Wis., 1909), 174–178.

pointment of Whiggish delegates to the Second Congress, and for a clear statement of grievances. And they would oppose appropriations on principle. Beyond that they had no definite program. They would, of course, be outvoted, but they would at least make the Assembly show its Loyalist colors. In this they succeeded.

The majority suppressed the minority on January 26 when the Assembly refused to approve the proceedings of the Continental Congress. The vote was close, 11 to 10.[5] Clinton not only voted with the minority, but showed himself a "flaming republican" in debate. According to a Tory contemporary, he declared that while he could not draw his sword against the King in any but an urgent cause, the time was drawing near when the colonies must arm—and the sooner men realized it the better. The chair called him to order; he made some sort of apology for his brusqueness, and the Assembly's decision stood.[6] One is reminded of certain of Patrick Henry's early indiscretions.

Throughout the session the minority remained much the same. Whether the vote concerned the Continental Congress, or the publication of letters received by the committee of correspondence,[7] or a grant of funds for the protection of Cumberland County,[8] the defeated cabal generally included Schuyler of Albany, Ten Broeck of Rensselaerwyck, Peter Livingston of the Livingston Manor, Pierre Van Cortlandt of Cortlandt Manor, Captain Zebulon Seaman of Queens, Woodhull of Suffolk, Thomas of Westchester, and Clinton of Ulster. Significantly enough the four members from New York County with Philipse and Wilkins of Westchester were the directorate of the majority—New York and Westchester Counties were to be the great centers of Toryism in the state.

The sole accomplishment of the Assembly that pleased the radicals was the adoption of a "Statement of Grievances." Clinton, Schuyler, and Brinckerhoff of Dutchess were the only members of the opposition among the eleven members of the Assembly's committee on grievances.[9]

[5] Cf. Colden to Dartmouth, March 1, 1775, Jones, New York, I, 494.
[6] Jones, New York, II, 328.
[7] Assembly Journal, February 26, 1775.
[8] Ibid., March 30.
[9] Appointed January 31; Peter Force, comp., American Archives (9 vols., Washington, 1837–53), series 4, I, 1288.

The committee reported a rigorous statement of grievances on February 23 and a month of debate began.

The many tedious pages of argument and resolution on the journal of the General Assembly show clearly where the extremists of both camps stood. Clinton and Schuyler alone objected to de Lancey's resolution that King and Parliament had a right to regulate the trade of the colonies and lay duties on foreign imports which might compete with the products or manufactures of Britain or her other dominions. It is perhaps surprising that this Assembly of reactionaries was willing to add to de Lancey's resolution Schuyler's amendment excluding from the right of King and Parliament to regulate and lay duties, "every idea of taxation, internal and external, for the purpose of raising a revenue on the subjects of America without their consent." But reactionaries may turn ultra in defense of their property interests.

The body resolved unanimously that the operation of the admiralty courts in such a way as to deny the accused a trial by a jury of the vicinage, the prohibition of the emission of paper money, the tax on tea, and the encouragement of Roman Catholicism in Quebec were grievances. Clinton probably voted emphatically against popery, for later in the same debate he was to suggest as a synonym for "the Roman Catholic religion," the term, "a sanguinary religion equally repugnant to the genuine simplicity of Christianity, and the maxims of sound philosophy." By votes somewhat less than unanimous the Boston Port Act and the Massachusetts Government Act were declared grievances.

McDougall wrote to Josiah Quincy Jr., that after the Assembly had passed its excellent Statement of Grievances, many of the country members went home. The "wicked and designing members of the House" then seized upon their opportunity and ignored the spirit of the List of Grievances in framing a Petition to the King, a Memorial to the Lords and a Remonstrance to the Commons.[10] Clearly, the country members were the firebrands.

Clinton, however, stayed on to take a prominent but largely fruitless part in the debates on the petition, memorial, and remonstrance. On March 24 he moved to substitute for a mild objection to the Boston

10 *American Archives*, series 4, II, 282f. There was, however, no noticeable decrease in the voting strength of the radicals.

Port Act and the Massachusetts Government Act, a resounding condemnation of ministerial policy in general, adding, "nor can we avoid declaring, that we view those acts with that jealousy which is a necessary result of a just sense of the blessings of freedom, and abhor the principles they contain, as establishing precedents subversive of the rights, privileges and property, and dangerous to the lives of your Majesty's American subjects." His motion was defeated by the usual vote, 15 to 8. And it was by this vote that the Petition to the King was adopted by the Assembly. Clinton, Schuyler, DeWitt, Van Cortlandt, and Woodhull were among the eight.

Later on the same day the Remonstrance to the Commons was under discussion. Paragraph four stated the colonists' right to exemption from internal taxation as the undoubted and unalienable right of Englishmen. Clinton moved to claim complete exemption from parliamentary taxation by deleting the word "internal," but his motion met the inevitable defeat. Subsequently the Remonstrance, the Memorial, and the Petition were all adopted by the Assembly.

Before the Assembly adjourned for the last time on April 3 it appointed a committee to obtain information of all acts of the British government which affected the liberties of America and to maintain a correspondence with the sister colonies. Clinton was made a member of this mock committee of correspondence. Its substantial Tory majority insured its entire ineffectiveness.[11]

As early as February the radicals, who saw that the Assembly would wash its hands of the extra-legal Continental Congress, were urging that delegates to the Second Continental Congress be chosen whether the staid Assembly liked it or not.[12] They resolved upon a provincial convention which would represent the whole province and would sit for one purpose only. In this way they would get a new and more satisfactory delegation than the delegation of 1774 which New York City, left to itself, might name again.

The Committee of Sixty appealed to the counties to name their deputies. Only Tory Richmond and the distant and sparsely settled

---

[11] *Assembly Journal*, April 1, 1775.
[12] From Philip Schuyler and others to Abraham Yates Jr., February 25, 1775; Abraham Yates Jr. Papers.

counties which had no substantial body of independent yeomanry, Tryon, Gloucester, Cumberland, and Charlotte, failed to respond. Westchester was keenly contested, and there was opposition in Dutchess and on Long Island. But the Hudson River counties, excepting those mentioned, showed that they were strongly in favor of what might be called, not only an extra-legal, but a revolutionary meeting. In Ulster, for instance, every town but one, Mamacoting, either took part in the meeting at New Paltz, where the Ulster deputies were named, or approved of its action.[13] Ulster's deputies were Levi Pawling, Charles DeWitt, and George Clinton. This choice made possible Clinton's selection as a member of the Second Continental Congress.

His election to the Convention did not receive unanimous approval. His old neighbor, Cadwallader Colden, second, and two other Ulster Episcopalians, Peter and Walter Du Bois, registered a protest. The meeting at New Paltz, which had named Clinton, Pawling, and De Witt, was, they declared, without authority. New York had its constitutionally elected assembly and to create unlawful provincial and continental congresses had "a direct tendency to Sap, undermine, & destroy our most Excellent Constitution, and introduce a Republican Government with its Horrid concomitants, Faction, Anarchy, and finally tyranny."[14] They seem to have suspected that Clinton and his colleagues had already turned republican.

April 20, 1775, the day of the meeting of the provincial Convention, has been declared the birthday of the State of New York. However that may have been, George Clinton was present at the event.

The Convention was faithful to its mission. It chose a distinguished Whig delegation to represent New York in the approaching Continental Congress.[15] Seven of the twelve had been delegates to the Congress of 1774: Jay, Duane, Alsop, Floyd, Boerum, Wisner, and Philip Livingston. Five of them were new men: Lewis Morris, Francis Lewis, Robert R. Livingston Jr., Philip Schuyler, and George Clinton. These twelve men, or any five of them, were given full powers "to meet the Delegates

[13] *Ibid.*, 352.
[14] New York Secretary of State, *Calendar of Historical Manuscripts, Relating to the War of the Revolution, in the Office of the Secretary of State* (2 vols., Albany, 1868), I, 22–23.
[15] *American Archives*, series 4, II, 357.

from the other Colonies, and to concert and determine upon such measures as shall be judged most effectual for the preservation and reëstablishment of American rights and privileges, and for the restoration of harmony between Great Britain and the Colonies." The reëstablishment of American rights came before the restoration of harmony! The revolution was in full swing and Clinton was in the van!

Two days later the Convention, with a restraint unusual in revolutionary bodies, passed into history. And on May 12, when the Philadelphia Congress was assembling and when New York should have had at least five representatives present, instead of only Alsop, Duane, and Philip Livingston, George Clinton left for the Quaker City.[16] He was never to show any exaggerated zeal in the federal service. His first loyalties were always within the borders of New York, and his career at Philadelphia and later at Washington was too often one of regrets and might-have-beens. He took his seat in the Congress on the fifteenth with four other newcomers from New York, and was constant in his attendance, with the exception of one hurried trip to New York on military matters, until August 2. For this he received 32 shillings a day.[17]

Thomas Jones wrote that the Ulster arch-patriot took an active part in the business of the Congress. He was violent and quarrelsome, and derisive of all things British. He ridiculed all accommodation and would have no talk of reconciliation. In one enthusiastic speech he went so far as to wish a poniard in the heart of the royal tyrant of Britain and to promise a contribution towards a handsome reward for any who would act the Brutus part in "so religious, so glorious, and so patriotic an act." [18] But the journals of the Continental Congress only occasionally mention his name. It is altogether likely that he seldom asserted himself in full meeting and spoke infrequently. His reticence may have been due to embarrassment in the presence of the famed delegates of colonies more aggressive than New York or it may have been due simply to his lack of forensic ability.

[16] Stokes, *Iconography*, IV, 885.

[17] *Public Papers of George Clinton*, I, 664. The dates of Clinton's service in Congress are given in E. C. Burnett, ed., *Letters of Members of the Continental Congress* (8 vols., Washington, 1921–36), I, liii.

[18] Jones, *New York*, II, 328.

Clinton's interest even then, a year before the Declaration of Independence, was largely in military preparations. There is, as Thomas Jones indicates, no reason for believing that Clinton cared a fig for measures of reconciliation with the motherland. And in this he was doubtless representative of thousands of rural New Yorkers who only two years later were to put their stamp of approval upon Clinton's career by making him governor of the new born state.

New York had achieved the reputation of being a conservative colony, yet even there, months before Tom Paine's rousing *Common Sense,* men were getting ready to fight. When the news of Lexington arrived on April 23, Sears and Lamb paraded through the town with the mob, flags flying and drums beating, to invite all good patriots to take up arms. The arsenal was broken open and the arms distributed to the faithful—or rather, to the unfaithful. The troops were forced to confine themselves to their barracks, their supplies were seized, and provisions destined for the king's troops in Boston never reached their destination. McDougall, Sears, Van Zandt, and others were storing away gunpowder. On May 1 the New York Committee met and unanimously appointed a committee on the purchase of "Arms, Ammunition, and Provisions." Samuel Broome and his Military Association Company offered their services to the Committee. "The Spirit of army, and Military Parade still runs high in the City," Colden wrote on June 7. Colden soon retreated to his Long Island farm and the Tory President of King's College, Dr. Cooper, barely escaped a mob of patriots to take ship for England. It was said that the library he left behind him sold for £5, his liquors for £150. And early in the fall, October 19, Governor Tryon showed his discretion by boarding the *Halifax Packet* from which he soon moved his quarters to the *Duchess of Gordon.*[19] Clearly enough the Revolution was under way by the summer of 1775 and men like Clinton knew it.

The Continental Congress might listen to the proposals of its moderates, Jay and Duane, for another petition to the King, but it went quietly to work preparing for the coming conflict. It was perhaps due to George Clinton's efforts [20] that the Congress turned its attention on

[19] *American Archives,* series 4, II, 468, 479, 536–38; George Clinton, *Public Papers,* I, 200; Jones, *New York,* I, 39, 59, 61, 498–501; Becker, *Political Parties,* 225.
[20] *Olde Ulster,* IV, 103–04.

May 25 to the defence of New York and resolved that posts be selected
on either side of the river in the Highlands of the Hudson and that
batteries be erected in such a manner as to "effectually prevent any
vessels passing that may be sent to harass the inhabitants. . . ." On
July 27 the Congress appropriated a very substantial sum of money
for "importing gun powder for the continental armies." Half of this
sum was to be paid to Philip Livingston, John Alsop, and Francis
Lewis, who were not only merchants and as such ready to purchase
gunpowder for a five per cent commission, but who were also New
York delegates to the Congress which was voting the money. Four
days later George Clinton was named a member of the recess committee for investigating the supply of virgin lead and leaden ore and
the best methods of collecting, refining, and smelting it.[21] The Congress
was thinking more of bullets than of conciliation.

The movement of protest which had been guided through the era
of the Stamp Act and the Townshend duties by the moderate conservatives, many of them merchants whose trade was threatened, had
after the tea episode fallen into the hands of the radicals. These latter,
like Clinton himself, were concerned with more than duties and taxes;
they talked of natural rights, of the equality of all men, and of other
doctrines that were anathema to the conservatives. Now that the
mechanics, artisans, tradesmen, and yeoman farmers had joined the
protest movement, the merchants found themselves and their policy of
moderation overwhelmed in the flood of rebellious radicalism. Many
of the conservatives made the best of the situation, joined with those
who defied the King, voted for independence, and then worked
steadily for half a generation to win back the leadership they had lost,
and, incidentally, to win for themselves the privileges and prerogatives
of the dethroned court party. Their victory about the year 1790 ushered
in the Hamiltonian or Federalist era in American history.

While men were reciting cant phrases of loyalty to George III, May
of 1775 saw Ethan Allen and Benedict Arnold seize Fort Ticonderoga
from His Majesty's troops; it saw Seth Warner capture Crown Point;
and it heard the request of the Committee of One Hundred, which

[21] Library of Congress, *Journals of the Continental Congress* (32 volumes, Washington, 1904–36), II, 210, 224.

had replaced the Sixty in New York City, that the people save canvas for tent cloth. In June the New York Congress offered a bounty to makers of gunpowder and ordered that Continental troops be raised in the province. During the same month the Continental Congress made Washington its commander-in-chief and elected Philip Schuyler a major general and placed him in command of the American forces in New York. In August James Clinton was named colonel of the third regiment. In November Montgomery captured Montreal from the forces of the King to whom the "colonists" still proclaimed their loyalty, and in December, as we shall see, George Clinton was appointed by the Provincial Congress a brigadier general of militia.

Clinton's attendance upon the Continental Congress at Philadelphia from May 10 to August 2 was broken by a hurried trip of about ten days to New York "on troop business," and while in New York City he took charge of the preparation of a public spread that was given to the newly chosen commander-in-chief when he passed through the city on his way to take command of the troops at Boston. Washington, leaving Philadelphia on June 25, narrowly escaped an embarrassing encounter with the royal governor William Tryon who arrived in New York on the same day. But Washington, fortunately for all concerned, came in the morning, enjoyed Clinton's dinner, and left for the northward before Tryon landed in the late afternoon.[22]

By now an ardent revolutionary, Clinton was devoting most of his time to the public service. There must have been but little left of his law practice and his family, especially his little daughter Catharine, were complaining bitterly of his long absences from home in the winter and spring of 1775.[28] It is likely, however, that he was with his family again in the early fall of that year when he suffered for some weeks from "an exhausting Dissease." He kept constantly in touch with his farm at New Windsor and with political developments in Ulster County, where he was a power to be reckoned with. According to Thomas Jones, Clinton was the terror of the Ulster Loyalists. He was "as absolute and despotic in Ulster, as the French King in France, and

---

[22] John C. Fitzpatrick, *George Washington Himself* (Indianapolis, 1933), 170; Martha J. R. Lamb, *History of the City of New York* (3 vols., New York and Chicago, 1877–96), II, 46.

[28] George Clinton, *Public Papers*, I, 214.

as cruel and arbitrary as the Grand Turk. He tried, condemned, imprisoned and punished the Loyalists most unmercifully. (They were by his orders tarred and feathered, carted, whipped, fined, banished, and in short, every kind of cruelty, death not excepted, was practised by this emissary of rebellion). . . ." [24]

Although this portrait of Clinton as a Tory baiter was doubtless much too highly colored for the political effect it would have at the time Jones was writing his history, there is no doubting that Clinton was completely carried away by the passions of the war that he and his kind had done so much to bring on. Clinton, as we shall see, accepted with all sincerity the ideals, the slogans, and the prejudices of the Revolution. Later, when other men like Schuyler and Jay and Hamilton had forgotten to hate aristocracy, to distrust distant governments, to detest Tories, to mistrust England, to oppose taxation from afar, and to struggle against restrictions on trade, Clinton clung passionately to the ideals of 1775.

It was not entirely clear why this country lawyer, and thousands like him, because fervid revolutionaries. Clinton had of course been concerned both as a clerk of court and as a lawyer with the stamp tax on legal papers, but that tax had been repealed. He could scarcely have relished the Townshend duties, but they had been repealed except for the tax on tea—and his account books, several of which have survived the Albany fire, show that tea was by no means the drink which most concerned him. There is nothing to indicate that Clinton, lawyer though he was, had been first aroused by the constitutional merits of the American cause. Rural patriots in '75 were not students of the British Constitution, and American lawyers and historians today are by no means agreed that the Americans constitutional position was a strong one. More important, perhaps, was the fact that business had often been poor in the late 'sixties and early 'seventies, and the trade restrictions adopted by the ministry had aggravated the situation. Men quickly forget their loyalty to a regime which cannot give them prosperity. Then there was Clinton's innate distrust of men and measures far removed from his provincial horizons. If he was later to distrust an administration no farther off than the shores of the Potomac,

[24] Jones, *New York*, II, 327.

how much more must he have suspected the motives of a government on the Thames! Certainly he did not intend to tax himself for the support of an empire that reached to Bombay.

But more than by the badness of the times or the remoteness of empire, Clinton was probably influenced by a compelling desire to play a part in the political life of the province. Under the regimes of Colden and of Tryon he found no career open to him. Naturally he drifted into the opposition and, being a man of strong character, impetuous and aggressive, he soon found himself in the van of the movement of protest. He must have detested the superciliousness of the self-styled aristocrats whom he faced in the courts and in the General Assembly, for he acquired a life-long aversion to all things aristocratical or monarchical. His detestation of New York's ruling class was to vent itself in his rigorous treatment of the Tories who fell into his clutches. George Clinton was representative of New York's newly fledged bourgeoisie, rural and urban, which had submitted long enough to the neglect of a snobbish ruling class and was now ready to contest with that ruling class the political control of the province.

Clinton's Ulster neighbors were but little less fanatical in their patriotism than was Clinton himself. Ulster, once its stolid Dutch and Scotch-Irish farmers had been aroused, ranked with Albany as one of the most aggressive of the rural counties. The rustics of Ulster, unconcerned with the restrictions on trade that exasperated the merchants of New York City, or with the ambitions of Clinton, Sears, McDougall, and their kind for political leadership, were vitally concerned with the natural rights philosophy of the Revolution. "Levelling principles are held up in Spencertown," Henry Van Shaack wrote his brother Peter from Albany County. "In short, the country is convulsed everywhere. God knows what the end will be." [25] Men spoke of "sons of liberty" and of "enemies of liberty." It is significant that New Windsor's Committee of Observation was chosen not only by the freeholders, who had enjoyed the franchise in the past, but also by the "other inhabitants." Those who read in their weekly gazettes long columns proclaiming the doctrine of the equality of all men could not be expected to resign themselves to perpetual disfranchisement. Clinton

[25] May 18, 1775; Van Schaack, *Henry Van Schaack*, 46f.

48 HIS EXCELLENCY GEORGE CLINTON

himself was a whole-hearted convert to the philosophy of the new democracy.

He devoted about three months of 1776 to the Continental Congress. The Ulster representatives in the New York Congress were instructed in no uncertain terms by the Ulster Committee to use their utmost influence to have him named a delegate to Philadelphia.[26] He received £148/16 for ninety-three days' service, March 10 to May 4 and June 6 to July 12, which included compensation for twenty-two days spent on the road. This was at the rate of thirty-two shillings a day.[27]

Clinton never appeared to relish legislative duty, and he took but little part in the debates of the Congress. Indeed, the New York delegation was not an inspired one. Edward Rutledge wrote to Jay from Philadelphia on June 29 that Jay was needed at Philadelphia to strengthen the New York delegation, for "Floyd, Wisner, Lewis and Alsop though good men, never quit their chairs. . . . Clinton has Abilities but is silent in general and wants (when he does speak) that Influence to which he is entitled." [28]

As might have been expected, Clinton's interests were chiefly military. He was a member of the cannon committee and New York's representative on the committee "to enquire into the cause of miscarriages in Canada," but was succeeded in this latter capacity on July 6, before the committee had made its report, by his colleague William Floyd.[29]

The repulse at Three Rivers of the American forces operating against Canada was responsible for a significant concession by the five New Yorkers in the Congress. A new battalion of four regiments was to be raised to support the forces in Canada and one of the regiments was to be raised in New York. The Congress itself on June 26, contrary to practice, had reluctantly named the officers for the new troops. The New York delegates protested at the time but offered no further opposition because, as Clinton wrote John McKesson on the twenty-sixth, they did not want New York to incur the odium of blocking an

[26] *American Archives*, Series 4, VI, 898.
[27] George Clinton, *Public Papers*, I, 664. According to his account rendered he left Philadelphia about July 6.
[28] Burnett, ed., *Letters of Members of the Continental Congress*, I, 517.
[29] *Journals of Continental Congress*, IV, 272; V, 474.

emergency measure.[30] This has been called the first indication of Clinton's infection with states' rights.

The weeks of Clinton's service to the Continental Congress probably saw the strengthening of his life-long friendship with Washington. The commander-in-chief had just returned from his victorious siege of Boston, and as it was likely that New York would be his next theater of operations, he needed advice respecting its men and resources and the Hudson Valley itself. This Clinton was able to furnish, and Washington conferred with him frequently during the weeks when both were at Philadelphia.[31] A real affection grew up between the two men who, in spite of the superficial dissimilarities produced by the very different Ulster and Virginia environments, were remarkably alike in those more substantial characteristics that were destined to make them the first chief magistrates of a great state and a great nation. Clinton showed his respect for Washington when in 1778 he named his only son George Washington Clinton and five years later had his fourth daughter christened Martha Washington Clinton.[32]

Clinton's failure to take rank with the more select immortals of American history has been to no small degree the result of his failure to sign the Declaration of Independence. He was in Philadelphia while the Declaration was being prepared and it is barely possible that he voted for it on July 4.[33] But he was back in New York on military duty weeks before the signatures were affixed in August. He must have regretted his inability to climax his long years of opposition to ministerial policies by affixing his signature to the great declaration.

If New York had not been the most conservative province in America, Clinton might well have achieved cannonization as a "Signer." New York's third provincial congress, which was elected in April 1776, was remarkably moderate in its politics—so moderate that it shied at any move toward independence. Yet it was scarcely practicable to

[30] *Ibid.*, V, 481f.; *American Archives*, series 4, VI, 1080. McKesson, a frequent correspondent of Clinton's, was a secretary of the New York Congress. *Ibid.*, 1310.
[31] Washington Irving, *The Life of Washington* (5 vols., New York, 1855–59), Book II, 70.
[32] She died in 1795.
[33] He may have been in Philadelphia to July 6, 1777. *Public Papers*, I, 664. Dr. Flick in *History of the State of New York*, III, 281, states that the tradition "seems to lack substantiation from the contemporary records."

drift along indefinitely without a decision. If the colonies were not to
come to terms with the King they must insist upon independence.
Business was bad; for trade with Britain was at a standstill, and even
intercolonial trade was suffering severely. The opening of the ports of
the colonies to the world in April might mean more trade but it also
meant friction with the royal authorities. Independence seemed inevitable. Many of the other colonies were ready for the step, but the
New York Congress held back.

Probably Clinton could have made more of a contribution to the
movement toward independence had he occupied his seat in the New
York Congress than he did at Philadelphia. But his membership in
both the third and fourth New York Congresses was scarcely more
than nominal; he sat only a few days.

The Committee of Mechanics on May 29 demanded that the New
York delegates at Philadelphia be instructed to vote for independence.
The Provincial Congress, unwilling to face the issue and entirely willing to delay action at Philadelphia, professed itself without authority
and on June 11 notified the delegates that they were not authorized
to commit the province. Richard Henry Lee had already on the
seventh introduced his famous motion, "That these United Colonies
are, and of right ought to be, free and independent States; . . ." This
had prompted the New York delegates on the eighth to appeal to the
Provincial Congress for instructions since, "Some of us consider ourselves as bound by our instructions not to vote on the question of independence." Nevertheless Robert R. Livingston, who had objected to
Lee's motion on the ground that the middle colonies were not yet ready
for the plunge, was placed with Jefferson, John Adams, Franklin, and
Sherman, on the committee to draft a Declaration of Independence.

Massachusetts and Virginia were ready for the decision. After all,
it would be only a perfunctory recognition of a *fait accompli.* Every
colony had already defied the King many times over. Even New York,
which, with its exposed position and its plentiful crop of Tories, was
the most conservative of them all, had come close to asserting its independence on May 27 when its Congress had decided to call a convention for constructing "a new internal form of government" to continue in full force "until a future peace with Great Britain." Yet the
Continental Congress delayed action on independence until July, and

even then, on July 2, the other twelve colonies voted themselves independent of Great Britain without the support of New York.

"The important Question of Indepency was agitated yesterday in a Committee of the whole Congress," Clinton and the other New York delegates wrote to the Provincial Congress on the second of July, "and this Day will be finally determined in the House. We know the Line of our Conduct on this Occasion; we have your Instructions, and will faithfully pursue them." Expecting, however, that the vote for independence would be nearly unanimous, they requested to be instructed whether they were to be considered as being bound by the vote of the majority. They urged that "it is our Duty nay it is absolutely necessary that we should not only concur with but exert ourselves in forwarding our military Operations." [34] Clearly, Clinton and his colleagues were impatient at the indecision of the Provincial Congress.

They were of course unprepared to vote for the adoption of the Declaration of Independence on the fourth, and George Clinton had left Philadelphia before the newly elected Provincial Convention which met at White Plains on July 9 relieved the doubts of the delegates by resolving unanimously, "that the reasons assigned by the Continental Congress for declaring the United Colonies free and independent States are cogent and conclusive; . . ." It authorized the delegates to concur in all measures which they might deem conducive to the welfare of the "United States of America." [35] When the Declaration of Independence was signed in August, William Floyd, Philip Livingston, Francis Lewis, and Lewis Morris signed for New York.

The radical democrats must have been jubilant. The June elections had eliminated the last Loyalist remnant from the new State's legislative body.[36] The conservatives of the Jay variety had been definitely repulsed in their efforts to block independence. And they were to suffer a further repulse on August 1 when the Convention appointed a committee of thirteen to report a bill of rights and a plan of government. The revolutionary democracy had for the moment overcome domestic opposition. It now had only the Tories and the King's troops to deal with!

[34] Burnett, *Letters . . . Continental Congress*, I, 524–25.
[35] *Journal of Provincial Convention*.
[36] Becker, *Political Parties*, 274.

CHAPTER V

BRIGADIER GENERAL

APPOINTMENT
THE GENERAL'S MODESTY
HIS BLUNTNESS
HE IS IMPATIENT WITH THE MILITIA
CLINTON TO THE DEFENSE OF THE HUDSON
WASHINGTON NOMINATES CLINTON
CLINTON URGES WASHINGTON TO HOLD NEW YORK
HE ENJOYS THE BATTLE OF HARLEM
BUT DOES NOT ENJOY WHITE PLAINS
CLINTON OBSTRUCTS THE HUDSON
HE INVADES NEW JERSEY WITH SUCCESS

I F there was to be war, steps must be taken to defend the Highlands
of the Hudson, which was perhaps the most important strategic
area in the entire thirteen provinces. It was for this purpose that the
Continental Congress in November 1775 called upon New York to appoint an officer with power to call out the militia of the Hudson River
counties, Ulster, Orange, Dutchess, and New York, if and when the
British attack should come. The Committee of Safety, which was act-
ing for the Provincial Congress during one of the many intervals when
the Congress was not actually sitting, responded on December 19 by
appointing George Clinton brigadier general of the Ulster and Orange
militia.

Clinton's appointment was a striking indication of the confidence
which New York had already come to have in his ability and loyalty.
He was only thirty-six. He had not served in the militia and had had

virtually no military experience since his campaign with Amherst as a mere subaltern, and yet he was preferred to men like his elder brother James [1] and a score of other prominent New Yorkers who had served with more distinction in the French and Indian War and who had more recently been active militia officers. His old friend, Charles De Witt, was to serve under him as colonel of one of the Ulster regiments and brother-in-law Christopher Tappen as major. His sudden elevation was indeed a bitter pill for some of the more ambitious of his compatriots to swallow, and certain of them, including Colonel Hasbrouck of Clinton's own county, curtly informed the New York Congress that if seniority was to be ignored, and Clinton favored, they would not serve. The harassed Congress offered to follow any recommendations the Ulster County Committee might choose to make. With few exceptions, however, Clinton retained the confidence of his colleagues and his commission was never revoked.[2]

Clinton's primary task at that time and for nearly two years thereafter was the all-important defense of the Highlands. If the thirteen provinces were to conduct the war as a unit, and if there was to be any effective co-operation between the so-called Eastern states of New England and the others of the feeble Union, the British must be kept out of the Hudson Valley. One of the principal objectives in the grand strategy of the Revolution was therefore the Hudson, and it is by no means easy to understand why the British, with their superior forces, did not make a determined effort to seize the entire valley up to Albany and to hold and patrol it. Instead they occupied Philadelphia; Burgoyne, left unsupported, surrendered his army; the French, encouraged, entered the war at a critical moment; and independence was won. Although the outcome was to be attributed much more to British blunders and misunderstandings than to the military genius of George Clinton or any other American officer who commanded on the Hudson, the fact remains that the defense of the Valley, to which Clinton contributed so much, made the winning of the Revolution possible.

Clinton was the first to admit that he did "not understand much of

[1] James Clinton was colonel of the Third (Ulster) Regiment of the New York Line, organized June 28, 1775. He was appointed a brigadier general August 9, 1776. O'Callaghan, *Documents Relative to the Colonial History of New York*, VIII, 806.

[2] *American Archives*, Series 4, V, 137-39, 379.

the refined art of war," [3] and historians of the Revolution have not claimed for him any profound knowledge of military science. When giving his reasons against the evacuation of New York City in the fall of 1776 he wrote, "I am not much read in the Art of War." [4] He never distinguished himself greatly on the field of battle. Yet it could be said of him by his friends "that the exertions made by this State [of New York] during the War are chiefly to be attributed to his influence." [5] He was not a great field general but he was a great war governor, and the work which he did as governor in recruiting, organizing, disciplining, feeding, and clothing the troops, and arranging for the defense of the Hudson Valley, he began as provincial brigadier general. And the reputation that he made in the field was of inestimable value to him in politics in later years. Democracies are lavish in the honors they bestow upon their war heroes.

With characteristic energy and stubborn insistence he persuaded, cajoled, and threatened the indifferent and unpatriotic. He wrote hundreds of urgent, encouraging letters to colleagues and subordinates, and long reports to his superiors and to the provincial congress. And he wrote what he thought, no matter who the correspondent. He wrote, for instance, on January 9, 1776, to his distinguished kinsman, Colonel DeWitt, who was some dozen years his senior: "It gives me great Concern to hear that (altho' the Congress have appointed you & other Gentlemen Field Officers of a Regim't to be formed in the Northern End of Ulster County) not one company is yet imbodied . . . You'll therefore not fail to exert yourself in filling up your Regim't with all speed agreable to the Directions of the Congress." [6] To one of his officers, Moses Phillips, he wrote: "I have received your letter of yesterday. The Reasons assigned for not furnishing your Quota of Men are by no means satisfactory, & such as I could not have expected from an Officer of whom I have always entertained so good an Opinion." [7]

[3] *Public Papers*, I, 399.
[4] Clinton Papers, Library of Congress.
[5] Reported by Hamilton in the Letters of H. G., February 22, 1789, *Works, Lodge*, ed., I, 544. See also the *New York Advertiser*, April 1, 1789, for letters referring to his military incapacity.
[6] *Public Papers*, I, 217.
[7] *Ibid.*, IV, 122.

Nor did he hesitate to speak plainly to the New York Convention it-self: "I observe by the resolves now sent me," he wrote that body late in 1776, "two of my Colonels, and other Officers, are put under the direction of a Secret Committee of your honorable House. In justice to myself, I beg leave to mention, I must consider this as a suspension of my command, at least as far as it respects the regiments and com-panies they command. As they cannot be subject to my orders, I can't be answerable for the conduct of my brigade." [8] Most of Clinton's letters show the same blunt sincerity and decision.

Intensely earnest himself in everything connected with the waging of the war against George III, he could not understand the indifference of others. He became at times especially wrathy over the way the militia conducted themselves. He was, for instance, compelled to in-struct his officers to jail any militiamen caught abusing the inhabitants of the country where they were stationed. When sheep disappeared on his own farm, he suspected the militia. The militiamen were constantly demanding leave to go home to tend their crops or they were simply taking leave without permission. During the summer of 1776 he persuaded the Committee of Safety to allow many of the troops in service on the Hudson to return to their farms for a few days to care for their crops; only to find, to his despair, that bad weather had delayed the haying and the return of his men. In September he reported many gaps in his lines as the result of desertion and the failure of men drafted to join their regiments. If he sent parties after the delinquents, he weakened the army still more. The situation was especially serious during the discouraging White Plains campaign in October when in the face of his enemy his brigade was melting away as a result of the ravages of sickness, a few deaths, and much desertion. Perhaps the case of Colonel Hoornbeek's regiment was one of the most serious. Hoornbeek's regiment of 251 men reported at the end of 1776, 50 men on furlough, 2 unfit, and 89 deserted! [9] That left 110 fit for service. At the same time Clinton was pleading with his officers to hold their men until new troops could be raised: "I am much distressed at the Militia's deserting me in the manner they do; some Regiments are gone off al-

[8] Letter of December 23, *American Archives*, Series 5, III, 1378.
[9] *Public Papers*, I, 517.

most to a Man." [10] This was campaigning under difficulties, to say the least.[11]

The army of the new American democracy was too much of a democracy to function smoothly. Soldiers complained of their officers and officers complained of their commands. Colonel Morris Graham and his officers, for instance, protested to General Clinton that they were unwilling to trust their lives to the medicinal knowledge of the regimental surgeon. The enlisted men at Fort Montgomery in August 1776 complained to Clinton of their officers who were "disagreeable" to them. As the higher officers had been appointed by the Congress, Clinton could do nothing for their men—if he would. His disgust with the whole system of choosing officers—officers up to and including the rank of captain were elected by the men of each company—came to a head in March of 1777 when he wrote the New York Convention of his intention to resign.[12] His purpose in resigning, he declared, was "not founded on any Disgust to the service other than that from fatal Experience I find I am not able to render my Country that Service which they may have Reason to expect of me, considering the importance of the Command they have honored me with." A few days later he admitted that he had entirely lost patience with the method of choosing officers which only elevated those who would stoop to court mean popularity. He stated that he would not withdraw his resignation but that he would serve as a private, believing that he would make an obedient soldier. His resignation was not accepted. He was too much needed.

The militia were constantly grumbling because their wages were overdue. Often when they grumbled enough, they got money.[13] Clinton was usually ready to champion their cause against the sluggishness and indifference of the indigent Provincial Congress. Always democratic in his sympathies, he saw that the war was bearing much more heavily upon the lower orders of men who filled the ranks than upon those

[10] *Ibid.*, 502.
[11] *Ibid.*, 216, 290, 315f., 338, 399, and 580; J. R. Simms, *The Frontiersmen of New York* (2 vols., Albany, 1882), I, 620.
[12] *Ibid.*, 281, 643, 654; Marius Schoonmaker, *The History of Kingston* (New York, 1888), 175f.
[13] *Public Papers*, I, 293, 329, 376.

who for one reason or another stayed home and financed or supplied the fighting. He wrote boldly to the council of safety in 1777 that service in the armed forces was so poorly paid as compared with other occupations that the difference was a virtual tax borne by the "Middling & lower Class of People." This, he believed, the militia fully understood.[14]

The war was developing rapidly in the weeks that followed Clinton's appointment as brigadier general in December 1775. Twelve days later the gallant Montgomery, one of the most promising of American officers, was killed before Quebec. In January 1776, Tom Paine published that most effective of all Revolutionary tracts, *Common Sense,* and Sir John Johnson, that staunch Loyalist, was disarmed by Schuyler's men. In February, General Charles Lee and Lord Stirling arrived in New York under orders from Washington to place the province in a condition for defense. More troops arrived in the months that followed, including Washington's forces who came fresh from the victorious outcome of the siege of Boston. The able-bodied part of the population of New York City was put to work building fortifications and the work of obstructing the river above the town was carried on by the population and troops of the upper counties.

The active campaign commenced when British war vessels ran by the American works on Manhattan on July 11 and on the next day landed some 9000 men on Staten Island. The Howes were about to attack the metropolis.

Warned by two river sloops of the appearance of the British at New York, Clinton at once left his New Windsor home, assembled a party of forty neighbors, set up his headquarters at Fort Montgomery on the Hudson, and called out three militia regiments, fresh from the farms, which he stationed at Fort Montgomery, at Fort Constitution six miles up the river opposite the present West Point, and at Newburgh a few miles farther north on the Hudson. By July 18 he had 600 men at Fort Montgomery.

Assisted by his brother James, who was a born soldier if not a dashing one, he pushed forward the construction work on Forts Mont-

[14] Letters of July 31, 1777, *Public Papers,* II, 142–43.

gomery and Clinton; he collected river craft near the forts and made preparations for stretching a chain across the river at Anthony's Nose, just below the forts, which would close the river to the British fleet.[15] He wrote Washington about his preparations and received in reply letters of encouragement and direction from his commander-in-chief.

It was fortunate that precautions were taken so promptly. Some of the British ships pushed up the river from Tarrytown to Haverstraw on the sixteenth where they fired shots at the curious provincials who lined the shore. The next two days the enemy ships, especially the *Rose* and the *Phoenix,* grew bolder, came farther up the river and sent out small landing parties; and one enemy sloop even risked the guns of Fort Montgomery.[16] The countryside was in consternation. General Clinton stationed militia along the banks of the Hudson to greet possible landing parties, caused neighboring livestock and supplies to be moved from the danger zone, and prepared large brush fires on the river bank below the fort to illumine the enemy vessels should they attempt to sail up the river during the night. These precautions, which Washington approved, seem to have been effective, and for a time the *Phoenix* and the *Rose* kept their distance.

The provincial convention, meanwhile, realized the necessity for keeping the King out of the Hudson Valley. It resolved on July 16 to call out a fourth of the militia of Westchester, Dutchess, Ulster, and Orange Counties for service until December, and to allow each man a bounty of twenty dollars with Continental pay and subsistence. Every militiaman was to provide himself with a knapsack and blanket and every group of six with a kettle. Of these levies the men raised in Ulster and Orange were to be stationed in the Highlands on the west side of the Hudson at points to be determined by Clinton, while the Dutchess and Westchester troops were to repair to Peekskill. General Washington was to be requested to name an officer to command the forces on both sides of the river.[17]

[15] *Public Papers,* I, 138, 187, 248–49, 251; F. L. Humphreys, *Life and Times of David Humphreys* (2 vols., New York and London, 1917), I, 88; E. M. Ruttenber, *Obstructions to the Navigation of Hudson's River* (Albany, 1869).

[16] *Public Papers,* I, 286–87.

[17] *American Archives,* series 5, I, 1409; *Public Papers,* I, 255.

Washington, being unable to send "an experienced officer" with adequate knowledge of the countryside to command on the lower reaches of the Hudson, recommended that George Clinton be appointed to that important command. "General Clinton," he wrote the Convention on July 19, "on all Accounts appears to me the most suitable Person, and as the appointment is made dependent on me, I shall nominate him, unless some objections should be made or difficulty arise which I do not now know." Washington later explained to the Convention that "His acquaintance with the Country, abilities and zeal for the Cause are the Motives that induced me to make choice of him." [18]

The Convention's emphatic approval of Washington's choice for the command on the Hudson shows how high Clinton had risen in the esteem of his fellow New Yorkers. Washington was told that it gave the Convention "great pleasure to find that [his] Excellency hath chosen for this important post a gentleman whose good sense and tried resolution do honor to the choice, which, united with his intimate knowledge of the country, cannot fail of rendering him useful to the public." [19] A few days later Robert R. Livingston wrote to "Dear George" from Fishkill: "You must lead us out of this labirinth which God grant you may shortly have it in your power to do by a victory so decicive as will amid only of one construction." [20]

Although the Convention understood that the Continental commander-in-chief had actually appointed Clinton to the new command, Washington himself promptly set the Convention right; and the Convention itself hastened to place Clinton in command of the levies of Ulster, Orange, and Westchester in the lower Hudson Valley. That was on August 8. Clinton was ordered to leave 200 men at Anthony's Nose and bring the rest of his command to the fort which had just been erected on the north side of Kingsbridge, one of the strongest positions north of New York City. He wasted no time for on August 9, the next day, orders were sent to Brigadier Generals Morris and Ten Broeck to march their brigades at once to Kingsbridge, which then

[18] George Washington, *Writings,* John C. Fitzpatrick, ed. (25 vols., Washington, 1931—), V, 309, 398.
[19] *Journal of the New York Convention,* August 6, 1776.
[20] *Public Papers,* I, 312.

became Clinton's headquarters.[21] Two weeks later the Committee of
Safety sent the Convention's records and papers and a chest belonging to the receiver-general to General Clinton's camp for safe
keeping.[22]

From his headquarters at New York Washington on August 12
issued general orders placing the brigades of Thomas Mifflin and
George Clinton under the immediate command of the newly commissioned major general, William Heath. Heath was a substantial
New England farmer but an uninspiring and decidedly mediocre
soldier. By the same order of August 12 the brigade of James Clinton, who had just received his commission as brigadier general, was
placed under Major General Putnam.[23] George Clinton's brigade at
about this time consisted of some 1800 men in five regiments commanded by Colonels Isaac Nichol, Thomas Thomas, James Swartwout, Levi Pawling, and Morris Graham; Albert Pawling was Clinton's brigade major. The brigade was, however, like most of the militia
brigades of the time, deficient in numbers and, in spite of the polite
admonition of a special committee of the convention in September
and, in spite of its officers who succeeded in bringing in a few de-
serters and recruits, the brigade in November still wanted nearly 700
men to complete its ranks.[24] In the late summer of 1776 New York
was furnishing about one-seventh of Washington's army—no small
proportion for one of the smaller states.

Then, late in August, came one of the most disheartening of the
American defeats of the war—a defeat that might easily have resulted
in the complete elimination of Washington's army. It was the Battle
of Long Island. Two American generals and 1100 men were captured and the rest of the army put to rout. It is entirely possible that
had there been no fog and rain on the night of August 29 to cover the
passage of the Continental Army with its supplies from Long Island
to the Manhattan shore, the war might have ended then and there.

[21] *American Archives,* Series 5, I, 852–54, 1489; *Journal of the New York Convention,*
August 6, 8, 1776; *Public Papers,* I, 298, 304, 312.
[22] *American Archives,* Series 5, I, 1546.
[23] Washington, *Writings,* Fitzpatrick, ed., V, 423.
[24] "The Campaign of 1776," *Memoirs of Long Island Historical Society,* III (Brooklyn,
1876), 128; New York Secretary of State, *Calendar of Historical Manuscripts Relating to
the . . . Revolution,* II, 478; *American Archives,* Series 5, III, 499.

It seemed to some that Howe allowed "the exact time necessary for his enemy to make his escape."[25] Apparently America owes much to Sir William Howe!

Washington's masterly retreat to Manhattan following the battle of Long Island brought Kingsbridge and Clinton's brigade closer than ever to the area of actual conflict. The Committee of Safety ordered him to hold his forces in readiness in case Howe should attempt to force his way up by the island of Manhattan, and Clinton made every preparation, even to the squeezing of £7000 from the niggardly committee to pay his restless militiamen. Following urgent orders received by General Heath from Washington, Clinton kept a sharp watch on the enemy's movements, sending out reconnoitering parties, despatching spies to Long Island, and laying plans to trap Tories who might be made to yield information on the enemy's movements. He himself planned to lead a party on the evening of September 9 across to Long Island, but the enemy's ships prevented the expedition and they got no farther than New Rochelle.[26]

Clinton found himself in complete disagreement with Washington on the vital question of the evacuation of New York City. General Greene believed that it would be too costly in a military sense to try to hold the city. The city and its suburbs should therefore be burned. Washington, who had already enquired of the Congress what should be done with the place, was inclined to agree with Greene; but the Congress was opposed to the policy of destruction although it was willing to have Washington decide whether the city should be evacuated or held at all cost. The final decision was made in Washington's council of war which met at the quarters of General McDougall on September 12.[27]

General Clinton attended the council.[28] He argued that although

[25] [Flick], *New York in the Revolution*, 151-53.

[26] Washington, *Writings,* Fitzpatrick, ed., VI, I; *Public Papers,* I, 343; George to Charles Clinton, September 12, 1776, State Museum, Newburgh.

[27] For Clinton's reasons against evacuation, see memorandum dated September 12, 1776, in Clinton Papers, Library of Congress. See also George Bancroft, *History of the United States* (10 vols., Boston, 1854-74), IX, 118 and Jones, *New York,* I, notes on pp. 612-14.

[28] He also attended the similar council on September 7. Washington, *Writings,* Fitzpatrick, ed., VI, 19.

the city itself was difficult to defend, it could be held by fortifying and holding the adjacent heights. He insisted that Washington's army outnumbered the enemy, although in other respects it might be inferior, and that to retreat, leaving the city for barracks for hostile forces and an asylum for the disaffected, would mean a serious loss of popular confidence in the Continental Army. If the enemy entrenched themselves in the city, so cutting off Long Island from the rest of the state and exposing New Jersey to attack by way of Paulus Hook, it might be very difficult ever to recover the town. It was better to attempt to hold it than meekly to give it up and then face the more difficult task of recapture.

The majority of the council, however, fearing that the British planned to surround the island and cut their lines of communication, decided to abandon the city, "none disenting," according to George Bancroft, "but Spencer from sheer ignorance and dulness, Heath from dishonesty, and George Clinton from stubborn zeal." [29] The other ten members of the council, including Greene, Putnam, McDougall, and Mifflin, were for evacuation. The withdrawal of the troops to the Harlem area began on September 14 and the British entered the town of New York on the fifteenth. Five days later a mysterious fire swept over a quarter of the area of the little city.

Clinton had a taste of real fighting on September 16 when General Howe attacked the center of Washington's line at Harlem Heights in an effort to clear Manhattan entirely of American troops. The Battle of Harlem was the culmination of several days of vigorous and active campaigning. It was also what the weary American forces so much needed to raise their morale, a decisive repulse for Howe's victorious army. Clinton came down from Kingsbridge with a portion of Heath's command. He spent several nights in the open, observing, but probably taking no part in the hurried retreat from New York City on Sunday and actually participating in more creditable operations at Harlem Heights on Monday. He saw the British advance, which had overwhelmed Colonel Knowlton's force at about ten in the morning, checked by an American attack in the hollow near

[29] *United States,* IX, 118. The statement is paraphrased from Alexander McDougall. *Cf.* J. C. Fitzpatrick, *George Washington Himself,* 253.

Martje Davit's Fly; he saw fresh American troops push back the enemy again early in the afternoon to the Buckwheat Field; and he saw the final British retreat later in the afternoon. He accompanied the troops during most of the action, encouraging and directing.[30] He afterwards wrote Dr. Peter Tappen that he wished he had had a pair of pistols with which he could, he believed, "have shot a Rascal or two." He thought it a pity that Peter's pistols should be lying idle. "I am sure I would at least have shot a puppy of an officer I found slinking off in the heat of the Action." [31]

Clinton wrote enthusiastically of the battle of Harlem Heights to the Convention: ". . . it has animated our Troops & gave them new spirits & erased every bad impression the Retreat from Long Island &c. had left on their minds. They find they are able with inferior Numbers to drive their Enemy & think of nothing now but Conquest." [32] The night after the battle his brigade formed on the extreme right between Scott's brigade and the Hudson on the ground where the action had commenced that morning.[33] Within a mile of the enemy, Clinton heard them working vigorously and, he thought, fearfully to prepare themselves against another attack in the morning. There was no attack, however, and on the evening of the sixteenth, the day after the battle, Clinton was back at Kingsbridge.

The fall of 1776 was a hectic one for the young brigadier general. Washington's confidence in him, which may well have been strengthened by his record at Harlem Heights, was responsible for several difficult assignments. The first of these was another abortive raid on Long Island. Washington wrote on September 30 to Major General Lincoln of the Massachusetts militia and to General George Clinton, requesting the former and ordering the latter to go at once to Fairfield, Connecticut, to plan a secret expedition to Long Island for the purpose of destroying stock and supplies that were in danger of falling into the hands of the enemy. Clinton spent several days in Connecticut, chiefly at New Haven, with General Lincoln, Colonel Henry B. Living-

---

[30] H. P. Johnston, *Battle of Harlem Heights* (New York, 1897), *passim;* George Clinton to the New York Convention, September 18, *Public Papers,* I, 351–54.
[31] Letter to Peter Tappen, September 21, printed in H. P. Johnston, *op. cit.,* 142–45.
[32] *Public Papers,* I, 353.
[33] General orders for September 16 in Washington, *Writings,* Fitzpatrick, ed., VI, 56.

ston, and John Sloss Hobart; but the expedition to Long Island hung fire. Late in October, with the enemy threatening a further advance in Westchester, Washington decided that Clinton could not be spared for the Long Island project,[34] and he returned to headquarters at Kingsbridge.

The next two weeks at Kingsbridge were filled with activity, rumors of British advances on land and river, removal of stores from threatened Kingsbridge to Dobbs Ferry, and, as always, letter writing. Peter Tappen, thinking it prudent to ignore Clinton's hint to lend his brace of pistols, sent down Clinton's sword with a letter of reassurance on the point of the health of Mrs. Clinton who had but recently been very poorly.[35]

After the removal of Clinton's camp to White Plains on the twenty-third, the fever of preparation continued. His headquarters was the center of activity for all business connected with the militia of the state as Washington's headquarters was the focal point from which the Continental forces were directed. It was said of Clinton that "judged by the volume of his mail, the number of his callers and the variety of duties entrusted to him by General Washington, General Clinton is one of the busiest men in America. His headquarters hourly presents a scene of the greatest activity and from his many callers, an interesting insight is gained . . ." into the whole exciting business of conducting the war.[36]

Reports of the enemy's advance reached White Plains on the night of Clinton's arrival when he was the only general officer in camp. He expected a battle at any time but asked John McKesson to reassure Mrs. Clinton for "it would be too much honor to die in such a cause." [37] Not until the twenty-eighth did General Howe, moving north, make his direct attack on Washington's army. The battle of White Plains was a disheartening affair for both sides. A providential rain put Howe's muskets out of commission and in the night Washington

---

[34] Clinton seems to have been at New Haven October 2 to 5; *Public Papers*, I, 372–73. Washington, *Writings*, Fitzpatrick, ed., VI, 141, 148, 222; *American Archives*, Series 5, II, 607–09.

[35] *Public Papers*, I, 378.

[36] Jonathan Rawson, *1766: A Day-by-Day Story* (New York), 1927), 335.

[37] *Public Papers*, I, 392.

retreated to a stronger position in the hills in the rear, leaving Howe, after some desultory maneuvering, to fall back to Dobbs Ferry. For several days, however, the Americans expected another general attack. General Clinton wrote McKesson on the thirty-first that for four days he had been closely confined to his post on the left flank, living in a soldier's tent and exposed to rain and weather. "We had reason to apprehend an attack last night, or by day-break this morning . . . Our lines were manned all night in consequence of this, and a most horrid night it was to lie in cold trenches. Uncovered as we are, drawn on fatigue, making redoubts, flashes, abatis and lines, and retreating from them and the little temporary huts made for our comfort before they are well finished, I fear will ultimately destroy our army without fighting." [38] His spirits were many degrees lower than after the more glorious clash at Harlem Heights.

Possibly the despondency of the battlefields of White Plains had something to do with Clinton's mysterious decision on the day following the battle to offer his resignation. The faithful McKesson, who was charged with the delicate task of communicating the general's message to the committee of safety, found the committee entirely unwilling to consider it. Clinton would give them no reasons. Some suspected he wished to evade the Continental articles against dueling through resignation. They thought the whole business most unlike him. The committee was willing to grant a leave of absence, if that was what the general wanted, but it could not consent to even the shortest resignation of his command. Abraham Yates especially was insistent that Clinton could not be spared, "even for an hour." [39] The committee did not alter its determination and Clinton remained in the field where he was so much needed.

During the next few weeks the American commanders were busy with their plans for the defense of the Hudson Valley. On the eleventh of November George Clinton, together with his brother James, Stirling, Mifflin, and Heath, accompanied Washington on a hurried visit to Peekskill and the posts in the Highlands. [40] Clinton's headquarters

[38] *Ibid.*, 400.
[39] *Public Papers*, I, 408, 410–11. McKesson apparently knew Clinton's reasons.
[40] Humphreys, *Life and Times of David Humphreys*, I, 89. Washington left White Plains on November 10. *Writings*, VI, 272.

were then moved to Peekskill where he remained until the end of the month, attending Heath's numerous councils of war, including a meeting with General Charles Lee, surveying the countryside and the river, and suggesting to the Convention his plan for obstructing the Hudson at Polopel's Island, a plan that, much to Clinton's indignation, Gilbert Livingston carried about with him for some days before it received the attention and the approval of the committee of safety.[41]

He must have been somewhat assuaged by the committee's whole-hearted adoption of his Polopel's Island project. It resolved at Fish-kill on November 30 that the work was to start immediately. Three hundred axes were to be delivered to Clinton at New Windsor; boats and scows were to be assembled there; Gilbert Livingston was to pro-vide Clinton with three tons of iron and with spars and timber, and a special committee was named to provide other necessaries. Re-enforcements were to be sent to Clinton at Constitution Island, and he on his part was to hold the Ulster and Orange militia in readiness to defend the west shore of the Hudson.[42] Major General Schuyler was asked to confer with him. The latter arrived at Constitution Island with 500 men promptly on the same day he received his orders. There followed the inevitable appeals for essential provisions and men, teams, anchors, rope and especially axes. There was flour enough at New Windsor; but salt and rum were just as essential, the latter because the men were working in the icy water and the weather was "so extream bad." [43] Clinton himself was sometimes at Fort Constitution supervising the work; at other times he was directing operations from his home at New Windsor just above Polopel's Island, or superintend-ing the procurement of equipment at such points as Murderers' Creek close to Newburgh.

This task of obstructing the Hudson received a serious setback the second week in December. Washington had been some days in New Jersey pursued by the victorious but dilatory Howe. The New York committee of safety, uneasy at the lack of news from the commander-in-chief and alarmed by the progress of the enemy, sent a special

---

[41] Public Papers, I, 430–33; American Archives, Series 5, III, 663, 751, 842, 860.
[42] Public Papers, I, 435–38.
[43] Ibid., 446.

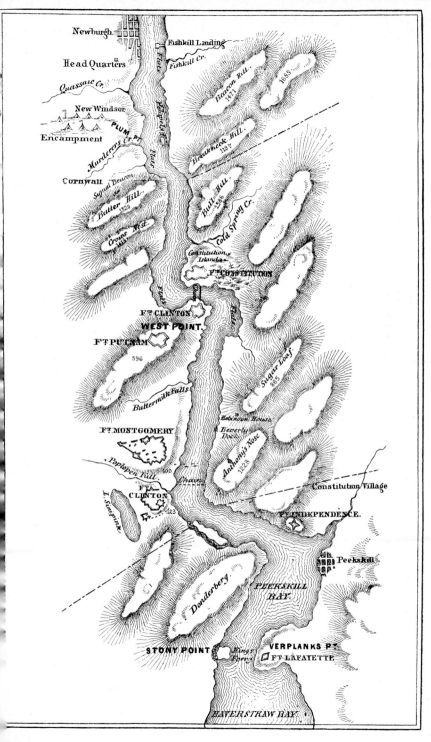

THE HIGHLANDS OF THE HUDSON

From Ruttenber's *Observations to the Navigation of Hudson's River*

committee of three, General Scott and Messrs. William Duer and Robert R. Livingston, to confer with George Clinton at New Windsor. They met on the eighth and, in all probability, concocted the plan for an expedition into New Jersey to relieve the pressure on Washington through an attack on the enemy's rear, a plan which was formally adopted by the committee of safety at Fishkill the next day.

Clinton was to assemble an army of New York troops at Kakiate in Orange County, and this force, together with such New Jersey, Connecticut, or other New England militia as might be induced to come, was to join Major General Gates or Major General Lee, provided the forces of either were to operate against the enemy's rear in such a position as to make it possible for Clinton to coöperate with them and still protect the Highlands of the Hudson.[44] If those two officers were to join Washington's main army, then Clinton was to march into New Jersey alone, raising the spirits of the Jersey militia and over-awing the disaffected in that state. As it happened it was not possible for Clinton to join either Gates or Lee.

Preparations took some days and it was not until the fourteenth that Clinton was at Fort Constitution hurrying on to the rendezvous at Kaki-ate where several militia regiments, already gathered, were protesting the general lack of food and shelter. The next day he was near Kakiate with 1200 militia, and a day later he rode to Hackensack with a small detachment of light horse to see Heath and offer him any assistance that he might need. Heath, however, had put the enemy to rout and needed no assistance. On the evening of the nineteenth Clinton and General Samuel H. Parsons, with 500 men, conducted a successful raid into enemy territory near Bergen, New Jersey, where Clinton had gone surveying some fifteen years before. Although the enemy discovered the movement before Colonel Woodhull, with a force of 200 men, was ready to cut off their retreat at Bergen Woods, 23 prisoners were taken with some supplies and the enemy cleared out of the district.[45]

Clinton, returning to Pyramus to prepare his report for the convention,

---

[44] *Calendar of Historical Manuscripts Relating to the Revolution*, I, 547–54; *American Archives*, series 5, III, 362–73; *Public Papers*, I, 454–57.
[45] Charles S. Hall, *Life and Letters of Samuel Holden Parsons* (Binghampton, N.Y., 1905), 79; *Public Papers*, I, 477–78.

was now in high spirits. The expedition had apparently accomplished its purpose [46] and two days later Clinton was ordered back to the east shore of the Hudson to secure the position at North Castle against an expected attack. There he was set to act in conjunction with General Alexander McDougall whom Washington was placing in command of the Continental forces in that Department with headquarters at Peekskill. Heath was to join Washington who thought that the British would not attack the Highlands at that season of the year.[47]

It was the end of a disastrous year for the American forces in New York. They had lost Long Island, Staten Island, New York City, and much of Westchester County, and only the half-heartedness of Howe's campaigning had spared them from additional losses. The state found itself shut off from the sea and from its greatest center of trade and population, seriously handicapped at the very commencement of the war. And its peripatetic convention, occupied when it did meet with the problems of war, had not yet been able to devise a state government worthy of the name. All in all, the situation was not an enviable one and it is unlikely that Clinton's small successes on the New Jersey frontier or even the glad news of Washington's Christmas success at Trenton dispelled any considerable proportion of the gloom that hung over the state of New York.

[46] Calendar of Historical Manuscripts Relating to the Revolution, I, 559, 573.
[47] Washington, Writings, Fitzpatrick, ed., VI, 417–19, 442.

CHAPTER VI

COUSIN HENRY ATTACKS THE HIGHLANDS

THE British attack on the Hudson Valley that Clinton had long been preparing for, came in 1777. With the shifting of the center of conflict to New Jersey and Pennsylvania at the close of 1776, the operations in New York assumed for the time a relatively minor importance. Yet frequent assignments from the committee of safety or the Convention and eloquent appeals from Washington, who was never too busy to watch every phase of the preparations in New York, kept Clinton occupied. He was placed with General Scott and William Duer on a committee for planning a secret expedition into Westchester County;[1] he was instructed to raise a thousand men in the four river counties, and he was admonished by Washington to bring these

---

[1] *Calendar of Historical Manuscripts Relating to the Revolution*, I, 578.

recruits into the service at the earliest possible moment[2] and to arrange in addition for the recruiting of companies for the Continental forces[3]—recruiting that Clinton did not relish and in all probability never entirely completed.[4]

The obstruction of the Hudson, however, which the Convention had entrusted to him, continued to take a major portion of his time and was undoubtedly the project in which he was most interested during the early months of 1777. Yet the works at Polopel's Island were, as events proved, of very little value. It must be admitted that Clinton was largely responsible for pouring too much of the state's scant resources and man power into the works at Constitution Island which was too low a position to be effectively fortified, and into the fortification of Polopel's Island which was several miles above the Highlands. The Highlands were the first line of defense and the state should have completed one or two strong positions there, including the present West Point, before it allowed Clinton to fortify Polopel's Island.

Late in March 1777 the enemy were again active in the lower Hudson Valley. Clinton hurried to Fort Montgomery on the twenty-fourth the moment he heard of General McDougall's retreat from Peekskill and a day later the Convention at Kingston, expecting the enemy to attack the Highland forts, empowered him as the ranking brigadier general to call out the militia of Dutchess, Ulster, Orange and Westchester, or any part of them, at his own discretion or at Washington's order.[5] Five days later Clinton held a council of war with his officers at Mrs. Falls' house in Little Britain and there it was decided to call out one-third of the Ulster and Orange militia to re-enforce the posts at Fort Montgomery and Sydman's Bridge.[6] The British did not, however, press their advantage. The real attack on the defenses of the Highlands was to come later in the year.

George Clinton's friends, including Washington himself, had meanwhile been recommending him for a Continental appointment. The

---

[2] Letter of January 19, 1777; A. Elwood Corning, *Washington at Temple Hill* (Newburgh, N.Y., 1932), 42.

[3] Washington, *Writings*, VII, 33.

[4] *Public Papers*, I, 662, 666.

[5] *Ibid.*, 679, 682.

[6] *Ibid.*, 687. He also ordered men raised in Dutchess County, *ibid.*, 695.

Continental Congress finally, on March 25, 1777, "elected" him Continental commandant of the posts in the Highlands with the title of brigadier general, a rank that he kept until after the close of the war. He wrote modestly to Washington, who had sent him his warm congratulations, that because of the precarious state of his health and his want of military knowledge he would have preferred a more retired life than that of the army, but he added, "as early in the present contest I laid it down as a maxim not to refuse my best, though poor services, to my country in any way they should think proper to employ me, I cannot refuse the honor done me in the present appointment." [7]

Although the Continental appointment brought with it no great change in Clinton's work, it did bring additional responsibility and he found less time than before for pressing the Polopel's Island project and for the always irksome business of recruiting militia. With the transfer of his brother James from Fort Montgomery, George found himself obliged to stay constantly at that place, neglecting some of his other tasks. Consequently on May 9 he asked the Convention to accept his resignation as brigadier general of militia. But the Convention, which could find no one to replace him, begged him to postpone his resignation. This decision, Pierre Van Cortlandt told Clinton, was influenced by "the high Sense they entertained of your Abilities to serve your Country in this important Hour" and "the Confidence reposed in your Zeal and abilities by the Militia in General." [8] Clinton, who may well have been flattered by the Convention's insistence, did not press the point. There was indeed no other state or Continental officer to whom both Washington and the New York Convention were so willing to entrust the vitally important defenses of the Hudson.

A few days later Washington ordered Major General Israel Putnam to leave Princeton and take command on the east shore of the Hudson at Peekskill,[9] and during the months that followed it was Putnam whom Clinton recognized as his immediate superior. Neither Heath nor McDougall had been conspicuously successful with the Peekskill

[7] Corning, *Washington at Temple Hill*, 44; *Journals of Continental Congress*, March 25, 1777; R. E. Prime, *George Clinton: An Address* (New York, 1902), 25.
[8] *Public Papers*, I, 808, 836-37.
[9] Washington, *Writings*, VIII, 51.

command, and Putnam was to be even less so. A brave, somewhat elderly gentleman, he was, it is said, unfit to command a battalion. He frequently misjudged the entire military situation in New York, and his nervousness as to his own position together with his unwillingness to accept Clinton's warnings were in October to help materially in bringing about the most serious military disaster of the year in New York. Washington himself was still the superior to whom Clinton turned with most confidence.

At the same time that Washington transferred Putnam to Peekskill he ordered Major General Nathanael Greene to visit the posts in the Highlands, especially Fort Montgomery, and make recommendations for their defense. The conference that Greene called in New York a few days later with Brigadier Generals Knox, McDougall, Wayne and George Clinton, concluded that if the obstructions on the river could be made effective, four or five thousand men could defend the passes. For this purpose they proposed to support the chain that, thanks largely to Clinton's efforts, had recently been placed across the river just below Fort Montgomery, with one or two cables and a boom. Two Continental ships and two "Row-Gallies" were to be placed just above the obstructions to rake the enemy ships with their fire. The consulting generals had confidence that these feeble measures would do much to keep open "the Communication between the Eastern and Western States [which] is so essential to the Continent . . ."[10]

With the appearance of General Burgoyne in northern New York early in June and St. Leger's invasion of the Mohawk Valley, the center of interest shifted to the northward. It was clear that the King intended to split the new union of American states by conquering the Hudson Valley from the north. When the harassed Schuyler called for reënforcements for the campaign against Burgoyne, Clinton responded promptly and generously. Although Washington asked him for only 500 militia, enough to release the Continentals in the Highlands, he ordered 1500 to join Schuyler at Albany, requested General Herkimer to provide 500 more, and called out 800 to serve in the lower counties, 2800 in all.[11] Clearly he realized the seriousness of the situa-

[10] The report is in the Library of Congress. Washington, *Writings*, VIII, 51-2, note; Corning, *op. cit.*, 12; *Public Papers*, I, 675.
[11] *Public Papers*, II, 142, 146, 167, 195.

tion. He informed the council of safety that, if they should approve, he was ready to go to Albany to take charge of the militia. Meanwhile, as he had become governor of the state, he postponed the meeting of the new legislature until the first of September.[12] Both Schuyler and the Albany committee wanted him to go north to reassure the threatened areas and as the council of safety had no objection, he was at Albany on the nineteenth.

Much to Clinton's regret Philip Schuyler was no longer in command at Albany. After months of sectional bitterness and controversy in the Continental Congress, of letters from Schuyler that Congress thought insulting, of criticism of his gloomy despondency and want of confidence in his troops,[13] the Congress had decided to replace him with Horatio Gates early in August. Perhaps the loss of Ticonderoga was the final straw that doomed the New Yorker. At any rate Clinton thought his removal without justification. James Duane wrote him from Philadelphia late in August that the New York delegation in Congress agreed with Clinton "that General Schuyler is sacrificed to unworthy Suspicion and unprovoked malace; and our State left to struggle almost alone under a powerful Invasion . . ."[14]

Whether or not Clinton approved of the appointment, it was necessary for him to coöperate constantly with General Gates who, as Continental commander of the Northern Department, was authorized to make requisitions on the State of New York. And it was due largely to Governor Clinton's generous coöperation in reënforcing Gates at a critical time that Burgoyne was defeated at Saratoga. Clinton stayed about a week in and near Albany, rejoicing in the news of St. Leger's retreat from Fort Schuyler and of the Battle of Bennington, receiving appeals and petitions for aid from the aroused northern counties, threatening contumacious militia, and arranging for necessary troop movements. By August 31 he was back at Kingston ready to meet his first legislature.

When Governor Clinton, usually so wary of possible enemy troop movements, harangued the legislature on September 10, he assured it

---

[12] *Ibid.*, 184, 230.
[13] *Ibid.*, 200; Flick, ed., *History of the State of New York*, III, 302–03; Samuel Adams to Roger Sherman, August 11, 1777. Meshech Weare Papers, Force Transcripts, Library of Congress.
[14] Letter of August 25 (typed copy), Library of Congress.

that the Highlands were "in so respectable a state of defense, as to promise us security against any attack in that quarter. This, together with the several obstructions in Hudson's River, has probably induced General Howe to alter his original plan . . ."[15] Once more Clinton showed too much confidence in his cherished obstructions.

Late in July the indecisive Howe had sailed southward from New York leaving Sir Henry Clinton with a small force in the state's metropolis. Believing that, so long as Howe was absent, no very determined assault on the Hudson Valley would be made, George Clinton left Fort Montgomery under the command of his brother and went to Kingston to assume the duties of the governorship. Sir Henry had only about 4000 men and until he received the reënforcements that he expected from England, or until Howe returned to New York, if he should, there was little or no danger of an assault on the Highlands. Sir Henry was, however, an excellent soldier, perhaps the best of the British commanders of the American Revolution, and he would bear watching. He was, incidentally, the son of George Clinton, the provincial governor, and therefore a distant cousin of the American Clintons who stood between him and Burgoyne.

Even with Howe away, George Clinton found it next to impossible to settle down to affairs of state. Only a week after the British fleet had left New York, Washington heard that it had turned eastward again from the capes of the Delaware and, suspecting that this promised a sudden attack on the Hudson Valley, he sent urgent appeals to Putnam, Sullivan, and McDougall to reënforce the garrison at Peekskill, and urged Clinton to call out the militia and, if possible, go himself at once to the important position at Fort Montgomery.[16] Governor Clinton received the startling news on August 5. He at once called out virtually all of the remaining militia, prorogued the legislature because of the emergency, and himself hurried to the Highlands[17]—only to learn some hours later that Howe apparently had no intention of returning to New York.

During the late summer of 1777 everything conspired toward re-

---

[15] C. Z. Lincoln, *Messages from the Governors*, Vol. II, 8.
[16] Washington, *Writings*, IX, 1–6.
[17] *Public Papers*, II, 180–86.

ducing the American forces in lower New York: the expiration of periods of enlistment, the reënforcement of Schuyler and Gates in the north, and, finally, the despatching of a major share of Putnam's Continentals from the Peekskill region to reënforce both Washington and Gates in mid-September. Only a few hundred militia and Continentals were left to defend the all-important Highlands. Washington on September 14 was still urging Putnam to send him more men— men who, according to the plan, were later to be replaced in part by 2000 Connecticut militia.[18] With Burgoyne threatening in the north and Sir Henry Clinton stirring now and then in the south, the situation was critical. Governor Clinton at once ordered six regiments to Peekskill to reënforce Putnam, three to McDougall at Ramapo over the New Jersey line, and two to Fort Montgomery. This was all of the militia south of Poughkeepsie.[19]

There had, however, been many cries of "Wolf!" during the preceding months, and as the militia were impatient to be back at their farms to sow their wheat and to harvest the late crops, the easy-going Putnam released several hundred of them. This left only about a thousand Continentals and four hundred militia to defend the Highlands, and General Clinton was somewhat irked by Putnam's untimely generosity.[20] On September 18 it was necessary for the governor to order more militia regiments northward to join Gates. When Putnam appealed to him nine days later for still more militia, he could only suggest, perhaps none too tactfully, new regulations to compel the militia "to their Duty & keep them in the Field."

On the twenty-eighth of September [21] the bewildered Putnam heard that Sir Henry Clinton had received the long-expected reënforcements from England—three thousand added to Sir Henry's four thousand at New York. An attack on the Hudson Valley was now almost a certainty. George Clinton ordered seven of his colonels to send half of each of their regiments to Putnam at Peekskill and three others to

[18] Letter of September 14. Washington, *Writings*, IX, 218.
[19] *Public Papers*, II, 323.
[20] Clinton's letter to Washington, Little Britain, October 9, 1777, in Library of Congress; Hoffman Nickerson, *The Turning Point of the Revolution* (Boston, 1928), 337; Hall, *General S. H. Parsons*, 116.
[21] *Public Papers*, II, 348.

send half regiments to reënforce Fort Montgomery where General James Clinton was in command. These were the same regiments that the benevolent Putnam had allowed to return to their crops.

On the day that Clinton issued these orders, the twenty-ninth, his cousin Sir Henry received a note from the stranded Burgoyne appealing to him to create a diversion by attacking Fort Montgomery.[22] Now that Sir Henry had his reënforcements a diversion was clearly in order, and he set sail up the Hudson with 3000 men on October 3. The next day, which was Friday, an artillery officer just arrived at Fort Montgomery from Peekskill gave James Clinton the startling information that the enemy had come up the valley as far as Tarrytown. General James, expecting that Putnam would of course send him warning of the British advance or have the alarm guns fired, "waited some time," and then despatched a letter to his brother at New Windsor. George Clinton received the letter at seven o'clock on Saturday evening, at once replied to his brother advising him to call out the Orange militia, and two hours later wrote the legislature that he intended to go southward himself the next morning. He did not change his plans although he was inclined to believe, after reading a letter from Putnam which probably arrived in the early hours of the morning, that the British attack was aimed at Westchester County and not at the Highlands.[23]

On his way to Fort Montgomery on Sunday he heard the guns down the valley calling the scattered militiamen to their stations. According to his own account he found Fort Montgomery garrisoned by only about 500 men.[24] Probably the two forts together, Montgomery and Clinton, had a combined garrison of a meager 600, for only a few score of the reënforcements he had recently ordered out had arrived. And of his small force he sent sixty men that night at Putnam's order "to repair to the top of Anthonies Nose" directly across the river above Fort Independence. Men were coming in from the farms, but it was clear that it had been much easier for Putnam to release the militia

[22] Nickerson, op. cit., 343.
[23] Public Papers, II, 360–62.
[24] Clinton's statement submitted to the court of inquiry early in 1778 explains fully the action taken by him on his arrival. New York Historical Association, Quarterly Journal, April 1931, 167–71.

to return to their crops than for Clinton to get them back to their posts.

Unfortunately the Hudson divided the American forces. When Sir Henry Clinton arrived at Tarrytown on October 4 Putnam fully expected an attack on his position at Peekskill which was only fifteen miles up the river.[25] On Sunday the fifth when the British seized and made an early camp at the very indifferently fortified Verplanck's Point, only three to four miles below Peekskill, Putnam had even less inclination to send reënforcements to Clinton at the forts. On the other hand, as we have seen, he ordered sixty of Clinton's men to Anthony's Nose on the Peekskill side of the river. He himself had only 1200 Continentals and 300 militia to defend Peekskill and its valuable supplies.[26] Sir Henry Clinton's highly successful strategy kept the divided Americans ignorant until the last moment of the point where his attack was to be made, and so prevented any union of their forces.

George Clinton himself took command of Fort Montgomery which stood with its unfinished works on the north side of Popolopen's Kill, more than a hundred feet above the Hudson. He placed his brother in command of Fort Clinton which stood on somewhat higher ground just south of the Kill, a stronger position if adequately manned. The two forts overlooked the chain which had been stretched from the promontory of Anthony's Nose to the Hudson's western shore[27]—the chain in which comtemporaries had such confidence. Both forts were intended primarily to resist attack from the river side.

The British attack came on Monday the sixth. About nine that morning Major Logan, a trusted officer whom Clinton had sent out the night before to reconnoitre, returned to Fort Montgomery to report his belief that the enemy had landed at King's Ferry almost opposite Verplanck's Point on the western shore of the Hudson only about four miles as the crow flies below Fort Clinton. The morning was foggy, however, and he could not say for certain. Clinton then sent out Lieutenant Jackson with twenty-eight men on the Haverstraw road. This detachment was only too fortunate in locating the enemy

[25] Nickerson, op. cit., 344–45.
[26] Hall, Parsons, 117.
[27] See the map of the Highlands opposite page 66.

at ten o'clock near Doodletown between Bear Mountain, and its twin, the Dunderberg. To support Jackson Clinton risked weakening his garrison by one hundred Continentals and militia under Colonel Bruyn and Lieutenant Colonel James McClaughry, Clinton's brother-in-law. But the reënforcement only delayed the enemy's progress by some sharp skirmishing before it joined Jackson in a retreat to Fort Clinton.[28]

Whether or not he had as yet received the letter of warning that the bewildered Putnam wrote him early on Monday, it must have been clear to Clinton by noon that the long-expected British attack on the Highlands and the obstructions in the river was under way and that he must face it with his few hundred men. He immediately asked Putnam for reënforcements but the appeal never reached its destination. The British did not, however, have 5000 men as Clinton suspected.[29] Very early on the foggy morning of the sixth Sir Henry Clinton had left Verplanck's Point with 2000 of his 3000 men. Landing near Stony Point, just north of Haverstraw Bay, they had been guided northward across rough, almost mountainous country, by Brom Springster, a Loyalist who belonged in the region. Five miles of laborious marching brought them by eight in the morning to the "Timp," a formidable passage, several hundred feet above the river and the forts, which might have been effectively defended by even a small force of Americans—but was not.[30] At that time George Clinton had not even received Major Logan's report that the British had crossed the river.

Arriving in the valley between Bear Mountain on the north and the Dunderberg on the south, Sir Henry Clinton divided his forces for a simultaneous assault on the two forts. He himself took Generals Vaughan and Tryon with a majority of the troops for the shorter and more direct attack on Fort Clinton, while Lieutenant Colonel Campbell with 900 men, including some Loyalists under Colonel Beverly Robinson and German chasseurs, were to circle Bear Mountain for an attack on the west and more vulnerable side of Fort Montgomery.[31]

[28] George Clinton reported the events of October 6 to the Council and to Washington in letters of October 7 and 9 printed in *Public Papers*, II, 380 and 389.

[29] *Public Papers*, II, 381.

[30] Hoffman Nickerson's *Turning Point of the Revolution*, p. 346, blames Clinton's negligence for the failure to guard the "Timp."

[31] Nickerson, *op. cit.*, 347-51, contains an excellent account of the attack on the forts.

Believing that Putnam would send reënforcements across the river above the chain and under its protection, Governor Clinton tried to delay the British assault until they could arrive. He not only sent out the Bruyn-McClaughry party, but he also posted his one field piece and over a hundred men at the "Hell Hole" about a mile west of the fort on the road that Colonel Campbell would arrive by. This was undoubtedly good strategy. The force at the "Hell Hole" resisted manfully when Campbell's advanced guard arrived, giving the British a taste of grapeshot and musket balls and spiking the field piece before making the inevitable retreat to the fort. Only Captain Fenno, who was in immediate charge of the field piece, fell into Campbell's hands.

It was over two hours later, nearly five, before the British were ready for the assault on the two forts. Just before commencing the final action Lieutenant Colonel Campbell himself came with a flag to demand the surrender of the fort and George Clinton sent Lieutenant Colonel Livingston to receive him. Livingston, under orders from Clinton, informed Campbell that he had no authority to treat and unless Campbell wished to give himself up he might better continue the attack on the fort since it would be defended to the last.

After these impressive preliminaries Campbell attacked, the German troops in the center, the British on the right, and Robinson's Tories on the left. The struggle was short but bloody, for the British used their bayonets and the fighting was at short range. If, as is probable, the British casualties were over three hundred, Clinton's little garrison, greatly outnumbered as it was, gave an excellent account of itself. Colonel Campbell himself was killed together with a number of his officers.

Fort Montgomery was first occupied at about half-past six, and the stronger works at Fort Clinton fell to the British shortly afterwards. The garrisons were of course completely routed. Many escaped in the dark, but a number were killed by fire or by bayonet and over 250, including Colonel McClaughry and the governor's aide, Stephen Lush, were taken by the British.[32] James Clinton received a bad bayonet wound in the thigh and although his brother thought for a time that he had been captured, his knowledge of the country enabled him to escape down

[32] *Public Papers*, II, 623.

the steep sides of Popolopen's Kill and home to Little Britain. Governor Clinton himself narrowly escaped capture by a precarious descent of the precipitous hillside to the Hudson where he was persuaded to enter an already overladen boat that escaped in the darkness to the eastern shore.[33] Sir Henry Clinton very nearly had the pleasure of escorting his cousin the governor back to New York City a prisoner.

There is no doubt but that the defense of Fort Montgomery was spirited and courageous. In spite of its disastrous but inevitable outcome, it enhanced the military reputation of virtually every man in the heroic little garrison, including that of its commander. General Parsons of Connecticut, like other contemporaries who commented on the engagement, had only admiration for "the courage and bravery displayed by the troops (principally militia from New York) who defended the Post . . . No terms would be accepted," he went on in his letter to Governor Trumbull written on October 7 from Danbury, "but with fortitude seldom found, they undauntedly stood the shock, determined to defend the Fort or sell their lives as dear as possible. The Fort was finally taken, merely for want of men to man the lines, and not for want of spirit in the men. But about five hundred was afforded to man the Post and outworks . . ."[34] Four days later John Palsgrave Wyllys wrote to his father from Little Britain: "You must have heard by this time, the favourable news from the Northern & Southern Armies, as well as the loss of Fort Montgomery—if ever place was well defended, that was—by a handful of men—& with little Loss—Of near four hundred men, scarce a third is missing—it was carried by storm after repeated attacks; with the loss of numbers & some principal Officers, both British & Hessians—The Post might easily have been held, had our Generals thought of an attack upon that place—but unluckily they did not know of it soon enough for a reënforcement to reach the Fort—"[35] "The noble defense of Fort Montgomery," declared General Gates, "will, to the latest posterity, adorn the name of Clinton."[36]

[33] Nickerson, op. cit., 351; Corning, Washington at Temple Hill, 50; Leake, John Lamb, 176–77; Public Papers, II, 382.

[34] Hall, Samuel H. Parsons, 118.

[35] George Dudley Seymour, Captain Nathan Hale and Major John Palsgrave Wyllys (New Haven, 1933), 189.

[36] Leake, Lamb, 179.

Washington himself added his commendation when he wrote George Clinton from near Philadelphia: "It is to be regretted that so brave a resistance did not meet with a suitable reward. You have however, the satisfaction of knowing that everything was done that could possibly be, by a handful against a far superior force. This I am convinced is the case." [37] Clinton himself had declared to Washington that whatever blame might fall upon him for the loss of the forts, "the officers and men under me of the different corps behaved with the greatest spirit and bravery." [38] The defense was a gallant one and it seems to have raised, rather than depressed the morale of the troops.

When George Clinton reached the further shore he may well have encountered the five hundred men of Putnam's who were ready to cross to his aid just as the forts fell into British hands. With such a re-enforcement the outcome of the struggle might have been very different. Later that night he may have seen two sad bonfires on the river, the ship *Montgomery,* which got out of the control of her crew and was fired at Captain Hodge's own command to save her from the enemy, and the *Congress,* the other continental frigate, which seems to have had an equally clumsy crew, that went aground near Fort Constitution and had to be burned.[39] Clinton was somewhat provoked that these defenders of the great chain should have given up so easily. The burning of Fort Constitution a few miles upstream opposite the future West Point, he did not condemn.

Governor Clinton at once joined Putnam at Continental Village where a council of war agreed that it was Sir Henry Clinton's purpose to join the threatened Burgoyne in the north—a view that subsequent events proved to be wrong—and that Putnam should retreat to the hills up the river near Fishkill while Clinton, with reënforcements from Putnam and from the Orange and Ulster militia, should rally his troops to protect the chevaux-de-frise in the river at Polopel's Island. If the chevaux-de-frise should provide as little hindrance to Sir Henry as the great chain was providing at that moment, then both Putnam and the governor were to give ground, defending the countryside, especially

[37] Washington, *Writings,* IX, 372.
[38] *Public Papers,* II, 395.
[39] *Public Papers,* II, 382, 394.

Kingston, and making Sir Henry's advance as difficult as possible.[40] During the days that followed this convincing plan was only indifferently carried out.

Part of the stores were removed from Fort Constitution and the fort destroyed by its own defenders. Clinton himself returned to New Windsor and established his headquarters at the home of his widowed cousin, Mrs. Falls, on the Goshen road in Little Britain.[41] Here he waited for his reënforcements to arrive. "We are at present on the West Side of the River, under the command of Governor Clinton—," wrote one of his New England soldiers. "Never had a man a more absolute Ascendancy over people, than he has over the Inhabitants of this part of the Country—They are now gathered round their *Chief*— a stout hardy race—armed with good, long Musquets—in high Spirits —exulting in their behavior at Fort Montgomery & wishing for another opportunity—In short they do not appear like Dutchmen; but have the manners of N. England, from whence I believe they sprang—Their Governor deservedly has their Esteem—few men are his Superiors—." [42] Clearly George Clinton was an inspiring leader of men.

On October 9 while Clinton was at Mrs. Falls', his men captured David Taylor, the famous spy of the silver bullet. Taylor had been sent by Sir Henry Clinton with a message of encouragement to General Burgoyne, a message that was enclosed in a little capsule of silver, the size of a bullet, that could be opened by unscrewing it in the middle. When taken before the governor Taylor cautiously swallowed the bullet. Clinton later reported to the Council of Safety that he had "mistrusted this to be [the] case from information [he had] received, and administered him a very strong emetic, calculated to operate either way. This had the desired effect; . . ." Yet Taylor managed to conceal it a second time, but "brought it forth" again when the governor promised to hang him instantly and cut him open to search for it.[43]

[40] *Public Papers*, II, 388.
[41] Corning, *Washington at Temple Hill*, 35–36. The Falls house, which was of wood except for the north wall, was destroyed by fire in 1914. It was an inn in 1777.
[42] Seymour, *Captain Nathan Hale and Major John Palsgrave*, 189–90.
[43] *Public Papers*, II, 398, 403, 404, 413–414; James P. Baxter, ed., *The British Invasion from the North* (Albany, 1887), 33–35; Corning, *Washington at Temple Hill*, 51–53. Taylor was tried by court martial October 14 and hanged October 18.

Another more fortunate messenger succeeded in delivering the message to Burgoyne. The message did not, however, promise that Sir Henry would come to Albany and Burgoyne's aid, and there is little to indicate that Sir Henry had any intention of pushing his advantage to the extent of attacking Gates from Albany.

In spite of the enthusiasm of his men and his bold appeals for aid, all was not going well with Clinton. The chevaux-de-frise at Polopel's Island was broken by Sir James Wallace's "musquito fleet" which was able to sail up the river without opposition. Clinton complained that he had no suitable shot with which to plague the enemy shipping. And more serious still, the promised reënforcements did not arrive. The night of the fall of the Highland forts Putnam had promised him 3000 men as soon as the New England militia should arrive; yet over two weeks later, on October 21, Putnam had sent him less than 400.[44] He had also appealed to the Council of Safety, to Gates, and to the state of New Jersey; but he still had only about 1000 men in his entire force.

Meanwhile, on the sixteenth of October, the day before the tremendous victory at Saratoga, the governor's little army had failed entirely to prevent the sacking and burning of Kingston by the main body of Sir Henry Clinton's forces under General Vaughan. On the evening of the fifteenth, while the British were landing at the little town of Esopus about six miles below Kingston, which they burned, Governor Clinton was hurrying down from Albany[45] and his militia were pushing up from New Windsor in the hope of saving Kingston. His troops probably camped that night at Shawangunk while the governor hastened on, reached Kingston that night or the next morning and reported to Gates at noon that there was little hope of saving the town.[46] Neither his own little army nor the six hundred New Jersey militia that General Dickinson had promised him, would come in time. Vaughan arrived in the late afternoon, burned the entire town, plundered the countryside, and reëmbarked his troops within three hours.[47] The sacking of Kingston was one of the most brutal, indefensible actions of the entire war.

[44] Clinton's letter of October 24 to Gates printed in Schoonmaker, *Kingston*, 317.
[45] Clinton wrote Washington from Albany, October 15; Washington, *Writings*, IX, 393.
[46] *Public Papers*, II, 444; *Olde Ulster*, X, 303–04.
[47] Schoonmaker, *Kingston*, 301, 318; *Public Papers*, II, 457–59.

After the fall of Kingston Governor Clinton went to Hurley to guard the supplies that had been saved from the British, and Vaughan continued his plundering of the countryside until, after receiving the news of Burgoyne's surrender, he fell back down the river to rejoin Sir Henry Clinton. Sir Henry's "diversion" in the Hudson Valley, successful as it had been in every detail, had failed to save Burgoyne, and late in October, after demolishing the works in the Highlands, he retired to New York City.[48] Simultaneously the troops at Hurley were ordered back to headquarters at New Windsor where the governor arrived on the twenty-seventh. It was some time before his Cousin Henry was to trouble the governor again; but twelve years later, in April 1789, Clinton was to write to George Clinton to entreat him to interest himself in saving his estates in America.[49]

Both Putnam and Clinton have been blamed for the loss of the forts in the Highlands; Clinton because he had not fortified the passes in the hills behind the forts, especially at the "Timp," and because he had not sent out more scouts to warn him of the enemy's moves; and Putnam because he allowed himself to be outmaneuvered by the British and because he did not reënforce Clinton in time to save the forts. So convinced were the people of New York that Putnam was incompetent that exactly five months after the burning of Kingston, Washington found it wise to remove him from the command on the Hudson and put McDougall in his place.[50] Perhaps it was the death of Mrs. Putnam that rendered "Old Put" especially ineffective at that time.

Meanwhile, on November 28, the Continental Congress directed Washington to make an inquiry "into the loss of Forts Montgomery and Clinton, in the State of New York . . . and into the conduct of the principal officers commanding these forts." The following February Washington named a court of three to conduct the investigation: Alexander McDougall president, Brigadier General Huntington and Colonel Edward Wigglesworth.[51] Although the court finished its inquiry on April 4, Governor Clinton received no official notice of its findings until

[48] *Public Papers,* II, 490.
[49] Letter of April 24, 1789. Copy in the Wisconsin Historical Society.
[50] Hall, *Parsons,* 167.
[51] *Journals of the Continental Congress;* New York Historical Association, *Quarterly Journal,* April 1931, 165–66.

September when, in response to his request, the president of Congress sent him "an Act of Congress of the 21st," with an apology for having neglected him. "The Act of the 21st," President Laurens pointed out, "signifies the entire approbation by Congress of your Excellency's conduct as Commander of the Forts on Hudson's River which I repeat with great pleasure in obedience to the order of Congress . . ." [52] Certainly Clinton had come off much better than Putnam.

It is, as a matter of fact, unfair to try to assess the blame for the fall of the Highland forts in October 1777. Once Sir Henry Clinton had received his reënforcements from England the defenses of the Hudson were at his mercy. The American forces were not only greatly inferior in numbers but they were inevitably divided by the river and, what was often more serious, by the more or less coördinate authorities of state and nation. Clinton was not supreme on his side of the Hudson yet he could not depend upon Putnam for effective direction. This division in the American command was one of Sir Henry Clinton's greatest advantages. A unified command under a general officer far more skilful than Putnam might have made Sir Henry's progress up the Hudson much less of a triumph than it was, but even unity of command could only have delayed the British. The American forces were numerically inferior to the British and because of the great urgency of reënforcing both Washington's main army and Gates' northern army, the forces on the Hudson could not be materially increased. The Highlands and Kingston were sacrificed, and properly sacrificed, so that Washington might not fall prey to Howe and Gates might take Burgoyne. For these necessities Putnam and Clinton were in no way to blame.

[52] *Public Papers*, IV, 14, 99.

CHAPTER VII

FIRST GOVERNOR OF THE STATE

CLINTON NEGLECTS THE CONSTITUTIONAL CONVENTION

THE STATE'S FIRST CONSTITUTION

CLINTON AGAINST SCHUYLER, SCOTT, AND JAY

THE SOLDIERS MAKE CLINTON GOVERNOR

DISAPPOINTMENT OF THE FIRST FAMILIES

THE GOVERNOR'S CONSTITUTIONAL POWERS

HE HARANGUES THE LEGISLATURE AT KINGSTON

GEORGE CLINTON played only an insignificant rôle in the New York Convention of 1776 and 1777 that framed and adopted the harassed little state's first constitution. War and administration had a far greater appeal for Clinton throughout his entire career than the tedious, humdrum business of legislation; and even the plaintive urgings of the faithful John McKesson, who was then a secretary to the Convention, brought Clinton to Kingston to attend legislative sessions for only a few days during the ten months of the Convention's existence. It was perhaps that Clinton's tough, burly frame felt out of place in legislative halls.

The Convention of 1776–1777 was the fourth of the extra-legal provincial congresses which had followed one another in those kaleidoscopic years, 1775 and 1776. It met in the courthouse at White Plains on July 9, 1776, but it was soon to earn for itself the designation, "a government on the run," by migrating, as the British pushed northward, from Harlem to Kingsbridge to Philipse Manor to Fishkill to Poughkeepsie and, finally, to Kingston.[1] On the very day it met, it

---

[1] Allan Nevins, *The American States . . . 1775–1789* (New York, 1927), 158.

approved the Declaration of Independence. George Clinton, the member from Ulster who had just returned post haste from the Congress at Philadelphia on a military mission, was of necessity absent on July 9 and was therefore for a second time deprived of the distinction of voting for the Declaration.

Its second major task, the framing of a state constitution, took the convention over nine months. For weeks constitution-making was neglected. But then, as Gilbert Livingston and Christopher Tappen pointed out, it was advisable to secure a state to govern before discussing a form to govern it by. The group of thirteen statesmen that the Convention named on August first to frame a form of government and a bill of rights was distinguished and at the same time properly representative of both the conservative and radical points of view. It included John Sloss Hobart, William Smith, William Duer, Gouverneur Morris, Robert R. Livingston, John Broome, John Morin Scott, Abraham Yates, Henry Wisner, Samuel Townsend, Charles DeWitt, Robert Yates, and, most important of all, John Jay.[2] The Convention requested a report on August 26, but some of the committee, including Jay, were off on military missions and the report was rendered after a bewildering number of delays, not on August 26, 1776, but on March 12, 1777. Then followed over five weeks of discussion and revision before the adoption of the completed constitution with only one dissenting vote on Sunday evening, April 20. The Convention decided not to submit it to a popular vote since the Convention itself had been chosen expressly for the purpose of framing an instrument of government—a decision that the more radical patriots did not at all relish.

During the tedious sessions of the winter of 1777 George Clinton had only occasionally visited Kingston to spend a night or two in the Tappen's big stone house and take part in the deliberations of the Convention. During the discussions on the proposed constitution he seems to have been present for only one day, Friday, April 11, when he voted for Jay's plan for a council of appointment and against Robert Yates's amendment to strengthen the governor by allowing him to choose the council from among persons nominated by the senate and assembly.[3]

[2] Duane was later added.
[3] *Journal of the Provincial Convention*, April 11, 1777.

The first governor of the state of New York must often have regretted this vote—for of all the institutions established by the constitution of 1777, the council of appointment was to cause him the greatest amount of grief. His vote to weaken the governor's power was, however, understandable. The democrats of the time were resolved that the state governors should have far less power than the colonial governors who had so long been thorns in the flesh of all native Americans, and some of the radicals wished to deprive the governor entirely of the appointing power by conferring it on the legislature. As a compromise Jay, Morris, and Robert R. Livingston [4] seem to have worked out the plan for a council of appointment of four senators presided over by the governor, a plan that was to provide an effective curb on the governor's power of appointment.

The new constitution, hastily drawn as it was by a little group of provincial lawyers, farmers, and proprietors, was to outlive the Continental Articles of Confederation by over thirty years. Robert R. Livingston told Clinton he believed it would prove to be the best yet adopted in America. It was proclaimed on April 22 from a platform mounted on a hogshead in front of the court house at Kingston,[5] and almost simultaneously steps were taken to put it into operation. On the day of adoption the Convention named a committee to set up the machinery of government and some days later, upon the committee's recommendation, the Convention chose judges, sheriffs, and county clerks. It named Robert R. Livingston first chancellor of the state, John Jay chief justice—both in preference to that capable but radical Presbyterian lawyer, John Morin Scott—and chose Egbert Benson, whom a contemporary described as "a Person of Probity and plain Understanding, who will be guided by John Jay and R. R. Livingston,"[6] to be attorney general. The Convention chose senators and assemblymen for the occupied southern counties of the state and named a Council of Safety to carry on the state government after its own final adjournment on May 13. It was this Council of Safety that instructed the sheriffs to

[4] Nevins, *American States,* 162.

[5] It was ordered published at the court house at eleven o'clock, April 22. [Flick], *The American Revolution in New York,* 85, 92.

[6] B. F. Stevens, *Facsimiles of Manuscripts in European Archives Relating to America, 1773–1783* (London, 1889–1895), No. 438, Box 4.

hold state-wide elections in June for the choice of governor, lieutenant-governor, senators, and assemblymen.[7]

For the first time in its history New York was to elect a governor— a privilege for which, among others, the Revolution was being fought. Yet there seems to have been only a mild interest in the elections. There were no political parties to organize the campaigns; there was no outburst of campaign oratory; and with New York City in British hands there were but few newspapers to drum up an interest in the issues of the day. It was perhaps the most dignified gubernatorial campaign in the history of the state. What interest there was, as indicated in the press and in the private correspondence of the time, centered on the personalities of the numerous candidates.[8]

Of these the most indifferent to high office was John Jay. Allied by blood or marriage to such traditionally powerful families as the Livingstons, Van Cortlandts, and Philipses, Jay was probably the finest candidate that the New York aristocracy could offer. A Kings College graduate, an excellent lawyer, a gentleman in every sense of the word and a pious Anglican, he was the candidate *sans peur et sans reproche*. Conservative in his political philosophy, he had long hesitated at crossing the Rubicon of independence, but by 1777 no man doubted his patriotism. Men might, however, doubt his democracy; for he never relinquished his conviction that those who own a country are most fit to govern it. Able and talented as he was, he had no ability to win the confidence of the masses of men and he was never a strong candidate for public office.[9] In 1777 he disclaimed all desire to be governor. He told Abraham Yates that he preferred to be chief justice and he hoped that the electors might unite upon some other candidate.[10]

The other leading candidate put forward by the New York aristocracy was General Philip Schuyler of Albany. His mother was a Van Cortlandt and his wife a Van Rensselaer; he was wealthier than

---

[7] C. Z. Lincoln, ed., *Messages from the Governors*, II, 6.

[8] Col. Morris Graham wrote Clinton that in his county there were seven candidates for governor. *Public Papers*, II, 36.

[9] S. F. Bemis, ed., *American Secretaries of State and Their Diplomacy* (10 vols., New York, 1927–29), I, 193–97; S. F. Bemis, *Jay's Treaty* (New York, 1923), 203–05; Frank Monaghan, *John Jay* (New York, 1935).

[10] John Jay, *Correspondence and Public Papers*, Henry P. Johnston, ed. (4 vols., New York and London, 1890–93), I, 136–37.

Jay and an even more forbidding patrician. In spite of his very great services to the cause of American rights in the colonial assembly, he had little or no sympathy with the democratic urges of his time. He was virtuous, honest, and able; but he could not inspire confidence in men and he could not win votes. It has been said that people respected but did not love him. A veteran of the French War, he was in 1775 created a major general in the Continental service, but during his command in northern New York he managed to arouse so much antagonism that he was to be replaced in the late summer of 1777, as we have seen, by Horatio Gates. Always an intense partisan, Schuyler was probably the most eager of the candidates, and there were many indications that he would be elected. Even George Clinton's neighbor, Charles DeWitt, and his brother-in-law, Christopher Tappen, as well as John Jay, supported Schuyler's candidacy and recommended Clinton for only second place.[11]

John Morin Scott, aged forty-seven, was the oldest of the four principal candidates. He was a thorough-going democrat. John Adams, who remembered with pleasure the excellent fare that he received at Scott's "elegant seat" on the Hudson, labelled that gentleman "a very sensible man and an open one," an eminent lawyer and a ready speaker, who could "sit up all night at his bottle, yet argue to admiration next day . . ."[12] He had served in the Continental Congress as well as the provincial congress, and he was at the time of the election in 1777 a brigadier general and a member of the council of safety. He was a graduate of Yale College, a prominent Son of Liberty, and, like George Clinton and so many other radical whigs, a Presbyterian. He was, however, in spite of his wealth, too ardent a democrat and too fanatical a patriot to appeal to the moderates.[13] When Jay and his friends met at Kingston on June 2 and wrote to George Clinton in favor of Schuyler's candidacy, it was in all probability Scott whom they had in mind in warning against those without "Stability, uniformity or Sobriety to recommend them."[14]

[11] *Olde Ulster,* IV, 229.
[12] C. F. Adams, *The Life of John Adams* (2 vols., Philadelphia, 1871) II, 345–57.
[13] *Biographical Directory of the American Congress, 1774–1927* (Washington, 1928), p. 1502; *Public Papers,* I, 73.
[14] *Olde Ulster,* IV, 229.

It was remarkable that, in an age when family connections and property counted for much in public life, and when the franchise was confined to a select few, a man with George Clinton's modest background should have been recognized as an outstanding candidate for both the governorship and the lieutenant governorship. His humble Ulster County origins, his inconsiderable education, his small estate, his modest family connections and his complete indifference to the pretentiousness of social life, must all have handicapped him. On the other hand, he had been since 1768 an outstanding champion of the American cause in the colonial assembly, Continental Congress and provincial congress. He was in the prime of life, his thirty-eighth year, and physically a giant. Most important of all, he had contributed more to the waging of the war than any other general officer from New York with the possible exception of Philip Schuyler. His intense devotion to the American cause, his long months of service in the field at the expense of his health and personal interests, his rugged straightforward qualities, his preëminent common sense, his energy—these factors and others had won Washington's confidence and the admiration of thousands of New Yorkers. He has been rightly called "the most masculine" of all New Yorkers of the Revolutionary period.[15] The first families of the state, although they did not at the moment realize it, had no such candidate to offer.

Many conservatives, like John Jay, recognized Clinton's strength and were willing that he should have the lieutenant governorship. In Albany and Tryon Counties, for instance, where Schuyler led the balloting for governor, and in Charlotte County in the northeast, where Scott was the favored gubernatorial candidate, Clinton received heavy votes for second place.[16] But in other districts Clinton was from the first the candidate for governor. Jay thought his being pushed for the two offices might result in his obtaining neither, especially as Scott's candidacy had made inroads upon Clinton's vote.[17] It is said that some

[15] Statement by E. F. de Lancey in his edition of Jones, *New York in the Revolution,* II, 591.
[16] A. Ten Broeck, however, received more votes than Clinton in Albany. New York Secretary of State, *Calendar of Historical Manuscripts Relating to . . . Revolution,* II, 242.
[17] Jay, *Correspondence and Public Papers,* I, 144.

months before the elections a number of the most influential republicans met at Clermont, Robert R. Livingston's manor on the Hudson, and there they considered who was to be the first governor of the state. One well-qualified gentleman could not be spared from the important position he already occupied; this was presumably Philip Schuyler. Objections were offered to every person named until Margaret Beekman Livingston, the mother of Robert R. Livingston, proposed George Clinton, and her suggestion, the story goes, was received with acclaim. "He is the man! Why did not we think of him at once?"[18] Whether or not there is any truth in this story, Clinton did carry Dutchess County where Clermont was situated.

The general himself exhibited a proper indifference toward the outcome of the elections. Men might feel strongly on such matters even in those days, but they did not tour the state to harangue the electors.

The decisive factor in the balloting for governor was probably the soldier vote. The troops in the field felt that they should not be disfranchised and after some discussion it was agreed that officers and soldiers who had the right to vote might go to the nearest election place if they could be spared from their posts. These soldiers seem to have been very nearly unanimous for General Clinton.[19] We have the returns from six counties, not including Orange or the occupied southern counties, and of the six Schuyler carried Albany and Tryon; Jay obtained a plurality in Westchester; Scott, a majority in Charlotte; and Clinton, majorities in his own Ulster and in Dutchess. The total vote for the six counties, however, gave Schuyler 1012 ballots to 865 for Clinton. But somewhere, probably from Orange and from the soldiery, Clinton received 963 additional votes to only 187 additional votes for Schuyler. The complete returns gave Jay 367 votes, Scott 368, Schuyler 1199, and Clinton 1828.[20] Clinton's plurality came within 159 votes of being a majority. The general himself must have been amazed at the result.

Nor was that all. Clinton was also elected lieutenant governor by a

[18] Julia Delafield, *Morgan Lewis* (New York, 1877), 33; Marghenta A. Hamm, *Famous Families of New York* (2 vols., New York, 1902), I, 30–31.
[19] [Flick], *American Revolution in New York,* 93; *Public Papers,* I, 850; Hamilton, *Works,* Lodge, ed., I, 544.
[20] *Calendar of Historical Manuscripts Relating to . . . Revolution,* II, 242.

substantial plurality. He received 1647 votes to 1098 for Pierre Van Cortlandt, 746 for Ten Broeck, 108 for Jay, 84 for Scott and 57 for Schuyler.[21] Of the six counties for which we have returns, only one, Albany, failed to make Clinton its choice for either governor or lieutenant governor. It was indeed a spectacular victory for the young soldier.

Clinton's election must have caused consternation in the camp of the old patrician families of New York. With the British Crown eliminated, they had fully expected to rule the state. Yet an upstart Ulsterite of modest family and less estate had carried off the greatest prize of all. The dismayed Schuyler wrote Jay on June 30: "General Clinton I am informed has a majority of votes for the Chair. If so he has played his cards better than was expected." And he added a few days later that, "Although his [Clinton's] family and connections do not entitle him to so distinguished a predominance; yet he is virtuous and loves his country, has abilities and is brave, and hope he will experience from every patriot what I am resolved he shall have from me, support, countenance and comfort . . ."[22] Making the best of the recent holocaust, Schuyler sent his congratulations to the newly elected governor and received a gracious and friendly letter from Clinton in reply.[23]

However his social betters in New York might feel about Clinton's elevation to high office, Washington was undoubtedly sincere in his expressions of pleasure at that event: "The appointment of General Clinton to the Government of your State," he wrote to the Council of Safety on August 4, "is an event, that, in itself, gives me great pleasure, and very much abates the regret I should otherwise feel for the loss of his Services in the Military line. That Gentleman's Character is Such, as will make him peculiarly useful at the head of your State, in a Situation so alarming and interesting, as it at present experiences. For the future, agreeably to your desire, I shall direct my applications to him."[24]

Although the Convention had contemplated setting up the new state

[21] *Ibid.*
[22] Jay, *op. cit.*, I, 144, 147.
[23] Clinton to Schuyler, New Windsor, August 7, 1777, MS, Library of Congress.
[24] Washington, *Writings*, IX, 15.

government on July first, it was the ninth of the month before Pierre Van Cortlandt, president of the council, officially notified Clinton of his election to two high offices and invited him to come with all convenient speed to Kingston to accept one of the offices and decline the other. Clinton replied on July 11, declining the lesser office and promising to come to Kingston as soon as his "Duty to the Continent" allowed him.[25] It took a formal resolution of the Council of Safety, passed on July 21, to bring the busy general to Kingston. He requested Putnam's permission in a letter of the 26th, arrived in Kingston two days later, and on the afternoon of the 30th in front of the court house he took the oath of office from Pierre Van Cortlandt. The companies of Captain Evert Bogardus and Captain John Elmendorph were present to add dignity to the occasion, and the new governor was proclaimed in the presence of the council of safety by Sheriff Dumont standing, it is said, on the same hogshead platform that had served more than three months earlier at the proclamation of the new state constitution.[26]

After this simple ceremony Clinton remained about a week at Kingston before returning to Fort Montgomery and he did not again quit the field for any length of time until after Burgoyne's surrender. For those first few months the war governor of New York was primarily a warrior and only secondarily a governor.

The state constitution of 1777, which gave a legality to the state government during Clinton's administration that the earlier congresses and committees had not possessed, was one of the most enduring and at the same time the least liberal of the group of constitutions framed in 1776 and 1777. It has been called the best state constitution prior to that of Massachusetts of 1780. Although the radical Whigs in the convention's committee which drafted the constitution were able to elect one of their number, Abraham Yates, chairman, they somehow allowed John Jay and such moderate colleagues of Jay's as Livingston and Gouverneur Morris to do most of the actual drafting.[27] The resulting document, framed in the midst of revolution, was by no means radical.

[25] *Public Papers*, II, 105, note.
[26] *Ibid.*, 128, 140; *Olde Ulster*, IV, 262–63; Alexander, *New York*, I, 22; R. R. Hoes, *The Old Court House of Ulster County, New York* (1918), 16.
[27] Flick, ed., *History of the State of New York*, IV, 156.

It contained substantial property qualifications for the suffrage, allowing only twenty-pound freeholders, occupants of tenements valued at forty shillings a year, and freemen of Albany or New York to vote for assemblymen, and only hundred-pound freeholders to vote for governor and senators. Its elaborate system of checks and balances and its carefully contrived threefold separation of powers gave the popular branch, the legislative, no such ascendancy as it enjoyed under certain of the other more liberal state constitutions. "Another turn of the winch," Jay declared, "would have cracked the cord." [28] It was perhaps fortunate for the fate of the constitution that it was not submitted to a popular vote.

The constitution did, however, give to Governor Clinton power enough to make him far more than a figurehead. "A wise and discreet freeholder" elected by ballot every three years, the governor of New York was the only governor in all of the states who was not elected by the legislature. This distinction alone made Clinton perhaps the strongest executive in the confederation. He was to possess "the supreme executive power and authority"; he was to be both commander-in-chief of the militia and "Admiral of the navy" of the state; he was given power to convene the legislature on extraordinary occasions; and to grant reprieves and pardons. It was his duty to inform the legislature of the condition of the state and to recommend matters for their consideration; to correspond with the Continental Congress and with other states, and to take care that the laws be faithfully executed. The power of appointment, civil and military, the governor shared with four senators elected by the Assembly from each of the four senatorial districts. Of this Council of Appointment the governor was president with a casting vote and he could make appointments only with its "advice and consent." [29] As long as the governor could dominate the Council of Appointment, as Clinton did for more than fifteen years, it was relatively innocuous; but it was later to prove itself the most unfortunate achievement of the framers of the constitution of 1777 and to force the calling of a constitutional convention.

Almost as disastrous was another innovation of the framers of 1777,

[28] Becker, *Political Parties*, 276.
[29] Article XXIII.

the Council of Revision.[30] When Gouverneur Morris proposed to arm the governor with the veto power, the representatives of the commercial and landed interests of Albany, Dutchess, and New York Counties were in favor; but the majority of the delegates from the more democratic, more strongly Whiggish counties of Ulster, Orange, and Tryon cast their votes against the veto.[31] A radical Whig himself, Clinton probably shared the point of view of the men of the river counties. It was agreed, however, that there should be a check on hasty, ill-advised legislation. The resulting institution, designed to curb the legislature without adding materially to the powers of the governor, was the Council of Revision. This monstrosity consisted of the governor, the chancellor, and the judges of the supreme court, or any three of them, always including the governor; and it was empowered to offer objections to legislative measures inconsistent with the spirit of the constitution or with the public good—a generous grant of power which could be overruled only by a two-thirds vote of both houses of the legislature. It provided more than judicial review; it added to the state legislature a third chamber which lacked little more than the power to initiate legislation. It brought the judges into politics and it deprived the governor of the veto power that any effective executive should enjoy. It was a conservative check on the legislature and many progressive measures were its victims. In less than a third of its vetoes was it overruled,[32] but during the twenty-one years that Clinton was governor there were 76 vetoes by the Council of which 37, one less than half, were passed over the veto by the legislature.[33] Governor Clinton seems generally to have left the drafting of the council's veto messages to the chancellor or the justices of the supreme court. Possibly he did not always find himself in agreement.

The conservatives in the convention of 1777, some of whom had feared that Scott's radicals would not agree to the creation of a governor with any degree of power,[34] were tolerably content with the

[30] Article III.

[31] *Journals of the Provincial Congress,* March 13 and 14, 1777.

[32] In 45 years the Council vetoed 169 measures, 51 of which were passed over its veto. D. L. Colvin, *Bicameral Principle in the New York State Legislature* (New York, 1913), 37.

[33] Lincoln, *Messages from the Governors,* II.

[34] Jay, *Correspondence,* I, 136.

governorship they were able to obtain. The governor would have to share with senators and judges two very important powers, those of appointment and of veto of legislation; but otherwise he would possess most of the powers essential to a vigorous executive. During the years when Governor Clinton and his legislatures were politically harmonious, Clinton never complained of the powers given him by the constitution of 1777.

Five days after his inauguration the new governor prorogued the legislature until August 20; two weeks later he set the day at September 1;[35] and it was, as a matter of fact, September 9 before the first meeting of a New York State legislature in the old stone court house at Kingston. Jay and Schuyler would have preferred a meeting at Albany, but there was clearly some opposition.[36] Kingston was nearer to the center of population and it was near enough to New Windsor to satisfy the new governor and his family. Furthermore, the Tappens' large two and a half storey house was on North Front Street in the heart of Kingston, midway between the court house and the long stone house where the state senate was to hold its sessions, and the Tappens would be more than glad to make George and Cornelia Clinton welcome during the legislative sessions.[37]

On September 10 his Excellency harangued the legislature for five or six minutes. His messages were almost invariably short. Later, Governors John Jay and Morgan Lewis were to be a third again as verbose as Clinton in their grist of messages; and Governor Tompkins more than half again as wordy. Clinton was always, in official life at least, a man of few words. It was also worthy of some note that he adopted the courtly custom of reading his messages in person to the assembled law-makers, a custom that was followed for many years by New York governors[38] and by Presidents Washington and Adams. This first message was optimistic in tone. The governor explained that the western frontier was secure for the moment; that there was little

---

[35] Mabel C. Weaks and Victor H. Paltsits, *Calendar of Messages and Proclamations of General George Clinton* (New York Public Library, 1927), 5.

[36] Jay, *Correspondence*, I, 143.

[37] *Olde Ulster*, III, 331; VI, 111. The old senate house is still standing, but the court house and the Tappen residence have been replaced by other buildings.

[38] Lincoln, *Messages from the Governors*, II, 2.

likelihood of an immediate attack on the Highlands; that Stark had won Bennington; and that he, Clinton, had sent generous reënforcements to Gates for his campaign against Burgoyne. He advocated a revision of the state's military laws and attention to the sorry subject of finance; and he promised to respect the division of powers among the executive, legislative, and judicial branches as arranged by the new constitution.[39] The message was blunt and scarcely inspiring, but there was no time for eloquence even if the young governor had been capable of it—which he was not.

During the hectic days that followed the new state government functioned as best it could. To obviate the necessity for a new election, Pierre Van Cortlandt, the president *pro tempore* of the senate, performed the duties of the lieutenant governor until June 30, 1778, when he assumed that office in his own right.[40] And as the state had adopted no seal, and as proclamations must be issued with some ceremony, the governor issued them under his own Clinton "seal at arms" until the adoption of a state seal by a law of March 16, 1778.[41] His Excellency found time to pardon the English Shaker, Ann Lee, founder of the Shaker Community at Watervliet, who was charged with being an English spy,[42] and he found time for his usual prolific correspondence with officers and friends. But despite his inauguration into civil office his primary concerns for many months were military. Enlistments, troop movements, supplies, and new fortifications continued to occupy a lion's share of the war governor's time.

[39] Governor Clinton's messages are printed in Lincoln, *op. cit.*, II.
[40] Mabel C. Weaks, *op. cit.*, 4. Walter Livingston became speaker of the assembly.
[41] *Ibid.*, 5; Stokes, *Iconography*, V, 1054.
[42] Gaillard Hunt, *Life in America One Hundred Years Ago* (New York, 1914), 239-40.

CHAPTER VIII

HAMILTON VISITS LITTLE BRITAIN

THE LEGISLATURE LEAVES KINGSTON
THE CLINTONS LEAVE NEW WINDSOR
CLINTON COMMANDS THE NEW YORK TROOPS
WASHINGTON WANTS HIM IN THE FIELD
HE LEAVES THE HUDSON TO PARSONS
HE DISLIKES HORATIO GATES

ON October 7, 1777, the day after the fall of the Highland forts, the little legislature at Kingston hastily adjourned. To provide for the government of the state in the emergency the chameleon legislature converted itself into a convention which in turn appointed a council of safety over which the governor, with a casting vote, was to preside.[1] This council, which met frequently in the smaller towns of Ulster County and in Poughkeepsie, gave way again, on January 7, 1778, to the convention which lasted only eight days before the legislature met at Poughkeepsie pursuant to Governor Clinton's proclamation of December 15.[2] Meanwhile the Falls house on the Goshen road at Little Britain had been for some weeks the executive capitol of the state.

After his conference with Putnam on October 7 Clinton had hurried to New Windsor where he arranged for Mrs. Clinton and the children to leave the New Windsor farm to which they were never to return. The Clinton household and personal effects were sent by sloop up the river to Esopus; while Mrs. Clinton with her brother, Dr.

---

[1] Lincoln, *Messages from the Governors*, II, 16. The legislature was not prorogued by the governor when Henry Clinton attacked the Highlands, as is often stated.
[2] *Ibid.*, 17. The date set by the proclamation was January 5. The Council probably determined upon Poughkeepsie; *Public Papers*, II, 500.

Peter Tappen; his wife, Elizabeth Crannell Tappen, who was then in a most interesting condition; Elizabeth's sister, Catherine, who was Mrs. Gilbert Livingston; and Captain Machin, who was Clinton's factotum at the time, sought refuge with a Mr. and Mrs. Barnes of Pleasant Valley some eight miles from Poughkeepsie.[3] Here they were comfortable enough, but Colonel Hughes thought that they were too near the army's supplies and might better be moved to Sharon in Connecticut. At any rate the governor did not propose to bring Cornelia back to New Windsor; he planned to rent the New Windsor farm, and he soon had Peter Tappen, Major Billings, and Captain Machin house-hunting for him in and near Poughkeepsie which was to remain his home for several years. The only hitch in the moving was that Captain Machin forgot to send the governor his razors.[4]

The house that the Clintons occupied at Poughkeepsie for all or at least part of their stay there was the Crannell house on Main Street not far from Dr. Peter Tappen's home. Crannell was a Tory who was forced to take refuge behind the British lines as early as 1776, leaving behind him his substantial mansion which had been built over thirty years before on the outskirts of the town. His two sons-in-law, Peter Tappen and Gilbert Livingston, may very naturally have been reluctant to see the property pass out of the family and so have suggested to the governor that he occupy the mansion, which since May 1777 had been in the hands of the Commissioners of Sequestration. It is entirely possible that the governor also used the Everitt house which had also been owned by a Tory and which in the twentieth century was to become the Clinton Museum; but certainly he was in 1780 paying for repairs on the Crannell house and a map of the town of 1790 labels that house as one occupied by George Clinton during the Revolution. It was purchased by Gilbert Livingston and Peter Tappen in 1788, five years after the Clintons had left Poughkeepsie.[5]

Almost a year after the governor's arrival in Dutchess county the

---

[3] Helen Wilkinson Reynolds, "The Mill-Site by the Bridge at Pleasant Valley and the Visit there of Mrs. Clinton," Dutchess County Historical Society, *Year Book, 1932*, 77–78; *Public Papers*, II, 409, 411, 417.

[4] Simms, *The Frontiersman of New York*, I, 620; Duane to Gates, *Letters . . . Continental Congress*, Burnett, ed., II, 590.

[5] Helen Wilkinson Reynolds, "Bartholomew Crannell," Dutchess County Historical Society, *Year Book 1922*, 40–49; Edmund Platt, *History of Poughkeepsie* (Poughkeepsie, 1905), 46–49, 57; *Public Papers*, VI, 50.

Clinton's third child and only son was born. It was fitting and proper that he should be named George Washington Clinton and his fourth sister, the Clintons' fifth child, who was born in October 1783 was called Martha Washington Clinton. Washington Clinton was to live only long enough to dash his father's fondest hopes; for he died a young man in 1813, innocent of all serious achievement. Martha was to die in her twelfth year. Another daughter, Elizabeth, the future wife of Matthias B. Tallmadge, was born at Poughkeepsie in July 1780. The last of the six children of George and Cornelia Clinton was Maria who was to be born in New York City in 1785.[6] The Clintons were a prolific tribe.

The governor's mansion at Poughkeepsie, however, housed more than Clinton's own growing family. During those five years when the legislature met more often than not at Poughkeepsie—it met in 1778 at Poughkeepsie; in 1779 at Poughkeepsie and Kingston; in 1780 at Poughkeepsie, Albany, and Kingston; in 1781 at Poughkeepsie and Albany; and in 1782 at Poughkeepsie only—notables were constantly in or passing through the town. James Kent in his memoirs comments on the singular advantages to be gained from this parade of "the great men that visited there, such as George Clinton, Washington, Hamilton, Lawrence, Schuyler, Duer, Duche," and many others.[7] Among those who visited Governor Clinton was Kosciusko who came to consult him on his way to West Point to work on the fortifications.[8] On February 14 and 15, 1778, the governor was visited by Lafayette who was traveling to Albany, presumably to take charge of an expedition into Canada. Lafayette wrote Washington that he had conferred with Clinton "and was much satisfied with that gentleman."[9] The satisfaction seems to have been mutual, for the governor regretted that the marquis had been chosen to lead what he considered a quixotic enterprise and wished that he might instead have been given Putnam's command on the lower Hudson.[10]

[6] *New York Genealogical and Biographical Record*, XIII, 129; Ruttenber, *History of New Windsor; Olde Ulster*, February 1905, 56–57.

[7] Platt, *History of Poughkeepsie*, 50.

[8] *Ibid.*, 49.

[9] J. B. Nolan, *Lafayette in America Day by Day* (Baltimore, 1934), 44; Charlemagne Tower, *The Marquis de La Fayette* (2 volumes, Philadelphia, 1895), I, 283.

[10] Clinton to Lafayette, February 26, 1778, Clinton Papers, Library of Congress; same to same, March 8, *Public Papers*, III, 4–5.

Although there had been some doubt in Clinton's mind whether he would ever be able to return to the field after he assumed his new civil office, he did, as we have seen, return to the Highlands early in August to direct preparations for the expected British attack; he made a hurried trip to Albany later in the month to see for himself the military situation in the north and west; and he took the field in person to oppose Sir Henry Clinton in October. His headquarters was now headquarters for the entire militia of the state. It was now his responsibility to direct the movements of the militia, to coöperate with the Continental officers, to protect and reassure the frontier settlements, to call the militia to arms or to excuse them from service, to see that supplies were available for the men in the field—in brief, to direct the whole strategy of war as far as the New York forces were concerned. In addition, he must send militia to reënforce Putnam at Peekskill and Schuyler or Gates in the north and must replace with state troops the Continentals that Washington had had to order away from the state. He had to keep Washington informed of all important developments; it was probably from Clinton and certainly not from Gates, that Washington first heard of the great victory of Saratoga.[11] The task was gigantic; but the young war governor was in his element; he enjoyed the work of direction for which he was, as a matter of fact, much better fitted than for active command in the field; and from few states, if from any, did Washington receive better and more sustained coöperation than from New York.

That George Clinton still enjoyed Washington's confidence to a high degree was apparent in July when Washington, fearful that the enemy were "upon the point of making some capital move," wrote to the New York Council of Safety.[12] He understood, he said, that the Council had authorized Clinton to call out the militia of Ulster, Dutchess, and Westchester until August first when the new legislature was expected to meet; he feared that Clinton's successor might not be promptly appointed, an eventuality that might prove fatal in its consequence; and he asked that the power to call the militia be extended, if

[11] Washington received the news from both Clinton and Putnam on the same day, October 18. Washington, *Writings*, IX, 393, 400.

[12] Washington, *Writings*, VIII, 454–55.

possible, to Clinton himself whom he, Washington, would prefer to any other. This confidence must have been flattering to the young governor. President Van Cortlandt replied for the Council that they expected Clinton to take his oath of office almost immediately at which time he would become by the provisions of the state constitution the commander-in-chief of all the militia of New York; a special authorization would not therefore be necessary. Just why General Scott had his dissent recorded in this common-sense reply to Washington, is difficult to understand.[13]

In November when Clinton's headquarters was at Little Britain he received a visit of several days from Colonel Alexander Hamilton who, under Washington's orders, had just seen Putnam and was on his way to visit Gates. The object of his mission was to persuade Putnam and Gates to send reënforcements to Washington's army. Putnam, however, wanted to attack New York City, which Hamilton thought would be suicidal; consequently, the old general paid little attention to the young aide's orders even though they were given in Washington's name. The indignant Hamilton wrote to Washington on November 10[14] that Putnam had refused to coöperate and that Governor Clinton was the only one who had done anything toward moving the two brigades that were to join Washington. The governor had borrowed five or six thousand dollars for the purpose and made it possible for one of the brigades to march. Furthermore the governor had advised Colonel Hamilton to send an emphatic order to Putnam to send all his Continental troops to Washington's assistance, and the order was sent. It is of considerable interest to note that Hamilton, who in the heat of politics in later years was to belittle George Clinton's military abilities, expressed to Washington the wish that Putnam, whose "blunders and caprices are endless," might be removed from his command and Clinton substituted.[15] Whatever his abilities, Clinton was at least entirely loyal to Washington. That was more than could be said for Gates.

A violent attack of fever and rheumatic pains kept Hamilton with

[13] *Public Papers*, II, 136–37.
[14] Hamilton, *Works,* Lodge, ed., VII, 528–30.
[15] *Ibid.,* 530.

Clinton at Little Britain for two or three days. Dr. John Jones, whom the governor called on to attend the young colonel, was himself ill; so Hamilton had no doctor and he left only partially recovered.[16] At Peekskill a day or two later he fell ill again and it was the end of the month before he was pronounced out of danger.

One consequence of Hamilton's visit to New York was the inauguration of a friendly correspondence between him and Governor Clinton in the course of which the two men wrote scathingly of Gates, showed themselves to be of one mind as regards the Conway cabal and commented bitterly on the shortcomings of the Continental Congress. Hamilton, for instance, denounced its "Folly, caprice, a want of foresight, comprehension, and dignity," and Clinton replied in the same vein with the comment that "Could our Soldiery subsist on Resolves, they would never want Food or Cloathing."[17] Only a few years later these two men were to be in complete disagreement on the subject of the Congress and its powers.

The state of New York, fortunately for itself, did not occupy the center of the military stage during 1778. Most of Governor Clinton's time, however, continued to be given to such major wartime problems as the defense of the northern and western frontiers, the procurement of supplies, the suppression of the remaining Loyalists, and the fortification of the Hudson. During the first weeks of the year his concern was chiefly with the new works on the river. He had been credited by some with having been the first to suggest the fortifying of West Point;[18] although others would award the paternity of West Point to Putnam. Certainly Clinton was writing Gates as early as October 26, 1777, that he thought it necessary to fortify some strong post on the Hudson to prevent future excursions up the river by British vessels and suggesting New Windsor or, better, Fort Constitution which was opposite West Point. Eleven days later Colonel Hughes wrote Gates that, "The General, Governor Clinton, and General James [Clinton], an Engineer, and your humble servant, were at the forts yesterday, viewing the River, Bluffs, Points, &c., in order to erect some further

[16] J. J. Smertenko, *Alexander Hamilton* (New York, 1932), 84–5; *Public Papers*, II, 541–42.

[17] *Ibid.*, II, 865; III, 30; Hamilton, *Works*, Lodge, ed., VII, 536–40; IX, 127–28.

[18] *Public Papers*, II, iii; R. E. Prime, *George Clinton . . . An Address*, 27.

obstructions, which are immediately set about. The Boom will be near Fort Constitution; and a work on the west shore to defend it."[19] The works on the west shore would be at West Point. On November 24 and again on December 20 Governor Clinton wrote to urge upon Gates the necessity of strong works at West Point.[20] He had at last realized the possibilities of that superb promontory.

No one wanted the task of directing the fortifying of West Point. In November Congress asked Washington to remove Putnam and give Gates command in the Highlands, but Gates made no move to assume the new post. Meanwhile Putnam, who was still the Continental general officer in charge on the lower Hudson, was ordered by the commander-in-chief to consult with Governor Clinton and General Parsons whose brigade was to assist in the actual work; and Washington, who had no reason to expect coöperation from Gates, told Governor Clinton that it was entirely possible Gates would not serve, in which case he would be greatly pleased if Clinton would take the chief direction of the business.[21] The governor replied, urging at great length the importance of the river fortifications but regretting that the meeting of the legislature in January and other public affairs would prevent his giving proper attention to the task on the Hudson. Little wonder that the work did not get under way until January.

General Parsons arrived in mid-winter to find West Point under two feet of snow, few tools or workmen or materials, and no one to give directions. "In Short," he wrote to Clinton, "I come to this Command in the most disagreeable circumstances, nothing done, every Thing expected & wish'd for & every Thing in confusion, I have every thing to pick from perfect chaos."[22] "Old Put" had dillied and dallied for two long months; Gates had chosen to sit on the board of war and Clinton had been at Poughkeepsie busy with his correspondence and with his reconvened legislature. To bring order out of chaos the Continental Congress turned again to Clinton. It resolved on February 18 to authorize and request him to superintend the business of securing the passes in the Highlands, and to accomplish this it gave him sweep-

---

[19] E. C. Boynton, *History of West Point* (New York, 1863), 48.
[20] *Ibid.; Public Works,* II, 589.
[21] Washington, *Writings,* X, 136.
[22] *Public Works,* II, 756.

ing powers—to employ the militia of Massachusetts Bay and Connecticut as well as that of New York, to receive "every assistance" from the commanding officer at Peekskill including money from the military chest, and to receive fifty thousand dollars from the loan office in New York to defray the cost of the work.[23] It was, however, too much to expect of the governor of the state. Clinton made every effort to furnish artillery, materials for the works, teams and provisions; he gave advice when requested to Gates, Putnam, and Parsons; he asked Massachusetts and Connecticut for 2300 militia and his own legislature to raise 700 men to work on the Hudson; and he even called upon the commanding officer at Peekskill for fifteen thousand dollars for the purpose; but he made it clear that he could not, in all probability undertake to superintend the work himself.[24] He told the legislature in a message of March 10 that he could not undertake to supervise the work while that body was sitting.[25]

Although the legislature was to adjourn early in April the governor was both relieved and pleased when it was learned that Major General McDougall was expected to take command on the Hudson at the end of March. He was probably not nearly so well satisfied when Congress on April 15 ordered that Gates be placed in charge of the whole northern department with authority to call out the New England and New York militia and with instructions "to confer with & take your Excellency's advice & assistance."[26] Clinton told Gouverneur Morris that he had been well satisfied with McDougall and regretted the change. McDougall, who felt himself ill-used, was to evince some satisfaction the next fall when he learned that Gates had finally been shelved, far from all possibility of active duty, at Boston. "In short, Sir," McDougall wrote the governor, "he is as weak as water"![27] Horatio Gates had never been popular in New York.

[23] Public Papers, II, 776, 801.
[24] Ibid., 811; Hall, Samuel H. Parsons, 153; Lincoln, Messages from the Governors, II, 31. An act to provide for the raising of 700 men was passed over the veto of the council on March 31, 1778.
[25] Lincoln, op. cit., 31.
[26] Public Papers, III, 197.
[27] Ibid., 310; Hall, Samuel H. Parsons, 199.

CHAPTER IX

THE WAR GOVERNOR

THE recovery of New York City from the British, so important to the commercial life of the state, must have been one of George Clinton's fondest hopes. Yet in the spring of 1778 Clinton, who two years earlier had so strenuously opposed the evacuation, was advising Washington against an immediate attack on the city. Washington had consulted McDougall, Parsons, and Clinton on the project; and Clinton for one had urged delay until the new fortifications in the

Highlands should be ready, an adequate force of militia in reserve, and sufficient hay and provisions on hand.[1]

Clinton hoped, however, that it would soon be possible to strike. Yet the plan hung fire for months. Washington fully expected to attack the city in the fall of 1779 and Clinton's legislature had adjourned at Kingston on October 25 after a brief session in the expectation of the arrival of the French fleet and the commencement of operations. To coöperate with Count d'Estaing, Washington asked Clinton for 2500 New York militia. Clinton replied five days later that he flattered himself "with the Hope that no Failure will take Place, for want of a prompt & full Compliance . . ." on the part of New York.[2] More months went by; Washington made preparations in the spring of 1781; but the attack was never made. The projected attack on the metropolis, nevertheless, played its part in the winning of the war, for by feigning an attack upon New York in the late summer of 1781, Washington prevented Sir Henry Clinton from reënforcing Cornwallis until it was too late.

Among the tasks of the war governor in 1778 was the not entirely agreeable one of serving as a member of the court martial assembled in October to try that devoted but not always popular patriot, Major General Philip Schuyler. Schuyler was accused of neglect of duty and consequent responsibility for the loss of Ticonderoga. Clinton thought the charge "vague & general" and probably concurred heartily in the verdict of the court that Schuyler was not guilty.[3] There is nothing to indicate that the court martial of 1778 was in any way responsible for the later coolness between Clinton, who up to that time had admired and frequently supported Schuyler, and Schuyler, who never could quite bring himself to accept Clinton.

It was not, however, always possible for the governor to come officially to the rescue of old friends; and where his passionate devotion to the great cause of the Revolution clashed with personal friendships, the friendships were sacrificed. One of those friend-

---

[1] Hall, *Samuel H. Parsons*, 170.

[2] *Public Papers*, V, 292, 317, 520; Washington to Clinton, October 4, 1779, in *Magazine of History*, March 1907, pp. 138-39.

[3] *Public Papers*, III, 621. The minutes of the court martial are reprinted in the New York Historical Society, *Collections, 1879* (New York, 1880).

GOVERNOR GEORGE CLINTON

MRS. GEORGE CLINTON

ships was that with Clinton's old mentor in the law, William Smith,
the historian. The governor was constantly called upon to allow the
passage down the river into the enemy lines or to Canada of all
descriptions of people—Loyalists, wives and families of Loyalists,
prisoners, persons having property or business in New York, or persons
going to England. It was not easy to prevent the abuse of such
privileges. The governor felt it necessary in the winter of 1778 to
refuse permission to the eminent Tory lawyer, Peter Van Schaack of
Kinderhook, to visit his consumptive wife in New York City. He was
ready to exchange prisoners of equal rank but he was unwilling to
exchange British soldiers for American civilians. In the case of Loyalist
women, Clinton's rule was to give permission only when the British
authorities were willing to reciprocate by allowing American women
to visit husbands in state territory.[4] He did not intend to allow able-
bodied Loyalists to cross the line unless a satisfactory exchange could
be arranged. Consequently when, in the summer of 1778, his old
friend William Smith, who had recently announced his loyalty to the
Crown and his willingness to accept exile, applied to the governor
for permission to take with him his several male servants, Clinton
refused. His slaves, Clinton pointed out, he might sell in New York
State, and his white servants, "hardy Scotch Hierlings," he might take
with him by securing their exchange for any two New Yorkers in the
power of the enemy. When Smith complained to Washington of
this verdict, Clinton thought him "unjust and unreasonable." Yet
Clinton went to much trouble to have the historian's effects transported
under a flag into New York.[5]

The governor was a thorough-going Whig with almost as little
sympathy for men like William Smith, who tried to compromise
their loyalties to both King and country, as for out and out Tories like
his neighbors, the Coldens. A member of his family was later to
"reflect with pleasure, and even with exultation, that not one branch
of our *Families,* have ever been *Tories,* or in *Synonymous Terms
Federalists.*"[6] It was one of Governor Clinton's principal policies to

[4] *Public Papers,* III to VII, *passim.*
[5] *Ibid.,* IV, 7, 326, 348.
[6] Joseph Young to DeWitt Clinton, May 25, 1812, DeWitt Clinton Papers, Columbia
University Library.

stamp out disaffection and loyalism in the state, and in general he was successful. At his order Tories were tried, proscribed, jailed, or exiled even before he became governor, but the Tory's lot became an even more unhappy one after the establishment of the new state government in 1777.[7] Even the pacific Quakers became subjects of his displeasure and he suspected their loyalty.

Vigorous anti-Tory measures seemed necessary, for New York had a larger proportion of Tories in its population than any other state. In 1776 the state Convention decreed death for the disloyal and it appointed a committee for detecting and defeating conspiracies. This committee was revived in the fall of 1777, perhaps because of the new governor's urging, and it continued its purgative work until the end of the war. The governor kept in constant touch with it[8] and also with many of the local committees engaged in the crusade against the Tories. Loyalist property was seized and sold for the benefit of the impecunious state treasury. By the famous confiscation act of October 22, 1779, drafted by John Morin Scott and James Jay and approved by George Clinton, fifty-nine prominent Loyalists lost their estates. Commissioners of forfeiture were appointed, who began in 1780 the sale of forfeited estates and a veritable revolution in tenures took place in the state through the division of many of the great Tory estates into small holdings. The Trespass Act became law in 1783. Loyalists were attainted; thirty or forty thousand were driven from the state to Canada, Nova Scotia, or England; and those who remained were to be disfranchised by the act of May 12, 1784.[9]

George Clinton probably approved whole-heartedly of all the anti-Tory measures. Thomas Jones declared that Clinton "had rather roast in hell to all eternity, than consent to a dependence upon Great Britian, or show mercy to a dammed tory." According to the Marquis de Chastellux, Clinton "governs with the utmost vigor and firmness, and is inexorable to the Tories, who he makes tremble, though they

---

[7] A. C. Flick, *Loyalism in New York* (New York, 1901) is the standard treatise on the subject. See also article on "George Clinton," *Olde Ulster,* IV, 226.

[8] Flick, ed., *History of the State of New York,* III, 348–50; *Public Papers,* I, 253, 360.

[9] [Flick], *The American Revolution in New York,* Chapter IX; Flick, *Loyalism in New York.*

are extremely numerous in the State of New York." [10]   However rigorous his measures, they seem to have been approved by the great majority of New Yorkers north and west of the Westchester line and they served to enhance his popularity. Futhermore, his measures and those of his legislature were effective. In 1782 Hamilton told Morris that although half the population of the state had been loyal to the Crown when the war broke out, the government's energetic handling of the Tory problem had reduced the fraction to one-third.[11] Only the southern counties had any considerable number of Tories at the end of the war.

Yet in spite of some tar and feathers, rides on sharpened rails for 'non-associators," duckings in convenient ponds, and smashing of windows by over patriotic mobs, there were on the whole surprisingly few excesses in the treatment of New York Tories throughout the war. 'Americanus" complained in the *New-York Packet* of October 20, 1785, that New Jerseyites had cut off the ear of a Tory and he added, 'I thank God, no such thing has happened in this state; the first step of that nature being stopped by the spirited and praiseworthy interposition of the Governor, who in person, secured the ring leaders, and brought them to justice." "Americanus" was probably referring especially to an incident in New York City soon after its evacuation by the British when Governor Clinton intervened in person to save two British officers from tarring and feathering by the mob.[12] Indeed, Clinton was usually ready to intervene on behalf of abused or unfortunate individual Loyalists. The notorious Tory, Cadwallader Colden, 2nd, wrote the Governor in 1778: "I think myself under an obligation to give you many thanks (as I now do) for the regard which my wife tells me you paid to her complaints of some insults and abuse she met with from some of the low class of officers." [13] The governor allowed Peter Van Schaack to go to England on parole in 1778 to have an operation performed on his eyes.[14] And in the years following

[10] Jones, *History of New York*, II, 329–30.
[11] Hamilton, *Works*, Lodge, ed., VIII, 69.
[12] *New-York Gazette*, June 25, 1784; Stokes, *Iconography*, V, 1159, 1167; Street, *Council of Revision*, 106–07.
[13] Joseph Bragdon, "Cadwallader Colden, 2nd," *New York History*, October 1933, 420.
[14] Clinton to Jay, November 8, 1784. Copy obtained by Dr. Frank Monaghan.

the war the governor seems to have made little or no effort to enforce some of the most drastic of the anti-Tory enactments which would have sent many of them into exile.[15]

The treatment of the Tories remained a burning issue in state politics for four or five years after the peace. When John Jay wrote to Clinton from Spain that the passage of the Confiscation Act of 1779 disgraced New York "by injustice too palpable to admit even of palliation,"[16] he was representative of a considerable body of moderates who were to press more and more for leniency towards the Tories. Hamilton, who had always had sympathy for the Loyalists and some for their cause, was to become the leader of the moderate group and men like Schuyler, Duane, Hobart, and Robert R. Livingston were to join him in opposing the Tory-baiting policies of George Clinton and his radical Whigs.

So important was this division of opinion that it has often been called the beginning of political parties in New York.[17] It was Hamilton's contention that all of the laws complained of as being unduly abusive of the Loyalists were promoted by the political adherents of George Clinton, and that those favoring their moderation were politically opposed to Clinton. Certainly it is a fact that Whiggish counties like Orange, Ulster, Dutchess, Montgomery, and Washington, which were generally to support Governor Clinton and his policies during the years after the war, were usually anti-Tory; while New York, Albany, Richmond, Kings, and Queens Counties, which were later to be politically hostile to Clinton, were most friendly toward the Loyalists.[18] The pre-war alignment of liberal Whigs against conservative supporters of the royal governors and the British ministries was being supplanted by a new but very similar alignment of liberal Whigs against conservative Whigs and their partially disfranchised allies, the recent Tories. The Tory issue was to play an important rôle in disrupting the friendship between Clinton and Hamilton so auspiciously begun at Mrs. Falls' house in 1777.

[15] Dixon Ryan Fox, *Decline of Aristocracy in the Politics of New York* (New York, 1918), 12-13.
[16] William Jay, *The Life of John Jay* (2 vols., New York, 1833), I, 111.
[17] Nevins, *The American States*, 268.
[18] E. Wilder Spaulding, *New York in the Critical Period* (New York, 1932), 126–128.

The civil business of state went on during the last years of the war despite the general indifference of New York's wartime statesmen. That it went on at all was due in large part to the amazing energy of the young war governor. When Secretary of State John Morin Scott explained that lingering attacks of rheumatism had kept him from his duties,[19] the skeptical governor suspected that it was laziness, not illness, that had held up the issuance of important commissions. And the legislature was always days late in responding to the governor's call. On January 20, 1779, the governor, who could speak and write his mind, wrote to his friend, John Lamb, that: "Our Legislature were to have met at this place on the 8th instant, but a sufficient number of members have not yet appeared, to proceed on business; when these will, God only knows. So little attention is paid to the public weal, by the guardians of the rights of the people, as to discourage me, more than I can well express."[20] It was January 28 instead of January 8 when a quorum was ready to hear the governor's message. Furthermore, it was as difficult to hold a quorum as to assemble it. Because of the absence of a number of members who left suddenly to join their militia regiments, the session ended on March 16 with its work unfinished. It met again for two months in the late summer—this time at Kingston, for the legislators had developed an aversion to Poughkeepsie.[21] The next session was to commence on January 4, 1780, at Albany; but there was a heavy snow and the governor could not welcome his legislators until January 27. The spring session, which was called to meet at Kingston on May 9 could not report a quorum until May 26. This remarkable inability to gather promptly characterized the legislators of New York even during the years after the war. Their sessions during the seventeen-eighties assembled on an average over ten days late.

In spite of its short-comings the legislature turned out a great deal of legislation of vast importance. It ratified with considerable promptness the Articles of Confederation which, according to a great historian of the Revolution, "proposed the strongest confederation that the world

---

[19] *Public Papers*, III, 313.
[20] Leake, *John Lamb*, 216.
[21] *Public Papers*, III, 313.

had ever known, and its daring astounded the men of the time." [22]
The Congress submitted the articles to the states on November 17,
1777; Governor Clinton sent them to his legislature on January 16
and a month later they had been approved by both governor and legislature. It was over three years before Maryland, the last state, was
to ratify.

The legislature and the governor also had to grapple with what
was the most vexatious wartime problem of all, that of finance. On
this subject Clinton had very definite views—views that were to change
in some respects after the wartime crisis had passed. He wanted a
sound system of currency supported by heavy taxation. He realized
that his state was, generally speaking, entirely capable of seeing the war
through to a victorious conclusion provided only that it did not collapse
financially. In discussing the impoverishment of the country with
Jay in 1781 the governor wrote optimistically that "Our resources as
a Nation are, however, yet great; we abound in Provision and the
Prices in Specie are nearly the same as at the Commencement of the
War." He added, however, that "The Situation of our Finances is
perhaps the only Thing in human probability that can distress me." [23]
Clinton was indignant when men refused to take state or Continental
paper money at par as when Mr. McCurdy of his own county offered
to sell a horse for £32 in Continental currency or £26 in hard cash,
and he advocated punishment for such "criminal practices." [24] But
he fully realized that the real solution was adequate taxation that would
maintain the credit of both state and nation and of their all too abun-
dant currencies.

The first fruit of his drive for adequate taxation was the act of
March 28, 1778, providing for a small levy on the value of both real
and personal property. For the first time the legislature had admitted
that the war could not be won on printing presses alone. [25] Prices,
however, continued to rise at staggering rates and the wartime issues of
state and Continental paper money to fall to amazing lows. Clinton
told the legislature in October 1778 that price-fixing was only a tem-

[22] Claude H. Van Tyne, *The American Revolution* (New York, 1905), 185.
[23] *Public Papers*, VI, 747–48.
[24] In February, 1777. *Public Papers*, I, 630.
[25] *History of the State of New York*, IV, 122–23.

porary expedient; it was essential to reduce the quantity of money through taxation. In 1779—a year when Livingston was paying £537 for "a plain suit of cloaths" and £21 for plain buttons for a servant— the governor was urging additional taxes to rescue the state's credit. The legislature responded and on March 2 raised the rates on real and personal property drastically, but there was much tax-dodging and in the fall the entire system of direct taxation was changed. During the remainder of the war period the legislature simply determined the total sums it expected to raise and apportioned them among the counties—a system that was quite generally denounced but which was perhaps the only practicable one at the time.[26]

There were other sources of revenue such as the sums advanced by the Continental Congress, the £260,000 that the sale of Tory personal property in the seven upstate counties brought to the state, the much larger amount that the state garnered from the sale of Tory real estate [27] and the new tariff laws which of course yielded very little while the British occupied New York City. Compared with the systems of revenue in effect in many of the other states, New York's system was tolerably adequate. Yet there were times when the treasury ran dry, as when in the spring of 1781 the distressed legislature admitted to Washington that "the treasury is entirely destitute of money; nor is there the least prospect that any will come in until a new State currency which we have directed to be issued can be prepared for emission . . ." [28]

George Clinton seems to have been ready to pledge his personal credit and his own savings in the risky business of winning a revolution. As early as 1776 he expended over £1000 on flour for the troops at Kingsbridge. He advanced nearly £2800 in specie from his own pocket to satisfy the needs of American prisoners behind the British lines on Long Island and from time to time he advanced his own funds or pledged his own credit to purchase supplies for troops in the field or even for the expenses of the civil government. For most, if not all, of these advances he received compensation even before the

[26] *Ibid.*, 123–25; *Olde Ulster*, V, 69, 175; *Public Papers*, IV, 157, 820–21; VII, 366.
[27] [Flick], *The American Revolution in New York*, 221, states that the state realized over $3,000,000 from forfeited lands.
[28] *Public Papers*, VI, 729.

end of the war. He stated, however, in appealing to the Congress for compensation: "I have for these several years past by an Attention to the public utterly neglected my own private Business"; and if the sale of his farm at New Windsor was not primarily to recoup his fortune, the specie that it brought was most welcome.[29]

The story has often been told of how Governor Clinton obtained specie from Long Island for the campaigns of the revolution and for American prisoners within the British lines. It seems that Washington's spies had reported that many patriots on the island had hard money in plenty which they were willing to turn over to the state or federal authorities. Washington asked Clinton to do what he could to obtain this specie. The governor called in a number of agents, probably including Major Brush, Major Hendrick Wyckoff, and John Sands, and furnished them with notes signed and executed by himself pledging the credit of state, paying six per cent, and payable after the peace. Sir Henry Clinton was told early in 1781 that a number of Long Islanders who expected an American victory were paying for these notes in specie which found its way to the American governor. It is said that George Clinton, unlike the financiers of most wars, received no commission.[30]

However successful the state's fiscal program may have been, there was often too little money available to keep two delegates—the minimum number—in attendance on the Continental Congress. The business of attending was evidently a burden that was by common consent rotated among the several reluctant delegates. Governor Clinton wrote often, both officially and unofficially, to the New York delegates, severally and collectively, exchanging news, newspapers, and recent enactments of the Congress or the state legislature; and year after year this correspondence was strewn with appeals from the delegates for funds and with appeals from the governor to the delegates to remain

[29] Ibid., IV, 40, 251; VII, 501, 535, 540; Clinton to Gerard Bancker, July 9, 1780[?], MS in Wisconsin Historical Society; E. C. Knight, compiler, New York in the Revolution (Albany, 1901), 162–63; Lincoln, Messages from the Governors, II, 161; Clinton to Stephen Lush, December 8, 1782, MS in New York State Library.

[30] According to Olde Ulster, X, 146–48, this story is told in the Ulster Plebeian, September 25, 1819, and the New York Columbian of the same month, and is confirmed by vouchers in the Comptroller's office. See also E. C. Knight, op. cit., 168 and Magazine of American History, 1883, pp. 414–15.

at their posts.[31] Occasionally the president of Congress would take a part in the correspondence to point out "the deficiency of a Representation from your State." Or Hamilton would enquire of the governor why the states kept their best men at home. "You have a Duane, a Morris, and, may I not add, a Duer? But why do you not send your Jay and your R. R. Livingston . . ." or General Schuyler? When, however, Clinton urged Schuyler to go to the Congress a few weeks later, that gentleman sent his regrets as "Mrs. Schuyler expects to lay in about the first week in May, . . ."[32] General Scott seems to have been a particularly unfortunate delegate for he was habitually appealing for funds and at one time, in the fall of 1780, it was reported that he was out of funds, had been ill for a month, "and is really in a bad way having lost his Appetite. . . ."[33]

Not only were there constant appeals from New York delegates who could not pay for their lodgings at Philadelphia, but there were more serious appeals from the Congress itself, from Robert Morris who was its superintendent of finance, and from Washington, for men and money. Governor Clinton seems always to have done his best to comply with Washington's requisitions. Certainly Washington was able to write Clinton in June 1780, that "New York is among the few that has felt the necessity of energy and considering its situation has done everything that could be expected of it."[34] But the governor was not always entirely responsive to the innumerable demands from the Congress itself and its committees, and while he might do what he could to comply, he did not hesitate to argue the point with the Congress. When Congressional demands became too pressing, Clinton defended his state's position without equivocation. For instance, he wrote on July 8, 1780, to Samuel Huntington, the president of the Congress, that the New York legislature had fully intended to comply punctually with the congressional requisitions; but, he added diplomatically: "it is not to be numbered amongst the least of our misfortunes that we were unable to fulfil these Intentions, but were obliged by

[31] Burnett, *Letters . . . Continental Congress, passim.*
[32] *Ibid.*, III, 35, 142; Hamilton, *Works*, Lodge, ed., VII, 539; *Public Papers*, III, 77, 177.
[33] Duane to Clinton, October 6, 1780, copy in Library of Congress.
[34] *Writings of Washington*, XIX, 84.

subsequent appropriations to apply the monies to different purposes. Hence I suppose our arrears are considerable. How far tho', we are to be considered as Defaulters, we submit to the Justice and Generosity of Congress." He then proceeded to plead eloquently the distressed condition of the state:

The Enemy in the entire Possession of our Capital and four Counties; our Southern, western & northern Frontiers exposed and ravaged, our Subjects on the Grants in a State of Revolt, the Staple of the Country restricted from Exportation and limited in Price, for near three years past, solely with a view to retain it for the army, all purchases & impresses for the Continent within the State for many months past upon Credit and still unpaid, the Expence of our civil administration when we are thus reduced to the mere Epitome of a State, equal as if we were in the full possession of our whole Territory, in short if our peculiar Situation, the Difficulties we have had, and still have to contend with, our former Exertions and present Efforts (when we shall call into the Field for three months at least one fourth Part of our enrolled militia) are considered, I trust we shall stand acquitted and that none of the public Embarrassments will be imputed to us.[35]

Unfortunately it was only too easy to show the "peculiar situation" of New York which had had to bear so many of the direct burdens of the war. "We should be justified in not furnishing any supplies of any kind," the governor told the New York delegates to Congress in 1781, "as we have heretofore made advances ruinous to the state and greatly distressing to individuals, and much beyond our quota." [36] He restated New York's position late in 1781 in a long letter to John Hanson, then president of the Congress. "This State I flatter myself has for its Spirit & Exertions in the War stood equal in point of Reputation with any other in the Union, and notwithstanding our Misfortunes & Injuries, and notwithstanding our Legislature is, with respect to the Individuals who compose it, fluctuating, I am confident the People at large and their Representatives in Gov't. still retain the same Spirit & are equally disposed to every possible Effort in the common Cause. I mention this, lest it be supposed that we were sinking under our Distresses . . ." [37]

[35] Public Papers, V, 939–40.
[36] Letter of March 28, 1781, in Duane Papers, quoted from in Thomas C. Cochran, New York in the Confederation (Philadelphia, 1932), 49.
[37] Public Papers, VII, 520–21.

In these letters of the governor there was evident a growing impatience with the Congress—an impatience that both Clinton and Hamilton had expressed in their correspondence in 1778. In the letter of 1781 to John Hanson the governor gave it as his personal opinion that "the Defects in the Powers of Congress are the chief Source of present Embarrassm'nts, and as a Friend to the Independence & True Interests & Happiness of America," he expressed the earnest desire that these defects might be remedied. Indeed, he said, New York had already indicated its willingness to give the Congress more adequate powers by promptly agreeing to the proposal for granting Congress a duty on imports.

New York was later to block the plan for fortifying Congress with this power to collect a five per cent tariff on imports for federal use, thus producing an impasse that was broken only by the adoption of the federal Constitution of 1787. But in 1781 New York considered herself co-author of the plan and her legislature was prompt to adopt it. Indeed, George Clinton himself had more to do with this early movement for the enlargement of the powers of the Congress than has been generally recognized. Hamilton, to be sure, did propose increased powers in his famous letter of September 3, 1780, to Duane, and Schuyler championed the cause of the Congress in the legislature in late September and October of that year. But Governor Clinton made an effective, and for him eloquent appeal for increased congressional powers when he addressed the legislature at Poughkeepsie on September 7, only a few weeks after a convention of three states at Boston had proposed a stronger Congress. Clinton told his legislature that "our embarrassments in the prosecution of the war are chiefly to be attributed to a defect in power in those who ought to exercise supreme discretion, for while Congress only recommend and the different States deliberate upon the propriety of the recommendation, we cannot expect a union of force or counsel. From this conviction," he went on, "I take the liberty of submitting to you whether further means ought not to be devised for accelerating the proposed confederation, and thereby vesting Congress with such authority as that in all matters which relate to the war, their requisitions may be peremptory." [88]

[88] Lincoln, *Messages from the Governors*, II, 105–07.

In view of George Clinton's later opposition to the extension of federal powers, these statements of his in 1780 are most interesting.

The legislature acted upon the governor's suggestions. It agreed to send delegates to a convention to be held in November at Hartford—the purpose of which was also the propping up of the federal Congress—and it instructed the New York delegates at Hartford, as well as those in Congress, to urge that body to assume more adequate powers for the strenuous prosecution of the war. The most amazing of the resolutions was that proposing that the commander-in-chief march his army into any state delinquent in furnishing men, money, or supplies, "and by a Military Force, compel it to furnish its deficiency." [39] This vigorous proposal, which might have revolutionized our federal system even before the Articles of Confederation went into effect, was adopted at Hartford. But Duane and Scott thought it far too advanced to broach to Congress, [40] and Governor Clinton may have agreed with them. The outcome of this agitation for increased congressional powers was the proposal of 1781 to give Congress a five per cent impost. Although New York promptly agreed, Rhode Island objected; and when Congress again asked for the impost grant, in 1783, New York and its governor had concluded that the impost was too rare a jewel to be entrusted to the ne'er-do-well Congress and the grant was refused. While the war lasted, however, Clinton was as persistent as any in urging increased federal powers.

It was with some reluctance, nevertheless, that the governor consented to the cession of New York's western lands to the federal government. Jay wrote Clinton in October 1779, that in his opinion the territory west of Niagara was too extensive to govern and Livingston suggested to him only a few weeks later that it would be prudent to forestall any decision to appropriate the western lands by ceding all New York's claims west of the northwest corner of Pennsylvania. [41] New York's title to this western country was shadowy enough, [42] yet Clinton was clearly loath to give it up. He replied to Livingston in

[39] *Ibid.*, 107, note; Burnett, *Letters . . . Continental Congress*, V, 445.
[40] *Ibid.*, V, 445; VI, v.
[41] *Public Papers*, V, 314, 382.
[42] *The Territorial Papers of the United States*, C. E. Carter, ed., II (Washington, 1934), 5.

January that "it may be to our Interest to give up a Part of our Western Lands, if by this we shall be able to Injoy the Remainder free from every Claim," and he admitted that the boundary described by Livingston would give New York all it could properly administer. The act of February 19, 1780, made New York the first state to cede its western claims. Other states followed and Maryland, which had refused membership in the Confederation while her neighbors claimed great areas in the west, ratified the Articles. New York had made a real contribution towards the building of the confederation and once again Clinton might well be proud of his state's record.

The war governor's first winter in his new office was the winter of Valley Forge and Washington's eloquent appeals for supplies for his hungry, ragged troops must have convinced Clinton that it is often easier to direct troop movements in the field than to feed and clothe armies. Desperate, Washington wrote his Excellency in February regarding "the present dreadful situation of the army for want of provisions." [43]

The governor acted at once. Within a few days a hundred head of cattle and one hundred and fifty barrels of salt pork were on their way to Valley Forge in wagons impressed for the purpose under the governor's own authority. [44] And it is interesting to note that the governor wrote Washington on March fifth that he would make every effort to obtain more supplies although he had only a day earlier told Horatio Gates, president of the board of war, that "no beef or pork can be procured in this state." [45] It depended on who made the request. The several hundred additional barrels of pork that were sent to Washington a few days later were undoubtedly a major factor in enabling the Continental Army to survive the winter. [46]

The procurement of supplies remained Governor Clinton's most troublesome task through the entire period of the war. If the new democracy could not feed and clothe its armies, it would not survive and its champions might end their promising careers in the Tower of London. This Clinton fully understood. Yet production of most

[43] Letter of February 16, Washington, *Writings,* X, 469–70.
[44] *Public Papers,* II, 799, 818, 823, 866.
[45] *Ibid.,* 842, 866.
[46] *Ibid.,* III, 5.

of the essentials—grain, meat, clothing, shoes, and munitions—was sadly reduced by the lack of man power, by the loss of the southern counties occupied by the enemy, and by the state's too frequently empty treasury. Furthermore, the farmers were by no means eager to sell provisions for state or Continental paper notes that were constantly depreciating in value. They waited for higher prices or sold to New England where food shortages were also chronic and prices were also high. Other produce sifted through the lines and found its way into Westchester and Long Island from which it soon reached the enemy in New York City. The governor believed that provisions illegally exported to New England later helped the British in New York City to survive the winter of 1778.[47] Then there were the "engrossers" of foodstuffs who bought up supplies and held them for higher prices. This kind of profiteering was sometimes penalized but not always. The Livingstons, for instance, were accused of selling iron to the state at prices that were more than double those paid by private persons and they were also accused of refusing to sell it to the state when New Englanders would offer more. Nevertheless, Governor Clinton diplomatically declined to seize their iron or adopt coercive measures, contenting himself with asking Walter Livingston to approach his father, Colonel Robert, on the delicate subject.[48]

It was the war governor's task to prevent the leakage of supplies from the state. An act of March 14, 1778, renewed the embargo on the exportation of grain and flour that had first been established by the Committee of Safety in 1776. This act the governor heartily approved and endeavored to enforce in spite of fervid appeals from New England for wheat and flour. The suspicious governor guessed that New England requests in 1778 for grain for the French fleet were mere pretexts, and he insisted that the New York troops should be supplied before those of Massachusetts, Rhode Island, or Connecticut. Exportation of flour and grain forced up the New York prices and in spite of the legislature's attempt at price-fixing in 1778, prices rose so sharply that it was sometimes necessary to pay for supplies twice as much as

[47] Jones, *New York in the Revolution*, I, 267–70; *Public Papers*, II, 868.

[48] *Public Papers*, II, 654–60, 713–14; Corning, *Washington at Temple Hill*, 11–12; Flick, ed., *History of the State of New York*, IV, 137. The Livingstons received £45 a ton from the state although they sold to others for £17 to £20. Corning, *op. cit.*, 12.

Congress had authorized in order to fill the state's quota.[49] In June 1779 the price of rum reached thirty dollars a gallon although it was "so weak that half a pint of it makes but a Pint of what they stile Grogg." [50] Price-fixing was abandoned in 1780. Meanwhile the legislature had turned to confiscation, authorizing the seizure of a quarter of the wheat raised by the reluctant farmers, and the unpopular task of appointing officers to make the seizures fell to the governor. He did not at all relish it. "Where will extortion End?" he demanded of one of his officers. "What have we not to dread from it? More I am perswaded than from the arms of our Common Enemy." [51]

The winter of 1780 was the worst period of the war for the procurers of supplies. There had been drought in the fall of 1779; the winter was a heavy one; there was little or no water to turn the mill wheels; and prices were higher than ever. While the governor was convening his commissaries at Poughkeepsie in December the troops in the Highlands were virtually without food. It was in 1780 that the legislature created the office of purchasing agent for the state of New York with an annual salary of £800, an office that was occupied for three years by the Clintons' good friend, Udny Hay. The creation of this office was an attempt to coördinate the state's purchasing which had previously been done by a number of free-lance commissioners, some of them appointed by the governor. Udny Hay was a capable Scot who had arrived at New York as recently as 1776 and had served valiantly as assistant deputy quarter-master general for the Continental Army. He came to Poughkeepsie in 1780, bought a house on Main Street not far from the Crannell house where the Clintons stayed, and was to sell his place and leave for Vermont at a time when a man of his Antifederalist views might have been of considerable value to the governor.[52] During the last months of the war the governor leaned heavily on Udny Hay when supplies were in demand.

There were innumerable other aspects to the problem of supplies.

[49] *Public Papers*, IV, 92, 496, 732; VI, 240–41, 397; *History of the State of New York*, IV, 119–20.
[50] B. F. Stevens, *Facsimiles*, Box I, Number 123.
[51] *Public Papers*, III, 681; IV, 639, 691.
[52] *History of the State of New York*, IV, 141–42. For Hay, see H. W. Reynolds' article in Dutchess County Historical Society, *Year Book 1925*, 49–58.

There was, for instance, the decision to accept wheat and rye for taxes in the place of paper and currency. There was the draining of cattle from Westchester into the enemy lines until the legislature in 1780, at Clinton's request, empowered the governor to prohibit the driving of cattle south of any line he might assign. There was the adoption of the policy of offering bounties to encourage the establishment of new powder mills, the board of war's success in getting Clinton to have certain abandoned and almost useless lead mines reopened, and the designation in 1777, probably by Clinton and McDougall, of Fishkill as the central depot for munitions and supplies.[53] The governor's indefatigable pen was busy at Poughkeepsie sending out instructions to subordinates and counsel to superiors on these and a multitude of similar subjects in such quantity that the letters for 1777 to 1782 now fill nearly eight ponderous volumes of the printed *Public Papers of George Clinton*.

It would be easy to defend the proposition that the Revolution was won in the wheat fields, cowpens, and pigsties, and at the looms, mills, and forges of America. It would be scarcely less easy to show that the sturdy men who held the frontiers against Tory raiders and hostile Indians made the winning of the war possible. Certainly Governor Clinton realized that unprotected frontiers meant not only burned villages and lost lives but also lost crops and demoralized populations. During the last five years of the war the governor was more concerned with the always threatening problems of defending New York's endless frontiers than with any other single task. Most of the time he was at Poughkeepsie directing operations from the comparative tranquillity of the Crannell house; but occasionally, when the situation was threatening and when his rheumatism did not prevent, he hurried in person to the area of operations. It was, to be sure, still vital to hold the lower Hudson Valley and keep the British confined close to New York City. West Point was the most important fortified position in the entire state. But aside from Anthony Wayne's heroic seizure of Stony Point in July 1779 and Arnold's amazing treason somewhat over a year

[53] Lincoln, *Messages from the Governors*, II, 89–90; *Journal of the Assembly*, March 7, 1782; Washington, *Writings*, VIII, 4; *History of the State of New York*, IV, 136–138. The legislature authorized the governor Jan. 7, 1778, to draw £5000 to work lead mines at Continental expense. M. C. Weaks, *Proclamations of General George Clinton*, 7.

later, most of the spectacular developments of the last years of the war
were on the frontiers.

If so many of the warriors of the Six Nations had not remained
faithful to the king, the defense of the frontiers would have been far
easier. That the Indians were pro-British was largely the work of the
Johnson family and especially of that very influential member of the
family, Joseph Brant. Brant, who was years later to strike up an interesting friendship with George Clinton, was a Mohawk chief and
the brother of the sprightly and talented Molly Brant who was for
many years the common-law wife of Sir William Johnson. Brant had
attended Dr. Eleazar Wheelock's Indian school at Lebanon and he
had married the half-Indian daughter of the Tory Indian agent,
George Croghan. Secretary to Sir Guy Johnson after Sir William's
death in 1774, Brant was naturally enough ready to side with the
Johnsons against the colonies. Colonial agents met with the chiefs of
the Six Iroquois Nations at Albany in 1775 in a vain attempt to keep
them at least neutral; but although the Oneidas and the Tuscaroras remained more or less friendly, the Senecas, Mohawks, Cayugas, and
Onondagas were often on the war path and Brant soon became the
bête noire of northwestern New York.[54] He attacked the Unadilla settlements in 1777 and it was known that he planned more raids early the
next year.

At the request of Congress, Governor Clinton appointed a New
York commissioner, James Duane, to join with two Congressional commissioners in holding a treaty with the Six Nations in February and
March 1778. But even Lafayette's persuasiveness failed and the commissioners extracted promises of friendship only from the already
friendly Oneidas and Tuscaroras.[55] Nothing could ward off the approaching storm. By May there was a reign of terror on the borders
of western New York. Crops and stock were stolen or destroyed,
houses and barns burned to the ground, settlers murdered or taken
prisoner. Schoharie was threatened, Cobleskill was destroyed with a
loss of nineteen lives, and Albany was in a panic. The governor from

[54] Ruth L. Higgins, *Expansion in New York* (Columbus, Ohio, 1931), 97–98;
History of the State of New York, IV, 294, 324. Brant's Indian name was Thayendanagea.
[55] Copy of letter from Duane to Clinton, March 13, 1778, in Library of Congress;
William L. Stone, *Joseph Brant* (2 vols., New York, 1838), I, 304–06.

Poughkeepsie urged Generals Ten Broeck, Gates, and Stark to send troops into the Schoharie region and he ordered Colonel Cantine's regiment north from West Point. Not only Tryon and Albany Counties, but Ulster and Orange as well, were appealing to him for help.[56] He proposed an attack upon the enemy rendezvous at Unadilla; and after consultation with Generals Ten Broeck and Stark agreed to the former's suggestion that it should be led by that gallant soldier and hero of Fort Schuyler, Colonel Marinus Willett; [57] but Willett was not available and the expedition was put off.

Springfield was burned in June and there were massacres in the Wyoming Valley in July. When Washington returned to New York in mid-July, Governor Clinton at once waited on him to appeal for troops to use on the frontiers. At about the same time the Continental Congress advanced a hundred thousand dollars for New York's use— too modest an amount, the New York delegates believed—but the sizeable expedition into the Indian country that Congress had authorized in June was soon given up. Gates as usual was indifferent; and even Stark, deciding late in July that an Indian expedition was impossible at the time, delayed Lieutenant Colonel William Butler, whom Clinton had sent to Albany, with Washington's permission, to begin an offensive against the Indians. General Stark finally allowed Butler to proceed to Schoharie but, much to the impatient governor's disgust, the general continued his opposition to plans for a determined offensive against the Tories and their Indian allies.[58] In short, very little was being accomplished in spite of Clinton's appeals. He felt that Congress and its generals were indifferent to the fate of western New York.

Then, in September, German Flats was devastated for miles along the Mohawk and early in November a force of seven hundred Tories and Indians led by Captain Walter Butler and Joseph Brant laid waste the settlements at Cherry Valley. This was one of the most notorious raids of the war and it convinced even the far away Congress that something vigorous must be done in 1779. The war must be carried into the enemy's territory, the governor wrote Jay.

Months of preparation followed. On November 4 the state legisla-

[56] *History of the State of New York*, IV, 187; *Public Papers*, III, 377, 388, 391, 403, 424, 467.
[57] Clinton to Schuyler, July 3, 1778, Clinton Papers, Library of Congress.
[58] *Public Papers*, IV, 13, 54.

ture gave the governor £20,000 for the payment and subsistence of the militia [59] who had been unreliable and even mutinous during the fall campaigns. The uncoöperative Stark was replaced in the command at Albany by General Hand. Washington himself began a systematic campaign of preparatory fact-finding; Congress authorized the proposed expedition on February 26; and a few days later Washington gave command to the young and energetic General Sullivan.[60] Gates had most ungraciously refused it—fortunately for the state of New York. As Sullivan's second in command Washington appropriately enough chose a New Yorker who knew the Indian country well— General James Clinton.

Meanwhile Governor Clinton continued to bombard Washington with appeals for action. He suggested giving Willett command of a regiment of state troops and assigning him to raid the Indian country provided Washington would supply a force of Continentals to coöperate with the expedition. In reply on March 4 the commander-in-chief confided to Clinton that measures for a major campaign against the Tories and Indians had been under way for some weeks, and he asked the governor what troops the state of New York could furnish.[61] A few days later he was representing to the governor the need of General McDougall for support from the local militia in the region of the Highlands and the need of more militia to hold the western borders until Sullivan could get under way. Clinton did what he could to comply, authorizing McDougall to call out the Westchester and part of the Orange militia, promising for Continental service half of the force of a thousand men that the legislature had just empowered him to raise for frontier service, and ordering General Ten Broeck to confer with Schuyler and James Clinton at Albany on the defense of the western frontier. Washington was appreciative. "The readiness, with which you comply with all my requests in prosecution of the public service, has a claim to my warmest acknowledgments," he assured the governor early in May. Washington's confidence in Clinton was as great as ever.[62]

---

[59] *Messages from the Governors*, II, 53, note.
[60] *History of the State of New York*, IV, 190.
[61] *Public Papers*, IV, 612, 615–16. Willett refused the command that Clinton offered him. *Ibid.*, 656.
[62] *Ibid.*, 796; Burnett, *Letters . . . Continental Congress*, IV, 75.

There was one more nerve-wracking interlude before the Sullivan expedition could get under way. At the very end of May some forty sail of enemy shipping under Sir Henry Clinton himself left Manhattan and started up the Hudson to Kings Ferry. General McDougall appealed to Clinton for advice, troops, and teams to move his supplies. Colonel Udny Hay wrote frantically from Fishkill, "We want animation. I wish to God you were here." The governor issued the usual orders to the militia and hurried down from Poughkeepsie to Fishkill where he informed McDougall that he meant to act under him in the character of a brigadier general in Continental service "unless an Officer superior to you in Command shoud arive in which case I cannot. The Militia would not submit to it. You understand without Explanation what I mean." [63] The militia behaved excellently and the governor had a considerable force at his command at Camp Highlands when he wrote the president of Congress on June 7. The Americans had, however, promptly withdrawn from the unfinished works at Stony Point and the garrison at Verplanck's Point surrendered rather ingloriously. The British now controlled the Hudson up to the posts in the Highlands. Yet only six weeks later Wayne was to recapture Stony Point.

"Your march to the Highlands has given occasion to many handsome things being said & written of you here," John Jay wrote Governor Clinton from Philadelphia early in August.[64] Indeed, his presence in the Highlands had had such salutary effects that Washington persuaded him to take no part in the Sullivan-Clinton expedition, insisting that in case of another crisis on the Hudson the Governor's presence might be essential. In spite of his chronic rheumatism Clinton probably regretted the necessity for this decision. He was under no delusions on the score of his ability to direct armies in the field of operations. In the summer of 1779 he had planned to give himself a distinctly minor rôle in the campaign. His plan was to march a force of five hundred men from Warwarsing on the frontier west of Kingston, to create a diversion in the Delaware country by scouring the Tory and Indian settlements there, and to join at Onoquaga with

[63] *Public Papers*, V, 6.
[64] *Ibid.*, 199.

James Clinton's army as the latter pushed south from Canajoharie on the Mohawk down the long Susquehanna Valley to Tioga to unite with Sullivan.[65] Sullivan's main force was to come up to Tioga from Easton, Pennsylvania. But Washington feared that the governor's great influence with the militia might be needed in the Hudson Valley in case of another British advance and Colonel Pawling was chosen to take his place.[66]

The Sullivan-Clinton campaign was successful in almost every respect. It was, to be sure, delayed some weeks in starting—a circumstance of which Brant took advantage by destroying Minisink in July while Clinton fumed over Sullivan's "unaccountable delay" at Wyoming.[67] James Clinton's army of 1500 men floated down the Susquehanna with the assistance of an artificial flood created by damming the waters of Otsego Lake, burned a number of Indian towns and arrived safely and promptly at Tioga to join Sullivan on August 22. General James found time to write his brother several newsy, enthusiastic letters during the course of the expedition—letters that are among the historian's best sources for the events of those weeks. Together Sullivan and Clinton pushed into the Indian country, fighting a little battle at Newtown and burning dozens of Indian villages, in the country of the Senecas, Onondagas, and Cayugas, by Seneca Lake and westward to Genesee Castle. They were back at Tioga on September 30. The Indians had been almost completely driven out of central and western New York, and the power of the Six Nations was never to recover from the blows dealt it during this campaign. For some months at least the frontiers of western New York were safe. A great granary of the British and Indians had been destroyed; and, by no means least important, extensive areas were cleared for American settlement at the end of the war. According to the State Historian of New York, "the Sullivan-Clinton campaign and the expedition under George Rogers Clark in the northwest were intended to stake out claims which would assure to the United States not only western New York and Pennsylvania, but likewise the rich terri-

[65] George to James Clinton, Poughkeepsie, June 12, 1779, Historical Society of Pennsylvania; same to same, Poughkeepsie, June 20, 1779, Huntington Library.
[66] Ibid.; Washington to Sullivan, June 21, 1779, Magazine of History, March 1907, 137.
[67] Public Papers, V, 162–66, 180.

tory south of the Great Lakes, farther westward." [68] It was an important step in the building of an empire.

Like the surrender of Burgoyne in 1777 and the French alliance in 1778, the Sullivan-Clinton expedition raised the morale of all New York patriots and strengthened the will to win. Indeed, in spite of the constant demands upon the state for men, money, and supplies, in spite of the loss of the southern counties, and in spite of the constant hammering of British irregulars and Indians upon the open border settlements, there had been remarkably little defeatist sentiment in New York even during the darkest weeks of the war. When Lord North's peace commissioners arrived in America in June 1778, to offer the Americans virtually everything that they had quarreled over with the British ministry since 1765, their proposals received almost no consideration whatsoever in New York State. Governor Clinton expressed the sentiments of his state when he declared that, "Lord North is two years late with his political manoevre." [69]

[68] A. C. Flick in *History of the State of New York*, IV, Chapter 6.
[69] George Bancroft, *History of the United States* (10 vols., Boston, 1854–74), IX, 498.

CHAPTER X

WASHINGTON AND CLINTON ENTER NEW YORK

1780 REELECTED GOVERNOR

KIDNAPERS

CLINTON LETS SIR JOHN JOHNSON ESCAPE

SIR JOHN ESCAPES AGAIN

WASHINGTON DEPENDS ON CLINTON

YORKTOWN AND EVACUATION OF NEW YORK

NEW YORK WELCOMES WASHINGTON AND CLINTON

THEY CELEBRATE THE NEW ERA

BY 1780 George Clinton had achieved recognition as one of the greatest of the war governors. In New York he was almost universally respected and his reëlection to the governorship should he consent to stand was inevitable. Rivals were few. Schuyler was no more popular than he had been in 1777 and Jay, who had been for a year president of Congress, was in 1780 on a fruitless diplomatic mission at Madrid.[1] Except for Schuyler the first families of New York had not succeeded in producing any war leader of the first rank to contest the leadership of the state with Clinton. Clinton expressed some reluctance to serving another three years. Yet Stephen Lush was able to write him from Albany shortly before the elections that in spite of numerous contending candidates for the Assembly who were "divided into parties," and in spite of some campaigning against the new taxes and the raising of more levies for the frontier, Clinton's name and that of Lieutenant Governor Van Cortlandt appeared on every list of candidates that he

---

[1] He was not received at court, however, and left Madrid for Paris in May, 1782.

had seen.[2] Clinton must have been pleased. The New York democracy had not been disappointed in the man it had chosen in 1777.

Under the provisions of the elections act of March 27, 1778, the elections were held on the last Tuesday in April and the voting was *vive voce* for senators and assemblymen but by ballot for governor and lieutenant governor. Although the voting in 1780 may have produced "some Heats," very few electors found time to visit the polling places. Some days after the balloting Robert R. Livingston was able to congratulate the governor, expressing pleasure at "the great superiority of ballots in your favor at the last election, that the people notwithstanding the endeavors of some designing men are disposed to do justice to your merrits." General Lewis Morris added to his congratulations the wish that Clinton might preside over the state for life. Clinton had won by 3264 ballots.[3] His second gubernatorial term began on July 1, 1780.

The Clintons were of course still living at their Poughkeepsie home, but the governor's life was a peripatetic one. Legislative sessions took him for weeks at a time to Fishkill, New Windsor, Newburgh, or even Saratoga. He pretended that he did not enjoy this roving. "One month at most, out of the last twelve, have I enjoyed the Society of my Familly & that not without Interruption by claims from one quarter or another," he wrote in 1781.[4] Possibly on some of these trips he used the phaeton that James Bloodgood sent down to him from Albany in the fall of 1781.[5]

The Christmas of 1780, Governor Clinton and his wife or daughter dined with General and Mrs. Washington at the general's headquarters, the Ellison House at New Windsor. The company was a large one comprising as it did the officers of the general's staff, two French officers, and certain of the neighbors, including Mrs. James Clinton who had furnished three turkeys for the occasion. Mrs. Washington had only recently rejoined the general and this was the first occasion on which she entertained. Mr. Corning tells us that the guard band

[2] *Public Papers,* V, 614.
[3] *Ibid.,* 691, 896; F. B. Hough, *New York Civil List* (Albany, 1860), 29; Lincoln, *Messages from the Governors,* II, 10.
[4] *Public Papers,* VI, 736.
[5] *Ibid.,* VII, 388.

played while the guests challenged the beef, mutton, and poultry. "After dinner spiced wine was passed round, followed by pies, puddings, apples, nuts, and cider."[6] Men and women ate heartily in those days.

The practical Clinton was no patron of the fine arts. Yet during these busy years he found time for an interesting but not always spirited correspondence with the Swiss artist, Pierre du Simitiere. The artist usually wrote from Philadelphia, explaining his plans for pencil drawings of great Americans, hinting broadly to Clinton of his wish to acquire collections of documents and of Indian relics, and complaining of Clinton's neglect. Clinton usually succeeded in finding time to write and even supplied the persistent Swiss with the desired collection of Indian relics.[7]

Even residence at Poughkeepsie in friendly territory did not protect the war governor from attempted kidnapings. In early August 1781, Washington wrote Clinton to warn him of a plot to seize him and take him to New York. A considerable group of British partisans were involved and the prizes offered were a hundred guineas each for the four men who were to make the actual seizure. Attempts were made to kidnap Generals Schuyler and Gansevoort at about the same time. Early in 1782 Hendrick Wyckoff warned Governor Clinton that a plan was afoot to abduct him, that the prize was two hundred guineas, and that the kidnapers had recently been routed near Poughkeepsie by the governor's guard. In acknowledging Wyckoff's letter Clinton stated that although he had no guard at present, he was not much concerned for his safety.[8]

For two and a half years after the fall of the Highland forts George Clinton did no active campaigning. In 1780, however, he made two last appearances in the field, both of them attempts to capture that wily Tory, Sir John Johnson. The chastisement that Sullivan and James Clinton had administered to the Indians in northwestern New York had left the Indians and Tories of the frontier momentarily subdued but thirsting for revenge, and the years 1780 and 1781 saw a succession of terrifying border raids. It was not until after the ar-

---

[6] Corning, *Washington at Temple Hill*, 59–60.
[7] *Public Papers, passim.*
[8] *Ibid.*, VI, 568–69; VII, 193–94; *Olde Ulster*, V, 370.

rival of news of the treaty of peace with Britain that the governor could relax his efforts to provide for the defense of the frontiers. One of the most troublesome of the enemy raids was Sir John Johnson's famous return to Johnson Hall in May 1780.

Governor Clinton was at Kingston waiting for a quorum of the legislature to gather to hear his recommendations when the news came that Sir John with five hundred Tories and Indians had entered the Mohawk Valley. They destroyed Caughnawaga and Sir John recovered some of his family plate that had been hidden at Johnson Hall. The governor delivered his message to the legislature on the twenty-fifth and then left immediately for Albany. Quite apart from the crisis in the Mohawk Valley it was a pleasant time of year for a trip into the northern woods. General Ten Broeck was ill, but Clinton ordered Colonel Van Schaick to start the pursuit of Sir John while he himself went north to Saratoga and Fort George to gather the militia.[9]

He had at first two primary objects: to cut off Sir John and his company and, secondly, to prepare for an expected attack by a much larger force from Canada on Fort Schuyler. But, suspecting that the attack on Fort Schuyler was a British ruse "calculated to favour Sir John's Incursion," he turned all his available militia and those which came in from the Vermont country to the task of intercepting Sir John. Van Schaick was to harass the enemy's rear to delay their retreat, yet Van Schaick lacked supplies as well as men and Clinton, realizing the colonel's ineffectiveness, planned to give himself more time by moving up from Lake George to Lake Champlain before attempting to check Sir John's march. He felt that he was making good time, but Sir John made better and embarked at Crown Point on Lake Champlain some six hours before the governor and his militia could arrive. He told Washington that while he regretted the failure to trap Sir John, he hoped that that gentleman's close escape might deter him from similar enterprises.[10] By June 13 Clinton was back with the legislature at Kingston writing to Abraham Yates that "Mrs. Clinton, after waiting till the alarm below and the great hurry

[9] *Public Papers*, V, 761, 766, 769, 818.
[10] *Ibid.*, 819.

of Business was over very decently presented me with a fine Girl." [11]

That summer Washington was again in New York and General Benedict Arnold took command at West Point. When Arnold's shocking treason was discovered late in September Governor Clinton was one of the first that Washington notified. The governor's attention was, however, shortly transferred to the north, for it was only a few days after Arnold's flight to a British sloop of war that Sir John Johnson showed by a new raid that his close escape that spring had been no deterrent to similar expeditions. He came from Canada by way of Oswego with a large force of regulars, Greens, and Butler's rangers, was joined by his Indian allies at Unadilla and in mid-October fell on the Schoharie Valley. Houses and barns at Schoharie were burned, great amounts of newly harvested grain destroyed and Caughnawaga given to the flames. The frontiers were in terror. Once again the governor thought it necessary to go himself to the scene of battle. He wrote Washington on October 14 that he was leaving Poughkeepsie immediately for Albany and he appealed for Continental troops. With militia under General Robert Van Rensselaer of Claverack the governor hurried by forced marches to the threatened region and arrived on the eighteenth at Caughnawaga in time to see it burn.

Then followed a series of inexcusable errors and delays for which General Van Rensselaer was probably directly responsible as Clinton had placed him in command of the expedition. But the governor as commander-in-chief of the militia possessed the authority, if not the wisdom, to prevent Van Rensselaer's blunders and must to some degree share the blame with that lackadaisical officer. Van Rensselaer ordered Colonel John Brown to attack Sir John but failed to support him and in the ensuing skirmish Brown was killed and his little force routed. Sir John then found time to desolate Stone Arabia and pillage the countryside. On the twenty-first the Americans came on the enemy at Klock's Field, near Canajoharie, defeated them, but again allowed them to get away. Van Rensselaer's pursuit brought him to Fort Herkimer just behind Johnson, but he soon gave up and the enemy returned to Canada by the Oswego route. The governor overtook his general at Fort Herkimer but did not, it is said, even then inter-

[11] Platt, *Poughkeepsie*, 52.

fere in the command. The expedition accomplished its prime purpose of running Sir John Johnson out of the state but with proper direction it might have captured or destroyed the whole enemy force.[12] Somewhat mortified with the results, Clinton returned to Schenectady and Albany, spent the night of October 27 with Colonel Livingston and was back to Poughkeepsie on the 28th.[13] Not only mortification but also a bad siege of rheumatism followed the trip.

Two months later Washington called on Clinton for assistance in what might have proved a very serious emergency. Washington wrote the governor from New Windsor on January 4 that there had been a mutiny in the Pennsylvania line stationed near Morristown. If there should be further outbreaks it would be necessary to depend entirely on the militia. Knowing Clinton's influence with the militiamen, Washington thought it "indispensably necessary that your Excellency should be as near the posts as possible" and added that "your advice upon such an occasion would be of infinite service to me. . . . If the Session [of the legislature soon to assemble at Albany] can be carried on by the Lieutenant Governor, I shall be glad to see your Excellency as soon as possible." Clinton replied the next day that he would give up his Albany trip, and on January 6 he was with Washington at the New Windsor headquarters. He returned to Poughkeepsie before Washington was satisfied that the Morristown mutiny was completely disposed of, but he promised Washington that if necessary he could throw a thousand militia into West Point in three or four days."[14]

George Clinton was in conference again with Washington at Peekskill late in June when he agreed to the withdrawal of the Continental regiments at Albany provided he could get reënforcements for Albany from Massachusetts. Washington promised six hundred Bay State militia but found it easier to promise than to produce them. Governor Clinton was, however, as insistent as Governor Hancock was reluctant.[15]

[12] Public Papers, VI, 291–338; Benson John Lossing, Empire State (New York, 1887), 306–07; Stone, Joseph Brant, II, 115–23.
[13] Public Papers, VI, 345–47.
[14] Public Papers, VI, 547–50, 572.
[15] John C. Fitzpatrick, ed., Diaries of George Washington (4 vols., Boston and New York, 1925), II, 229, 247.

There was of course great rejoicing and much exchanging of congratulations upon the arrival of the great news of Yorktown in October 1781. At Poughkeepsie the legislature convened in the Dutch church to offer thanks while the good folk of the town expressed gratitude in bonfires and salutes. Chancellor Livingston wrote enthusiastically to the governor; General Heath asked him to join the army on October 31 in its celebration of the great event; and Colonel Hamilton called on him early in November with first-hand news from Virginia.[16] The news must have given great satisfaction to the governor who could develop a deal of satisfaction over any event that he could consider "humiliating to British pride and arrogance."

Yorktown was not the end of the war. There was nevertheless after the surrender of Cornwallis a very natural feeling in the states that the war was virtually over and that further sacrifices in the Continental cause were not essential. In spite of this let-down of morale George Clinton worked, much as before the victory, to raise and maintain troops and to keep the always threatening frontiers adequately defended. The problems of supplies and finance were more pressing perhaps than ever. "I sincerely wish the people would be persuaded to forego the use of Luxuries & even of Articles which habit has in some measure made the Necessaries of Life & apply the monies they expend in that way to the support of the War," the governor told Gouverneur Morris in 1782.[17] He must have been gratified when Steuben wrote him in April of that year: "I have the pleasure to inform your Excellency that the appearance of the New York line which I inspected last week does them the greatest honor. The men are exceedingly well cloathed, and armed & by the attention of their Officers I have reason to believe they will be disciplined the ensuing campaign equal to any troops in the army."[18] On the other hand, the decision of the Continental Congress to refuse James Clinton a commission as major general on the ground that the New York line

[16] Platt, *History of Poughkeepsie*, 53; *Public Papers*, VII, 459; Heath to Clinton, October 30, 1871, letter in Huntington Library; Livingston to Clinton, October 27, 1781, photostat in Library of Congress.
[17] *Public Papers*, VIII, 23.
[18] Letter of April 10, 1782 in State Museum, Newburgh.

was not entitled to a second major general probably did not increase the governor's fondness for that body.[19]

There was time during these months for the less serious duties of war. Among the more frivolous was a splendid dinner of five hundred plates that Washington gave at West Point to Governor Clinton and other gentlemen on May 31, 1782. The occasion being the celebration of the birth of a Dauphin, eight of the thirteen toasts were to France and the alliance.[20] Late in June the governor accompanied the commander-in-chief on a visit to Albany, Saratoga, and Schenectady. Schuyler entertained them royally at Albany and wherever they went their trip became a kind of triumphal progress. In the fall Washington and Clinton were received with similar acclaim in Kingston where Washington viewed "with indignation the marks of a wanton and cruel enemy," but rejoiced that Kingston's calamities had only added to its patriotism.[21]

The preliminary articles of peace with Great Britain, which were signed at Paris on November 30, 1782, and ratified by the United States the following April, provided among other things that his Britannic Majesty should "with all convenient speed, & without causing any Destruction or carrying away any Negroes," withdraw all his armies, garrisons and fleets from every port, place and harbor within the United States. The provision also appeared in Article VII of the definitive treaty which was signed at Paris on September 3.[22] Yet to persuade his Britannic Majesty to evacuate southern New York occupied a good deal of George Clinton's time in 1783 and it was to be nearly thirteen more years before his still reluctant majesty could be induced to yield up the western posts which included Niagara, Oswego, Oswegatchie, and two stations on Lake Champlain in New York.

Even before the ratification of the preliminary articles of peace the impatient governor sent Egbert Benson, his attorney general, to New York City to congratulate Sir Guy Carleton on the peace and to sug-

---

[19] Burnett, *Letters . . . Continental Congress*, VI, 322, 554; *Public Papers*, VIII, 55.
[20] *New York Packet*, June 6, 1782.
[21] *History of the State of New York*, Flick, ed., V, 72. *New York Packet*, December 5, 1782.
[22] *Treaties and Other International Acts of the United States*, Hunter Miller, ed., II (Washington, 1931), 96, 151.

gest politely a speedy evacuation of the parts of New York held by the British. Carleton was courteous but evasive. He thought that the initiative in formulating plans for evacuation should come from the governor. Washington then took a hand in the negotiations and Sir Guy agreed to meet the American commander-in-chief at Tappan. Governor Clinton accompanied Washington at this conference, which took place on May 6, but the two together succeeded only in getting Sir Guy to promise to withdraw from Westchester County. Six days later, after some further urging by Clinton, Carleton wrote the governor that his troops were leaving Westchester.[23] That was something.

The council for the southern district of New York, which had been rather prematurely appointed by the legislature in 1779 to take over the administration and policing of the southern counties when they should be evacuated, met at Poughkeepsie on May 20 and viewed with regret Carleton's failure to hasten evacuation. The council, of which the governor was a member, reviewed Clinton's correspondence with Carleton and approved the governor's action. Encouraged, Clinton returned to the attack. He urged the evacuation of Long Island, rebuked Carleton for his refusal to turn the records and archives of New York City over to young Scott, the son of the secretary of state, and complained that patriot property was still kept from its rightful owners and even leased by the British authorities. Not until November 12 did Sir Guy yield and write Clinton that he expected to retire from New York and Long Island on November 22. It was as a matter of fact the 25th before the Americans could enter the metropolis.[24]

It was only natural that the governor of the sovereign state of New York should share the honors with the Continental commander-in-chief when the American forces entered New York. Shortly before the time set for evacuation Washington came down from his Newburgh headquarters to meet Governor Clinton and his staff and General Knox with his troops at Harlem. On the 25th Knox led the troops amid cheers down Bowery Lane and Chatham Street into the city as the British withdrew, leaving their flag, it is said, nailed to a

[23] *Public Papers*, VIII, 134–40, 156–68, 176.
[24] *Public Papers*, VIII, 183, 186, 203, 207, 211, 239–40, 278–83, 298; James Grant Wilson, *Memorial History of the City of New York*, III (New York, 1893), 10–12.

greased pole. The city having been occupied, Knox and a group of citizens proceeded to the Bull's Head in the Bowery to call for Washington and Governor Clinton while the citizens who were to march afoot assembled "at or near the Tea-water-Pump at Freshwater." Then took place a triumphal progress through the city. A troop of horse led the procession, followed by Washington with Clinton at his side, Lieutenant Governor Van Cortlandt, the members of the council for the temporary government of the southern district, other notables, and a body of citizenry. The troops marched up Broadway and the gentlemen and officers through Queen Street to join forces at Cape's Tavern.[25] The citizenry that crowded the streets to welcome the American conquerors to the harassed little city that had suffered two major fires since the British occupied it in 1776, seems to have been properly enthusiastic. The thousands who regretted the departure of the red coats discreetly held their peace.

The climax of the day was a dinner given at Fraunces' Tavern by Governor Clinton to Washington and his officers. Here at Samuel Fraunces' the assembled guests consumed, among other things, ten pounds' worth of punch, 24 bottles of spruce, 24 of porter, 16 of port, 18 of claret, and 75 of Madeira, which was always Clinton's favorite. And an even more lavish dinner was given by Clinton and his council to the Chevalier de Luzerne, the French Minister, and to General Washington a few days later at Cape's. The dinner must indeed have been a gay one for the 120 diners broke 60 wine glasses and made away with 135 bottles of Madeira alone, not to speak of 36 bottles of port, 60 of English beer, and 30 bowls of punch. There was coffee for the few who wished it; fruits, nuts, and music for all. The state received from John Cape a bill for £156/10.[26]

Little wonder that Clinton and his fellow Whigs forgot frugality, and possibly temperance too, in the jubilation of that great moment.

[25] Broadside of November 24, 1783 in Edward Ten Broeck Perine, *Here's to Broadway* (New York, 1930), opp. p. 14; Humphreys, *David Humphreys*, I, 283–84; *Historic New York*, edited by Maud W. Goodwin and others (2 vols., New York and London, 1897–99), II, 261. James Clinton was among the officers present. John Romeyn Brodhead, *Documents Relative to the Colonial History of the State of New York* (Albany, 1853–87), VIII, 806.

[26] The itemized bills for both banquets are printed in E. C. Knight, *New York in the Revolution*, 167.

For eight years certainly, and possibly for fifteen, Clinton had fought to make his New York the cornerstone of a new-world republic. To him and his fellow democrats, naive and confident as they were, monarchy meant tyranny, corruption, absentee government and all that was reprehensible. Republicanism, on the other hand, would bring liberty, justice, and civic virtue; it would open the door of opportunity to all men—excepting only Tories; and it would make possible government based upon the social contract, that good government of, by, and for the people that had been the goal of Clinton and his radical Whig compatriots since 1776. It was perhaps too simple and democratic a faith that these men possessed, and some disillusionment was certain to follow. But in December 1783 Clinton and his democrats were jubilant in their belief that a new era had dawned.

CHAPTER XI

STEPFATHER OF VERMONT

GEORGE CLINTON'S political and economic philosophy was radical enough to make him a revolutionary in 1776 and, in the eyes of men like Hamilton and Jay, a radical democrat in the critical period that followed the Revolution. Yet there were certain striking limitations to his radicalism. There was, for instance, his firm belief in the sanctity of property rights in land—so long as the owners were not Tories. Himself an owner of extensive lands it was only natural that he should uphold the inviolability of land titles. There was also his insistence upon the territorial integrity of his state which involved a denial of the right of self-determination that, as asserted by the American colonies, had justified the Revolution. It had seemed to him entirely proper for New York to secede from the British Empire in 1776, but for Vermont to secede from New York a few years later was nothing short of treason. And as Vermont's secession would not only reduce New

York's area but would also threaten the titles of a number of prominent New Yorkers to choice northern lands, Clinton became the declared
enemy of any concession to the Vermonters. He has consequently come
down in Vermont history as a kind of unnatural stepfather to that state.

The Vermont controversy, to which Clinton fell heir, began in 1749
when Governor Benning Wentworth of New Hampshire ignored New
York's claim to the area west of the Connecticut River by granting
away whole townships in that region. New York objected; Lieutenant
Governor Cadwallader Colden obtained from the king in council an
edict recognizing the Connecticut River as New York's eastern
boundary north of the Massachusetts line, but it took over forty years
to settle the dispute. Even before the Revolution Ethan Allen and
his famous Green Mountain Boys were rioting and intimidating New
York settlers in the so-called New Hampshire Grants and Governor
Tryon was retaliating by reasserting the validity of the New York
titles and outlawing Allen.[1]

George Clinton became involved early in 1774 when he served as
chairman of a committee of the New York Assembly to investigate
conditions in the Grants. New York subjects had complained of violence done them by the Bennington mob and petitioned for armed
protection. Clinton reported that "a dangerous and destructive Spirit
of Riot and Licentiousness" existed in the Grants and he asked that
Governor Tryon offer a reward for the capture of Ethan Allen, Seth
Warner, Remember Baker and others. This Tryon did on March 9.[2]

Clinton himself had speculated in lands in the area of the Grants
—properties that were of course held under New York titles.[3] John
Morin Scott, William Smith Jr., Robert, Robert R. and William Livingston, Leonard Lispenard, Richard Morris, and, probably, Peter Van
Schaack were among the prominent New York claimants. The most
extensive New York claimant seems to have been that "squint-eyed,"

---

[1] *History of the State of New York,* Flick, ed., III, 162; V, Chapter 1; John Pell,
Ethan Allen (Boston, 1929), 28–40.
[2] Edmund Bailey O'Callaghan, *Documentary History of the State of New York* (4
vols., Albany, 1850–51), IV, 856, 869, 870.
[3] Letters of January 19 and February 1, 1779, from Thomas Fanning and Andrew
Elliot in Stevens, *Facsimiles,* Box 1, Numbers 114 and 115; R. C. Benton, *The Vermont
Settlers and the New York Land Speculators* (Minneapolis, 1894), 136; *History of the
State of New York,* Flick, ed., V, 21.

plodding, but wealthy and influential lawyer, James Duane. His claims to 60,000 acres or more in the Grants made him for years Vermont's most formidable opponent in the Continental Congress and Clinton's most effective lieutenant in the long years of political warfare against Ethan Allen and his confederates. Naturally enough, the group of New Yorkers who had invested heavily in Vermont lands were violently opposed to recognizing either the grants of Governor Wentworth or the independence of Vermont.

Ethan Allen's capture of Ticonderoga from the British in 1775 made him the hero of the moment even in New York. But when a convention, meeting at Westminster in January 1777, proclaimed the Grants a free and independent state and appointed delegates to Congress, it was virtually declaring war on New York. Later in the year Vermont adopted a constitution. Nevertheless, when Governor Clinton took office he was willing to try conciliation before attempting coercion, and consequently in February 1778, he issued a proclamation offering to confirm the titles of persons claiming Vermont lands under the grants of other states on the condition that they recognize New York's sovereignty. The Allens, who had themselves invested heavily in Vermont lands, wanted no conciliation, and Ethan Allen replied to Clinton's overtures in terms that showed there could be no agreement. "There is quaintness, impudence, and art in it," Jay wrote regarding Allen's philippic.[4] Certainly it was effective enough to offset Clinton's proclamation. Later in the year Clinton tried again, offering to submit the contested land titles to Congress if the Grants would only submit to New York's jurisdiction; but again Ethan Allen replied and Clinton's proposals received scant consideration.[5]

Clinton was now losing his patience. He had already, in April 1778, asked of Congress "an explicit and unequivocal Declaration" of disapproval of the action taken by the people of the Grants. As Congress took no action, the governor in June urged the New York delegates to press the matter. There would be civil war, he believed, if Congress did not interfere.[6] But with so many of the New England

[4] Stone, *Joseph Brant*, II, 182–83; Pell, *Ethan Allen*, 146–51.
[5] *Ibid.*, 159.
[6] *Public Papers*, III, 144, 416, 531, 533.

and Southern delegates more or less openly favoring the Grants, little was to be expected from the Congress except delay. By February of 1779 it was rumored that the indignant governor was ready to send troops into the Vermont country to protect the "Yorkers" from violence and assert his state's sovereignty.[7] When in May, Ethan Allen led his troops to Brattleboro and there seized a number of New York militia officers, insulted the Yorkers, assaulted and wounded several, and bid defiance to the state of New York, Clinton prepared to send militia into the region to "repel this Outrage."[8]

Clinton's threats finally brought Congressional action and a resolution of apology for its delay from the Congress to the governor.[9] Congress decided on June 1 to send a committee into the Grants to obtain an amicable settlement. Clinton was astonished, however, that Congress took the Brattleboro incident so lightly as to make no mention of it in the resolution and he predicted that the legislature would consider the Congressional resolution as highly unsatisfactory. He himself did not approve.

Certainly the outcome of the Congressional committee plan was unsatisfactory; for only two members of the committee ever reached Vermont and their report to the Congress brought no settlement of a condition that now threatened civil war. Clinton realized that every delay favored Vermont and he wrote constantly and persistently to the New York delegates to force Congressional action.[10] In September of 1779 Congress undertook to make the settlement itself, but there were interminable delays and late the next year the governor made a scarcely veiled threat to withdraw New York's entire Congressional delegation.[11] The whole unfortunate episode of the Grants had much to do with the impatient governor's declining confidence in Congress.

By 1781 it was becoming evident that New York's jurisdiction in the Grants was to be sacrificed for expediency's sake, and that New York must try to secure the best possible terms. Yet Clinton was not

---

[7] Letter of Andrew Elliot in Stevens *Facsimiles,* Box I, No. 115.
[8] *Public Papers,* IV, 846, 859. Washington wrote a friendly letter of remonstrance. Washington, *Writings,* XV, 275.
[9] *Ibid.,* V, 84.
[10] Burnett, *Letters . . . Continental Congress,* IV, *passim.*
[11] Cochran, *New York in the Confederation,* 90.

willing to make the final concession. He was, on the other hand, ready to use all his constitutional powers to block it. The show-down came in February 1781, when the state Senate passed a resolution for the appointment of commissioners to settle with the commissioners from Vermont the terms for a cession of jurisdiction. This was a virtual admission of Vermont's statehood. On February 27 Governor Clinton sent a message [12] to the Assembly pointing out that the resolutions just passed by the Senate completely reversed the position that the legislature had previously taken. He concluded with the bold statement that:

Should you, therefore, agree to carry into effect these resolutions, the duties of my office will oblige me to exercise the authority vested in me by the Constitution, and prorogue you, and by that means prevent you from pursuing measures which, from the repeated declarations of former legislatures, I am warranted to believe would not only be ruinous to this State, but also destructive to the general peace and interest of the whole confederacy.

The Assembly did not concur in the Senate resolution. George Clinton had effectively blocked a settlement of the Vermont dispute.

It is not of course possible to say to just what extent Clinton's action was dictated by his ownership of Vermont lands. It is, however, clear that his most steadfast ally in his opposition to Vermont's claims was James Duane, the greatest New York claimant of all, and that other New Yorkers, like Gouverneur Morris, who had no considerable direct interest in Vermont were much less ardent champions of New York's sovereignty.[13] Had Clinton had no personal interest in Vermont, that region might have become a state some ten years earlier than it did.

Realizing that the tide was turning in their favor, the Vermonters grew bold and extended their territorial claims in 1781 up to the Hudson. Clinton was wrathy. To emphasize New York's sovereignty in the Grants he had several arrests made for minor delinquencies, arrests that Governor Chittenden of the Grants denounced as an un-

---

[12] Lincoln, *Messages from the Governors*, II, 142–45.
[13] Morris was not reëlected to Congress in 1779 because he had not pressed New York's case against the Grants. *Dictionary of American Biography*, XIII, 210.

warranted invasion of friendly territory. To add to his resentment Clinton was now certain that the Vermont leaders were occupied in treasonable correspondence with the British—a suspicion for which there was some justification. And mutinies in regiments raised in northeastern New York seemed to be attributable to the treason of the Grants.[14] Consequently, Governor Clinton sent General Peter Gansevoort with some 200 militia into the Grants in December. He had, he told Gansevoort, tried to avoid altercation and he wished even yet to prevent any break before the close of the campaign; but if it was necessary to enforce the laws of the state and protect loyal Yorkers by force of arms, Gansevoort was not to hesitate to take the necessary action.

Gansevoort's little force ran into formidable opposition and he found it necessary to make a strategic retreat. General Stark, whose natural sympathy for the cause of the Grants had stirred Clinton's ire on more than one occasion, refused to authorize Gansevoort to proceed against the insurgents;[15] and Clinton had to content himself with more protests to the Congress. A few weeks later a certain Luke Knoulton wrote Haldemand, "that Govr. Clinton by Information had solemnly promised that if Congress did not settle the matter Relative to Vermont, in January he would march with a force himself in February and would subdue Vermont or lose his life; he [Ethan Allen] said he was not afraid to fight Clinton & all the troops he could raise within his Government if he had a sufficient quantity of powder for his Men."[16] Evidently both Clinton and Allen were ready to force the issue.

When the legislature met at Poughkeepsie late in February, Clinton laid before it papers that showed conclusively the treasonable intrigues of the Vermonters. He was, he told the legislators, convinced that it was necessary to enforce New York's jurisdiction over the rebels of the Grants. The legislature responded by again proffering the olive branch to the Vermonters,[17] but Congress was now so strongly pro-Vermont that the insurgents felt that, with statehood virtually as-

[14] Stone, *Brant*, II, 183, 184, 185, 205; *Public Papers*, VI, 770.
[15] *Ibid.*, VII, 611–15.
[16] Pell, *Ethan Allen*, 235.
[17] Lincoln, *Messages from the Governors*, II, 164n.

sured, they could afford to ignore any advances from New York.[18] In this they were correct.

Yet it was nine more years before Vermont's statehood was recognized through its admission to the Union. By 1789 a number of New Yorkers, including Hamilton, were advocating recognition of Vermont's statehood; but George Clinton was still irreconcilable. When the legislature passed an act appointing commissioners to declare New York's assent to the creation of the state of Vermont, the Governor objected strenuously. He told the council of revision that the bill would take property without compensation by destroying rights to land; it would violate the contract clause of the federal Constitution, and it would injure New York land claimants in any one of several ways.[19] In brief, the bill was unconstitutional. Yet the commissioners were appointed; Vermont paid $30,000 to New York for the claims; and New York recognized the independence of Vermont. On July 4, 1791, Vermont became a state in spite of George Clinton.

Clinton was opposed to the dismemberment of New York, but he was always an ardent expansionist. His numerous investments in unsettled lands plus his faith in the expansive powers of the new-world democracy that he had helped to create made him a consistent advocate of the extension of settlement northward and westward. Indeed, the Clinton dynasty in New York was largely responsible for the rapid settlement of the old Northwest. George Clinton's valiant, if sometimes ruthless, policy of acquiring Indian lands for white settlement made possible DeWitt Clinton's great canal and the press of settlers westward even beyond the New York frontiers.

In 1784 the legislature established the state land office. The commissioners, who were to grant bounty lands from the great public domain, were the governor, lieutenant governor, speaker, secretary of state, attorney-general, treasurer, and auditor. So onerous were the governor's duties as a member of the commission that in 1790 at his urgent request the legislature empowered any three commissioners, not necessarily including the governor, to act for the commission.[20] Greatly restricted in their powers at first, the commissioners received

[18] *Public Papers,* VIII, 7.
[19] Street, *Council of Revision,* 416–17.
[20] Lincoln, *Messages from the Governors,* II, 308–09.

in 1791 almost unlimited powers to dispose of the public lands "in such parcels, and on such terms, and in such manner as they shall judge most conducive to the interests of the state." As we shall see, the commissioners took advantage of the generous grant of power to make some enormous sales on such reasonable terms that Clinton and his associates were accused of violating their trust, and the charge was used against the governor in the state elections of 1792. Whatever the merits of the case, the commissioners' liberal sales hastened the settlement of northern and western New York, kept the state treasury well supplied and so spared the state from direct taxation. Thus his friends were able to maintain that Governor Clinton "devised the plans of finance which have placed the citizens beyond the calls of the tax-gatherer, and furnished for them an actual fund of near four million." [21]

The state's surveyor general from 1784 and for many years thereafter was Simeon DeWitt, a nephew of George Clinton. This capable young graduate of Rutgers had served during the war as an assistant geographer to the Continental Army; he was a man of varied scientific interests, and he was later to become chancellor of the University of the State of New York.[22] It is said that during his forty years of service as surveyor general he avoided criticism by never purchasing a single acre of the public lands. If Simeon DeWitt was immediately responsible for the crop of classical names that were affixed to the new towns on the New York frontier during this period, the Land Office Commissioners must assume the ultimate responsibility. Yet not quite all of the place names of the period were those of Greece and Rome. A town that was organized in Dutchess County in 1786 and a place near Utica in Oneida County were named "Clinton" after the governor, of the state and Clinton County in the northeast was organized in 1788.[23] The New York Clintons have helped to make Clinton one of the most popular place names in the United States.

One of the major barriers to New York's expansion during the colonial period was the Iroquois. The Revolution gave the New Yorkers

[21] Anon., *An Address to the People of the American States* (Washington, 1808). For New York land policy see also Don C. Sowers, *Financial History of New York State* (New York, 1914), 38–40, and Cochran, *op. cit.*, Chapters IV and V.

[22] *Dictionary of American Biography.*

[23] Philip H. Smith, *General History of Duchess County* (Pawling, 1877), 144; R. L. Higgins, *Expansion in New York*, 102; *History of the State of New York*, Flick, ed., V, 190.

an opportunity to break down that barrier, for four of the Six Nations were openly hostile to the patriot cause. During the war Governor Clinton coöperated with the federal Indian commissioners for the Northern Department, the most important of whom was Philip Schuyler, in keeping the Oneidas and Tuscaroras faithful to the Americans. He was asked to appoint one of the commissioners to meet those tribes at a treaty held at Johnstown in 1778. The next year the legislature appointed him and four other commissioners to hold a treaty of pacification with the Indians.[24]

After the war many New Yorkers contended that the hostile Iroquois had forfeited their claims to their lands by disloyalty to the American cause. It was largely through the influence of Washington and Schuyler with the federal Congress and of George Clinton with the state legislature that this contention was abandoned; and the Congress and the legislature adopted the policy of easing the Indians out of their holdings by a series of treaties. The governor and a board of commissioners were designated in April 1784, to begin the easing-out process.[25]

In the field of Indian affairs, as in so many others, the governor found himself embarrassed by a conflict of authority between state and nation. After a conference of the Six Nations in June 1784, the Mohawk chief, Joseph Brant, wrote the governor that the Iroquois chiefs and warriors would be glad to meet the New York commissioners at Fort Stanwix to renew their ancient friendship, but it was clear that they also wanted to meet the federal commissioners.[26] Accordingly, Governor Clinton wrote rather frigidly to the federal commissioners that he had requested the Six Nations to convene at Fort Stanwix and that he would have no objection if the commissioners wished to improve "the incident to the advantage of the United States, expecting however and positively stipulating that no long agreement be entered into with Indians residing within the Jurisdiction of this State, with whom I only mean to treat, prejudicial to its rights."[27] Whatever

[24] Journal of the Continental Congress, VI, 456; Cochran, New York in the Confederation, 98–99.
[25] Ibid., 128–29.
[26] Public Papers, VIII, 323, 327, 328.
[27] Ibid., 332–33.

Clinton meant by this vague assertion of state's rights, the federal commissioners went ahead with their plans, making it clear to the Indians that the governor's proposed negotiations were unauthorized by Congress. Clinton was piqued. He had less love than ever for the Congress.

The resulting conference at Fort Stanwix was a dual one. The first phase was the meeting of the Indians with Clinton and his commissioners on August 31 to September 10. The conference was amicable enough but in reply to the governor's request for a cession of lands near Niagara and Oswego as compensation for the ravages of the Iroquois during the Revolution, Brant only promised that the assembled chiefs would consult with their peoples.[28] Governor Clinton returned to New York City to meet the legislature, leaving Major Peter Schuyler at Fort Stanwix to attend the meetings of the Congressional commissioners with the Indians in October and to use his "most undivided influence to counteract and frustrate" any measures that might prove detrimental to the state.[29] By the treaty of October 22, 1784, between the United States and the Iroquois, the latter gave up a large part of their western lands. The line was to run from a point just east of Niagara south to Buffalo Creek on Lake Erie, down to the Pennsylvania line, and west and south on that line to the Ohio River. The friendly Oneidas and Tuscaroras were, however, to be secured in the possession of their lands.[30] This was the first of the series of federal treaties that took the American West from the Indians and opened it to white settlement.

Even the Oneidas and Tuscaroras found it wise to cede lands in 1785. Governor Clinton and his commissioners met them in June at Fort Herkimer where in return for the modest sum of $11,500 in cash and kind they ceded lands between the Unadilla and the Chenango Rivers north of the Pennsylvania line in the later counties of Chenango, Broome, and Tioga.[31] Three years later Clinton conducted further negotiations with the Oneidas persuading them to yield all of their

[28] *Ibid.*, 349–76.
[29] *Ibid.*, 379; J. A. James, *George Rogers Clark* (Chicago, 1928), 307.
[30] *Indian Affairs: Laws and Treaties*, C. J. Kappler, ed., II (Washington Government Printing Office, 1904), 5–6.
[31] E. A. Werner, *Civil List* (Albany, 1889), 219.

lands north of the cession of 1785 excepting a reservation; this tract was henceforth known as "the Governor's Purchase," or "Clinton's Purchase." Other cessions followed and by 1789 virtually all of the Iroquois lands east of Seneca Lake had been given up.[32]

One great cession of the Iroquois Governor Clinton succeeded in having annulled. In spite of the provision of the state constitution that all land purchases from Indians must have the consent of the legislature, Colonel John Livingston and some eighty others, who styled themselves the New York Genesee Company of Adventurers, obtained a great tract for 999 years at 2000 Spanish milled dollars a year. Although the company had considerable influence in high places, the legislature voided the leases and instructed the governor to use force if necessary to keep trespassers off the disputed lands. This scandal, which involved several of the most prominent Federalist families of New York enabled the governor to pose as the defender of the Indians and the western lands against the selfish forces of speculation.

By 1790 George Clinton had struck up a warm personal friendship with Joseph Brant, the same Mohawk who had been the terror of the frontiers during the Revolution. Through Brant, who placed a great deal of confidence in Clinton's honesty and fairness towards the Indians, the governor exerted a considerable and a very useful influence over the Iroquois. When the Indians protested too vehemently from Canandaigua in July 1789 against white intrusions, the governor replied to Brant's letter as a father might to a disrespectful child, rebuking him for having any part in the sending of a letter "so highly exceptionable in every point," but promising that, if the legislature should revive the law establishing state Indian commissioners, or at least authorize him to hold a treaty with the Iroquois, he would see that justice was done.[33] The result of this correspondence was a series of conferences and, on the whole, a satisfactory settlement of the difficulties. Clinton seems to have attended at least one of the conferences, that at Fort Stanwix in the summer of 1790; for Brant wrote him on July 21 that he was "at a loss for words to express my

[32] R. L. Higgins, *Expansion in New York*, 105.
[33] Clinton to Brant, New York, September 19, 1789, Draper Collection, Wisconsin Historical Society.

gratitude for the civility and attention I received from your Excellency and the rest of the Gentlemen at Fort Stanwix." [34] As Brant's biographer has stated, Clinton always treated Brant not only with respect "but with evident personal kindness and regard." [35] When Clinton's letters grew less frequent in 1792, Brant reproached him, declaring that nothing on his part should "be wanting to cultivate a good understanding between us." The friendship between the two did continue, and as late as 1802 and 1803 Brant was expressing his appreciation of the governor's "known disposition to give satisfaction to all reasonable Indian requests." [36]

Washington and his Secretary of War found it more difficult to get on with Brant. They thought he had tried to frustrate all agreement between St. Clair and the Indians at Fort Harmar and they feared he would make trouble for the Americans in the anticipated campaigns in the northwest in 1791. To prevent this they turned to Clinton. Secretary Knox wrote the governor on April 12 to ask him to use his influence to induce Brant "to undertake to conciliate the western Indians to pacific measures, and bring them to hold a general treaty" with Colonel Pickering, the federal commissioner. Clinton was not enthusiastic over the plan. He told Knox that he thought it unwise to bring the Six Nations together at that time for any purpose; that it was wise to keep them divided; but that, if Knox desired it, he would do what he could with Brant. Whether Clinton helped or not, Colonel Pickering was able to hold his conference with the Iroquois on the Susquehanna in mid-summer. Later in the year the governor invited the Mohawk chief to visit him at New York. [37]

Clinton's administration was much more successful in pushing back the Indians than it was in ousting the British from New York territory.

Washington had sent Steuben in 1783 to try to persuade Governor

---

[34] Draper Collection, Wisconsin Historical Society.

[35] Stone, *Joseph Brant*, II, 289. Typical is the letter of August 17, 1792, from Clinton to Brant in Historical Society of Pennsylvania; Clinton asks assistance in finding the murderer of an Onondaga chief.

[36] Letters of December 11, 1792; February 16, 1802; and November 15, 1803, Draper Collection, Wisconsin Historical Society.

[37] *American State Papers: Indian Affairs* (2 vols., Washington, 1832–34), I, 167–69. For later Clinton negotiations with the Indians see *ibid.*, I, 655, 663–64, 667.

Haldimand to have the garrisons withdrawn from Oswego and other posts, but Steuben had had no success. Haldimand was equally unresponsive when Governor Clinton sent Lieutenant Colonel Fish to Canada in March 1784 with a copy of the American proclamation of the definitive treaty of peace. In the letter to Haldimand that Fish carried with him, the governor asked to be informed when Niagara and the other posts would be given up, since it would be his duty to provide for receiving those that were in New York. He had no doubt, he said, but that Haldimand would soon be withdrawing the garrisons. But Haldimand had no intention of evacuating them. He replied that unfortunately he had received no official notice of the treaty and no authorization to give up the posts.[38] These reasons were of course valid only at the moment. To justify the retention of the posts the authorities in Canada soon took the position that they were under no obligation to return the posts so long as New York continued on its side to violate the treaty by persecuting the Loyalists. Possibly they were right. Nevertheless it is probable that the real causes of their policy of hesitation were Canadian anxiety to retain the very valuable fur trade and a fear of Indian reprisals should the Indians be abandoned to their recent enemies, the Americans.[39] Not until 1785 did the British government announce frankly that while America prevented the collection of British debts and persecuted its Loyalists, the posts would not be returned.

Meanwhile the governor's anglophobia grew as he heard of New Yorkers' being ejected from frontiers that by the terms of the treaty were New York's own.[40]

He never tired of showing his resentment at British aggression. In 1790 he was complaining to Washington that the British were ordering New Yorkers to move away from the western shores of Lake Champlain; in 1791 he was urging federal action to protect the New York boundaries in the north; he was angry at the closing of

[38] Clinton to Haldimand, March 19, 1784, and Haldimand to Clinton, May 10, 1784, Force Transcripts, Meshech Weare Papers, Library of Congress.

[39] W. E. Stevens, The Northwest Fur Trade, 1763–1800 (Urbana, 1926), 44–45; A. C. McLaughlin, "Western Posts and the British Debts," American Historical Association Report for 1894, 415–28.

[40] Clinton to James Monroe, August 20, 1784, Monroe Papers, Library of Congress.

the Oswego River in 1793; a few months later he was denouncing the British to the legislature for taxing New York properties, and shortly afterwards he was outraging Canadian opinion by referring in a speech to the "natural right" of Americans near the lakes to use the St. Lawrence. Clinton was not twisting the lion's tail for mere effect or for political advantage; many of the grievances he stressed were real enough. New York had in 1788 passed its act for repealing all state laws inconsistent with the treaty of peace with Great Britain and the governor felt, more than ever, that the British had no right in his state.[41]

Clinton seems to have kept an agent or agents at Montreal in the heart of the enemy's country. This enabled him in March 1794 to send Washington a copy of Lord Dorchester's amazing speech of February 10 to the western Indians that seemed to show so conclusively that the British were attempting to stir up the Indians against the Americans. Washington feared a break with Britain and asked Clinton to get further information that would be of value in case the break should come.[42] Little wonder that Lieutenant Governor Simcoe of Upper Canada heartily disliked Governor Clinton and declared that control of the states of New York, Pennsylvania, and Virginia by "those violent and able Antifederalists, Clinton, Mifflin and Lee, is no favorable circumstance for peace or security."[43] It was John Jay's diplomacy, however, and not Clinton's protests, that finally evicted the British from New York. Jay's treaty of 1794 provided for the evacuation of the posts by June 1, 1796, at which time Jay himself was governor of New York.

That George Clinton was always interested in westward expansion and the settlement of the western lands is evidenced by his advocacy of the earliest canal projects. Gouverneur Morris and Philip Schuyler have both been given the enviable title of father of the New York canal system, and Dr. Fox has pointed out that the Federalists with their great holdings in western lands were stronger advocates of the

[41] Clinton to Washington, May 21, 1790, in U. S. Department of State, Miscellaneous Letters; E. A. Cruikshank, ed., *Correspondence of Lieutenant Governor John Graves Simcoe* (4 volumes, Toronto, 1923–26), I, 399–400; II, 135–36, 158, 165, 171.
[42] S. F. Bemis, *Jay's Treaty* (New York, 1923), 195; Simcoe, *op. cit.*, II, 196, 263.
[43] In a letter of July 26, 1793, in Simcoe, *op. cit.*, I, 400.

development of inland waterways than were their Antifederalist opponents.[44] Yet Clinton deserves to rank high among the early advovates of a canal system. Brought up as he was near the banks of the Hudson where his neighbors were largely dependent upon water transportation, he was quick to see the need of waterways. As early as 1779 he sent Thomas Machin into the Mohawk Valley to take the level of the river from Albany to Schenectady and above, to see whether a canal to supply water to Albany would be practicable.[45] His tour to northern New York with Washington in 1783 may have been largely responsible for the interest in canals that both men were to show in later years.

It was perhaps a consequence of the agitation for canals carried on by Elkanah Watson, recently of Rhode Island, that Governor Clinton urged upon the legislature in 1791 the necessity for facilitating communication with the frontier settlements in order to prevent the diversion of their produce to other markets. The legislature responded within a few weeks by directing the commissioners of the land office, of whom the governor was one, to make surveys for canals both north and west of Albany. The surveys were made the same year and in 1792 Clinton told the legislature that both projects were entirely practicable and at a very moderate expense. Schuyler seems to have fathered the bill passed at the same session for establishing two canal companies. The northern canal project was to come to nothing; the western project was to unfold gradually during the 1790's, pointing the way toward the Erie Canal in later years.[46]

The governor retained his interest in canal transportation developments to the end of his life. A few weeks before Clinton died, Robert Fulton expressed in the warmest manner his appreciation of the venerable gentleman who had supported his "claims on the public with a friendship and even zeal which I could not presume to request of him and which being voluntary I consider as the greater favor." About the same time John Jacob Astor, who was planning to wrest

[44] Fox, *Aristocracy*, 148–53.
[45] *American Historical Record*, II, (1873), 162–63.
[46] Lincoln, *Messages*, II, 311–21; J. S. Davis, *Essays in the Earlier History of American Corporations* (Cambridge, 1917), 158–65. Clinton advocated support of the two canal companies in his message of January 7, 1794.

the fur trade in the far West from the British in Canada and was so-
liciting President Jefferson's support, received enthusiastic endorse-
ment from his friend George Clinton.[47] Whether it was a turnpike,
a canal, a steamboat, or a project for the conquest of the West, Clinton
showed a life-long interest in any development that advanced the path
of empire on its westward way.

[47] Fulton to DeWitt Clinton, January 17, 1812, DeWitt Clinton Papers, Columbia
University Library; K. W. Porter, *John Jacob Astor* (2 volumes, Harvard University Press,
1931), I, 166–67.

CHAPTER XII

HONORS FOR THE GOVERNOR

THE MOST POPULAR NEW YORKER

INVITATION TO MOUNT VERNON

CLINTON NEGLECTS WASHINGTON

HE WELCOMES THE CONGRESS TO NEW YORK

REËLECTIONS

A SUCCESSFUL ADMINISTRATION

THE GOVERNOR EJECTS GENERAL SHAYS

THE end of the Revolution found Governor Clinton at the height of his fame, perhaps at the zenith of his career. He was everywhere recognized as one of the foremost heroes of the war and as one of the most capable of the war governors. Furthermore, he had accepted high office without abandoning that rugged simplicity and democratic indifference to the pretensions of office that his neighbors so admired. He was faithful to the libertarian principles upon which the Revolution had been agitated and fought, even after the war when many other patriots were finding it difficult to apply the principles of 1776. He was therefore long to remain the political idol of the masses who accepted him as one of themselves. It is no wonder that Clinton, known both as a fervid democrat and as a war hero, became the most popular man in his state.

Among the honors bestowed on the governor was a brevet major-generalcy that the Continental Congress, which had never been able to make up its mind to bestow the distinction on him during the war, gave him in the fall of 1783.[1] In the same year he was named vice

[1] Corning, *Washington at Temple Hill*, 42; F. B. Heitman, *Historical Register of Officers of the Continental Army* (Washington, 1914), 161.

president of the New York State Society of the Cincinnati, an office that he held for three years. Yet Clinton probably came to share the growing distrust of the aristocratical tendencies of the Society of the Cincinnati, its secrecy, and its advocacy of special privilege, and by the middle eighties he was no longer an officer. The control of the society was by that time in the hands of the prominent Federalists of the state and Schuyler and Hamilton in turn received the vice presidency. This withdrawal from the Cincinnati was one more piece of evidence that there was a growing breach between the democratic Clinton and the more conservative group of New York Whigs.

Possibly the departure of Washington from the New York scene was one cause of Clinton's break with the moderates during the 1780's, although it is certain that even Washington's restraining influence could not have made a thorough-going Federalist out of him. He saw a great deal of Washington in 1783 and Mrs. Clinton came to know Martha Washington intimately. When Washington returned to Mount Vernon after the reoccupation of New York City he wrote the governor one of his friendliest letters:[2]

I am now a private Citizen on the banks of the Potomack, where I should be happy to see you, if your public business would ever permit, and where in the meantime I shall fondly cherish the remembrance of all your former friendship.

Although I scarcely need tell you how much I have been satisfied with every instance of your public conduct, yet I could not suffer Colo Walker . . to depart for New York without giving your excellency one more testimony of the obligations I consider myself under for the spirited and able assistance, I have often derived from the State under your administration.

The scene is at last closed—I feel myself eased of a load of public care —I hope to spend the remainder of my days in cultivating the affections of good men, and in the practice of the domestic virtues.

Permit me then to consider you in the number of my friends, and to wish you every felicity.

Mrs. Washington joins me in presenting the compliments of the season, with our best respects to Mrs. Clinton and the family.

Clinton seems to have neglected his correspondence with Washington, for in the late fall of 1784 the latter was acknowledging one of the

[2] On December 28, 1783. Anon., *Revolutionary Relics or Clinton Correspondence* (New York, 1842), 8. The letter is quoted here only in part.

governor's letters with the statement that although he had felt pain from Clinton's silence, he now realized that he should have imputed it to any cause rather than a diminution of friendship, "the warmth of which I feel too sensibly for you, to harbor a suspicion of the want of it in you, without being conscious of having given cause for the change—having ever flattered myself that our regards were reciprocal." [3]

Clinton sent Washington lime and balsam trees, ivy, corn, pease, and certain nuts, which were duly planted at Mount Vernon. And as some of the trees did not stand transplanting well, he also sent assorted evergreen seeds for Washington's use.[4] The gentleman farmers of the time had a passion for experimentation with crops and livestock.

The legislature celebrated the reoccupation of New York City by meeting in January 1784 in the metropolis where it was to assemble for every succeeding session until 1788. The Clintons moved down from Poughkeepsie in 1784 beginning a period of residence in or near New York City that was to continue until they should move to the new state capital, Albany, in 1801. Clinton was one of five, together with Washington, Lafayette, Steuben, and Jay, who were honored by the Common Council of New York in the fall of 1784 with formal addresses and gold boxes containing the freedom of the city.

Here at New York new horizons were opened to the governor and his family. The Continental Congress which was there at intervals, brought to the city the prominent and notorious from all of the other states and even from abroad. When Richard Henry Lee, the president of the Congress, and a group of delegates entered the city in January 1785 amid the discharge of cannon and the applause of the populace, they were met at Whitehall by Governor Clinton and conducted to his very respectable residence in Queen Street. Clinton could never be accused of trying to ape the ceremonials of the old world by holding a gubernatorial court of his own, but he did play the host when occasion demanded. When the Fourth of July was celebrated in 1786 "with every demonstration of joy," the governor visited the president

[3] *Ibid.*, 8.
[4] In 1784 and 1785. *Ibid.*, 9; Washington, *Diaries*, Fitzpatrick, ed., II, 343.

of the Congress and presented the compliments of the day.[5] It is difficult to understand Hamilton's contention, made a few years later, that George Clinton was personally unfriendly to the Congress while it was in New York.

During the 1780's the three oldest sons of General James Clinton, Alexander, Charles, and DeWitt, were much of the time in New York City. Of these the eldest, Alexander, was a pleasant young man who had received a lieutenancy during the Revolution, joined the Cincinnati, and gone to Queen Street to live with his Uncle George and serve him as his private secretary. In 1787 Alexander met a tragic death by drowning while crossing the Hudson just above New York City in a "ferry periagua."[6] The death left a void in two households and to replace him the governor selected Alexander's brother DeWitt who graduated from Columbia College in 1788 when he was not yet twenty. The choice was the foundation of the Clinton dynasty in New York politics.

Clinton must have been greatly pleased to be reëlected both in 1783 and in 1786 with virtually no opposition. In 1786, to be sure, Schuyler tried to find a candidate to put up against him, contending that Clinton was fortifying himself in public office through his influence over appointments. Schuyler thought that he himself, Jay, or Livingston should oppose Clinton. He told Jay that the "person, at present in the chair of Government, so evidently strives to maintain his popularity at the expense of good government, that it has given real concern to many."[7] Jay, however, did not think the situation critical; he had heard no general demand for a change, and he himself did not wish to run for the governorship.[8] He knew, as apparently Schuyler did not, that Clinton's reëlection was inevitable.

At first glance it may be difficult to see just why Clinton was so strongly entrenched in his office. As a general rule the political effect of bad times is to oust the "ins" and bring in the "outs." In the middle

[5] Stokes, *Iconography of Manhattan*, V, 1198; *New-York Packet*, July 6, 1786.
[6] He was born on June 20, 1765 and died March 15, 1787. (Poughkeepsie) *Country Journal*, March 28, 1787; Ruttenber, *New Windsor*, 139; DeWitt Clinton Papers, Columbia University Library.
[7] Jay, *Correspondence*, Johnston, ed., III, 151.
[8] *Ibid.*, 154–56, 187. Jay was then Secretary for Foreign Affairs.

1780's the United States were experiencing one of the greatest depressions of their history. Trade was at a standstill; money was scarce; thousands were in bankruptcy or hounded by their creditors; and prices, which had reached amazing heights during wartime inflation, fell to distressing lows in 1785 and 1786. Men did not realize at that time that serious depressions follow great wars, and they inclined therefore to throw the blame on their governments. It was the great depression of the so-called Critical Period of American history that made it possible for such nationalists as Hamilton to curb the powers of the states by substituting the Constitution of 1787 for the Articles of Confederation. Yet not only the New York constitution but also the Clinton administration weathered the economic storm. Hamilton and his associates somehow failed in their attempt to brand the governor with responsibility for the bad times.

The explanation lies in the fact that only a minority of the good people of New York were so concerned over the depression as to want to change their government; and even Hamilton's eloquence and wit could not make them so. The merchants of New York, Albany, and certain of the Hudson River towns suffered seriously when foreign trade all but ceased in 1785. The traders of Albany wanted the fur trade that Canada was taking to itself. The bankers of New York City feared that the state might depreciate its currency by turning on the printing presses. The ex-Loyalists in southern New York were afraid that the radical Whigs would never observe the treaty with England. And creditors and men of wealth and property generally, including the great patroons and landlords of the Hudson Valley, wanted no levelling movements. All of these classes could rally about Hamilton, Jay, Schuyler, Duane, and Robert R. Livingston in the movement for a more vigorous central government that would protect commerce, maintain credit, enforce treaties, and uphold law and order. These merchants, bankers, traders, ex-Loyalists, and great landlords were, however, only a minority of the population of the state.

The majority of New York's population consisted of farmers, farm laborers or tenants, artisans, and modest tradespeople. They lived for the most part in small towns or in the rural districts where men were not directly concerned with foreign trade, where currency of any kind was seldom seen but was always welcome, and where men had not forgotten the recent war against centralized government and haughty Tories. Many of these people were forced into bankruptcy during the lean years, but suits at law by impatient creditors only convinced them that they already had too much government, not too little as Hamilton would have them believe. By and large, however, the depression did them no great harm. The farmers lived much as usual. After a week in New York during the worst year of the depression, David Humphreys wrote to Jefferson that, "to judge by the face of the country, by the appearance of ease & plenty which are to be seen everywhere one would believe a great proportion of the poverty & evils complained of, must be imaginary." [9] This relatively contented majority had no complaint against the Clinton administration or, for that matter, with the Articles of Confederation, and its votes kept George Clinton in office throughout the depression.

Unfortunately for George Clinton's place in history this great body of his followers,—farmers, laborers, and tradespeople,—was largely inarticulate. They might vote faithfully for him at the polls, but unlike their Federalist opponents who knew how to use the pen and who controlled virtually the entire press of the state,[10] they have left comparatively few written records for the historian. History has been written, therefore, from the point of view of the Hamiltonian school which "viewed with alarm" so many of the measures for which Clinton and his friends stood, and statesmen of Clinton's school have been damned with very faint praise or carefully ignored.

Indeed, New York was during the Critical Period among the best governed of the states. A successful fiscal policy is one essential test of a good administration, and in New York the tax burden was very small. Yet the state was to emerge from the decade with a per capita debt of only $3.50 as compared with about $22 in South Carolina.[11] The impost was yielding approximately £50,000 in currency each year which helped to relieve the citizenry from direct taxation. The state's paper money was circulating at par by 1787 although there

[9] Letter of June 5, 1786. Humphreys, *David Humphreys*, I, 353.
[10] Spaulding, *op. cit.*, 39. *The New-York Journal* was the only Antifederalist newspaper in the state.
[11] *History of the State of New York*, IV, 332.

had been an emission of paper—the only one in New York during the period—the previous year. This issue of paper had been approved by George Clinton and favored in the legislature by the representatives who were generally partial to the measures of his administration.[12] The amount of the issue, £200,000, was not extravagant; for money was very scarce and the demand for more of it was overwhelming. Clinton was generally conservative in his fiscal policies, but he realized that if the state made no concessions to the paper men, agitation and violence were certain to follow as they did in Massachusetts.

Clinton wanted no Shays' Rebellion in New York and he took vigorous steps to prevent the Shaysites from crossing the Massachusetts line. In February 1787 after the suppression of the Shays movement in the Bay State and when there was danger that the agitators would make New York their center of operations, Governor Clinton offered a reward for the capture of the intrepid Shays and his associates. The legislature authorized him to call out the militia. He ordered out three regiments and hurried without any guard to New Lebanon "in very ungenial weather for the purpose of chassing away Captain Shays." The malcontents were dispersed. It was said, however, in later years by a certain rude critic of the governor, that only a few months afterwards he set "a pious example of humility and forgiveness by cordially shaking the hand of the said Capt. Shays." [13] Certainly he saw to it that there was no Shays' Rebellion in New York.

Another indication that Governor Clinton would not tolerate disorder or mob rule was the suppression of the famous doctors' riots in April 1788. The sight of an anatomy student at work on a human specimen in the New York City hospital aroused an intolerant mob that broke into the hospital and rioted for hours in the streets. Governor Clinton later enjoyed telling the story of how he, Mayor Duane, Jay, Steuben, and a number of other prominent gentlemen tried to quiet the rioters by persuasion. Clinton had called out the troops but although a number of citizens had been injured, the troops had been kept out of the fray. Soon the governor's patience became ex-

[12] Ibid.; Humphreys, loc. cit.; Spaulding, New York in the Critical Period, 151.
[13] New York Daily Advertiser, April 16, 1792; Clinton to General Lincoln, March 6, 1787, New York Historical Society; Stokes, op. cit., V, 1215; John Bach McMaster, People of the United States (8 vols., New York, 1883–1913), I, 328.

hausted. Steuben was remonstrating with him against ordering the militia to fire when Steuben himself was struck by a rock, at which he quickly changed his advice and cried to Clinton, "Fire, Governor, fire!" The soldiers fired and several were killed.[14]

The Shays episode and the doctors' riots show that even in an era that was notorious in other states for governmental laxity, Governor Clinton ruled New York with a firm hand. Clinton's conception of the functions of government was a narrow one, but within the narrow range of its powers Clinton expected the government to tolerate no interference. It was difficult for the political opposition to Clinton's administration to brand as weak or demagogic a government as vigorous as New York's.

[14] R. W. Griswold, *The Republican Court* (New York, 1868), 102. Jay was severely injured.

CHAPTER XIII

MR. HAMILTON SCORES A VICTORY

WHETHER the United States were to become a nation or remain a federation, was the great issue of the 1780's. The controversy was to be settled by the triumph of the nationalists, but it must not be forgotten that there was at the time a large group of able and patriotic men who sincerely believed that a consolidated national government was not only unnecessary but was extremely dangerous to civil liberty. This group included such distinguished names as Patrick Henry, Richard Henry Lee, George Mason, James Monroe, Luther Martin, and Elbridge Gerry. Samuel Adams and Governors Hancock and Randolph also hesitated before crossing the Rubicon of consolidation. Historians may doubt the wisdom of such men, but they cannot doubt their sincerity and patriotism. They have, as a matter of fact, credited the nationalistic Federalists with a virtual monopoly of political wisdom and studiously overlooked the patriotism of the Antifederalist opposition. The latter our Federalist historians have not attempted to understand.

To George Clinton and his Antifederalist friends a strong centralized government represented the direct antithesis of all that they had fought for in the Revolution. They did not wish to be governed from a far-away capital, taxed by the representatives of other states, and disciplined by standing armies over which they had little or no control. These were just the things that they had objected to under British rule and they wanted no more of them. Wars might have to be fought by federal armies, and treaties negotiated by the agents of a distant Congress; but most of the functions of government could be far better and more safely conducted by their own representatives in the city council or state legislature. They wished to be ruled by their own neighbors in their own state, not by the representatives of a dozen other states gathered at a distant capital. Why was it necessary to create a super-state? After all, the federation had succeeded in winning a major war. These arguments were so convincing to thousands of Americans that had it not been for the great depression of the so-called Critical Period, the federal Constitution would never have been ratified by the states.

George Clinton was one of the towering figures among those in the American states who preferred federation to consolidation. In spite of their protests that they were the true "Federalists," since they wanted to retain the federation, Clinton and his friends became known as "Antifederalists." They preferred to be called "Federal Republicans" but the name never took.

Vigorously as he opposed the extension of the powers of the central government, Clinton always advocated endowing Congress with full authority to carry out the few powers it did possess. As we have seen, he grew impatient of the ineffectiveness of the Congress during the last years of the Revolution. Months before the evacuation of New York he was agreeing with Washington that they ought "to have an Eye to the Support of the Federal Union as the first and principal Object of national Concern," and in the same letter he was expressing his distrust of the militia system and advocating a permanent Continental army.[1] Many of his fellow Antifederalists were to dissent vigorously on the subject of a standing army. Hamilton himself could not have objected to Governor Clinton's opening address to the legislature in January, 1784: As the legislators must realize that the blessings they were enjoying flowed from the federal union, he recommended attention to "every measure which has a tendency to cement it, and to give that energy to our national councils which may be necessary to the general welfare."[2]

Not long after this, however, it became evident that there was in New York a difference of opinion as to how the federal union should be cemented. When the enterprising corporation of Kingston in Ulster County invited the federal Congress to settle in that city, the legislature offered to incorporate the Congress so that it could hold the preferred lands but refused to grant it "exempt jurisdiction" in criminal cases and tied other ungenerous strings to the offer.[3] The growing jealousy towards Congressional pretensions was most evident in the long controversy over the proposal to give Congress a five per cent tariff on imports. Even in 1781 when the legislature so promptly voted Congress the right to collect the impost, George Clinton seems to have had serious doubts. New York's principal port would soon be restored to the state; New York needed revenue sadly; and its treasury would welcome the revenue from the customs. One of Clinton's friends remarked that the "Congress being a single body and consequently without checks would be apt to misapply the money arising from it."[4] Clinton must have agreed that it would be safer in the coffers of the state.

Impelled by these doubts the governor's party repealed the impost grant to Congress in 1783 and substituted for it another arrangement for collection by state agents, an arrangement that was so unsatisfactory to Congress that nothing came of it. Clinton was later to point out that he had never opposed granting the impost to the Congress so long

[1] *Public Papers*, VIII, 145.
[2] Lincoln, *Messages from the Governors*, II, 196.
[3] *Journal of New York Assembly*, March 14, 1783. The governor transmitted the offer to the president of Congress.
[4] *Public Papers*, I, 179–80; Hamilton, *Works*, Lodge, ed., I, 553.

as the grant did not involve collection by federal agents.[5] Hamilton, however, declared years later that Governor Clinton did not care in 1783 how the impost was collected so long as Congress got none of it.[6] It was the northern and river counties of the state, so generally Clintonian in their politics, that were responsible for this refusal to let Congress have the impost on Congress's own terms.

With the return of peace Clinton saw less reason than ever for the impost grant. Congress was managing to make itself less and less popular with the governor—by its Vermont policy, its policy of dealing directly with the Indians, and its inability to drive the British out of the northern posts. The legislature, which was becoming markedly Antifederalist in its politics, ignored another Congressional request for an unconditional grant of the impost in 1784, and began sending hostile delegations to Congress, delegations including such men as John Lansing Jr., Melancton Smith, Peter W. Yates and Abraham Yates Jr., who had no great love for Congress or its works.

By 1785 and 1786 federalism was the most important issue in state politics. Toryism and even paper money were secondary. The new issue was welding together a group of men and interests that by 1787 could properly be called a political party—a party pledged to revolutionize the existing political system by changing the very nature of the federal union. Robert Livingston indicated the nature of the new alliance when he wrote Hamilton in 1785 from Livingston Manor, deploring the depravity of the times but rejoicing in the political union recently achieved in his part of the state. We have, he told Hamilton, now succeeded in "uniting the interests of the Rensselaer, Schuyler and our [Livingston] family, with other Gent-m of property in the County in one interest; by which means we carried the last Election to a man. . . ."[7] By 1786 it became evident that the leader in New York of these "gentlemen of property" was the capable young son-in-law of General Schuyler, Colonel Alexander Hamilton.

It was also evident by 1786 that Governor Clinton and Colonel Hamilton, who had found so much to agree upon during the war, were

[5] In the Poughkeepsie Convention, June 28, 1788.
[6] Hamilton, *op. cit.*, I, 554–55.
[7] Letter of June 13, 1785, in Hamilton Papers, Library of Congress.

not at all in agreement on the federal issue. Three months after the legislature had voted another unacceptable impost grant to the Congress, the latter body recommended to Governor Clinton that he call a special session to reconsider. This the governor promptly and firmly refused to do. He was, he said, empowered by the constitution to call the legislature into special session only on "extraordinary occasions." As the legislature had voted only a few weeks earlier after due deliberation, fully aware of the importance of the issue, Clinton failed to see what was to be gained by asking it to vote over again.[8]

This reply only served to infuriate the Hamiltonians. Clinton was contemptuous of Congress and his excuses were frivolous. He interpreted "extraordinary occasion" so narrowly only because he did not wish to call the legislature. As for the unwillingness of the legislature to reconsider, the legislature that would have met in August was a new one chosen in April which had had no opportunity to vote on the impost.[9] The fact that Hamilton himself, who had not been a member of the Assembly of 1785–86, was to represent New York City in the new Assembly, probably accounted in a large part for his desire to have the governor convene the legislature.

When the new legislature finally met in New York in January 1787, Hamilton was there to wage war against Clinton. The governor in his message of January 13 gave his reasons for not having responded to the Congressional request that he call the legislature in the summer of 1787. "I have only to add," he told the lawmakers, "that a regard to our excellent constitution, and an anxiety to preserve unimpaired the right of free deliberation on matters not stipulated by the confederation, restrained me from convening you at an earlier period."[10] Jones, Gordon, and Hamilton were named by the Assembly to prepare the customary reply to the governor's message. They drafted a reply that ignored Governor Clinton's explanation respecting the special session and thus tacitly condemned it. This was the work of Hamilton and Gordon; for Samuel Jones, the third member of the committee, was an Antifederalist. But the Assembly made plain its intention of standing by the

---

[8] Clinton wrote twice to the President of Congress. See letter of August 25, 1786 in George Clinton Papers, New York State Library, duplicates.

[9] Hamilton, Works, Lodge, ed., I, 556–57.

[10] Lincoln, Messages from the Governors, II, 264.

governor. Only 5 New Yorkers, 3 Albanians, and 1 Richmondite objected, and 39 members approved when Speaker Varick moved to amend the reply to the governor by inserting "approbation of your Excellency's conduct in not convening the Legislature at an earlier period."[11] Clinton, and not Hamilton, was master of the situation.

To make it doubly clear that it would have been futile for the governor to assemble the legislature in the summer of 1786, the Assembly again rejected the unconditional impost grant to Congress, 38 votes to 19. Hamilton's first session in the legislature was so far barren of achievement. But perhaps there were other ways to get what he wanted. A federal convention was meeting that summer at Philadelphia.

George Clinton was not enthusiastic over the plan for a convention to revise the Articles of Confederation.[12] He sent the Congressional resolution on the subject to the legislature without comment or recommendation, phrasing his brief message in such a way as to make it clear that the legislature could not offend him by ignoring the matter altogether.[13] Although the convention was not ignored, the Antifederalist legislature sent to Philadelphia two friends of Clinton, Robert Yates and John Lansing, and only one Federalist, Hamilton himself. Both Yates and Lansing had voted against the federal impost grant. Furthermore, these delegates were appointed "for the sole and express purpose of revising the Articles of Confederation"; they were not empowered to help draft a new frame of government.

The three New York delegates found little to approve in the work of the Philadelphia Convention. Hamilton wanted a strongly centralized national government that would leave the states mere administrative units. Yates and Lansing found their worst forebodings confirmed. One of the first decisions of the convention was, "that a national Government ought to be established consisting of a supreme Legislative, Executive and Judiciary."[14] A new government was to be created! The

---

[11] *Journal of the Assembly*, January 19, 1787.

[12] According to Hamilton's "Letters of H. G." written in 1789. These campaign letters should be used with considerable caution. Hamilton, *Works*, Lodge, ed., I, 563.

[13] Lincoln, *Messages from the Governors*, II, 270. He referred to the resolution without comment and in the next sentence went on to another "subject which appears to me to merit the attention of the Legislature."

[14] From Yates's notes on the convention printed in *Records of the Federal Convention*, Max Farrand, ed. (3 vols., New Haven, 1911).

states were to be submerged! Yates and Lansing fought valiantly against every feature of the nationalistic "Virginia Plan" and rather approved Mr. Paterson's mild "New Jersey Plan." Lansing reminded the convention that New York had sent him to Philadelphia only to revise the Articles, and he ventured "to assert, that had the legislature of the state of New-York, apprehended that their powers would have been construed to extend to the formation of a national government, to the extinguishment of their independency, no delegates would have appeared on the part of that state." In this he was undoubtedly correct.

According to Hamilton it was Governor Clinton who recalled Yates and Lansing from Philadelphia early in July. Hamilton himself remained to the end to brave the governor's displeasure by signing the new Constitution.[15] In a letter addressed to Clinton following their withdrawal, Yates and Lansing explained their reasons for leaving Philadelphia—reasons that fell into two main categories: first, they had been authorized to revise the Articles of Confederation but not to draft a new constitution of government; and, second, they could not give their approval to the consolidation of the states into one national state. A single government, they believed, could not administer the vast area of the United States; such a government would be expensive to operate; and such a government, located far from the homes of most of its citizens, would be unresponsive to public opinion and dangerous to civil liberties.

This letter to Clinton was a fair summary of the position that he and his Antifederalist allies were to take during the coming year of struggle and controversy. Satisfied as they were with the existing political system, they protested their loyalty to it, and attempted to brand the innovators who opposed them with the stigma of advocating the illegal and unconstitutional. For very practical reasons these men, most of whom were radical Whigs who had only recently fought to overturn a system of government in America, were strict constructionists and constitutionalists. They could not agree with their opponents, the Hamiltonians, that a great economic depression constituted an emergency which

[15] Hamilton, *Works,* Lodge, ed., I, 404; J. J. Smertenko, *Alexander Hamilton;* De Alva S. Alexander, *Political History of the State of New York* (3 vols., New York, 1906-09), I, 32.

justified changing the very bases of their federal system of government.

Long before the work of the Philadelphia Convention was finished, the whole state of New York knew that George Clinton disapproved of the convention's plan for a consolidated central government. Late in July the *Daily Advertiser* printed a letter that denounced the governor for prejudicing the country against the convention's work before it was done.[16] This letter was Hamilton's declaration of war on Clinton. "Republican" came to the governor's defense and the war of words was on. The champions on either side were too much in earnest to avoid personalities and the air became charged with insinuations and accusations. Hamilton wrote that Clinton's course showed a "greater attachment to his own power than to the public good," and some Antifederalist insinuated that Washington had once been forced to dismiss Hamilton from his family. Even young DeWitt Clinton joined the fray with his effective "Countryman" letters.[17]

The very day that the new Constitution was first printed in New York, Governor Clinton published in the New York *Journal* the first of his famous series of "Cato" letters,[18] a series which brought forth an even more famous reply, "The Federalist" letters of Hamilton, Madison, and Jay. The governor's letters were dull and ponderous, full of the usual tedious allusions to such classic names as Montesquieu, Hume, Locke, and Sidney, and intemperate in their dogmatism and exaggeration. Yet they show far better than such scholarly productions as "The Federalist" what men were thinking and talking.

"Cato" urged against undue haste in making a decision. At the end of the Revolution Americans astounded the world by establishing "an original compact" between themselves and their governors, and that compact should not be lightly put aside. We did not throw off the yoke of Britain only to find new masters! If we do not approve the Constitution, we are under no obligation to accept it; yet Hamilton insinuates

[16] July 21, 1787.
[17] Published in the *New-York Journal.* George Clinton wrote him that the letters were well adapted to the "understanding of the Common People." Letter of December 22, 1787, DeWitt Clinton Papers.
[18] "Cato" I appeared September 27, 1787 and "Cato" VII on January 3, 1788. The series is printed in Paul Leicester Ford, ed., *Essays on the Constitution of the United States* (Brooklyn, 1892).

that it is better to give Washington the presidency under the new plan than to have him lead an army to force it on you. Hamilton "treats you with passion, insult and threat."

The new plan creates one sovereignty, a consolidation of states in one government. Clinton quoted Montesquieu as his authority that a republic must have a small territory in order to exist. Governments that are too large tend to break up, just as Maine was ready to break away from Massachusetts, Franklin from North Carolina, and Vermont from New York. To prevent disintegration, armies are necessary, and armies destroy liberties. Large states fall of their own weight. "The ties of the parent exceed that of any other," and as the circle is enlarged, affection diminishes. New Yorkers, schooled in a democratic tradition, could have little in common with Southerners who were attached to slavery and aristocratic distinction. New York should take care before risking its liberties in the common pool.

Clinton had a number of more specific objections to the plan evolved by the Philadelphia Convention. There were too few representatives; the senatorial term of six years was much too long; the necessity for annual elections was ignored; standing armies might be established; and the vice presidency, an unnecessary office, improperly blended the legislative and executive powers that should have been kept separate. The presidency itself savored too much of monarchy. The president's term was too long; he would rule like a king in his ten square miles. It may be said that Americans will always resist prerogative, but they may change, for "the progress of a commercial society begets luxury, the parent of inequality, the foe to virtue, and the enemy to restraint." Clinton, like Jefferson, always believed that only an agricultural civilization could remain sound and virtuous.

He was also convinced that the Constitution meant more taxes. The new government cannot exist on import duties alone and the landholders will oppose taxes on land just as they have in New York. The result will be such taxes as the poll and the window tax—and the federal tax gatherer will thunder on your door for the duty on the light furnished by Heaven! The new government will, then, be costly as well as dangerous to our liberties. Consider well before accepting it.

Some of these arguments were the hasty and ill-advised conclusions of an irreconcilable foe of centralization who had not yet had adequate time to analyze the proposed form of government. But many of "Cato's" arguments had some validity. It was criticism of this kind that led to the prompt adoption of the first ten amendments to the Constitution, the federal bill of rights.

Five days after "Cato's" first blast, Hamilton returned to the attack with his first "Caesar" letter.[19] He called George Clinton a demagogue, one of these "designing croakers" who are always exclaiming, "My friends, your liberty is invaded!" He pointed out that "there are Citizens, who, to gain their own private ends, enflame the minds of the well-meaning, tho' less intelligent parts of the community, by sating their vanity with that cordial and unfailing specific, that *all power is seated in the people.* For my part," he added, "I am not much attached to the *majesty of the multitude,* . . . I consider them in general as very ill qualified to judge for themselves what form of government will best suit their peculiar situations; . . ." He thought even "Cato" would admit that men of good education and deep reflection are the only judges of a form of government.

This form of attack was so ill-tempered and politically so ill-advised that Hamilton soon decided to attempt something more dignified and less revealing of his own personal animus against democrats in general and Governor Clinton in particular. He persuaded Jay and Madison to contribute to the proposed series of essays and the result was "The Federalist," a truly great treatise that has had far more influence with later generations than it had at the time of its composition upon the skeptical voters of New York.

Governor Clinton did not wish to hasten the calling of the state convention to consider the Constitution.[20] Possibly five other states would reject the new plan and make it unnecessary for New York to come to a decision at all. That would please the governor, for he was not quite certain that a New York convention could be trusted to follow his wishes. Some of his own friends were willing to compromise by

[19] "Caesar" Numbers 1 and 2, printed first in the *Daily Advertiser,* are reprinted in P. L. Ford, *Essays on the Constitution.*

[20] (Boston) *Independent Chronicle,* December 13, 1787; *Maryland Journal,* November 30, 1787; Samuel Blachley Webb, *Correspondence and Journals* (3 vols., New York, 1893), III, 89.

accepting the Constitution with reservations. And there was rumor that if the Clintonians rejected the plan, southern New York with its commercial interests would secede.[21] It was better to wait than to force the issue.

Nevertheless the governor placed the proceedings of the Philadelphia Convention before the state legislature on January 11, 1788, but without comment. After a delay of three weeks it was agreed to hold the New York convention at Poughkeepsie in June. Five states had already ratified and three more were to ratify before June. New York might have an opportunity to be the all-important ninth state.

The result of the April election of convention delegates was a staggering blow to the constitutionalists. Both sides had been confident. The press, which was overwhelmingly Federalist in sympathy, had created the impression that Federalist arguments were carrying all opposition before them and that the governor had been discredited and his leadership rejected.

When the returns came in, however, it was found that the Clintonians had carried 46 of the 65 seats in the convention![22] Only Westchester, Kings, Richmond, and New York Counties, all clustered around Manhattan Island, had elected Hamiltonian delegates. Even Albany County had broken away from its alliance with the merchants of New York City; Queens and Suffolk on Long Island, not always hostile to federal measures, had gone over to Clinton; and the river counties, Ulster, Orange, and Dutchess, were faithful to the governor. Clearly the yeomanry of eastern Long Island and the modest farmers and tenant cultivators of the Hudson Valley had accepted "Cato" as their prophet.

The struggle against the Constitution as George Clinton conceived it, was the old struggle of democracy against privilege. The Antifederalists he called "The friends of the rights of mankind," and the Hamiltonians "the advocates of despotism."[23] And there were many who agreed with him.

One fervid democrat expressed this feeling in the New York *Journal* when he wrote that "our modern federalists, namely the advocates of

[21] Spaulding, *New York in the Critical Period*, 197.
[22] *Ibid.*, Chapter XII.
[23] Clinton to John Lamb, June 21; Force Transcripts, Library of Congress.

the new constitution, evidently aim at nothing but the elevation and aggrandisement of a few over the many. The liberty, property, and every social comfort in the life of the yeomanry in America, are to be sacrificed at the altar of tyranny . . ."[24] The leaders of the Federalists were referred to disparagingly as the "well born." One of the newspaper scribblers of the time, "Brutus Junior," pointed out that it was generally known that many of the members of the Philadelphia Convention were "possessed of high aristocratic ideas, and the most sovereign contempt of the common people; that not a few were strongly disposed in favor of monarchy . . ."[25] Governor Clinton's young secretary, DeWitt Clinton, prophesied that if the Constitution should be adopted, even its supporters would exclaim: "From the insolence of great men —from the tyranny of the rich—from the unfeeling rapacity of the excise-man and Tax-gatherer—from the misery of despotism—from the expense of supporting standing armies, navies, placemen, sinecures, federal cities, Senators, Presidents and a long train of et ceteras Good Lord deliver us!"[26] We may suspect that the secretary's views were not radically different from the governor's.

George and James Clinton were among the six delegates chosen to represent Ulster County in the convention. The governor had led the balloting in Ulster with 1,372 votes while General James brought up the Antifederalist rear with 905. The leading Federalist candidate in Ulster received a scanty 68,[27] thus demonstrating that Ulster had lived up to its reputation of being the most Antifederalist County in the entire state. But in New York County the tables were turned. There John Jay led the balloting with an impressive 2,735 while Governor Clinton, who was also a candidate in that county, had to content himself with leading the Antifederalist candidates with a mere 134 votes. He seems to have been without honor in the county of his adoption.

When a group of Federalist delegates left New York on June 14 for Poughkeepsie where the convention was to be held, they embarked amid the acclaim of the populace and the discharge of cannon. When the governor and certain other Antifederalist delegates took ship for

[24] April 30, 1788.
[25] Ibid., November 8, 1787.
[26] Letter of April 25, 1788, in New York State Library.
[27] New-York Packet, June 2; New York Advertiser, June 4, 1788.

Poughkeepsie on the same day, the governor's request that there be no demonstration was complied with. Possibly the governor's request was a needless one.[28]

At Poughkeepsie the convention met and organized in the new court house on June 17 and chose George Clinton to be its president. This was fitting and proper. Yet it might have been better tactics for the Antifederalists to have kept Clinton on the floor where he could speak freely and furnish that leadership which they so much needed.

Although Clinton was an avowed partisan, his good faith and impartiality as a presiding officer were not challenged. Young James Kent, who was at Poughkeepsie but was not a member of the convention, wrote later that although he himself was strongly prejudiced against the governor as the leader of the Antifederalists, he nevertheless "became very favorably struck with the dignity with which he presided, and with his unassuming and modest pretensions as a speaker. It was impossible not to feel respect for such a man, and for a young person not to be somewhat over-awed in his presence, when it was apparent in all his actions and deportment he possessed great decision of character and a stern inflexibility of purpose." [29]

It was possible for a Federalist to write with considerable accuracy that his party would be able to "boast all the Good Sense and Shineing Abilities" in the convention.[30] For among the nineteen Federalists were such able debaters as Robert R. Livingston, John Jay, James Duane, John Sloss Hobart, and Hamilton himself. The Antifederalists, on the other hand, included very few who were adept at argument and debate. Aside from the governor, John Lansing, who was listened to with considerable respect; Samuel Jones, the ex-Tory of Queens County; John Williams, one of the few great landed proprietors among the Clintonians; John Bay of Columbia; and Melancton Smith of Dutchess were the only Antifederalists who spoke with any frequency. Of these the most capable was Melancton Smith, the merchant-lawyer of New York City who represented Dutchess County in the convention. A man "of remarkable simplicity, and of the most gentle, liberal, and

[28] Letter of June 15, Abraham Yates Jr. Papers, Box 3, New York Public Library.
[29] William Kent, *Memoirs and Letters of James Kent* (Boston, 1898), 306.
[30] Webb, *Correspondence*, III, 99.

amiable disposition," his mind was keen and logical and he spoke well. He was in fact the only Antifederalist capable of standing up against Hamilton. George Clinton spoke occasionally and with some effect, but in the main his influence with the members of the convention was personal and not oratorical.

The governor was the recognized leader of the Antifederalist majority in the convention and he found the task of marshaling and directing his following an impossibly difficult one. Composed for the most part of village lawyers, farmers, and small town politicians, the Antifederalist majority was as unable to unite upon any definite, positive program as it was to rebut the arguments of Hamilton and Livingston on the floor of the convention. Some of them wanted nothing but an opportunity to vote against the Constitution and return to their crops or their law offices; others were willing to flirt with the idea of ratifying the Constitution on condition that certain amendments be attached to the ratification; and still others were ready to listen when the impressive battery of Federalist orators told them that rejection would force the southern counties of the state to secede or would leave New York entirely out of the Union. The 19 Federalists had only one goal: ratification; the 46 Clintonians had no program.

Clinton himself was evidently prepared from the first to accept ratification provided a series of vigorous amendments could be written into the Constitution. At least some of his Antifederalist colleagues, when they sailed with the governor for Poughkeepsie on June 14, had a number of draft amendments stowed away in their breeches' pockets.[31] And in the convention the governor cast his vote in favor of ratification with conditional amendments.[32] Beyond that, however, Clinton would not go.

Like most of the Antifederalists in the convention, the governor only assumed the negative rôle of critic. He insisted that representation of such a vast territory in the House of Representatives would be inadequate. So few men could not know the entire Union thoroughly. In the states, the legislators were under the eye of their fellow citizens;

[31] Letter of June 15, 1788, in Abraham Yates Papers, New York Public Library.
[32] July 23. On July 25 Clinton voted for Lansing's motion that New York recede from its ratification after a period of years in case the desired amendments should not be adopted. The latter vote is given in the McKesson Papers, New York Historical Society.

in the far away federal district they would not be. He admitted he had often criticized the feebleness of the Articles of Confederation. He solemnly declared that he was a friend to efficient and energetic government, but he warned against erecting a system that would destroy our liberties. "Because a strong government was wanted during the late war, does it follow, that we should now be obliged to accept of a dangerous one?"

He was quite unable to see why New York could not ratify with conditional amendments. It surely could not be argued that Congress might not legally accept New York into the Union on such terms, for, if the question of legality were to be raised, the Constitution itself was illegal under the existing Articles of Confederation. He was convinced that to ratify without conditions would be to ignore the wishes of a large majority of the people.

He was as firm as ever in his belief that the Constitution would set up a consolidated government that would soon destroy the states. Although free, sovereign states were the very foundation of the federation, the Constitution for the most part ignored them. The very expression, "We the People of the United States," signified that the powers granted the new government originated, not in the states, but in the people themselves. Hence the proposed instrument of government must be considered "an original compact, annulling the state Constitutions as far as its powers interfere with them and thus far destroying their distinct rights." The powers of the new government were enormous. They included "every object for which government was established amongst men, and in every dispute about the powers granted, it is fair to infer that the means are commensurate with the end." It was not safe to delay; the rights and liberties of the people must be protected at once by far-reaching amendments. For there is no example in all history of a government once established which has been willing to relinquish its powers.[33]

These objections, Clinton said, he offered only to give the gentlemen on the other side an opportunity to answer them. He was open to con-

[33] Clinton's speeches and notes will be found in Francis Childs, *Debates and Proceedings of the Constitutional Convention of New York, Poughkeepsie, June 17, 1788* (reprint, Poughkeepsie, 1905), in the Bancroft Transcripts of Clinton Papers, New York Public Library, and in the Clinton Papers, New York State Library.

viction. But as the debate extended through the last weeks of June and well into July,[34] the governor was not convinced. On the contrary he was indignant when Samuel Jones, Gilbert Livingston, and Melancton Smith began to give ground.

Jones led the retreat of the Antifederalists when on July 23 he moved to change the formula of ratification from "on condition" to "in full confidence" that the New York amendments should be accepted by the other states. This was nothing more nor less than unconditional ratification. When Jones's proposal was carried in committee of the whole by 31 votes to 29, George Clinton voted with the minority. The next day the irreconcilable Clintonians tried to retrieve their lost ground by attaching to ratification the condition that if a second federal convention should not be called within a given period of years, New York might withdraw from the Union. Twelve Antifederalists deserted the governor in the vote on this amendment and it was defeated, 31 to 28.[35] The battle was lost.

The convention hurriedly put in order the 32 amendments it had agreed to recommend to the other states, appointed a committee to draw up the circular letter that Governor Clinton was to send to the governors of the states, and cast the final vote for unconditional ratification by the narrow margin 30 to 27, the closest vote in any of the state ratifying conventions. In this final vote not a single delegate from any county north of Orange and Dutchess cast his ballot for the Constitution; and, with one exception, no delegate from the counties south of Orange and Dutchess voted against it. It was the victory of New York County and its neighbors over the bloc of river and frontier counties in the north. Furthermore, it was Alexander Hamilton's first triumph over George Clinton.

Clinton's leadership was not entirely to blame for the defeat of the Antifederalists. It was expediency and not conviction that finally persuaded New York that it must ratify the Constitution even though a majority of New Yorkers thoroughly mistrusted the document. The principal consideration in bringing New York Antifederalists to terms was the fact that ratification by New Hampshire and Virginia, while

[34] Final adjournment came on July 26.
[35] The vote will be found in the McKesson Papers, New York Historical Society.

the Poughkeepsie Convention was sitting, made the Union a certainty. Rejection by New York would mean isolation. New York merchants might be excluded from the ports of the other states, and imports for New Jersey and Connecticut would no longer pay tribute at New York's customs houses. Possibly the southern counties would secede, leaving northern New York cut off from the sea and from its neighbors. Certainly, if New York did not come to a prompt decision, the federal Congress would desert its chief city for Philadelphia or a site on the Potomac—and this consideration alone was a weighty enough one with the business men of the metropolis to make the Antifederalist governor decidedly unpopular in his own city. While the convention was still sitting at Poughkeepsie General Webb wrote his fiancée from New York that if Congress should depart for Philadelphia it "will be a fatal stroke to our Commerce & when it will end God only knows. . . . I do not believe the life of the Governor and his party would be safe in this place." [36]

New York state politics were embittered as never before in the struggle over the Constitution. While Governor Clinton entertained delegates of both parties pacifically enough at Poughkeepsie on the Fourth of July, the little Federalist city of Albany saw bloodshed in the streets. A Federalist procession encountered an Antifederalist one; a battle of swords, bayonets, sticks and stones ensued; the Antis were outnumbered and put to rout; one was killed and eighteen were wounded. Albany took its politics seriously.

It was on July 26 that the news of ratification reached New York City. The citizenry paraded through the streets cheering the victory. Overjoyed merchants cheered the Constitution at the coffee houses and salutes were fired from the federal ship *Hamilton,* a float that had been used in the great pre-victory parade a few days earlier. It was said that even the Antifederalists forgot their disappointment and joined in a concerted attack on what was known as the "Federal Bowl." But all was not harmony. The hoodlum mob broke into the house of Mr. Green-leaf, the editor of the Antifederalist *Journal,* broke the windows, and carried off his type. And to complete the day's demonstration, they paraded to the home of Governor Clinton, beat the rogues' march

[36] Webb, *Correspondence,* III, 111.

around the building, and gave three lusty hisses. Fortunately George Clinton had not yet returned to town.

The contest over the Constitution marked the end of the "era of good feeling" in New York politics. Clinton was to serve ten more years as governor of the state, but after 1788 he was only the leader of a party. The period of his unchallenged personal ascendancy was over.

CHAPTER XIV

THE FEDERALIST ERA

GEORGE CLINTON was aging. His great frame was becoming stooped; his rugged features were betraying his years; his greying hair, plentiful enough where it was gathered behind in a queue, was now scanty in front; and his chin had developed a whole hierarchy of folds. Yet he had no intention of abandoning politics in his early fifties.

From 1788 to his death, Clinton was a national figure and a perennial candidate for the vice presidency or for the presidency itself. The governorship of New York has probably produced more candidates for the presidency than any other office, state or federal. Yet only two New York governors, Cleveland and Franklin D. Roosevelt, have achieved the chief magistracy of the nation without the aid of the vice presidency; four have become president by ballot or by mischance only after serving as vice president; and six others, including George Clinton, have had to content themselves with the vice presidency. New York's location, size, and generally even balance of political parties, have given the state an influence with the electoral college that dates back to the first elections under the Constitution.

Paradoxically it was Governor Clinton's provincialism and his stubborn championship of the rights of his state that made him a national figure. As Henry Adams has pointed out, Clinton's protest against the Constitution made him the leader of the northern Republicans long before Jefferson appeared upon the national scene as his rival. Because he was the outstanding Antifederalist in the northern states many people thought him the logical selection in 1789 to serve as vice president under a president who would most assuredly be Washington, the outstanding Federalist in the South. He was, consequently, the candidate of a small group of Antifederalists in New York and the South who felt that they should be represented in the new administration by a vice president pledged to secure the inclusion of the much-desired bill of rights in the new Constitution.

Patrick Henry, the aged Virginia Antifederalist, put Clinton's name "in agitation" in the fall of 1788 and William Grayson of the same state was "warm in such an election." At Fraunces' Tavern on November 13, 1788, the Federal Republican Society met and sent letters to kindred spirits in several other states. The letters urged Clinton's election as vice president and stated that gentlemen in Virginia had already agreed to support him.[1]

Hamilton, however, wanted none of Clinton in the vice presidency. He knew that the governor had no love for the new system and he did not intend to have the federal establishment contaminated if he could help it. Consequently he supported John Adams as a trustworthy opponent of the plan for a second convention, and warned the Federalists to keep watchful eyes on the governor who might garner votes in South Carolina as well as in New York and Virginia. Yet he professed to doubt very much whether Clinton would exchange the governorship for the vice presidency or risk his popularity by holding both.

In the choice of electors Clinton's own state failed him. Although the Congress had determined that the presidential electors would meet to cast their votes on January 7, 1789, the governor did not call the New York legislature into special session until December 8, so late as to

[1] William Wirt Henry, *Patrick Henry* (3 vols., New York, 1891), II, 431; Hamilton, *Works,* Lodge, ed., VIII, 203–05; John Lamb Papers, Force Transcripts in Library of Congress; Louis Clinton Hatch, *A History of the Vice Presidency* (New York, 1934), III, 117–18.

invite a rebuke from the Federalist state senate when it replied to his message on December 26. His message contained a politically timely but obviously futile appeal for a second convention and he mentioned the necessity of preparations for putting the new government into operation. In response the two hostile houses chose representatives to the federal Congress by joint ballot, a procedure that enabled the numerically superior Antifederalist Assembly to elect the Antifederalist candidates. The Federalist Senate countered by proposing three days later that the two houses compromise in the choice of presidential electors by choosing four each. The Assembly insisted upon election by joint ballot; a conference failed to bring peace between the factions; and New York named no electors.[2] The Federalists had carried the day. When the votes of the electors of the other states were counted, it was found that Clinton had received only three votes, all from Virginia. John Adams was to be vice president. This was the first of the numerous failures that were to block Clinton's way to the elusive presidency. Possibly, however, he preferred a fifth term as governor.

To win the governorship both parties were prepared to make every legitimate effort—and perhaps more. The era of good feeling in New York politics that began with Clinton's election in 1777 had failed to survive the momentous struggle for the Constitution and by 1789 state politics was coasting disastrously towards the disgusting depths where the generation of Cheetham, John Wood, and W. P. Van Ness was to crown it with new infamy.

The veteran governor was no longer the master of a political situation that had become very much muddled. He had failed at Poughkeepsie; the hundred pound freeholders had given him a hostile state senate; and New York had failed to present him with its electoral vote. Perhaps it was even more unfortunate for him that crops had been bad in 1788. Nevertheless the Antifederalists showed no hesitation in supporting him for his fifth term as governor. To oppose him the Federalists would have preferred a dyed-in-the-wool Federalist like Justice Richard Morris. Pierre Van Cortlandt, who had served patiently for twelve years as lieutenant governor, was more than willing to accept a nomination for governor from any party that would offer it. Mor-

[2] Lincoln, *Messages*, II, 292–300.

GEORGE CLINTON

From a crayon drawing presented to the Oneida Historical Society
by Miss Julia Clinton Varick

ris, that portly old patriot whose "full, rounded face and commanding presence appeared to advantage among the stately and dignified
personages who supported knee breeches and silk stockings," [3] would
probably have been delighted with the nomination. But as a wealthy
aristocrat and an enthusiastic champion of the new Constitution he
could win no votes from the moderate Antifederalists who must be
tempted away from Clinton if the election were to be won. Hamilton, never at a loss, rationalized the situation by explaining that the
Federalists must not expose themselves to criticism for undue partisanship or for encouraging the "heats of party." Consequently the
Federalist party leaders resolved to give the nomination to a renegade
from Clinton's own camp.

The renegade who offered himself was Judge Robert Yates, the
man who had left the Philadelphia Convention to protest its work. He
had more recently made judiciously conciliatory remarks to an Albany jury indicating his conviction that all good citizens should support the Constitution—with, apparently, no reference to a second
convention. On February 11 Judge Yates was nominated by a meeting of Federalists in New York City; he accepted thirteen days later
and the campaign was on. It was a bitter one.

Most of the Antifederalists of 1788 were to be found in the Clinton ranks and many of them, such as Melancton Smith and Marinus
Willett, on the Antifederalist campaign committees. The earnest
energetic chairman of the New York City Federalist committee was
Alexander Hamilton, actively seconded by none other than Aaron
Burr, an intimate friend of Judge Yates.[4] The committee published
an address charging the governor with planning to subvert the federal
Constitution, and its chairman wrote a series of political letters—clever,
malignant, and often dishonest—which appeared in Childs' newspaper. Hamilton called them the "Letters of H. G." In them he traced

---

[3] Quotation from Alexander, *New York,* I, 39. See also *Dictionary of American
Biography.* James Clinton discusses the candidates in his letter of February 13, 1789, to
William Cross, Clinton Papers, Library of Congress.

[4] Jabez Delano Hammond, *A History of Political Parties in the State of New York*
(3 vols., Syracuse, 1852), I, 39; James Cheetham, *A View of the Political Conduct of
Aaron Burr* (New York, 1802), 13; *New-York Advertiser,* March 31, 1789. Parton's life
of Burr states that Burr and Hamilton never again joined in politics, Volume I, 173.

Governor Clinton's career, belittling each phase of it, and painting the governor a sly, cunning mediocrity inveterately opposed to the union of the states. Clinton was not a brilliant lawyer nor even a good soldier, "H. G." maintained, and as governor his record had been a shameless one. He had, for instance, behaved contemptuously toward the federal Congress, had continued his opposition to the new Constitution, and was unfriendly to the residence of Congress in New York.[5] It is difficult to believe that these shrewd but malicious and unprincipled letters did not cost the governor hundreds of votes.[6] His party had no penman with half of Hamilton's ability.

The Federalist press, finding but little to criticize in Clinton's twelve-year administration of the state, stooped to personal abuse. The governor was sneered at for "not keeping a house of elegant entertainment"; he was accused of dominating the Council of Appointment; of hoarding his salary until he had become a rich man; of seeking to overthrow the new federal system; and of accepting his salary during the war only in hard money.[7] Shortly after the campaign William Grayson wrote that,

"There has been a most severe attack upon Governor Clinton, he has been slandered and abused in all the public newspapers for these five months by men of the first weight and abilities in the state. Almost all the gentlemen, as well as all the merchants and mechanics, combined together to turn him out of his office: he has had nothing to depend on but his own integrity and the integrity of an honest yeomanry, who supported him against all his enemies. He did me the honor of a visit yesterday, and gave me such an account of this business as shocked me.—As this gentleman is the g't palladium of republicanism in this State, you may guess at the situation of anti-ism here . . ."[8]

The republican governor, without any lieutenants of note or influence, was still supported by his loyal yeomanry.

[5] For the "Letters of H. G.," February 20—April 9, 1789, see Hamilton, *Works*, Lodge, ed., I, 539–79.

[6] *Cf.* a letter from a gentleman in New York printed in *Daily Advertiser*, February 29, 1792, which states, "We were both of opinion at the last election, that the scurrilous letters of H. G. did the Governor no harm. He was detected in many misrepresentations, . . ."

[7] Hudson *Weekly Gazette*, March 17; *New York Daily Advertiser*, February 20, 21, March 23, 1789.

[8] W. W. Henry, *Patrick Henry*, III, 389–95.

As the elections approached the Federalists grew optimistic. Kiliaen Van Rensselaer wrote in mid-March that "A Change in Administration is the cry in Claverack and its neighborhood—*Col. H.* has taken a very active part in favour of Judge Yates from which circumstance much is expected—I believe old Clinton the *sinner* will get *ousted*—Columbia County is five Weeks gone with Electioneering sickness." The Federalist Webb replied hopefully a few days later that in New York City the governor was despised by all but a few sycophants whom he himself had put in office.[9]

Indeed, Clinton was to lose New York, the three counties on the east of the Hudson, and Albany and Montgomery. These were the counties which were dominated by the mercantile interests and the great landlords, always Clinton's opponents. On the other hand the more democratic counties of Long Island and the west bank of the Hudson stood by the governor. His own Ulster County backed him almost unanimously and faithful Orange rejected Judge Yates to the tune of four to one.

Clinton's victory, 6,391 votes to 5,962 for his opponent, was not an impressive one, but a margin of even four hundred votes was significant in a year when the Federalists captured a majority in the Assembly and strengthened their hold on the Senate. Hamilton had beaten Clinton at Poughkeepsie in 1788 but in 1789 Clinton held the governorship against the assaults of a carefully picked Federalist candidate that was no Federalist, and against the wily pen of "H. G." That was some satisfaction.[10] The Clinton men celebrated it on June fifth with a "Grand Jubilee" at Fraunces' Tavern.

In July the Clinton forces suffered a serious but inevitable defeat in the election of New York's two United States senators. During the winter session of the legislature the Federalist state Senate had blocked the election of United States senators by refusing to participate in a joint ballot. Consequently, when the first federal Senate met on March 4, 1789, New York was unrepresented. As soon as he was certain of his reëlection Clinton called a special session of the legis-

[9] S. B. Webb, *Correspondence*, III, 125; Stokes, *Iconography*, V, 1236.
[10] Werner, *Civil List*, 166. The vote by county appears in contemporary newspapers, especially the *New York Daily Advertiser*, issues for May, 1789.

lature to meet on July 6 expressly to select the two senators. Both houses were now Federalist and it was only a question of what two Federalists would be chosen. After ten days of debating and balloting Philip Schuyler and Rufus King were named. The choice of Schuyler was not a surprising one, for his son-in-law was now virtual dictator of the Federalist forces of the state; but King's selection was remarkable in more than one respect. He was chosen in preference to the plodding Duane, a Livingston son-in-law, who claimed the senatorship as his right; to General Lewis Morris of Morrisania; to Ezra L'Hommedieu the gentleman farmer of Long Island, and to Robert R. Livingston who had every reason to expect that Hamilton would support his pretensions. King was a Massachusetts man who had been only a few weeks in New York. Furthermore, King was probably Governor Clinton's candidate for the office.

Clinton talked frankly with King early in June, explaining that Lansing would not serve and Melancton Smith had disgusted many of his party by voting for the Constitution. Clinton thought that King would be a suitable selection and believed that many of the country members agreed with him. He then went on to explain that it was his aim to prevent the concentration of the great offices "in a certain party or family association." "Formerly," he pointed out, "there were two great Families or Parties, namely Delancys and Livingstons; that from their Opposition they kept a constant watch on each other, that neither dared any measure injurious to the mass of the people; that the case was now different, the Delancy party was extinct by the Revolution, and all the great and opulent families were united in one Confederacy; that his politicks were to keep a constant eye to measures of this Combination, and thought the people should be on their guard . . ." [11] Evidently Clinton hoped to make a democrat out of King and bring him into the Antifederalist camp. Usually an excellent judge of men, he failed to foresee that Rufus King would prove a thorough-going Hamiltonian and no defender of popular rights. But Hamilton also erred in supporting King for by it he deeply of-

[11] C. R. King, *Rufus King* (6 vols., New York, 1894–1900), I, 354–56, 363. The manuscript copy of King's memorandum of the conversation is in the New York Historical Society.

fended the Livingstons who were the most powerful of the great landed families of the state.

The governor whom Hamilton accused of treating the Congress with contempt was called upon to offer New York's hospitality to the new federal government. It is more than likely that the shrewd Clinton realized that the presence of Congress in New York City would contribute to the cause of Federalism there. Clinton nevertheless played the host with as much cordiality as he could muster, and insofar as his old friend Washington was concerned, his cordiality was genuine enough. He did not, however, exert himself to welcome many of the others who composed the federal invasion.

Unfortunately for the governor's prestige with those historians who have admired the dash and brilliance of the "republican court" that the Federalists created at New York in the first two years of the reborn republic, Clinton did not shine refulgent in the society of his time. Perhaps it was because Mrs. Clinton was not well that they did not entertain. Perhaps as a sturdy democrat he disliked the balls and ceremonial dinners that to him smacked of monarchy. His instinct for economy may have made him a reluctant host. Or perhaps it was merely because Clinton did not want to entertain. His brother General James had none of the social graces and his nephew and successor DeWitt was never noted for qualities of that kind. Although George Clinton had a faculty for winning men and cementing friendships that his brother and nephew lacked, he seems still to have shared the Clinton dislike for the social whirl. During the period in 1788 when all New York City was hostile toward the governor for his opposition to the Constitution, Colonel William Smith's "Lady" wrote the following illuminating comment: [12]

We were invited to dine with the Governor, which was a very particular favor. He nor his family neither visit, or are visited by, any families either in public or private life. He sees no company, and is not much beloved. His conduct in many respects is censured, perhaps unjustly. To me he appears one whose conduct and motives of action are not to be seen through upon a slight examination. The part he has taken upon the subject of the new Constitution is much condemned, . . . Mrs. Clinton is not showy, but a kind, friendly woman.

[12] K. M. Roof, *Colonel William Smith and Lady* (Boston, 1929), 197.

Certain more hostile critics complained of the governor's unsocial life in the midst of New York's Federalist gaiety. The anonymous author of *The Milkiad*,[18] for instance, enquired in heroic couplet:

> Fair first [?] C[hie]f M[agistrat]e of Y[or]k's fair state—
> Does dignity stand porter at thy gate?
> Does hospitality enhinge thy door,
> Prais'd by the great, and pray'd for by the poor?
>
> Why C[linton] stays here is what no man can tell,
> Unless condemned to Q[uee]n S[tree]t as his hell—
> For Q[uee]n S[tree]t is a fashionable place
> And folks live there in plenty with some grace,
> Not shut like Hermits in a gloomy Cell . . .

It was of course the socialites and social climbers of the time that resented Clinton's indifference to the society that exhibits itself at balls and banquets. Among that class he was clearly "not much beloved." The general run of mankind, that elected him seven times governor of New York, seems to have had considerable regard for him.

The governor might dislike the display and glitter of New York society, but he always enjoyed the company of his friends. Nor was he any foe of the cup that cheers. He is said to have frequented the Merchants' Coffee House at the corner of Wall and Water Streets. Years after Clinton's death Charles Carroll remembered "with pleasure a conversation at [John Jay's] house over a bottle of good old Madeira, between him and Mr. Clinton afterwards Vice-President, at which [Carroll] was present but not bearing any part . . ."[14]

It must also be admitted that the governor showed every courtesy to Washington. On March 10, 1789, six days after the first Congress met at New York City, Clinton wrote to Washington inviting him to use his house when he should arrive at the capital and until more suitable accommodations should be provided. Washington replied from Mount Vernon on the 25th, stating that he considered this kind

---

[18] M. S. Austin, *Philip Freneau* (New York, 1901); Martin Martial (pseud.), *The Milkiad* (1789).

[14] Kate Mason Rowland, *Charles Carroll of Carrollton* (2 vols., New York, 1898), II, 355.

invitation "as a testimony of your friendship and politeness, of which I shall ever retain a grateful sense. But," he added, "if it should be my lot (for Heaven knows it is not my wish) to appear again in a public station, I shall make it a point to take hired lodgings or rooms in a tavern until some house can be provided." [15] On April 23 the President-elect arrived at New York from Bergen Point in an "elegant barge of thirteen oars, with colored awnings and silken curtains," amid the thunder of cannon and the acclaim of the crowd. A carpet was laid at the wharf to guide him to his carriage. It is said, however, that instead of taking the carriage he walked arm in arm with his old friend Clinton, through the crowds, followed by a line of dignitaries, to his house at No. 3 Cherry Street. That evening he dined with the governor and a number of notables at Clinton's home which was near by on Queen Street. This was only the beginning of the governor's most active social season at New York.

The governor's home at No. 10 Queen, later Pearl Street, opposite the end of Cedar Street, was his city house. It was a large mansion of three storeys which had been built by the rich mayor Abraham de Peyster late in the seventeenth century and occupied by Washington in April and May 1776. The neighborhood was one of the most fashionable. The house was forfeited by its Loyalist owner Henry White, held by the Commissioners of Forfeitures and turned over in 1784 to the governor. Two years later the Commissioners sold the house to Henry White Jr., but the governor stayed on while the state paid White a rental of £300 a year. Later, probably from 1791 to 1794, he was to occupy the Government House which was built on the site of Fort George at Bowling Green, designed to be the residence of the President, but unfinished when the federal government moved away to Philadelphia. The Government House, with its two high storeys, Greek portico and elevated position, was an even more pretentious mansion for a democratic governor than was No. 10 Queen Street.[16]

[15] W. S. Baker, *Washington after the Revolution 1784-99* (Philadelphia, 1908), 119. In 1811 Caleb Street offered to rent the Pearl Street house from Clinton for $500. Clinton Papers, Albany, Vol. 30.

[16] T. E. V. Smith, *The City of New York in . . . 1789* (New York, 1889), 22, 23, 31; *Magazine of American History*, 1889, p. 185; New York City directories. The Government House is of course not to be confused with Federal Hall which was the old city

The home of which the governor and Mrs. Clinton were to make more and more use was their farm on the Hudson at Greenwich a suburb of the city. It had evidently been a part of the old Mandeville farm known as "The Burgomasters' Bowery," which was later acquired by that notorious old rascal, printer and bookseller, James Rivington. George Clinton bought a substantial portion of the property from Rivington in 1790, apparently untroubled at dealing with a man who only ten years earlier had been anathema to all good patriots. The house was a "long, low, venerable, irregular, white, cottage-like brick, and wood building, pleasant notwithstanding, with a number of small, low rooms and a very spacious parlor, delightfully situated on a steep bank, and some fifty feet above the shore, on which the waves of the Hudson . . . dashed and sported. There was a fine orchard, too, and a garden on the north . . ." [17] We can well imagine that it was this home of which the Clintons, in all the years after their precipitate flight from New Windsor, were most fond.

There is perhaps little wonder that Jefferson, when he arrived at New York from France, was amazed at the unrepublican character of the Federalist "court." There were levees and receptions and teas and fine dinners without end. The lean years had passed; Federalism was in its heyday, and it meant to enjoy it. It was an age of optimism, of lavishness, and of speculation. Bourgeois America was enjoying the liberty for which it had fought. Even the governor, sceptical Antifederalist that he was, seems to have become infected.

He was received by the President on May Day with "a great number of other persons of distinction." He attended the Columbia College commencement exercises on May 6 with Washington, Adams and the other notables. A day later he attended "an elegant Ball and Entertainment to his Excellency the President" which was given by the "Dancing Assembly." On the eleventh he and Mrs. Clinton were the President's guests at the old John Street Theatre to see the "Old Soldier" and "School for Scandal," which that crabbed democrat from

hall on Wall Street converted by L'Enfant to serve the federal government. Clinton's account book in the State Library shows he paid Henry White £130 on April 16, 1790 for the rent of the Queen Street house. See New York City Hall of Records, Liber III, pp. 4ff. for the sale of No. 67 Pearl Street in 1815 for the benefit of Clinton's heirs.

[17] Description in the *New York Evening Post*, December 17, 1831.

CORNELIA TAPPEN CLINTON

From a crayon drawing presented to the Oneida Historical Society
by Miss Julia Clinton Varick

Pennsylvania, Senator Maclay, branded "an indecent representation before ladies of character and virtue." On the fourteenth of the same month Washington and Clinton attended the French minister's ball. When the First Lady arrived at New York from Mount Vernon late in May, Clinton escorted her to her residence and later attended that truly "elegant entertainment," the so-called inaugural ball.[18] The Clintons were invited when the President and his lady entertained on August 27 at what Maclay called "a great dinner, and the best of the kind I ever was at." It was also, Maclay explained, the most solemn dinner in his experience. "Not a health drank; scarce a word said until the cloth was taken away. Then the President, filling a glass of wine, with great formality drank to the health of every individual by name round the table . . . Everybody imitated him, charged glasses, and such a buzz of 'health, sir,' and 'health, madam,' and 'thank you, sir,' and 'thank you, madam' never had I heard before. . . . The ladies sat a good while, and the bottles passed about; but there was a dead silence almost. Mrs. Washington at last withdrew the ladies." [19] Federalist society seems to have been elegant but scarcely hilarious.

During the fall of 1789 and the first half of 1790 the President and the governor entertained each other frequently. Washington not only called informally at Queen Street to chat with the governor or take tea with "the Governor's Lady," but he attended on December second what must have been for the Clintons a rather formidable dinner party, including, as it did, "Mrs. Washington and all the family, (except the two children)," Vice President and Mrs. Adams, Colonel and Mrs. William S. Smith and Mayor and Mrs. Varick. Washington's curt diary contains no comments on the success of this occasion.[20] In 1790 the vestry of Trinity Church set aside a pew for the governor as well as one for the President, a gesture that must have pleased Clinton with his views on the coördinate position of the state and federal governments.[21]

[18] Smith, New York in . . . 1789, Ch. VII; W. S. Baker, Washington after the Revolution, 1784–99, 132–35; Fitzpatrick, ed., Diaries of George Washington, IV, 17, 53, 55, 58.
[19] E. S. Maclay, ed., Journal of William Maclay, United States Senator from Pennsylvania 1789–91 (New York, 1890), 137–38.
[20] Diaries of Washington, IV, 58.
[21] Stokes, Iconography, V. 1262.

When Washington visited Rhode Island in late August, with Jefferson, the new Secretary of State, and several other gentlemen, he invited Clinton to join the party. Possibly the association with Jefferson was of more importance to the governor than the hasty visit to Newport, Providence and the college. On August 30, eight days after their return, the governor escorted the President to the pier on his way southward. The federal government was leaving New York and the Congress was to meet in Philadelphia in December. Clinton probably had but few regrets.

CHAPTER XV

JOHN ADAMS KEEPS THE VICE PRESIDENCY

DE WITT CLINTON REENFORCES HIS UNCLE

THE LIVINGSTONS JOIN THE CLINTONS

THE "HAYES-TILDEN CONTROVERSY" OF 1792

CLINTON RENOMINATED FOR A SIXTH TERM

ISSUES AND RHYME IN 1792

JAY IS COUNTED OUT

BURR SUPPORTS THE GOVERNOR

CLINTON AND THE VICE PRESIDENCY

DEFEAT BY FOURTEEN VOTES

JOHN ADAMS IS PROFANE

THE first serious check in Clinton's political career came with Mr. Hamilton's amazing victory at Poughkeepsie in 1788. The second check, as we shall see, was Mr. Jay's moral victory at the polls in the gubernatorial election of 1792. The governor's luck was deserting him. Federalism was in the ascendancy; politics was assuming new refinements and a new and involved technique that the now elderly governor did not quite understand. Clearly he needed a lieutenant who could lead him through the maze of practical politics.

George Clinton's nephew, DeWitt, the son of General James, had attended Columbia for two years; he had read law for three years in the Broadway office of that distinguished Antifederalist and ex-Loyalist, Samuel Jones; and had passed his law examinations "very reputably" early in 1790. The governor wrote General James that he had hardly expected DeWitt to do so well in certain practical parts of the examination as the boy had paid so much attention to the principles of law. Apparently General James intended DeWitt to return to little Britain to practice and to instruct his brother George. The governor objected strenuously, stressing DeWitt's abilities and his need for the contacts and experience that the city could offer to the young lawyer who had hitherto devoted himself entirely to books and treatises. There was, he said, danger of DeWitt's becoming "rusticated." He believed that he could be of service to the young lawyer.[1] It was finally arranged that DeWitt was to remain in New York City as his uncle's secretary. That decision made history.

The governor's decision in 1790 to retain DeWitt as his personal secretary did not, of course, mark the beginning of that portentous political comradeship between the two men that lasted as long as the governor lived. For DeWitt had already lived several years with his uncle in Queen Street, had been thoroughly saturated with the governor's views on all manner of political and economic subjects, and had more than once been able to serve him as in the writing of letters for the newspapers during the bitter campaign of 1788. He was already an outspoken Antifederalist and critic of Hamiltonian finance. He objected, for instance, to an order of the Supreme Court "That all process shall run in the name of the President," as smacking too strongly of monarchy.[2] DeWitt was still a very young man—scarcely more than a boy, but he was fast learning practical politics. He was the man that his uncle needed.

DeWitt, who was only twenty-two in 1791, was probably not responsible for that somewhat questionable deal that brought about the defeat of United States Senator Philip Schuyler. Schuyler was austere and a rabid partisan; in consequence he was not always popular, and he had alienated some moderates such as Chancellor Livingston by his dogged support of Hamilton's financial measures. It is likely, however, that the principal reason for the defection of the great Livingston clan, that caused Schuyler's defeat, was the failure of Hamilton and his Federal associates to satisfy the political ambitions of the Livingstons. Neither the Federalists in control of the New York legislature nor the Washington administration had recognized the Chancellor's claims to

[1] George to James Clinton, Apr. 27, 1790, State Museum, Newburgh.
[2] Dorothie Bobbé, *DeWitt Clinton*, 47–62; David Hosack, *Memoir of DeWitt Clinton*, 28–30.

high office and the lesser members of the family had been generally neglected. The Clintonians, on the other hand, having lost control of the legislature, needed allies who controlled votes. Burr saw possibilities in the situation. The outcome was that the Hamiltonians were caught napping; the thirty-four year old Burr was elected to the Senate in the place of Schuyler by a combination of Clinton and Livingston votes; and Morgan Lewis, brother-in-law of Chancellor Livingston, received Burr's office of attorney general.[3] This was a revolution in party politics. The Livingstons were never to return to the Federalist fold. Clinton's magnanimity in appointing Burr attorney general in spite of his defection in 1789, had borne fruit.

The "Hayes-Tilden controversy" of Clinton's career occurred the next year, 1792. The governor was still the outstanding figure of his party north of Virginia. He had opposed Hamilton's funding measures and had been suspected of fostering anti-Hamilton sentiment by writing Antifederalist papers for publication.[4] But if he was to succeed John Adams as vice president in 1793, he must show in the gubernatorial elections of 1792 that he could carry his own state.

There were four principal contenders for the governorship. Senator Aaron Burr was more than ready to accept the nomination. He was named by a group of his friends meeting in New York City; his candidacy was announced in the papers; and it was only after both the Clintonians and Federalists had nominated that he discovered that he was unwilling to run.[5] Naturally, Hamilton, Schuyler, whom Burr had replaced in the Senate, and Clinton, whom Burr now wished to replace, did nothing to support his candidacy. Judge Robert Yates, the Federalist candidate of 1789, was also seriously considered for the nomination, and it was not until February 9 at a meeting in New York that he announced that he would not stand. The meeting then voted against the renomination of Clinton and Van Cortlandt, and nominated Hamilton's candidates, John Jay and the young patroon, Stephen Van

[3] I. J. Cox, "Aaron Burr," in *Dictionary of American Biography;* Hammond, *New York,* I, 50f., 107; Alexander, *New York,* I, 49.
[4] For Clinton's political activities, see, e.g., Maclay, *Journal,* p. 194; and printer's bill of May, 1790 in Clinton Papers, Albany, Miscellaneous.
[5] S. B. Webb, *Correspondence,* III, 175f.; Cheetham, *View of the Political Conduct of Aaron Burr,* 17f.

Rensselaer. Six days later "at a Meeting of a respectable number of Free-holders from various parts of the state at Corré's Hotel" in New York, the governor and lieutenant governor were renominated to succeed themselves.[6]

The campaign was a bitter one. The two parties were organized with numerous committees of correspondence in the various counties and towns meeting frequently and hurling broadsides and open letters at their opponents. The Livingstons, again neglected by the Hamiltonians, deserted in a body to Clinton. The supporters of Yates turned to Jay.[7] Otherwise the party cleavages were similar to the divisions of 1788 and 1789. The issues were not always clear, for although the Clintonians condemned Jay on the ground that he represented the classes of leisure, wealth, and privilege, the Federalists countered with suggestions that Clinton had betrayed his people. He had allied himself with the lordly Livingstons; he had used state patronage to feather his own nest; and he had been found favoring his friends with enormous grants of pub-lic lands at nominal rates. Alexander Macomb in particular had been allowed to purchase over 3,600,000 acres at 8 d. each. The commissioners of the land office, of whom the governor was one, were accused in the state Assembly of indiscretion if not corruption; and although they were absolved a few days before the elections, many took the accusations seriously and the story survived to pester the governor in later years.[8] It was unfortunate that Clinton was to be connected, even so indirectly, with the great speculative disasters of 1792 that brought Macomb, Duer, and many other proud names to bankruptcy and jail.

The newspaper poets came to the assistance of their respective candi-dates. Typical was the effusion of "A Friend to Freedom" whom we may suspect of having been a Jay man, in the *Advertiser:*[9]

> "Three years I lay me down to sleep,
> Clinton I pray the state may keep,
> If I should oversleep my time,
> Clinton the state be wholly thine . . .
> That man's a sycophant or fool,

---

[6] New York *Daily Advertiser*, February 17, 25, 28, 1792; S. B. Webb, *op. cit.*, III, 175.
[7] *Ibid.*, 175f.
[8] *Daily Advertiser*, March and April, 1792; Jefferson, *Writings*, Ford, ed., VI, 94.
[9] Quoted in Monaghan's *Jay*, 331–32.

Who thinks that Clinton should not rule:
The Hessian fly Clinton can kill,
Our floods with fish and oysters fill,
Can bid our rivers ebb and flow,
Can call down rain, or dew, or snow;
Can legislate our wives with child;
Can make dame fortune harsh or mild;
Can take the Congress by the nose,
If, as they may, become our foes;
Can feed us, clothe us, give us drink,
Can talk for us, and for us think.
Jay is in all things the reverse,
A tool, a blockhead, sour, perverse;
Keeps up with friends eternal strife,
And scarcely deigns to kiss his wife;
Hates that the African should groan,
And kindly listens to his moan. . . .
Should Jay get in the state must tumble;
Hawl in her horns, eat pye that's humble;
Be scalp'd by Indians every night;
Live all the day in fear and fright; . . .
Be sold to Congress for a trifle,
For Hamilton to strip and rifle; . . .
Be branded, whip'd, like southern slaves,
Forc'd [to] hang ourselves, then dig our graves!"

Jay was accused of being the candidate of those who held fast to the wigs, silks, buckles, and other trappings of aristocracy and snobbery. He had enjoyed the generous emoluments of federal office, the ease of foreign courts, and the favors of the Secretary of the Treasury. In a typical letter to the press,[10] one of his opponents announced that he would support Clinton "because the principles of republican independence are struck at: because the officers of the United States, not content with the pageantry and glitter of their own court, and the infinity of offices, that their measures daily create, eagerly and systematically grasp at the little pittance they have left the separate states; and because, in conformity to the fashionable tenets of advancing the rich and *well born,* he sees a young man of 25 [Stephen Van Rensselaer], without any other pretensions than those which his estate

[10] *Daily Advertiser,* March 1, 1792.

and his relation to the Secretary gave him, led forward by Mr. Jay to the seat which has so long and worthily been occupied by an old and distinguished servant of the people." Jay was the candidate of the Tories of 1776,[11] it was said, and of those who believed that property should rule and that the unprivileged should remain unenfranchised. It was also objected that Jay, recently president of the Manumission Society, desired "to rob every Dutchman of the property he possesses most dear to his heart, his slaves . . ."[12] Jay was one of the finest figures of eighteenth century New York, and it was unfortunate that the rift between him and Clinton should be widened by the professional calumniators on both sides.

The success of Clinton's administration in avoiding virtually all direct taxation was probably a more important issue than the campaign literature indicated. From the late eighties to 1797, when Clinton was no longer governor, there was an annual surplus of revenues over expenditures. Small sources like auction duties and peddler's licenses contributed to meet the modest expenses of the state, but the sale of public lands and, in the nineties, the income from state funds carefully invested, furnished the bulk of the revenues. The assumption of state debts by the central government in 1791 was a boon to New York, the largest debtor. There were no debt payments until the Jay administration created a debt, and there was no state tax until 1800. While Clinton was in office the ordinary expenses of government never in any year reached $300,000.[13] A state which in 1792 could invest a surplus of over half a million dollars, derived for the most part from the sale of public lands, was naturally reluctant to risk a change of administration.

Nevertheless Clinton won only by a decision of the canvassers rejecting the votes of three counties—one of the scandals of early New York history.[14] Of the three rejected counties, Otsego County was decisive. There the Jay forces claimed a majority of six to eight hundred while Clinton's majority in the entire state was only slightly

[11] *Albany Gazette,* July 30, 1792.
[12] Jay, *Correspondence,* III, 413.
[13] Don C. Sowers, *Financial History of the State of New York,* 133, 140–41, 228, 257, 302–06, 324.
[14] Clinton won by 108 votes.

over one hundred. It seems, however, that the term of the sheriff of Otsego, whose deputy brought the county's votes to the office of the secretary of state, had expired, and, through certain machinations of Judge Cooper, the Federalist "Bashaw of Otsego," the newly designated sheriff had not received his commission.[15] This, and the fact that the ballots were not delivered in one box as required by law, were the grounds on which the Otsego vote was rejected. The Tioga and Clinton County votes were rejected on similar grounds.

Naturally the Federalists were furious. "Clinton and his worthy adherents [the Livingstons] . . . these virtuous protecters of the rights of the people, of the enemies of aristocracy, and the declaimers against ministerial influence," were, wrote Troup to Jay, quibbling upon technicalities. Schuyler thought the Clintonians violated "every principle of propriety."[16] And Jefferson wrote Madison from Philadelphia after digesting the latest New York news: "It does not seem possible to defend Clinton as a just or disinterested man if he does not decline the Office of which there is no symptom; and I really apprehend that the cause of republicanism will suffer and its votaries be thrown into schism by embarking it in support of this man, . . ."[17] Modern historians have been no kinder: Jay's best biographer has accused Clinton of "filching" the governorship in 1792.

The canvassers, a majority of whom were Clinton men, certainly came dangerously near to quibbling over technicalities in throwing out the returns from the three contested counties. They may very well, however, have been retaliating for the discriminations which the Clintonians were supposed to have suffered in Otsego at the hands of the influential Judge Cooper. "The Clintonians again tell strange tales about these votes of Otsego," wrote Jefferson.[18] A tenant testified that Cooper "had been round to the people and told them that they owed him, and that unless they voted for Mr. Jay, he would ruin them."[19] It was also claimed that Otsego ballot boxes were stuffed

[15] Thomas Jefferson, *Writings,* Paul Leicester Ford, ed. (10 vols., New York, 1892–99), VI, 93.
[16] Jay, *Correspondence,* III, 424; MS letter, Schuyler to Stephen Van Rensselaer, May 19, 1792, in Library of Congress.
[17] Jefferson, *Writings,* Ford, ed., VI, 89f.
[18] *Ibid.*
[19] Fox, *Aristocracy,* 140.

in favor of Jay.[20] The legislature later endeavored to impeach Judge Cooper for his election activities, and although the impeachment failed, it was concluded that the Judge's threats to his tenantry had gained 700 votes for the Federalists.[21] There were other complaints that the landlords had interfered, and altogether too successfully, in the elections. Columbia County, dominated by the Livingstons, went for Clinton by a two to one vote; while Albany, Rensselaer, and Montgomery Counties, where Federalist landlords held sway, gave large majorities to Jay.

All in all, the gubernatorial elections of 1792 were one of the most regrettable episodes in New York history. Governor Clinton's reputation has suffered more from his acceptance of the verdict of the canvassers than from any other incident in his entire career, with the possible exception of his opposition to the federal Constitution. Yet it must be admitted that his position in 1792 was much like that of Rutherford B. Hayes in 1876. Neither thought it his business to settle the contested election, and each refrained from interfering in the verdict.

It is of some interest that Senator Burr, between whom and Clinton there was little love lost, advised the canvassers that the Otsego votes should be thrown out. It had been suggested that New York's two senators, Burr and King, be invited to advise the canvassers, and although Burr was reluctant, King's insistence upon giving his opinion persuaded Burr. As the Federalist King contended that Jay had been elected, and as Burr dissented, the canvassers gained nothing by referring the dispute to the senators. Burr commented on the case in a letter he wrote on June 15:

It would, indeed, be the extreme of weakness in me to expect friendship from Mr. Clinton. I have too many reasons to believe that he regards me with jealousy and malevolence. Still, this alone ought not to have induced me to refuse my advice to the canvassers. Some pretend, indeed, but none can believe, that I am prejudiced in his favour. I have not even seen or spoken to him since January last.[22]

[20] *Albany Gazette,* July 30,1792.
[21] *Journal of Assembly,* 1792–93, pp. 150, 186ff.
[22] Matthew L. Davis, *Memoirs of Aaron Burr* (2 vols., New York, 1836–37), I, 357. Burr's statement, "The Reasons Assigned by the Majority of Canvassers," is printed in Davis, *Burr,* I, 346ff. The Assembly voted January 18, 1793, to uphold the decision of the canvassers. The statement of the canvassers appears in Hammond, *New York,* I, 65.

Burr had again thwarted Hamilton and yet he had not made a friend of Clinton.

When Jay first appeared in New York State after the verdict of the canvassers, he was given the reception of a victor. Such Federalist towns as Albany, Hudson, and New York City cheered, fêted, and dined him. Jay himself acted with becoming dignity, accepting the decision as definitive if unjust. Hamilton, the more vigorous partisan, urged that a spirit of dissatisfaction with the Clintonians be kept alive "for national purposes as well as from a detestation of their principles and conduct." He undoubtedly had the vice presidency in mind. Although "some folks are talking of conventions and the bayonet," he counseled moderation.[23]

The sympathies of the state were not entirely with Jay, however. Even Albany celebrated the news of Clinton's election with salutes at four in the morning.[24] Dutchess County some months later defeated James Kent, candidate for Congress, largely on the ground that he had opposed Clinton.[25] The governor was dined by his friends in New York City on July 19 amid toasts to Washington, Jefferson, and the French Republic. Although other speakers denounced the machinations of the partisans of Jay, Clinton in his address made every attempt to be concilatory and moderate.

Except for the unfortunate reverberations that followed the decision of the canvassers of the votes for governor, Clinton might in 1793 have succeeded Adams in the vice presidency.

Washington would of course be reëlected in 1792. It was generally known, however, as early as June, 1792, that the opposition to the Federalist administration planned to unite on Clinton for the vice presidency.[26] Hamilton was warning Vice President Adams late in June that the Clinton candidacy was under way. "If you have seen some of the last numbers of the National Gazette [Freneau's]," Hamilton wrote Adams, "you will have perceived that the plot thickens, and that something like a very serious design to subvert the government

[23] Jay, *Correspondence*, III, 435; Hamilton, *Works*, Lodge ed., VIII, 269, 271.

[24] "Vanderkemp Papers," *Publications of Buffalo Historical Society*, II, 41.

[25] William Kent, *Memoirs and Letters of James Kent*, 42.

[26] Jefferson, *Writings*, Ford, ed., VI, 74; John Adams, *Works*, C. F. Adams, ed., VIII, 514.

discloses itself." [27]   Consequently Hamilton concentrated during the summer on opposing the attempt "to subvert the government" by making Clinton vice president. But in September it was discovered that the greater menace, Burr, was a candidate. Dallas in Pennsylvania, Edwards in Connecticut, and friends like Nicholson and Willett in New York were working for Burr; and although some believed that Burr's activities were merely a diversion in George Clinton's favor, it soon became apparent that the Senator was a candidate in his own right.[28]

By October it was by no means certain but that Burr might replace Clinton, and Clinton let it be known that he was not eager for the nomination.[29] "Mr. Clinton's success I should think very unfortunate," Hamilton wrote at the time. "I am not for trusting the government too much in the hands of its enemies. But still Mr. Clinton is a man of property, and in private life, as far as I know, of probity. I fear the other gentleman [Burr] is unprincipled, both as a public and a private man." [30]   Burr had more strength than Clinton in New York City and probably also in New England, New Jersey, and Pennsylvania. There were party leaders like Jefferson and Monroe who felt that Clinton had lost caste by accepting the governorship, and who had no particular objection to Burr. Nevertheless, even Monroe advised strongly against the Burr candidacy on the grounds that Burr was young and untried and his political principles unknown.[31] Jefferson and Patrick Henry seem to have agreed with Monroe, and since Virginia votes were essential, the Burr candidacy was abandoned.

As Washington's reëlection was uncontested, the campaign of 1792 revolved about the candidates for the vice presidency. Other candidates, such as Thomas Mifflin, Samuel Adams, John Jay, and Thomas Jefferson, were mentioned; but by November it was apparent that either Adams or Clinton would be vice president.

The issue, it was maintained, was republicanism. Clinton had always

---

[27] Ibid.

[28] J. Q. Adams, Writings, W. C. Ford, ed. (7 vols., New York, 1913), I, 126; Hamilton, Works, Lodge, ed., VIII, 285.

[29] James Monroe, Writings, S. M. Hamilton, ed. (7 vols., New York, 1898–1903), I, 242.

[30] Hamilton, Works, Lodge, ed., VIII, 283.

[31] Ibid., p. 243.

been republican in sentiment and his maxim "had always been to keep the government connected with the people." Monroe wrote in all seriousness that "the partisans of monarchy are numerous & powerful." [32] It was important therefore to oust Adams who, it was believed, was attached to all the baubles of the British constitution. According to Freneau, Bache and the other journalistic opponents of Adams, that gentleman's "Discourses of Davila" and "Defence of the American Constitutions" showed him in his true aristocratical colors. The Federalists had monopolized Federal office; they had lined their pockets through their financial measures; and they had involved the country in an orgy of speculation in lands and securities. An honest old soldier and democrat like Clinton was needed in the vice presidency.

The Federalists ridiculed the contention that Governor Clinton was now loyal to the federal Constitution. Federalist sheets like the *Gazette of the United States* maintained that he had tried to keep New York out of the Union. They accused him of having recently usurped the governorship of New York and, more significant politically, of being hostile to the Potomac site for the national capital.[33] His supporters were called the "Jackalls of Mobocracy," demagogues, and "abettors of anarchy and confusion." The Federalists did not claim that Adams was of common clay; and to them Clinton's advocacy of old-fashioned finance, simple republicanism, and popular rights, was reason enough why he should not become vice president.

Party alignments in the United States in 1792 were surprisingly clear-cut and generally recognized. The leaders of both groups corresponded constantly among themselves, made plans, arrived at common decisions, and prepared political material for pamphlet and newspaper publication. It was of course the group that Jefferson and his friends had fused together in Congress and in the states in opposition to the Hamiltonian program that supported the Clinton candidacy. These party leaders, especially in Virginia and New York, kept in touch with opposition statesmen from New Hampshire to Georgia, urging the election of anti-Hamiltonian congressmen and of electors hostile to

[32] *Ibid.*, p. 238.
[33] John Dawson to Madison, November 12, 1792, MS, Library of Congress. See McMaster's account of the election, *People of the United States*, II, 86–88.

John Adams. Late in November Oliver Wolcott wrote that "it is now understood that a systematical effort has been made in every state, which has been conducted with great address and secrecy. The plan really is to elect George Clinton, and where a direct interest cannot be made in his favor, it is intended to diminish the votes for Mr. Adams. I think it is likely, unless some attention is given to the subject, that votes will be solicited for such men as Mr. Hancock, &c. &c. Not that they expect that any other effect will be produced than a plurality in favor of the real candidate." [34] The plans of the opposition were to the Federalists "insidious contrivances" and conspiracy. They feared Adams might really be defeated; and that gentleman, who frankly wished to be reëlected, was prevented only by Hamilton from sulking in his Quincy tent when Congress met.

If Clinton could have won fourteen more electoral votes from Adams, he would have been vice president. All the 21 electors of Virginia, the 12 electors of New York, the 12 of North Carolina, the 4 of Georgia, and one of Pennsylvania gave the governor their votes. Jefferson received 4 votes from Kentucky and Burr one from South Carolina. All the other vice presidential ballots, including the solid New England block, went to Adams, who was consequently reëlected by 77 votes to George Clinton's 50. For Clinton it was decidedly unfortunate that he did not enter the national political stage in 1793 at the vigorous age of 54 years instead of being forced to wait for national honors until he was 66. He aged more than most men do between 54 and 66, and when he finally arrived at the vice presidency he was too old to go on to the higher office as he might have done in 1797.

Nevertheless the closeness of the result was a great disappointment for Adams. When Langdon of New Hampshire commented to Adams in the Senate chamber about the size of the Clinton vote, Mr. Adams is said to have gritted his teeth and muttered, "Damn 'em, damn 'em, damn 'em! You see that an elective government will not do." [85]

---

[34] George Gibbs, *Memoirs of Administrations of Washington and John Adams* (2 vols., New York, 1846), I, 83. See also J. Q. Adams, *Writings*, W. C. Ford, ed., I, 131; J. S. Bassett, *The Federalist System* (New York, 1906), 55.
[85] H. C. Lodge, *Life of George Cabot* (Boston, 1877), 60.

CHAPTER XVI

THE GOVERNOR TURNS FRANCOPHILE

THE wars of the French Revolution added new fuel to the already blazing fires of New York politics. The democrats that donned tricolor cockades, organized Francophile clubs and greeted one another as "citizen" or "citizeness," were largely Clintonian Republicans. George Clinton's own enthusiasm for things French, which can probably be attributed in the first instance to the Revolution, was strengthened by one of the most picturesque marriages in American history.

In April 1793 Edmond Charles Genêt, the new French minister, arrived at Charleston, intent upon bringing America into the French camp. There followed his triumphal progress to Philadelphia, his tactlessness and his breach with the Washington administration, his recall and his retreat to New York. In New York City he met and charmed the Clintons, especially the governor's nineteen-year-old daughter, Cornelia, whom Colonel William Smith's lady had described four years earlier: "as smart and sensible a girl as I ever knew —a zealous politician, and a high anti-Federalist."[1] Before Citizen

---

[1] Roof, *Colonel William Smith and Lady*, 197.

Genêt returned to Philadelphia at the end of 1793 he and Cornelia were engaged. She was ardently devoted to him and he to her. He chafed at the distance between them, became petulant when she did not write, and, as time wore on, grew suspicious of the continued postponement of the marriage. Cornelia wrote to him frequently and tenderly, always explaining and urging patience. On July 14, 1794, she wrote her beloved Edmond from Greenwich:

"It is not possible for me my love to explain to you my Fathers conduct as I have not had Courage enough to speak to him let me intreat you my beloved Edmond not to attribute this to any want of Affection for you, but to a natural timidity . . . Papa would never make a promise unless he intended to execute it . . . [And she referred to] the fond hope of soon being united to you for Life." [2]

Apparently there were rumors that Genêt already had a wife in France, and Governor Clinton wished to make certain before the wedding that they were baseless. Finally Cornelia and Genêt were married at the Government House on November 6, 1794, by Doctor Rodgers the Presbyterian clergyman. After the wedding, which was attended only by Cornelia's sister and Doctor Treat, they "went to pay their respects to Papa and Mama, & from thence the same day proceeded to the Citizen's Sandhill upon Long Island." [3] For the Citizen, having decided that it would be decidedly unwise to return to France and finding himself "terribly poor," had bought a small farm at Jamaica on Long Island. After his marriage he called it "Cornelia's Farm."

There was in the years that followed much writing and visiting back and forth between the Clinton farm at Greenwich and Cornelia's Farm. The governor wrote often and both Cornelia and the Citizen replied. Mrs. Clinton and Cornelia exchanged long visits and the governor and Genêt shorter ones. It was on the occasion of one of Mrs. Clinton's visits to the Genêts soon after the arrival of a grandson

[2] Genêt Papers, Library of Congress, Box 1793–1801. The Genêt Papers contain considerable Cornelia Clinton-Genêt correspondence.

[3] King, *Rufus King*, I, 580. See also [George Clinton Genêt], *Washington, Jefferson and "Citizen" Genêt 1793* (1899?), 38–42; Meade Minnigerode, *Jefferson Friend of France* (New York, 1928), 346, 372–78.

EDMOND CHARLES GENÊT

From a painting by Ezra Ames

that the governor wrote, November 30, 1795, to his son-in-law that
he expected to set out for Long Island shortly to bring "mama" home.
"Tell her I can't think of suffering her to absent herself from my Bed
& Board any longer. If neither of those Days [suggested for Clinton's visit] will admit of my going out, you must bring her Home
without waiting for me if all is well with you; whether the young
Democrat is a Christian or not before that Time." And the governor
added that Mr. Taylor was sending two caps "to keep the Young
Citizen's bigg Head Warm." [4]

Later another young Citizen was born and the delighted old governor had new correspondents at Jamaica. As early as January, 1802,
one of them, George Clinton Genêt, was complaining of the governor's
failure to write him. Clinton wrote a grandfatherly letter in response,
insisting that he had written the boy only a short time before. To be
sure, he added, I also wrote to Miss Cornelia Clinton McKnight "but
this ought not to excite any Jealousy for I presume you have too much
Gallantry not to know that particular Attention is due to the Ladies. . . .
I hope you & your Brother continue to be good Boys and improve fast
in your Learning." [5]

During George Clinton's last term as governor the Genêts moved
to Greenbush near Albany, the new state capital, to be near the Clintons. In 1810 Cornelia died, still in her thirties, and four years later
the Citizen married again.

The Genêt marriage gave the entire Clinton family a lively interest
in the wars of the French revolutionary period. It was inevitable, however, that they, like the other democratic republicans of the time, should
be thoroughly sympathetic with French republicanism. The vehe-
mence of early pro-French sentiment in the state is reflected in a letter
of March 9, 1794, to DeWitt Clinton from John C. Ludlow, his boon
companion and close friend. Ludlow wrote of the French victory
at Toulon: [6] "This long looked for and much wished good news was
announced on Friday morning by the ringing of Bells firing of Cannon hoisting coulours singing & dancing to the tune of the Cavinagnole

[4] Genêt Papers, Box 1793–1801. There are numerous letters of this period from
Clinton to Genêt in this collection.
[5] Letter of Jan. 27, 1802, from Albany in the Genêt Papers.
[6] DeWitt Clinton Papers, Columbia University.

[*sic*] in the Tontine in the evening & the special meeting of the Democratic Society attended by congratulations & other expressions of republican Joy." Cornelia was of course enthusiastic when news of French triumphs arrived. Even the cautious George Clinton showed his sympathies from time to time as when he wrote DeWitt Clinton: "I congratulate you on the late important news from Europe. Britain will have her hands full."[7] In 1794 he addressed his good friend Monroe as "Citizen James Monroe." And such good republicans as Edward Livingston labeled the Federalists "the English party" and regretted that war with England had not already been declared.[8]

In spite of his Gallic sympathies Governor Clinton did not lose his head. Soon after the federal executive on June 5, 1793, ordered the seizure of all vessels being fitted out for privateering, Clinton learned that the sloop *Polly* was being refitted, armed and rechristened *The Republican* in New York waters. He at once called out the militia to detain the suspected vessel, notified the French consul at New York, Hauterive, and informed Washington of his action, suggesting, however, that the militia should be empowered to act in such cases under federal authority. Hauterive was indignant, Genêt protested to Jefferson, and Clinton's republican friends did not try to conceal their disappointment.[9] In view of Clinton's meticulous neutrality it is difficult to understand why John Adams should have written December 17, 1795, that "Had Mr. Clinton, . . . been in my place the winter before last, this country would now have been involved in all the evils of a foreign, if not a civil war."[10] Yet the governor was generally regarded as an enemy of English interests. According to Secretary of State Randolph, who retired under a cloud in 1795, there was a meeting in New York in the summer of 1794 attended by Mr. Hammond the British minister and a number of his sympathizers. The object of the meeting, Randolph asserted, was to destroy him, Randolph, and George Clinton in their respective capaci-

[7] Letter of Jan. 13, 1801, DeWitt Clinton Papers.

[8] Clinton to Monroe, Sept. 8, 1794, Hist. Soc. of Pa.; Livingston to DeWitt Clinton, Mar. 13, 1794, DeWitt Clinton Papers.

[9] Clinton letters of June 9, 1793, to Washington and Hauterive are in the Library of Congress. See also McMaster, *United States,* II, 104–07.

[10] Roof, *Colonel William Smith and Lady,* 229.

ties as secretary of state and as governor.[11] Whether or not the story is a true one, both offices were occupied a year later by staunch Federalists.

Feeling ran high in New York City between the French and the British factions. In August H.M.S. *Boston* challenged and fought a duel with the French frigate *L'Ambuscade* off the Jersey coast, and republicans celebrated *L'Ambuscade's* victory as though she had been an American ship.

The British, already cordially disliked by the rank and file of New Yorkers for their refusal to evacuate the western posts, added to their unpopularity by impressing American seamen. British ships that visited New York were guilty of the practice and Clinton wrote indignantly about it to the President.[12] New York Republicans were urging war with Great Britain. Realizing that the state was entirely unprepared, the governor, in what may be called his war message of January 7, 1794, reminded the legislature "of the naked and exposed condition of our principal sea port, and urg[ed] the necessity of immediately providing for its defense." New York's extensive commerce with both belligerents, he stated, rendered the preservation of its neutrality an object of the first magnitude.[13] The Federalist legislature was not entirely sympathetic and after considerable delay it voted the modest sum of £30,000 for the fortification of New York City and £12,000 for the northern and western frontiers. The governor was disappointed. He succeeded however in getting free labor for the work on the fortifications of New York harbor by calling on the patriotic citizenry. Columbia students dug trenches, carpenters gave whole days of labor without charge to the state, and the fifty-five-year-old governor himself organized parties of workers and showed them on Governor's Island how to use pick, shovel and wheelbarrow. It was probably while the work was still in progress that Clinton on June 12 ordered all ships and vessels of war the property of foreign powers, excepting only commercial vessels, to approach no nearer than one

[11] George Gibbs, *Memoirs of the Administrations of Washington and John Adams edited from the papers of Oliver Wolcott,* I, 265.

[12] Clinton letters of Aug. 1, 26, Sept. 14, 1794, and June 7, 1795, in Department of State.

[13] Lincoln, *Messages,* II, 333f.

mile south of Governor's Island.[14] Somewhat ironically the fortifications on Governor's Island were later christened Fort Jay by the Adams administration.

It was of course inevitable that Clinton and his following should fight the Jay Treaty. The governor himself described it as gratifying only to aristocrats and adherents of Great Britain but detested by all true republicans.[15] He might have added that the merchants, always his political enemies, also championed the treaty. Clinton's position on the treaty seems to have been known a few days after the treaty's publication, for Hamilton wrote as *Camillus* on July 22, 1795, that,

It is remarkable that the toasts given on July 4, 1795, whenever there appears a direct or indirect censure of the treaty, it is pretty uniformly coupled with compliments to Mr. Jefferson, and to our late governor, Mr. Clinton, with an evident design to place those gentlemen in contrast to Mr. Jay, and, decrying him, to elevate them. No one can be blind to the finger of party spirit, visible in these and similar transactions.

It is entirely possible that "the finger of party spirit" was involved. The verdict of history, however, has branded the Jay Treaty as one of the most unfortunate capitulations in American diplomatic history. The eminent author of the outstanding study of that treaty could only conclude that it was a necessary evil. Politics or no politics, the Clintons saw that a treaty that ignored impressments, that allowed trade with the West Indies only under a system of stifling restrictions, that provided no compensation for slaves taken by the British, but did provide for the settlement of debts owed to British merchants, and that had to be explained away to our old friends the French, came dangerously near to sacrificing our national self-respect. The Livingstons joined in the assault on the treaty. "May the present coolness between France and America produce, like the quarrels of lovers, a renewal of love," was a toast proposed at the time by Chancellor Livingston.[16]

The Clintonians in New York worked with the Pennsylvania republicans to defeat the treaty in the federal Congress. DeWitt Clinton

[14] E. C. Genêt, *Communications on the Next Election* (1808), 39; *New-York Journal*, May 3, 1794; *New-York Advertiser*, June 13, 1794.

[15] Clinton to Monroe, Apr. 14, 1796, Monroe Papers, Library of Congress.

[16] Alexander, *New York*, 79.

corresponded with John Beckley of Pennsylvania. He urged the circulation of petitions in upstate New York.[17] And at Little Britain George Junior, was occupied with preparing the way for the petitions, writing over the pen name "Polybius," and making arrangements to obtain signatures.[18] Jay was amazed at the virulence of the opposition. Those who fought the treaty were, according to him, Jacobins, "disorganizing politicians," and demagogues.[19] Fortunately for him he had been elected governor of New York in April 1795, over two months before his treaty was made public.

The legislature of 1792, which chose New York's presidential electors, was the state's last Republican legislature for some years. The state elections of April 1793 and 1794 gave the governor hostile legislatures which plagued him and annoyed his young secretary, DeWitt Clinton, in innumerable ways. Even his daughter Cornelia was distressed "at the conduct of the miserable Men you have in the Legislature: is the Devil in them—"! [20] They returned the Federalist King to the federal Senate. They filled the Council of Appointment with partisans who contested the governor's right to control the nomination of officers to serve in his administration. They called Clinton "a delectable Rascal" when, in his message of January 1795, he referred disparagingly to the "children of the opulent." [21] They procrastinated when the governor urged that the port of New York be better fortified.

Governor Clinton faced the Federalist majorities in the legislatures of 1793 and 1794 with all the assurance that he could muster and on certain issues he was even able to persuade them to follow his recommendations. In his statesmanlike message of January 7, 1794, he showed his old distrust of centralizing measures when he urged support for the Virginia and Massachusetts resolutions limiting the "suability" of a state. "The decision of the supreme federal court, which gave rise to these resolves," he declared, "involves so essentially the sovereignty of each state that no observations on my part can be necessary to bespeak

[17] John Beckley to DeWitt Clinton, July 24, Sept. 13, 1795; Thomas Tillotson to DeWitt Clinton, Oct. 24, 1795; DeWitt Clinton Papers.
[18] George Clinton, Jr. to DeWitt Clinton, October 19, 1795, DeWitt Clinton Papers.
[19] Jay, *Correspondence*, IV, 191–93.
[20] To DeWitt Clinton, January 15, 1794, DeWitt Clinton Papers.
[21] King, *Rufus King*, II, 2.

your early attention to the subject matter of them." [22] After Congress had passed a resolution a few weeks later proposing what became the Eleventh Amendment to the Constitution, to protect the states from suits by citizens of other states, Clinton was able to forward to President Washington notice of the prompt approval of the proposed amendment by the legislature of New York. [23]

In spite of a few such triumphs, the aging governor had had quite enough of the governorship by 1795, the gubernatorial year. He had been criticized for accepting office at all after the unfortunate contest of 1792. The legislature during his last term had been the most bitterly partisan of his career and it was clear that 1795 would be a Federalist year when a Republican governor would be completely stultified by another bitterly hostile legislature.

Entirely aside from these political reasons, there is reason enough to believe that Clinton's health, always uncertain, made it impossible for him to accept another term. The governor was so ill at the Greenwich farm that he had to have his message read for him when the legislature met on January 6, 1795, at Poughkeepsie. [24] A few days later James Kent, the future chancellor, wrote to his brother that there was little prospect that the governor would be able to leave his house that winter, that it was expected the legislature would remove from Poughkeepsie to New York to be near him! Kent added that "It is doubtful whether he ever recovers." [25] On the legislature's removal Kent prophesied correctly. Perhaps the Federalist legislature, always ready to meet in New York City, was only too willing to join the Republican governor. At any rate it voted on January 13 to meet at the metropolis a week later. Clinton seems to have been somewhat better in February but he was still decidedly unwell in the fall. [26]

"The declining condition of my health" was the principal reason for his decision not to accept a renomination as given by the governor in

[22] Lincoln, *Messages from the Governors*, II, 334–35.

[23] The President's message to Congress, Nov. 21, 1794; *Annals of Congress*, 3d Congress, p. 894. Senate, Assembly and Council of Revision approved the resolution on the same day, Mar. 27, 1794.

[24] Lincoln, *Messages from the Governors*, II, 348.

[25] Letter of Jan. 12, 1795, James Kent Papers, Vol. II, Library of Congress.

[26] George Clinton to E. C. Genêt, Nov. 30, 1795, Genêt Papers, Box 1793–1801, Library of Congress.

CORNELIA CLINTON GENÊT

his letter of January 22, 1795, addressed to the freeholders of the state.[27] He pointed out that he had served continuously in elective office for nearly thirty years and that his duty to his family as well as his health dictated his retirement. Two days later General Van Cortlandt, Clinton's lieutenant governor since 1777, announced that he also would not accept a renomination.

Burr, it seems, had already been working against Clinton's renomination. The only result, however, of the approaches made by Burr's friends to members of the legislature at Poughkeepsie was a meeting of the Republican members which determined to support the old governor should he run again.[28] When Clinton refused, as it was generally expected he would, the Republicans turned not to Burr but to Robert Yates who had run against Clinton in 1789. The Clintons were active in Yates' cause.[29] Eight years later a close friend of Burr's was to maintain that George Clinton brought about the defeat of of New York Republicanism in 1795 by his obstinate refusal to support Burr for governor.[30] But had the Clintons supported and helped to elect Aaron Burr, they would have elected a man who had gained his majority only by flirting with the Federalists—which Burr was doing as early as December, 1794.[31] There is little reason to believe that any Republican short of Clinton himself could have been elected governor of New York in 1795.

Jay, the grievance candidate, had agreed to run as early as 1793. He was, his friends urged, the only man who could beat George Clinton. His supporters, including Schuyler and Van Rensselaer, were campaigning for him in December 1794 and he was named by a kind of Federalist legislative caucus early the next year. A colorless campaign followed and the unpopular Republican candidate, who was accused of being place-hungry, received less than 12,000 votes to almost 13,500 for Jay. On July 1, after eighteen years' service as governor, George Clinton yielded the office to Jay.

[27] Printed in *Albany Gazette*, Jan. 30, 1795, and other papers.
[28] James Cheetham, *View of the Political Conduct of Aaron Burr*, 20.
[29] DeWitt Clinton served on a Yates campaign committee. DeWitt Clinton Papers.
[30] "Aristides" [W. P. Van Ness], *Examination of the Various Charges Exhibited against Aaron Burr* (1802), 9.
[31] King, *Rufus King*, I, 583–84.

The next five years was a period of retirement for the old patriot. He spent much of the time convalescing, enjoying his Greenwich estate, where the chronically peripatetic Clintons took root from about 1794 to 1799 or 1800, visiting Cornelia's family at Jamaica, and recouping his private fortune.

For months the state of his health was precarious. "My enquiries after your health have been constant," Washington wrote him in November of 1795, "and my concern for the ill state of it has been sincere." But by February 1797, Washington was congratulating the old warrior on his complete recovery and expressing the hope that he might visit with him at Mount Vernon.[32]

In 1796, when Burr, now his constant rival for national honors, aspired to the vice presidency, Clinton did not wish to become a candidate for vice president and his friends made no determined effort on the ex-governor's behalf. New York Republicans probably favored Jefferson for president and Clinton for vice president, but as it was clearly a Federalist year in New York, they had less voice than usual in the selection of candidates. Clinton himself favored Jefferson for president but showed no great enthusiasm in his behalf.[33] Nevertheless three Virginia electors and all four Georgia electors cast ballots for George Clinton. Governor Jay received five votes from Federalist Connecticut, and Burr a fairly imposing total of thirty votes from Pennsylvania and states farther south which gave him third place in the electoral balloting and left him a candidate to be reckoned with four years later. Burr was, however, chagrined and angry at the failure of the Republicans to unite on his candidacy.[34] Certainly the New York Republicans would be able to unite on no New York candidate until either Aaron Burr or George Clinton should be eliminated politically once and for all.

[32] Washington Papers, Library of Congress, copies, Vol. XV, 5, 15.

[33] Hammond, *New York*, I, 103. George Clinton to DeWitt Clinton, Dec. 13, 1803, DeWitt Clinton Papers.

[34] Hatch, *History of the Vice Presidency*, 127.

CHAPTER XVII

POLITICAL PARTIES IN NEW YORK

DEWITT CLINTON ORGANIZES THE REPUBLICANS

FEDERALISTS PLAN A WAR WITH FRANCE

THE PARTY SYSTEM IN NEW YORK

REPUBLICANISM *vs.* MONARCHY

POLITICAL GEOGRAPHY OF NEW YORK

BURR AND TAMMANY

CLINTON IS NO PHILOSOPHER

DURING the Clintonian interregnum of 1795 to 1801, when John Jay and the Federalists ruled the state, George Clinton paid less attention to politics than to grandchildren and real estate. DeWitt Clinton, was no longer his secretary. From 1798 to 1800 that post was occupied by James Tallmadge Jr., just out of Brown College, later to practice in Poughkeepsie, to become lieutenant governor and to serve as president of New York University. DeWitt was during the period of the interregnum more active politically than his uncle and he became generally recognized as his uncle's confidant and representative in matters political.

A year after his uncle's retirement DeWitt offered himself as a New York County Republican candidate for the assembly. The county had long been notoriously Federalist and young Clinton's ticket was defeated. The next year, 1797, the New York Republicans offered a more distinguished ticket that contained among others the names of DeWitt Clinton, Aaron Burr, and Samuel Latham Mitchill, that faithful democrat and "walking encyclopaedia" from Columbia College. This ticket carried the county. The triumph of 1797 in the most populous county of the state was significant in that it marked the revolt of New York

City's voters against Federalist domination and inaugurated a period of Republican ascendancy that has been perpetuated with but few lapses to the present time.[1] Consequently New York County, which had always been particularly hostile to George Clinton, was to give him majorities in 1800 and 1801.

It was in 1797 that the little Dutch city of Albany became the permanent capital of the state. For twenty years the legislature and the executive had migrated, meeting in Kingston, or Poughkeepsie, or New York, or Albany. The decision to settle finally at Albany is significant in view of a conversation that Rufus King had had with George Clinton eight years earlier, in June 1789. The legislature had recently selected Albany for one of its sessions in preference to New York. This, Clinton observed, was due to the indiscretion of the city members. The country members had sound judgment but little or no ability to speak, and their attempts at oratory were improperly reported and ridiculed in the Federalist press of New York City. On one recent occasion an address by Taylor of Albany had been printed to make it appear ridiculous and Taylor had consequently forced the removal to Albany. Clinton declared that if the city members had occasionally gratified the rustics with meetings at Esopus or Poughkeepsie, they never would have considered removal to Albany.[2] It was probably the country members' dislike of the sophisticated metropolis that dictated the selection of Albany in 1797.

In 1798 DeWitt went to Albany to take his seat in the state Senate. He worked steadily and effectively to build up a Republican organization in the state. He discussed plans for bringing Freneau, that fanatically Republican printer who had baited Hamilton at Philadelphia, to New York.[3] He probably helped to convert the Tammany Society, of which he had been "scribe" as early as 1791, to militant Republicanism. In 1798 he worked to concentrate Republican support to make Robert R. Livingston governor.[4] But the fortunate Jay profited

---

[1] The Federalists carried the city in 1799, but the Republicans won it in 1798, 1800, and 1801.

[2] C. R. King, *Rufus King*, I, 357. The legislature met at Albany in December, 1788. In 1797 Albany had a population of 5000.

[3] Philip Freneau to DeWitt Clinton, November 8, 1796, DeWitt Clinton Papers.

[4] [W. P. Van Ness], *Examination of the Various Charges against Burr* (1803), 30.

by the X.Y.Z. affair; the odds were overwhelmingly in his favor, and
he was triumphantly reëlected over the Francophile Livingston with a
majority of nearly 2500 votes in a total of less than 30,000.

Jay had let it be known that he would stand for a second term only
because of the imminent danger of war with France. "Nothing can be
more gloomy than the present prospect of our affairs with France,"
candidate Livingston wrote DeWitt Clinton on March 7, 1798, and he
added that the "English party" would probably see to it that there was
war.[5] Governor Jay called a special session of the legislature to prepare
for the anticipated hostilities and his message was a call to arms. The
legislature approved the vigorous policy of the federal administration
toward France and voted money for fortifying New York harbor. The
militia was busy with its preparations and Hamilton, who had always
longed for a military command, saw active service ahead. If it should
come, it would be a Federalist war.

The break with France proved, however, to be the undoing of the
Federalist party in New York as in the nation. Although there was
fighting at sea, war was never actually declared; and when in 1799
Talleyrand offered to negotiate, conscientious John Adams forgot
politics, named a commission to proceed to Paris, and so irremediably
alienated the belligerent Hamiltonian wing of his party. The Federalist cause never recovered from the injury done it by this Adams-
Hamilton break. In New York the Federalist Assembly indignantly rejected a motion commending Adams for making peace with France.[6]

Much more than the war issue itself, the ill-fated Alien and Sedition
Acts contributed to the unpopularity of Federalism in New York.
Hamilton and Jay approved heartily of the measures passed by the
triumphant Federalists and designed to protect the national administration from criticism by aliens or natives. Jay wished to go even farther
and amend the federal Constitution to increase the disabilities on the
suspected classes.[7] The Clintons, on the other hand, were known to be
friendly toward dissenters and recent comers and to be opposed to the
Alien and Sedition Acts. When the irascible Judge Cooper obtained the

[5] DeWitt Clinton Papers.
[6] Hammond, New York, I, 125.
[7] Jay, Correspondence, IV, 241; Alexander, New York, I, 183.

prosecution of Judge Jedediah Peck, a sturdy Otsego Republican, for circulating a satirical petition aimed at the Alien and Sedition Laws, and Peck was collared by a federal marshal and brought from remote Cooperstown to New York for trial, it became evident that the Federalists were overplaying their hand. The Republicans, on their part, were helping to raise a fund to pay the fine of at least one victim of the Sedition Act, that fierce Irish-American from Vermont, Matthew Lyon. It is entirely possible that DeWitt Clinton contributed to the fund.[8]

To add to its increasing burden of unpopularity, the Jay administration in 1799 introduced the first general property tax in the state's history.[9] The Federalists were riding for a fall. Yet during these years George Clinton showed no inclination to return to public life.

By the end of the Federalist period when Clinton was to reappear upon the political scene, the party system had become firmly established in America and especially in New York. "Aristides" could write in 1803 with entire accuracy that "Since the establishment of the federal government, no state in the union has been more agitated by the efforts of contending parties, than the one in which we live." [10] And he added that "It was at that period [of the establishment of the federal government] that the line was drawn between the two parties that have alternately prevailed . . ." Yet certain distinguished historians have asserted that it was not until Hamilton's financial program got under way that public opinion began to crystallize and parties evolved. Channing, for instance, believed there was no definite party alignment until 1796 and that it was then on new lines which bore no relation to the issues of 1787 and 1788.[11] As a matter of fact the divisions of opinion in New York over a federal impost grant in 1783 and 1786 were almost the same as the divisions over the Alien and Sedition Laws in 1798. Certainly in New York the forces that fought for the federal Constitution in 1787 were almost identical geographically with the Federalist interests that supported Jay for governor in 1792. Individuals like

[8] Gallatin's letter of January 30, 1799, to James Nicholson appealing for funds is now among the DeWitt Clinton Papers, Columbia University.

[9] D. C. Sowers, *Financial History of the State of New York*, 114. The tax was to be continued three years.

[10] [W. P. Van Ness], *Examination of Charges against Burr*, 4.

[11] Edward Channing, *A History of the United States* (6 vols., New York, 1905–25), IV, 151.

Robert R. Livingston or Samuel Jones might cross party lines, but basically party divisions remained the same—democratic-republicans against consolidationists; Clintonism versus Hamiltonianism.

Contemporaries realized that party lines and fundamental issues did not change materially after 1788. The Federalists clung to their designation for a generation to come. On the other hand, the term "Antifederalist" continued in use for some years and was long used interchangeably with the new party name "Republican," thus showing the virtual identity of the two. During the campaign of 1792, for instance, both Jefferson and Hamilton spoke of Clinton's supporters as "Antifederalists," [12] but the term "republican interest" was commonly used at the same time in the newspapers. Jay wrote in 1795 and 1796 that the "Antifederalists" were opposing his treaty.[13] Hamilton made frequent use of the term "Antifederalist" even in 1800 when "Republican" was generally accepted.[14] Party consciousness and organization may have grown stronger in the middle and late nineties, but the "fundamental party division which has been at the basis of American politics ever since," [15] did not originate during Washington's administrations. The Federalist Schuyler recognized its existence in 1786 when he tried to persuade Jay to stand for governor against the Antifederalist Clinton.

There was a remarkable similarity between the issues of 1788 and those of 1800 when Clinton returned to politics. The Republicans of 1800 like the Antifederalists of 1788 feared America might turn monarchical. As late as 1795 Clinton felt called upon to declare that "It has been my invariable object to promote and cherish the republican system of government." [16] During Washington's administrations men criticized the president's fondness for riding in semi-monarchial state behind four white horses and the celebration of the president's birthday exactly as the King's was celebrated in London. Indeed, the British party in New York "celebrated with great festivity" the birthday of

[12] Jefferson, *Writings*, P. L. Ford, ed., VI, 74; Jay, *Correspondence*, III, 452.
[13] Jay, *Correspondence*, IV, 192, 214. John Quincy Adams used "Antifederal" in the same connection; *Writings*, I, 418.
[14] *Works*, Lodge, ed., VIII, 560–61.
[15] S. F. Bemis, *American Secretaries of State*, II, 27.
[16] *Albany Gazette*, January 30, 1795.

George III as late as 1789![17] Three years later the lieutenant governor of Upper Canada was told that New York's British party was so strong that if West Point, Fort Montgomery and Stony Point could be seized, the whole state would go over to the King.[18] It was frequently pointed out in the press and private correspondence that the Federalists had always had a yearning for monarchy and its trimmings. In 1804, for instance, an elaborate tale was circulated regarding a conspiracy of Hamilton, Adams, and other Federalists before the adoption of the federal Constitution, to place an English prince on the American throne and to join Canada with the United States. "Monarchy was the object of the Federalists," James Kane declared in his affidavit on the conspiracy. John Adams himself was said to have discussed the selection of a proper prince with the King of England. This story Clinton was supposed to have heard, probably from Judge Purdy; but, pressed by Hamilton, Clinton admitted that he could not vouch for it. Hamilton remained, however, to the day of his death, the consistent foe of "our real disease, which is democracy."[19] The cry of "monarchy!" may occasionally have been a crying of "wolf! wolf!" to bring out the voters. But in those days, when the little American republic felt very much adrift in a hostile monarchial world, most republicans were entirely sincere. They knew that many men agreed with John Adams that monarchy was inevitable. And had not Gouverneur Morris declared that "there never was, and never will be a civilized Society without an Aristocracy?"[20]

The Republicans were the advocates of civil liberty. A toast of 1800, now among DeWitt Clinton's papers, illustrates this: "The American people—may they never be awed by power or cajoled by flattery into an abandonment of their rights!"[21] They denounced the tyrannies of the Alien and Sedition Laws, and they feared standing armies. "The militia of the United States—may they always supersede the necessity of standing armies!"[22] They rejoiced in the great reforms and in the

[17] Maclay, *Journal*, 68.
[18] J. G. Simcoe, *Correspondence*, I, 156.
[19] Box 28 of the Clinton Papers contains several letters on the subject. Cf. Hamilton, *Works*, VIII, 610, 612; and *American Citizen*, April 1, 1802.
[20] Max Farrand, *Records of the Federal Convention*, I, 545.
[21] Miscellaneous Volume, p. 38.
[22] *Ibid.*

republicanism of the French Revolution, and they aped the French revolutionaries by forming democratic clubs and societies. But while Federalists like Hamilton hoped for the introduction of British political institutions in America, the Republicans admired France, not because they wished to introduce French principles of government in America, but because they thought they saw France itself about to introduce American principles.

The Republicans championed the humble and the underprivileged. Hamilton admitted in a letter of May 4, 1796, that the elections in New York had, unfortunately, become "a question between the rich and the poor." [23] Their press supported the lower classes in city as well as country when, like the "carmen" of New York in 1799, they refused to follow the dictates of Federalist employers.[24] They demanded economy in government and objected to increases in the public debt. They advocated such democratic measures as the election of presidential electors by the electorate itself instead of by the legislature, a proposal that the Federalist legislature of 1800 is said to have rejected on the ground that "the Swinish Multitude" was incapable of such a responsibility.[25]

Geographically the position of the two parties had changed between 1788 and 1800 in only one important respect. The Clintonians still controlled the democratic west bank of the Hudson and their opponents the east bank with its great estates and Federalists towns. Albany County, with its recent accretion of population from New England, was more Federalist than ever. The conversion of New York City to Republicanism, however, threw the balance of power to the democrats and marked the doom of Federalism in the state.

Greenleaf's democratic *New-York Journal*, which was succeeded in 1800 by Cheetham's notorious *American Citizen,* may have played an important part in the conversion of New York. But the political astuteness and organizing ability of Aaron Burr has been properly given much of the credit for the city's espousal of Republicanism. Burr, who was a good deal of a humanitarian and a professed democrat, was prob-

[23] *Correspondence,* Lodge ed., VIII, 395.
[24] *Albany Gazette,* May 10, 1799; *Watch-Tower,* April 26, 1802.
[25] *American Citizen,* March 19, 1800.

ably the most influential figure in the metropolis—so influential that he was able again and again to cross Hamilton's path, thus incurring the enmity of that determined gentleman. Indeed, the youthful Burr was at that time probably a far more vigorous, if less sincere, democrat than the aging Clinton, and as such was much more cordially disliked by the Federalist leader.

Another important factor in winning New York City to Republicanism was the Society of Tammany. Founded about 1786 [26] as a nonpartisan organization, it soon became involved in politics. It worked to counteract the revolutionary Cincinnati, which Senator Maclay called "another of [Hamilton's] machines." [27] It included in its membership such Republicans as Melancton Smith, printer Greenleaf, Burr's faithful friends William P. Van Ness and Matthew L. Davis, DeWitt Clinton and George Clinton Jr. [28] It met in Barden's Tavern on lower Broadway, later in the Long Room of Martling's tavern, which the fastidious Federalists labeled the "pig-pen"; and in its more solemn moments it met, significantly enough, in Presbyterian churches near by. [29] Its badge was the bucktail:

> There's a barrel of porter at Tammany Hall,
>   And the Bucktails are swigging it all the night long.
> In the time of my boyhood 'twas pleasant to call
>   For a seat and a cigar 'mid the jovial throng.
>
> Halleck's Song. [30]

By 1800 Tammany was frankly partisan and Burr, although he was not a member, used it to carry the city for his ticket. It remained Burrite in its sympathies and when the Clintons broke with Burr, Tammany broke with the Clintons. George Clinton was never a member.

The New York Republicans had by 1800 a somewhat more definite, but still a vague and poorly systematized ideology. They had found in the state no prophet who could shape their philosophy of govern-

[26] Article on William Mooney, its founder, in *Dictionary of American Biography*.

[27] Maclay, *Journal*, p. 194.

[28] W. R. Werner, *Tammany Hall* (Garden City, 1928), 37; F. B. Hough, *Washingtonia* (2 vols. Roxbury, 1865), I, 131.

[29] *Valentine's Manual of . . . City of New York* (1865), 861.

[30] *Ibid.*, 863.

ment and present it in a form that would win converts. They had no Republican Bible as their opponents had Hamilton's *Federalist*. They were too Anglo-Saxon in their thinking and their background to turn readily to the French revolutionary thinkers, however enthusiastic they might be over the triumphs of French republicanism. Their greatest figure, George Clinton, was not a philosopher or a glib orator who could formulate a republican system of politics. Indeed it was Clinton's greatest weakness that he was not more a man of theory who could systematize the political democracy that he instinctively believed in. Had Clinton been more of a philosopher, he might have realized that his own party's land system and his own private speculations, for instance, were the kind of things that build bourgeois oligarchies of the Hamiltonian variety. Disappointed in Clinton, the Republicans of the nation were turning instead to Jefferson who, they realized, did have a definite ideology; and by 1800 the Virginian had far out-distanced his early rival. Much to the disgust of the Clintons, who were always jealous of Virginia leadership, Virginia seemed likely to recapture the presidency.

CHAPTER XVIII

THE BUSINESS OF SPECULATION

HAMILTON THINKS CLINTON PENURIOUS
MAN OF AFFAIRS
ASTOR AND CLINTON DEVELOP GREENWICH VILLAGE
WASHINGTON AND CLINTON IN PARTNERSHIP
BESETTING SIN OF THE GENERATION
CLINTON AND THE MACOMB SCANDAL

GEORGE CLINTON had a ruggedness of character, a stern integrity, a high degree of political courage, and a refreshing confidence in democratic institutions, which won men as few figures in public life have been able to do. He had, however, one trait which was less admirable—an inordinate fondness for his account book.

His bourgeois love for investments and speculations and his personal thrift, that often verged on parsimony, grew more marked as he grew older. His contemporaries knew this and, with many, his popularity suffered accordingly. Men like Knox, who lived far beyond his means to make his courtly household worthy of the Federalist hey-day; or like William Duer, who speculated like a Jay Gould, lived like a prince, and dragged scores with him into bankruptcy, did not approve of the economical old governor. Hamilton, who had very definite views as to what the dignity of high office demanded, thought that Clinton was not only frugal but penurious, and that by saving he neglected what was due the decorum of the governorship. Hamilton stated that in the six years subsequent to 1782 Clinton must have saved half of his salary which totaled over £8000. This, with his interest and his speculations, must have given him a fortune of nearly £20,000.[1] Yet,

[1] *Works*, Lodge ed., III, 113-30. The governor's salary was £1500 a year.

the first families of New York and Philadelphia complained, he seldom entertained and he maintained only a modest household.

Clinton's accounts show occasional mild extravagances, such as his maintenance of a coach and coachman in the 1790's, his purchase of a gold watch for £35/16 in 1793, and frequent sizeable entries for wines and liquors. Most of the accounts, however, are a bewildering series of loans and borrowings and land purchases and dealings with his men of affairs.[2] John McKesson, legislator and law partner of DeWitt Clinton, was the most faithful of George Clinton's business managers. His own son-in-law, Matthias B. Tallmadge, was another. In his dealings with his factotums and his tenants, and especially with those of his debtors who were in arrears, Clinton was business-like and insistent upon his rights. Typical is a letter that he wrote to John Pierce on April 19, 1784:[3]

Sir: After your repeated promises in the first instance and your letter afterwards it has not been without great surprise that I have seen the payment of the money you borrowed from Captain Rutgers and for which I was considered as answerable deferred so long. Besides the very great inconvenience the delay has occasioned the gentleman who lent it to assist the public it has put me in a very disagreeable situation by being repeatedly called on for the money without having it in my power to pay it—I must therefore beg, Sir, that there may be no longer delay in this matter and that not only the amount borrowed but the interest on it may be immediately discharged, . . . I am Sir Your Most Obedient Humble Servant Geo. Clinton.

By means of economical living and a succession of moderately successful business ventures, George Clinton managed to amass a respectable fortune. After his death his personal estate was estimated at about $100,000 and his property in real estate at $125,000 more. In addition, he had advanced a good deal of money to his children including over $25,000 to Cornelia and Edmond Genêt, an amount that was carefully deducted from Cornelia's portion by the executor of the estate, Matthias

[2] Clinton's account books and considerable correspondence regarding his business affairs are in the Clinton Papers at Albany.
[3] MS letter, Buffalo Historical Society. The Wisconsin State Historical Society has Pierce's letter of January 17, 1784, to Clinton promising to have the money paid without delay.

B. Tallmadge.[4] An estate of a quarter million was of course a substantial one for that time and quite large enough to account for the increasing conservatism of Clinton's later years. Yet it was not enough to rank him with the great patroons of the Hudson or the ranking merchants and bankers of New York.

Clinton might occasionally invest in the stock of such ventures as the Manhattan Company, the Phoenix Fire Company, or the Air Furnace Company, but most of his investments were in mortgages, direct loans, and real estate speculations. As early as 1766 he was petitioning for a thousand acres in the Captain John Evans tract.[5] During the later years of the Revolution he was salting away in land whatever funds he could obtain from the state on his salary or in repayment of the advances that he had made the state during the war. Philip Van Rensselaer was his partner in several of these purchases.[6] His farm and grist and saw mills on the New Windsor hillside overlooking the northern entrance to the Highlands of the Hudson, which Clinton never occupied after the British invasion of 1777, he rented throughout the following decade and sold with the assistance of his brother James in 1790 for £1500—a good price.[7] He received revolutionary bounty lands from the public domain. He paid General Lamb £1000 for lands in Albany County in 1793. Other properties that he bought were located in J. Banyar's patent, in the town of Sharon on the Schoharie, in Deerfield, and in those classical townships, Solon, Homer, Scipio, Virgil, Cicero, Lysander, Cincinnatus, Fabius, and Tully. In 1802 he was renting the house at 65 Pearl Street in New York City to a certain James Hunt.[8]

It was also during his last term as governor while his household was temporarily established at Albany that he decided to exploit the pleasant farm at Greenwich in the eighth ward of New York City. A certain young native of Baden, Germany, had migrated to America in 1784, settled in New York, and become a merchant of some

[4] Affidavit and other papers in Clinton Papers, Vol. 31.
[5] *Calendar of Land Papers* (Albany, 1864), 406.
[6] *Public Papers,* VI, 251–53, 825.
[7] Sold to Hugh Walsh, April 26, 1790. See James Clinton to DeWitt Clinton, April 19, in DeWitt Clinton Papers and George Clinton to James Clinton, April 27, 1790, in State Museum, Newburgh. The property consisted of 350 acres.
[8] Account Book; letters of November 11 and December 3, 1802, Samuel Osgood to Clinton, Vol. XXVII.

reputation. In 1805 this man, John Jacob Astor, who knew the Clintons well and agreed with them in politics, struck a deal with the governor. He bought a half interest in Clinton's great Greenwich Village estate for $75,000. The two men planned to lay out the property, put through the necessary streets, and divide the resultant city blocks between them by lot. This was done, but unfortunately a legislative commission provided for another survey and an entirely different system of subdivisions, and the result was such confusion that it took a special act of the legislature to straighten out the tangle when George Clinton died intestate. Whatever the outcome, Astor's $75,000 must have done much to add comfort to Clinton's last years, even though John Jacob was not always prompt in meeting his payments. Nor did Astor himself regret the purchase, for some of the lots which he sold soon after Clinton's death brought him a tidy profit of over 200%.[9]

None of Clinton's investments in real property was extensive when compared with those of the really great contemporary barons of speculation, and most of them were in suburban areas or areas soon to be settled where they could easily and quickly be made to yield a return by subdivision, sale, or rental.

For some years before the Revolution George Clinton was one of two American agents who administered the lands of his distinguished but distant cousin, Sir Henry Clinton. As early as 1767 he wrote Sir Henry that he owed that gentleman's father, the first Governor George Clinton, a debt of gratitude for the clerkship of Ulster County and would therefore be glad to help him with his 4,000 acres in Ulster and his smaller estate in Dutchess. Sir Henry lost his estates during the War and all of the good wishes of George Clinton, who wrote him a friendly but discouraging letter in 1790, were not enough to recover them.[10]

The best known of George Clinton's ventures was his purchase of a 6,000 acre tract in the Mohawk Valley in partnership with Washington. In July 1783 Washington was at Newburgh waiting for news

[9] K. W. Porter, *John Jacob Astor*, II, 921, 924, 1061; An Act for the Relief of the Heirs of the late George Clinton, Esquire, deceased. Passed March 12, 1813; MS book New York Hall of Records, Liber Conveyances 70, 106, 145 and 220.

[10] See correspondence in William L. Clements Library, especially George Clinton's letters of October 14, 1767, and January 3, 1790, and his memorandum of November 7, 1799, regarding the properties of the late Sir Henry Clinton.

of the definitive treaty of peace. He decided to improve the idle weeks by exploring northern New York that he had never seen. "I have therefore concerted with Governor Clinton to make a tour," he wrote Schuyler, "and will start on July 18th." It was a momentous trip for it left both Washington and Clinton enthusiastic advocates of canal and highway systems to open the west to settlement. Washington saw that in the Mohawk Valley New York had a westward course that was comparable to his own Potomac–Ohio route.

They went by boat to Albany; northward on horseback to Fort Edward and Lake George, by boat again to Crown Point on Lake Champlain, and back by way of what became Saratoga Springs to Schenectady. They then went west through the Mohawk Valley to Fort Stanwix, where Rome stands today, and followed the route of the later Erie Canal to Oneida Lake. Returning by approximately the same route with diversions to Cooperstown and Duanesburg, they arrived at Newburgh Headquarters on August 5.[11] They had covered 750 miles. Both men were inveterate land speculators but they tried in vain to buy the springs at Saratoga and the area on which Fort Schuyler was located. They did succeed, however, in purchasing jointly "6,071 acrs. on the Mohawk River (Montgomery Cty.) in a Patent granted to Daniel Coxe on the Township of Coxebourgh & Carolana." These fertile acres were located between the present New Hartford and Clinton a few miles southwest of Utica.

The purchase was financed entirely by Clinton, who had, it seems, already lent Washington £2000 in New York currency for the purchase of the Dow estate near Alexandria, Virginia.[12] Clinton lent Washington £2500 at six and a half or seven per cent in December, 1782, and this money was probably drawn upon to meet Washington's half of the purchase price of the Mohawk land. Before his death Washington had almost doubled the money he had invested in the project, and he still had one thousand acres worth five or six dollars each! It was

[11] U.S. Bicentennial Commission, *History of the George Washington Bicentennial* (3 vols. Washington, 1932), I, 407 (map); III, 442; E. E. Prussing, *Estate of George Washington Deceased* (Boston, 1927), 306–07; A. C. Flick, ed., *History of the State of New York*, V, 72–74; Anon., *Revolutionary Relics or Clinton Correspondence*, 7–8.
[12] *Ibid.*, 377–79, 308f.; Clinton, *Public Papers*, I, 188; J. C. Fitzpatrick, ed., *Diaries of Washington*, II, 356.

a profitable venture! Governor Clinton had been the business manager, receiving the necessary authorization from Washington and transmitting the profits from time to time to his partner.[13] The partners seem always to have been in complete harmony.

Yet the debt pressed heavily upon the Father of his Country. As late as 1786 Washington told Mercer that his debt to Clinton, "who was so obliging as to borrow and become my security for £2500 to answer some calls of mine," might compel him to sell land and negroes. He had engaged to repay the sum within twelve months after the peace but he found himself in 1786 still paying interest on about £800 of it at seven per cent, more than his credit could properly bear. Even Washington admitted that this was a high rate of interest.[14]

Speculation was the besetting sin of the generation. The revolution was no exception to the rule that wars breed speculation. Freed of imperial restraints and of many of the Indian tribes which had been pro-British in the war, the new nation began to look forward to rapid westward expansion that would fill the public coffers and, more to the point, line many a private pocket. Francis Vanderkemp on a tour of western New York in 1792 saw clearly what was taking place:

The increasing population, the rage of speculation in land, by Americans, Dutch and Englishmen, double actually the value of the lands. An acre sold four years since, from one to six shill., is now valued at ten. I speak of woodland; cultivated farms have risen from £4 to 6, and this prize is doubled in the neighborhood of villages. . . . The Western parts of this State Sir! are now generally considered, as its very richest and most valuable part, which spurrs every forehanded man, to appropriate a part of it to himself or his children. . . . The families of Livingston, Beeckman, van Renselaer, van Cortland, Schuyler, in one word, all the powerful families of this State, merchants excepted, acquired their actual wealth and respectability by the purchase of new lands, and their judicious settlements on these.[15]

---

[13] A manuscript of Washington's dealings with Clinton, in the former's hand, for 1782–1785, is in the Huntington Library. The land was sold in small parcels, for the most part from 100 to 300 acres.

[14] *Pennsylvania Magazine of History and Biography*, IV (1880), 256–57. On June 9, 1787 Washington wrote Clinton he had arranged to discharge his debt to him by paying him $840. Photostat in Manuscript Division, Library of Congress.

[15] Publications of the Buffalo Historical Society, II, "Vanderkemp Papers," 42 and 45.

The new American bourgeoisie, having in mind the great landed families of the colonial era, were now attempting to carve out landed fortunes for themselves. They were also busily engaged in making fortunes in securities of all kinds, in soldiers' certificates, treasury warrants, continental paper, loan office certificates and state as well as federal obligations. Such manipulations were of course most rife during the hey-day of Hamilton's financial policies. But many of the finer figures of the period, including George Washington and George Clinton,[16] seem generally to have avoided speculation in paper and to have confined themselves to ventures in real estate.

"Terraphobia" or land-jobbing was almost universal. Among the outstanding plungers of the period were William Duer, Alexander Macomb, Francis Lewis, and Robert Morris. Judge William Cooper of Cooperstown employed Hamilton to extricate him and his partner from the legal consequences of acquiring lands in Otsego "by questionable methods."[17] Hamilton put much of his own fortune into lands. Jay had purchased lands in New Jersey as well as in New York. Duane, also Federalist in politics, was a plunger, and James Kent was so sanguine about certain of his purchases in 1795 that he planned to retire in two or three years to the country.[18]

It has been said that throughout the course of American history, those of the Federalist-Whig school have been more ardent expansionists and plungers into land speculations than those in the opposing political camp. That was true in the era following the Revolution; but it cannot be said that all the Republicans neglected to put their money into good virgin lands when opportunity offered and when money was to be had. Among the Republicans Aaron Burr invested in the Holland Company and other enterprises, Melancton Smith in the Ohio Company, Patrick Henry in Georgia lands, and even Tom Paine in the Indiana Company. General James Clinton was always

---

[16] Charles A. Beard, *Economic Interpretation of the Constitution of the United States* (New York, 1929), does not list Clinton as a security holder. There seems to be no foundation for the statement referred to in John McConaughy, *Who Rules America?* (New York, 1934) that Clinton made $5,000,000 by speculation. His papers and the correspondence of his heirs do not show that Clinton was even once a millionaire.

[17] A. T. Volwiler, *George Croghan* (Cleveland 1926), 329–30.

[18] Letter to Moses Kent, March 1, 1795, Kent Papers, Library of Congress.

ready for a tempting deal in land and he surveyed many of his own properties.[19]

It was in 1791 and 1792 that the "reign of speculators" reached its zenith and that George Clinton was drawn into the malodorous game. "Bank bubbles, tontines, lotteries, monopolies, usury, gambling, and swindling abound," according to a contemporary, with "poverty in the country, luxury in the capitals, corruption and usurpation in the national councils." [20] Three of the greatest of the New York manipulators, William Duer, Walter Livingston, and Alexander Macomb, became involved, dragging many into bankruptcy, and Duer himself was thrown into jail. The Republicans blamed the crisis on Hamilton's funding and assumption measures, and in New York the Federalists countered with claims that Governor Clinton had showed favoritism in allowing some of his friends, including Macomb, to buy public lands in huge quantities at nominal prices. This, as we have seen, became an issue in the campaign of 1792 and it was dug up and used against Clinton again in 1801.[21]

If Governor Clinton was responsible for the sale of over 3,600,000 acres of public lands to Alexander Macomb at 8 d. each, on easy terms, he was unwise. But there is no evidence to show that he was corrupt or was influenced by corrupt motives. In 1791 the legislature had authorized the Commissioners of the Land Office, of whom the governor was an *ex officio* member, to dispose of public lands without restriction as to price and quantity. The commissioners were therefore well within their legal rights. Macomb was not an intimate friend of the governor's and he later took oath before the Federalist mayor of New York, Richard Varick, that the governor had no interest, direct or indirect, in the much criticized sale.

It was said in the governor's defense that the Macomb purchase contained many acres of rough and mountainous land, which reduced the value of the whole, and that Massachusetts had recently sold 3,000,000 acres of its lands in western New York for only 7 d. an acre, less than

[19] Letters of April 19, 1790 and November 8, 1798 to DeWitt Clinton, DeWitt Clinton Papers. General James Clinton took a long surveying trip in Northern New York as late as 1798.

[20] *New-York Journal*, quoted in Alexander, *New York*, I, 53.

[21] *Daily Advertiser*, April 16, 18, 20, 1792; March 23, April 20, 1801.

Macomb was to pay. Yet the Federalists naturally made the most of the situation. Late in the winter session of 1792, just before the elections, a vicious resolution condemning the commissioners was introduced in the state Assembly. Apparently, however, the Federalists intended that no action should be taken on this resolution until after the elections, when a vindication would be of much less value to the commissioners; but the champions of the governor and the commission offered a substitute motion approving the action of the commissioners, forced a vote before adjournment, and upheld the governor by the substantial majority of 35 votes to 20.[22]

There were other charges against the governor's land policy, but they were vague and brazenly partisan. The New York Historical Society has in its great collections a little memorandum in Peter Elmendorf's handwriting that accuses Clinton of squeezing a grant of 50,000 acres out of the legislature for the benefit of a speculator who in turn made over 9,000 acres to the governor. But some worker in dusty manuscripts has taken the sting out of the accusation by clipping to it the following: "I think this is the only insinuation I ever saw against the honesty of Clinton."

Certainly the land policy of the commissioners had been eminently successful. The state received in the one year, 1792, $325,000 from the sale of public lands, and half of the state's revenue for the years 1790 to 1795 was to come from that source.[28] We can well believe that the governor, with an eye to storing away a generous surplus in the state's treasury and with his boundless confidence in the future of western New York, yielded too readily, but without improper motive, to Macomb's offers. It was Clinton's weakness that he did not realize that speculators like Macomb were as predatory and baneful an influence in American life as those who sought to corner wheat during the Revolution or collected soldiers' certificates in the era that followed.

[22] G. D. B. Hasbrouck, "Gov. George Clinton," New York State Historical Association, *Quarterly Journal*, July, 1920, p. 159; D. C. Sowers, *Financial History of New York*, 39–40; "Prices of Land . . . 1791," *Documentary History of New York*, III, 1070; "Decius" and "Lucius" in *Daily Advertiser*, April 18 and April 20, 1792; Hammond, *New York*, I, 58–61.
[28] Sowers, *op. cit.*, 39.

CHAPTER XIX

THE HEYDAY OF REPUBLICANISM

JEFFERSON NEEDS NEW YORK VOTES

BURR USES CLINTON TO CARRY THE STATE

WIDOWERHOOD

CLINTON, BURR, AND THE VICE PRESIDENCY

CLINTON ACCEPTS JEFFERSON

"THE FRIEND OF THE POOR" REËLECTED GOVERNOR

JEFFERSON FINDS CLINTON WORTH CULTIVATING

THE RISE OF DEWITT CLINTON

IT has been said that in the elections of 1800 New York carried the nation; New York City carried New York; and George Clintin carried New York City.[1] It was, therefore, George Clinton who made Jefferson president. Jefferson himself saw the importance of New York City and State when on March 4, 1800, he told Madison that "In New York all depends on the success of the city election, . . . Upon the whole, I consider it as rather more doubtful than the last election [1796], . . . In any event, we may say, that if the city election of New York is in favour of the republican ticket, the issue will be republican . . . it would require a republican vote both from New-Jersey and Pennsylvania to preponderate against New York, on which we could count with any confidence."[2] In New York, leaders on both sides realized that the party which should elect its ticket in New York County would in all probability control the legislature that was to choose presidential electors in the fall of 1800.

In the Republican victory of 1800 George Clinton was only a passive

[1] Channing, *United States*, IV, 237.
[2] Davis, *Aaron Burr*, II, 55.

agent. It was Aaron Burr who turned up his political shirt sleeves, gathered together the party workers, and labored ceaselessly until the returns were in. He set Tammany to work; he organized his "Tenth Legion"; he guided the finance committee that filled the Republican campaign chest; he harangued and argued in the taverns; he worked at the polls while the election was on; and he consulted constantly with the more active of the Republican leaders. Burr knew that if he could engineer a Republican victory in New York, he would become indispensable to his party and might well receive his reward when the electors of president and vice president met early in 1801. Perhaps the fact that Hamilton himself was equally active in working for a Federalist victory in New York was an additional incentive to Burr.

His strategy was masterly. To secure the veteran vote he had General Horatio Gates nominated for the Assembly. On the same ticket he placed Brockholst Livingston as the representative of one important branch of the party and John Swartwout, his close friend, to represent another. And to represent the Clintonian interest Burr decided that none other than George Clinton should stand for election to the Assembly. Brockholst Livingston and Horatio Gates were reluctant enough to run, but Clinton was even more determined not to emerge from retirement. He refused the nomination. The party leaders interviewed the old governor on three different occasions, and it was not until a few evenings before the election at a meeting among Clinton, Burr, Swartwout, and several others that they arrived at a decision. Clinton's name was to be placed on the ticket and he agreed to make no public remonstrance—surely a back-handed way of accepting a nomination!

It is not difficult to understand Clinton's objection to offering himself as a candidate. There was serious illness in his family. A term in the legislature would have little attraction for a man who had served as governor for six terms. Then again, Clinton, who had appointed Burr attorney general and nominated him to the state supreme court, felt under no obligation to him; and he had, furthermore, no particular desire to see Jefferson president. Van Ness undoubtedly exaggerated for political reasons Clinton's coolness toward Jeffer-

son, when, writing as "Aristides" three years later, he paraphrased
Clinton as having said at the conference with Burr in 1800,

that he had long entertained an unfavorable opinion of Mr. Jefferson's
talents as a statesman and his firmness as a republican. That he conceived
him as an accommodating trimmer, who would change with times and bend
to circumstances for the purposes of personal promotion. Impressed with
these sentiments, he could not, with propriety he said, acquiesce in the elevation of a man destitute of the qualifications essential to the good administration of the government.

"Aristides" added that, "it is so notorious that these were Governor
Clinton's sentiments, that it is scarcely necessary to produce authority to prove it." Clinton was so emphatic on the subject, "Aristides"
added, that Burr insisted he pledge himself not to use during the campaign any expressions like those he had used during the conference.
The governor consented, but his son, George W. Clinton, spoke frequently "with the most vulgar severity" of Jefferson, and his nephew
DeWitt took no part in the campaign. Making all due allowance for
"Aristides'" partisanship, we must admit that Clinton and Jefferson
were never close politically or personally.[3]

Clinton himself explained three years later that he had had, indeed,
no enthusiasm for Jefferson's candidacy. He had felt that Jefferson's
eulogy of Adams in his first speech to the senate in 1797 was disloyal
to his friends and he, Clinton, did not therefore believe himself to
be under an obligation to support him at a great personal sacrifice.[4]

With Clinton's name included the Republican ticket carried New
York County by nearly 500 votes and a Republican legislature was
assured. Once more Clinton and Burr had given Hamilton's political
schemes a serious setback. "In a word," wrote DeWitt Clinton on
May 17, "the failure of the aristocracy which has been erecting with
so much care and whose architects have been exhausting their powers
upon it for nearly twelve years must tumble into ruin."[5] Indeed, the

[3] [W. P. Van Ness], *Examination of the Various Charges against Aaron Burr*, 22. For
the state election of 1800 see also Hammond, *New York*, I, 135–37; M. L. Davis, *Burr*, I,
433–35, II, 55–58.
[4] George Clinton to DeWitt Clinton, December 13 and December 17, 1803, DeWitt
Clinton Papers.
[5] Letter to S. Southwick, quoted in Howard Lee McBain, *DeWitt Clinton and the
Origins of the Spoils System in New York* (New York, 1907), 74.

victory of 1800 in New York marked the collapse of Federalism.

Some of the high Federalists, realizing that the New York elections would make Jefferson president, decided that it would be preferable to put aside "the scruples of delicacy and propriety . . . to prevent an *atheist* in Religion and a fanatic in politics from getting possession of the helm of the State." They urged Governor Jay to steal the election. Hamilton, who was one of the conspirators, asked Jay to convene the old Federalist legislature before the end of its term on July first. The legislature would then provide for the choice of presidential electors by district; the Federalists would carry a few of the districts, and Jefferson would not become president. Apparently not only Hamilton but also Schuyler, Marshall, and some other Federalists were involved in this plan for an election steal. Fortunately for the party's good name, John Jay ignored the scheme.[6]

George Clinton at Greenwich was more concerned with Mrs. Clinton's health than with state or federal politics. She was critically ill in the late fall of 1799 and his daughter, Cornelia, had left the farm at Jamaica to be with her. By February her condition was even more critical, and while Dr. Young gave "flattering hopes of her recovery," George Clinton realized that the end was near. The devoted Cornelia Genêt wrote constantly to the Citizen giving him the most recent bulletins but refusing to abandon hope. It was on Saturday, March 15, that Cornelia Tappen Clinton died at the age of fifty-six. On Monday she was buried from Mr. Benson's at Number 21 Pine Street. While there is little evidence that any close intellectual comradeship had existed between Clinton and his wife during the thirty years of their marriage, Cornelia Tappen had been a devoted wife and mother and it is probable that her husband felt her loss keenly. In his years of widowerhood he aged rapidly, becoming "the venerable Clinton," "the aged governor," to his friends and associates. During the last twelve years of his life he was a solitary, almost pathetic figure.[7]

[6] Letter of May 7, 1800 from Hamilton and Schuyler to Jay, printed in Jay, *Correspondence*, IV, 270–73. Monaghan, *John Jay,* 419–21. In the winter session of 1800 the Federalist legislature rejected a Republican proposal to choose electors by district. Hammond, *New York,* I, 133.

[7] Genêt Papers, Box 1793–1801; DeWitt Clinton Papers; *American Citizen,* Monday, March 17, 1800.

Except for the political maneuverings of Aaron Burr, Clinton might have become vice president in 1801. As soon as the news of the Republican victory reached Philadelphia in May 1800, a group of Republican congressmen met, decided to give the vice presidential nomination to a New Yorker and determined on Clinton, Burr, or Robert R. Livingston. Gallatin was asked to communicate with the New York Republicans to find which of the candidates might best be named. Gallatin entrusted the matter to his father-in-law, Commodore James Nicholson, who proceeded to canvass the situation.

Nicholson first eliminated Livingston because of his deafness and because there was some doubt about his democratic principles. He then turned to Clinton who had reason to believe that he was the first choice of the Congressional caucus at Philadelphia. Clinton was probably ready to accept the nomination but he made certain objections such as his age, the recent death of his wife, and his election to the state legislature. Nicholson urged that refusal might create divisions in the party and might even endanger Jefferson's election. Clinton finally consented to Nicholson's writing Gallatin that his name might be used if a refusal would seriously injure the party's chances of victory and if Clinton might be free to resign if elected. Nicholson prepared to send Gallatin a letter to that effect.[8]

For some unexplained reason Nicholson showed his letter to Burr. Burr was agitated and muttered something about being certain of the governorship and uncertain of the vice presidency, and left the room. Whereupon some of his friends entered, convinced Nicholson that Burr should be urged to accept, saw Burr, "persuaded" him to yield, and had Nicholson change the whole tenor of his letter before mailing it. Nicholson again consulted Clinton who, he afterwards declared, was happy to be released. It is probable, however, that Clinton was not a little irked at being replaced by Burr. His apologist, Cheetham, wrote two years later that Burr would not have been nominated had the New York Republicans been consulted and that the

---

[8] Clinton's account of the entire incident appears in his letters of December 13, 1803 and January 2, 1804 to DeWitt Clinton in DeWitt Clinton Papers. Hammond, *New York*, I,137–39; Hatch, *History of the Vice Presidency*, 129–30; [W. P. Van Ness], *Examination of the Charges exhibited against Aaron Burr*, 24–26. Nicholson's statement dated December 26, 1803, is in the DeWitt Clinton Papers.

Congressional caucus named Burr only because it was assured that Clinton would not run.[9] It was on May 11 that the caucus agreed unanimously to support Burr for vice president.

In all this there was no mention of Burr's candidacy for the presidency itself. Commodore Nicholson's mission was to determine upon a candidate for the vice presidency, not the presidency. DeWitt Clinton, in predicting a Republican victory at the polls in April and May, 1800, stated that such a victory would give Jefferson the state's vote for president. Burr himself wrote as late as December 16 to General Samuel Smith, the Republican leader in the House of Representatives, that he would not contest the presidency with Jefferson. Yet when it was found that Jefferson and Burr would have an equal number of votes in the electoral college, the politicians, instead of devising a way to give Jefferson the presidency and Burr the vice presidency as the great majority of men had intended, tried to take political advantage of the unfortunate situation. "The Equality of Votes for Jefferson & Burr is indeed much to be regretted as every improper use will be made of the Circumstance," George Clinton wrote to DeWitt on January 13.[10] "Indeed I have reason to believe from Burr's explicit Declaration to me that he will not countenance a Competition for the Presidency with Mr. Jefferson." There was nevertheless a competition for the presidency; but Hamilton, who feared that Burr was "not very far from being a visionary" and a believer in "perfect Godwinism," came to the aid of the Jeffersonians and Burr became only vice president. The New York delegation in Congress with the approval of the Clintons gave their ballots to Jefferson.

If Clinton was as decidedly anti-Jeffersonian as "Aristides" was later to make out, he was reassured even before the inaugural. He wrote DeWitt that the day Jefferson took office was a festive one for New York Republicans and that he himself was in high spirits.[11] While attending the sessions of the legislature at Albany, he declared to Genêt that "Jefferson's inaugural Speech cannot fail of the Approbation of true republican[s]. That the Sentiments contained in it proceed from

---

[9] Cheetham, *View of the Political Conduct of Aaron Burr* (New York, 1802), 40–41.
[10] Clinton's letter of January 13 is in the DeWitt Clinton Papers.
[11] Letter of March 5, 1801, DeWitt Clinton Papers.

the Heart I cannot Doubt . . . Kiss Cornelia, Maria & the Children for me." [12]

Clinton was again a candidate for governor. On the night of the adjournment of the legislature, November 8, 1800, the Republican members met in caucus and nominated him for a seventh term. The nomination was confirmed at a meeting on February 26 at Adams' Hotel in New York City; and Jeremiah Van Rensselaer, the only Republican in a Federalist family, was nominated for the lieutenant governorship.[13] As Governor Jay felt that his health would not permit him to run for a third term and as he wished to retire to private life, the Federalists at the Tontine Hotel on January 13 nominated the young patroon, Stephen Van Rensselaer, to oppose Clinton.[14] The latter does not seem to have been eager for a seventh term. Possibly, however, he thought it might serve as a stepping-stone to higher honors. Of the candidacy of 1801 he wrote to DeWitt Clinton in 1803:

> You are sensible that it was with great reluctance I consented to be held up as a candidate for the office I now hold or to enter again into public life in any station whatever. . . . The reasons which then influenced me no longer exist. The object is happily accomplished and whether my services have contributed to its success or not is immaterial. The cause of Republicanism is now so well established as not to require any new sacrifice on my part.[15]

The campaign that followed was on the low level that had come to characterize New York politics. The Federalists maintained that if George Clinton was old enough to retire to private life in 1795, he was too old to be governor in 1801. They raked up the Macomb land scandal of 1791 to use it against Clinton, and they asserted that he had made a great fortune in public lands. His French son-in-law was an object of attack. The Federalists, one of them declared, are still "the trunk of the body politic," and to their party "belong all the riches, dignity, virtue and physical power." [16] Prosperity was a Federalist issue. Hamilton, who had "been harranguing the citizens

[12] Letter of March 15, 1801, Genêt Papers, Box 1793–1801.
[13] *Daily Advertiser*, March 2, 1801; Hammond, *op. cit.*, I, 154.
[14] *Daily Advertiser*, February 5, 1801.
[15] Letter of November 16, 1803, DeWitt Clinton Papers.
[16] *Daily Advertiser*, March 6, 1801.

of New York, in different Wards, in his usual style of imprecation and abuse against the character of the venerable Mr. Clinton," [17] showed a Federalist meeting "that it was to the Federal party exclusively that we owe the unexampled prosperity which we have hitherto enjoyed." [18] The cartmen of New York resolved to support the Federalists because under them "the Country at large has rapidly increased in prosperity," and Jay stressed the same issue. The Federalists denied that Van Rensselaer would advocate taxes that would be oppressive to the landed interest. For the Republicans seem to have emphasized the tax issue, pointing out the increase in taxation under Governor Jay. In some parts of the state people were even led to believe that Clinton would reimburse the taxes they had paid to the Federalist administration. [19] A Federalist gentleman in Montgomery County, in predicting a Clinton victory, wrote that the Republican campaigners went from house to house, convincing

each voter that this election is a contest between the Rich and the Poor— that Governor Clinton is the friend of the poor, and will be supported by every poor man in the state—that Mr. Van Rensselaer is a rich man, and a friend to the rich men . . . —that Mr. Clinton is also an enemy to taxation —that during the eighteen years that he was at the head of the government we had no taxes, but as soon as he was out of office taxes began. [20]

There was much of populism in the campaign. Clinton, said one of his supporters, was "bred in the school of Liberty." And Hamilton pointed out that Burr, in taking an active part in the campaign in favor of Mr. Clinton, had again "shown the cloven foot of *rank* Jacobinism." [21]

Although the Federalist government of New York City managed to disfranchise a number of prominent Republicans, including James Cheetham, Daniel D. Tompkins, W. P. Van Ness and George Washington Clinton, [22] and appointed only Federalist partisans as watchers at the

[17] [Newark] *Centinel of Freedom*, April 28, quoted in Stokes, *Iconography*, V, 1384.
[18] *Daily Advertiser*, April 13.
[19] Bleecker to Lewis Atterbury, June 18, 1801, Harmanus Bleecker Papers, Albany.
[20] *Daily Advertiser*, May 13, 1801.
[21] *Works*, Lodge ed., VIII, 589.
[22] *Republican Watch-Tower*, December 15, 1801.

polls,[23] Clinton carried the city with 1266 votes to 1090 for Stephen Van Rensselaer.[24] The Federalists had lost their hold on the metropolis. Clinton and Burr had scored once more against Hamilton. Clinton carried the state as a whole by a majority of nearly 4000 votes in a total of 45,651. Stephen Van Rensselaer received substantial majorities only in his home territory, Albany and Rensselaer Counties, and in the western counties of Oneida, Ontario, and Chenango where Federalist landed interests were strong and where New England immigrants with Federalist politics were settling in considerable numbers. Clinton swept Long Island. He carried Columbia where the Livingstons ruled, as well as Dutchess and Westchester on the east shore of the Hudson. On the opposite shore loyal Orange and Ulster gave him their customary majorities, and in the north and west he carried, among others, Saratoga, Washington which was normally Federalist, Schoharie, Montgomery, Otsego, Herkimer, Cayuga, and Onondaga. The yeomanry was still faithful to Clinton but there were signs of growing Federalist strength in such small cities of the north and west as Troy and Utica. What the Democratic Republican interest was to lose in the north and west, however, it was to gain in the south. A political revolution, by which the two great schools of politics were to change positions geographically, was under way.

The victory of 1801 produced a rapprochement between the Clintons and the Virginia dynasty. Monroe, always a friend of George Clinton's, wrote to congratulate him on his triumph.[25] Jefferson added his congratulations in a letter of May 17.[26] In the same significant letter he wrote of the irksomeness of making appointments to office and of his disposition to make as few changes as possible. He believed, however, that circumstances in New York required a less conservative policy. It had been represented to him that the collector, naval officer, and supervisor were violent partisans who should be removed; and Colonel Burr

<hr/>

[23] Davis, *Burr*, II, 149.
[24] *The Daily Advertiser*, June 8, 1801, Supplement, contains complete election returns for all counties. Stephen Van Rensselaer during the campaign denied that his tenants would be coerced into voting for him. Albany County went Federalist by 1400 votes in a total of 2900.
[25] Letter of July 12, 1801, Monroe Papers, Library of Congress.
[26] Jefferson, *Writings*, P. L. Ford, ed., VIII, 52.

and certain of the New York members of Congress had made suggestions, including the naming of Matthew L. Davis for the supervisorship.
Some disagreement, however, existed. "There is no one whose opinion
would command with me greater respect than yours, if you would be so
good as to advise me, . . . We also want a marshall for the Albany
district . . . Will you be so good as to propose one?" As Matthew L.
Davis was an intimate and a close political friend of Burr's, Jefferson's
consulting Clinton on the appointment to the supervisorship was an
incident of great significance. Burr's good friend Swartwout had
already received a federal marshalcy, but Jefferson was being made to
believe that Burr would have stolen the presidency had he been able.[27]
Consequently, Jefferson was turning his back on Burr and offering
friendship and alliance to Governor Clinton.

Matthew Davis did not become supervisor, nor did Burr succeed
in getting him named naval officer. Months later Osgood, a Clinton
man and informer against Burr, received the latter post. Meanwhile
the Livingstons were being carefully weaned away from Burr. The
chancellor, who had refused to be secretary of the navy, was appointed
minister to France, and Edward Livingston became mayor of New
York, an appointive position. Thanks to the work at Washington
of DeWitt Clinton, Osgood, Cheetham, and a number of others who
disliked Burr, Burr's influence with the Jefferson administration approached the vanishing point. Burr was to be driven out of the party.

Albert Gallatin, who concurred with the Virginians in their belief
that Burr was disloyal, had little love for the Clintons or the Livingstons. In a long letter written September 14, 1801,[28] he discussed with
Jefferson the question of the succession to the presidency and the
vice presidency. Madison he considered the proper successor to the
presidency. He pointed out that if the Republicans nominated Burr
for vice president in 1804, the Federalists would probably make him
president by throwing some of their electoral votes to him. One rem-
edy was an amendment to the Constitution making it possible to vote
separately for president and vice president, but the Constitution was
difficult to amend. Furthermore, Gallatin did not trust Burr and

[27] Henry Adams, *United States*, I, 230–31; Hatch, *Vice Presidency*, 137.
[28] Gallatin, *Writings*, H. Adams ed. (3 vols. Philadelphia, 1879), I, 49–52.

DEWITT CLINTON, 1769–1828

From a painting by Charles Ingham

would never have supported him for vice president had he discovered earlier the "total want of confidence, which during the course of last winter [he] discovered in a large majority of the Republicans toward Burr." Yet he did not think the Clinton or Livingston factions in New York had sufficient influence.

Yet I do not believe that *we* can do much, for I dislike much the idea of supporting a section of Republicans in New York, and mistrusting the great majority, because that section is supposed to be hostile to Burr, and *he* is considered as the leader of that majority. A great reason against such policy is that the reputed leaders of that section, I mean the Livingstons generally, and some broken remnants of the Clintonian party who hate Burr (for Governor Clinton is out of the question and will not act) are so selfish and uninfluential that they can never obtain their great object, the State government, without the assistance of what is called Burr's party, and will not hesitate a moment to bargain for that object with him, . . .

The event was to prove that the Clintons and Livingstons were entirely capable of controlling the state without assistance from Burr. Politically Jefferson made no mistake in accepting the Clinton-Livingston, instead of the Burrite, wing of the party.

When the young United States senator, DeWitt Clinton, went to Washington early in 1802, his uncle provided him with a letter of introduction to President Jefferson.[29] There is no evidence, however, that the president made a confidant of the big New Yorker who, with all his scholarly interests, ability, and energy, had a brusqueness and imperiousness about him that repulsed men as often as won them. With Burr's exit from the New York scene, DeWitt Clinton had become the foremost of the younger generation in the state's politics and he was rapidly taking his uncle's place as the leader of the Republicans. Six feet in his socks, broad-shouldered and big boned, he was a powerful figure physically as well as politically. He was a hard-hitting politician, a master of invective, a dangerous enemy. "The meekness of Quakerism will do in religion, but not in politics," he is said to have remarked.[30] He was not so consistent in his democracy as was his uncle. Although his statesmanship was constructive and

[29] Clinton to Jefferson, February 9, 1802, Jefferson Papers.
[30] S. P. Orth, *Five American Politicians* (1906), 90.

of a high order, he was willing to employ the most selfish and shoddy of political methods to gain his ends. His manipulation of the council of appointment and his employment of the unprincipled Cheetham are cases in point. The passing of leadership from George Clinton to DeWitt signified a decided change in the tone of state politics, and the change was not for the better.

CHAPTER XX

SPOILS OF OFFICE

THREE YEARS AT ALBANY

THE GOVERNOR IS NO SPOILSMAN

HAMILTON THE PROPHET OF THE SPOILS SYSTEM

1794 THE FEDERALISTS CHALLENGE GOVERNOR CLINTON

GOVERNOR JAY AGREES WITH CLINTON

DEWITT CLINTON IN THE PATRONAGE SADDLE

TRIUMPH OF THE SPOILSMEN

GEORGE CLINTON'S final term as governor began on July first, 1801. The Clinton family moved northward from New York to Albany where they occupied "Mr. James Caldwell's elegant house in State street" that Governor Jay had also used as his executive mansion.[1] Here the Clintons lived for three years with occasional treks to New York where they took a house on Cortlandt Street west of Broadway. But they never took root at Albany as they had done earlier at Poughkeepsie and New York. Albany on its side never claimed Clinton.

The veteran executive found at Albany that the governorship had been sadly emasculated during the Federalist period. The strangle hold of the spoils system on state politics was generally deplored but universally accepted. The governor was no longer the chief appointing officer even though he must still assume responsibility for the conduct of the ever increasing number of state officers who were appointed,

---

[1] G. R. Howell and J. Tenny, *History of the County of Albany* (New York, 1886), 443. Governor Jay rented the Caldwell house, which was at 60 State Street, in the fall of 1797. Monaghan, *John Jay*, 412.

not elected. He found the personnel of the state's civil service thoroughly permeated with the stench of virulent partisanship, divided politically within itself. New York politics had reached the nadir of decency.

Governor Clinton, from the day he became governor in 1777 to his death thirty-five years later, was never a spoilsman. As governor he was an ex-officio member, with a casting vote, of the council of appointment. The clause of the state constitution empowering the governor, "with the advice and consent of the council, to appoint all officers . . . ," was very similar to the corresponding clause of the federal Constitution of 1787, and under it Clinton claimed and asserted, as the president of the United States has claimed and successfully asserted, the right of exclusive nomination. It was clearly the intent of the framers of the state constitution to give the governor, who was to be responsible for the administration of the state government, a preponderant influence in the appointment of other officers such as the provincial governors had enjoyed. Certainly Clinton's assumption of the right of nomination was not seriously challenged for over ten years.[2]

Meanwhile the state enjoyed political tranquility and honest, nonpartisan government. During the early years loyalty to the American cause was, in addition to fitness, the only prerequisite to appointment. The governor called the council together, notified it of vacancies, and nominated candidates for its approval. His nominations were made with tact and generally with honest impartiality; and during the period of his undisputed leadership they were seldom challenged. He was admirably fitted for the often troublesome task of making appointments. Vanderkemp wrote of him in 1792 that he, Vanderkemp, had "often indeed been surprised with admiration at [Governor Clinton's] knowledge of men, which is a distinguishing trait of his character—and, in my opinion, one of the chief means of his Political success."[3] A keen judge of men and a forceful political leader, Clinton completely dominated his council and dictated its appointments. Under

[2] H. M. Flick, "The Council of Appointment," *New York History*, July, 1934, is the best account of the Council. H. L. McBain, *DeWitt Clinton and the Origins of the Spoils System in New York* is excellent and Hammond's *New York* is useful.

[3] *The Vanderkemp Papers* (Publications of the Buffalo Historical Society, II), 54.

his regime removals were made sparingly and only after serious consideration by the council sitting in an almost judicial capacity.

The worst that can be said of the appointments during Clinton's first administrations was that they came to be confined more or less to a small group of chronic office-holders and office-holding families.[4] But they were not confined to men who agreed politically with the Antifederalist governor. In 1788 three of the chief legal officers of the state, Chancellor Livingston, Chief Justice Richard Morris, and Justice John Sloss Hobart of the Supreme Court, were Federalist, while only one of that group, Justice Robert Yates of the Supreme Court, was an Antifederalist. If Mayor Lansing of Albany was an Antifederalist and a friend of Clinton's, Mayor Duane of New York was well known to be Federalist in principle. Recorder Samuel Jones of New York was at the time a Clintonian; Adjutant General Nicholas Fish and Attorney General Egbert Benson were both Federalists nominated by George Clinton and appointed by his council. If Simeon DeWitt, a relative of the governor's, was made surveyor general, so also was Philip Schuyler, who had no fondness for the governor and his politics. Later the Federalist Varick was made attorney general and he in turn was succeeded by the most enigmatical of all of Clinton's appointees, Aaron Burr, an Antifederalist who had opposed Clinton's reëlection in 1789 by supporting Yates. Yates himself was made chief justice. And as late as 1791 that vigorous Federalist squire, William Cooper of Cooperstown, was named first judge of Otsego County.[5] Certainly the appointments of the first five Clinton administrations were notable for their impartiality.

Abuse of the patronage is, of course, a perfectly natural concomitant of democracy in its early stages. Men who have worked and even shed blood to establish popular governments soon come to feel that they have a right to hold office. In their minds office-holding ceases to be a duty or a privilege confined to the able and the experienced, and becomes a highly desirable right—evidence of their partnership in the new commonwealth. And as there are invariably too few offices to go round, these partners insist on rapid turnover so that all may

[4] H. M. Flick, loc. cit., 560.
[5] F. B. Hough, Civil List of New York (1860); Hammond, op. cit., 53–54.

have their day. Although the rise of the spoils system in America is popularly associated with Andrew Jackson, whose fame has suffered considerably thereby, the clamor of the young American democracy for office was heard years before Jackson, soon after the Revolution.

The prophet of the spoils system in New York was none other than that earnest partisan, Alexander Hamilton. It was he who first suggested that in giving the governor the sole right of nomination, the council was misinterpreting the constitution. In the letters of "Publius" he made vague, unsubstantiated assertions [6] that the broad powers of the governor of New York in filling positions had produced "scandalous appointments to important offices," but "in tenderness to individuals" he forebore to descend to particulars. "The governor," Hamilton wrote, "claims the right of nomination, upon the strength of some ambiguous expressions in the constitution; but it is not known to what extent, or in what manner he exercises it . . . from whatever cause it may proceed, a great number of very improper appointments are from time to time made." These statements were made in a campaign document in a time of stress when men were not carefully weighing their words. Historians generally have concluded that Hamilton's position regarding Clinton's exercise of the right to nominate was unsound and without any basis but politics. Yet Hamilton had sowed the seed that was in six years' time to convert New York's appointive system into a pathetic scramble for the spoils of office.

The crisis came in 1794. When the Federalist legislature met in January the Tory lawyer Hoffman launched the attack on the governor and the Republican council of 1793 for their failure to appoint a fifth judge to the supreme court. The governor had, as a matter of fact, allowed the appointment of a fifth judge to go over because he had not approved of Peter W. Yates, the Republican candidate. The Federalists now proceeded to revolutionize the whole appointive system as Hamilton had suggested in 1788, in order to appoint their candidate, Egbert Benson. Although the old council of appointment had not served the customary full year, the new Assembly named a Federalist council in which Philip Schuyler was the leading spirit. The governor, feeling secure in the right of nomination which he alone had exercised for

[6] *The Federalist*, Ford, ed., 464, 472, 514.

seventeen years, innocently called together the hostile council. One of
the three Federalist members at once nominated Benson and he was
confirmed by a vote of three to one. The governor protested the council's
right of nomination and refused to sign the minutes of the meeting,
but the Federalists had tasted blood and did not intend to draw back.
As offices became vacant loyal Federalists were appointed, and if vacancies did not occur in sufficient number, new offices were created. The
governor's nominations were ignored. The power of appointment had
been transferred from the executive to the legislature, and politics was
to have its day![7]

Governor Clinton, who seldom lacked the courage of his convictions,
filed with the clerk of the council a vigorous protest against the council's
usurpation of power. He insisted that as he alone was responsible for
the conduct of the executive branch of the state government, it followed
that he must have the principal voice in the appointment of his subordinates. He accused the Federalist majority of the council of making appointments for party reasons. The Federalist majority replied, admitting
that they had increased the number of offices and made certain removals
without hearings, but justifying themselves on the ground that Clinton
had formerly used the power of the patronage to his own advantage. Yet
they could cite against him only two cases in his entire seventeen years
of service. One of the two was the famous sheriff of Otsego who was
involved in the disputed election of 1792.[8] However weak the position
taken by the job-seeking council may have been, Schuyler and his
Federalist colleagues had their way. The spoilsmen were in the saddle.

The power of the patronage was turned against the Clinton administration in another field. The federal administrations of Washington
and Adams very naturally favored Clinton's political enemies when
offices were to be distributed. Washington, who believed that somehow
faction and partisanship might be avoided in American politics, made at
first every effort to be impartial. He appointed General John Lamb,
the Antifederalist, collector of the port of New York. His postmaster
general for two years was Samuel Osgood, the New York democrat and

friend of the Clintons; and certain lesser appointees, such as Henry Remsen, chief clerk of the new Department of State, were Antifederalists. But later in the administration, disillusioned by the appearance of the political opposition that he wished so much to avoid, the first president yielded to his Federalist advisers and his appointees were expected to be orthodox in their politics. And John Adams seems to have made no effort whatever to appoint Republicans. According to Channing, when Jefferson came into office in 1801 he found among the 228 principal federal officers only 30 who could be called Republicans.[9]

While capable Antifederalists like Melancton Smith, Yates, Lansing, Samuel Jones, Aaron Burr, and George Clinton himself, were neglected, loyal New York Federalists fell heir to some of the best of the federal offices. Jay became chief justice; Duane, Troup, Laurance, and Hobart in turn received federal district judgeships; Richard Harison was named United States district attorney; William S. Smith became federal marshal; and Nicholas Fish supervisor of revenue for the New York district. Hamilton's appointment to the Treasury made him perhaps the most influential man in the administration. Such a constellation of high federal dignitaries in the New York heavens may have aided very materially in the state's conversion to Federalist politics in the 1790's. Although Clinton was always on the friendliest of terms with Washington, he did not press the president for a share in the patronage. Even when his own party was in power, he seldom pressed his claims. He could state a few days before his death that, "it is contrary to [a] Rule I long since established not to interfere in state or indeed other appointments from which I have seldom erred."[10]

Governor Jay found himself in a dilemma. Like George Clinton he believed that the exclusive right of nomination belonged to the governor, but he could not publicly maintain that position without offending his own party. He tried to avoid the issue by asking in his first message that the legislature pass a declaratory act determining the question once and for all, but the legislature failed to respond. Nevertheless the governor again assumed the sole right to nominate and while the

---

[9] *United States,* IV, 252.

[10] Draft letter of February, 1812, recommending Charles Christian, Clinton Papers, vol. 31.

Federalists controlled the council of appointment there was no inclination to challenge the practice. Jay seems to have urged some restraint upon his colleagues, but without much success. Republicans were turned out of office and replaced with Federalists. New offices were added to provide more spoils.[11] "To the general rage for party spirit I think the State Government have not been far behind its people," wrote William Fitzhugh from Geneva, "and in my opinion they have degenerated much from their wonted dignity . . ."[12] By 1801 when the Clintonians returned to power, almost all the important positions were filled with Federalists. Certainly the spoils system in New York originated, as McBain has so conclusively proved, under Federalist auspices some years before DeWitt Clinton and his outraged Republicans seized control of the council of appointment in 1801.

Unfortunately for George Clinton his own party challenged Jay's assumption of the right to nominate before the end of the Jay administration, a challenge that paved the way for the final transfer of the disputed right from governor to council. The council which Governor Jay convened in February, 1801, was Republican by a margin of three to one. DeWitt Clinton was one of the three Republicans. Another was the ponderous figure of Ambrose Spencer, formerly a Federalist, later a member of the state supreme court, brother-in-law and close associate of DeWitt Clinton. The third Republican was a pliable individual named Robert Roseboom. The council was DeWitt Clinton's, not Jay's. Nevertheless it showed a remarkable degree of moderation in accepting many of the governor's nominations and leaving Federalists in office. Finally, however, the three Republicans on February 24 rejected the governor's nominee for sheriff of Orange and named their own man. Jay asked for an adjournment to consider the matter and, the adjournment agreed upon, the council did not meet again during Jay's term.

Meanwhile, on February 26, Governor Jay sent a message on the subject to the legislature.[13] Now that his political opponents were the avowed champions of the obnoxious system of nomination by the

---

[11] McBain, *Spoils System*, 45-50; H. M. Flick, *op. cit.*, 266; Fox, *Aristocracy*, 6.
[12] S. B. Webb, *Correspondence*, III, 217.
[13] Jay, *Correspondence*, IV, 290.

members of the council, Jay had no hesitation about stating his side of the case. In his message he referred tactfully and effectively to Governor Clinton's position:

> Doubts have long existed whether by this article [article 23 of the state constitution] the right of nomination was exclusively vested in the Governor, or whether it was vested concurrently in him and and the council. Questions arose on this article during the administration of my predecessor, and in the month of March, 1794, gave occasion to animated discussions between him and the then Council . . . [Becoming governor I maintained that the right of nomination was exclusively the governor's, since] the right to *appoint* necessarily included the right to *select* and *nominate;* and it gave me pleasure to find, on conferring with my predecessor, that this opinion was strengthened by his informing me that he had always claimed this right and never yielded or conceded it to be in the Council.

Jay went on to explain that he had asked his first legislature to pass a declaratory act, but without result. Finding himself now opposed by a council which differed with him, he was submitting the matter to the legislature for its consideration.

The whole state was agitated over the issue—especially, according to George Clinton, the vendue masters whose jobs were at stake. He wrote to DeWitt Clinton that "the general opinion is in favor of the measures you have taken," but he did not add that he himself approved.[14] There was tremendous pressure among the Republicans for jobs and it would have been bad politics for the Republican candidate for governor to criticize the Republican council in the midst of the campaign. Clinton was seldom blind to the political aspect of events.

The legislature again refused to pass any declaratory act to settle the wrangle between governor and council.[15] The Assembly, by a decisive vote of 61 to 35, insisted that it possessed no authority to legislate in such a matter,[16] but the impasse was finally broken in April when the legislature "recommended" that a convention be called to amend the state constitution. It was mid-October, over three months after Governor Clinton took his oath of office, that the convention met at Albany and

[14] Letters of March 5, and 28, 1801, DeWitt Clinton Papers.
[15] A statement of DeWitt Clinton's observations on a proposed decaratory act is in DeWitt Clinton Papers, Miscellaneous volume.
[16] *Daily Advertiser*, March 7, 1801.

named Aaron Burr its president. Although DeWitt Clinton himself was absent, the Republican spoilsmen were in control and the convention with much discussion but with virtually no dissent awarded to the members of the council of appointment, as well as to the governor, the right of nomination. John Henry, the Albany lawyer, was the leader of the small majority that stood by the governor.[17]

It was a serious defeat for the governor and marked very definitely the rise of DeWitt Clinton to party leadership in his uncle's place. The council under the nephew's domination had already in its August session swept aside the old governor's conscientious objections and made a number of obviously partisan removals and equally partisan appointments. Federalists like Richard Harison, William Coleman, Richard Varick, and Daniel Dale, a host of lesser officials and the numerous Federalist justices of the peace, were proscribed. During the August meetings, most notorious for their decapitations, from a quarter to more than half of the officers in many counties were removed, although few changes were made in Federalist counties like Albany. Governor Clinton protested and spread his protest on the minutes of the council. On several occasions he refused to sign the minutes that recorded the most outrageous of the removals.[18] But the Republicans could not forget the Federalist proscriptions of the last seven years and the job-hungry Clintonians and Livingstons were swept into the newly made vacancies. Edward Livingston became mayor of New York; a Livingston by marriage, Morgan Lewis, became chief justice; Brockholst Livingston was also elevated to the supreme bench; and Thomas Tillotson, the new secretary of state, was a brother-in-law of Robert R. Livingston. Certainly the Livingstons received their full share of the plums. Only the Federalists and the Burrites were forgotten.[19]

DeWitt Clinton, now in full control of the dominant wing of the New York Republicans, had no scruples against putting his own friends and connections into office. A few Clinton relatives and inti-

[17] The convention also fixed the number of state senators and representatives. Among its members were James Clinton (Orange) and DeWitt's son, George Clinton, Jr. (New York). S. C. Hutchins, *Civil List of . . . New York* (Albany, 1874), 55; Alexander, *New York*, I, 115–16; H. M. Flick, "Council of Appointment," 267–68.

[18] McBain, *Spoils System*, 119.

[19] Hammond, *New York*, I, 180, states that not one Burrite received an office.

mates were already in office; others like Sylvanus Miller, the friend of
DeWitt who became surrogate of New York, were appointed during
the great raid on the patronage of August, 1801; and still others were
appointed in the months and years that followed. A famous "Clinton
Catechism" of 1811 named about twenty-five of these, including Judge
Obadiah German, James Tallmadge the elder, and James Tallmadge
Jr., John Taylor, Samuel Osgood, Pierre Van Wyck, Theodorus Baily,
Ambrose Spencer, Matthias B. Tallmadge, Simeon DeWitt, Charles the
brother of DeWitt Clinton, Philip Spencer Jr., and William Stewart.[20]
Over half of the names in the "Clinton Catechism" were those of relatives of George Clinton, but most of the appointments responsible for
their inclusion belong to the period when DeWitt dominated the
council. "Plain Truth," in a broadside of 1804, complained that of the
two great families that ruled the state the Clintons held fourteen important places and the Livingstons twelve.[21] Certainly it was not
Andrew Jackson who introduced the spoils system into American
politics.

[20] Reprinted in Platt, *History of Poughkeepsie* (1905), 308–09.
[21] Fox, *Aristocracy*, 64.

CHAPTER XXI

THE ELIMINATION OF AARON BURR

A SCURRILOUS ATTACK

BURR IS FAIR GAME

THE CLINTONS ATTACK AND ARE ATTACKED

JEFFERSON ACCEPTS CLINTON'S EXPLANATIONS

THE TRIUMPH OF SOUND REPUBLICANISM

GEORGE WASHINGTON CLINTON

THE united forces of the Clintons and Livingstons had captured the state from the Federalists in 1801. Now that Hamilton had been returned to his law practice and Jay to his estate, the victorious allies, to entrench themselves still further, determined upon the purification of their own party by the elimination of that troublesome and altogether too clever political manipulator, Aaron Burr. Ink was the weapon used.

In that era of sensational political journalists like Fenno and Freneau, Bache and Duane, New York had a coterie of editors that yielded the palm to none for ability, partisanship, and scurrility. There was William Coleman, the Bostonian, whom Hamilton had appointed to a federal clerkship. When Hamilton founded the *Evening Post* late in 1801 he made Coleman its editor, and Coleman, "skilled in the low arts of a petty-fogger," soon made himself master of all the black arts of journalism—invective, thinly veiled misrepresentations, gross and unashamed partisanship. Hamilton himself met often with Coleman, supplied anonymous pieces for his paper, and inspired his wily editorial policies.[1] Dr. Peter Irving, editor of the *Morning Chronicle* that was

[1] *Dictionary of American Biography*, IV, 294; *American Citizen*, April 1, 1802.

established in 1802 to defend the maligned Burr, was less rigorous in his assaults on the Clintons and Livingstons than Coleman in his assaults on the Republican mobocracy. This elder brother of Washington Irving was referred to by James Cheetham as "Doctor Squintum." [2]

By far the most capable, effective, and malignant of the group of New York journalists was Cheetham. He had already served his apprenticeship as an agitator in England before coming to America at the age of twenty-six. Three years later he became the partner of the Clintons' cousin, David Denniston, who a few months earlier had converted Thomas Greenleaf's *Argus* into the bitterly partisan *American Citizen*.[3] Unprincipled and quarrelsome, Cheetham broke with Burr, challenged Coleman to a duel that was only narrowly averted, met and thoroughly disliked Tom Paine, provoked Burr's friend Matthew L. Davis to the point of violence, and a few years later severed relations with the Clintons over the embargo. It was said of him that he "forced the press to become the disturber of domestic quiet—the assassin of private reputation . . . the degraded vehicle of foul defamation."[4] Although the *American Citizen* may not have been so vitriolic and defamatory as these words suggest, it did mark a new low point in New York journalism. For that debasement DeWitt Clinton, as the patron of Cheetham, must accept considerable responsibility.

Burr was fair game. He had illicitly coveted the presidency in 1800. His flirtation with the Federalists, as seen in his vote on the repeal of the Judiciary Act and his famous toast to the "union of all honest men," had won him the enmity of the Jefferson administration. That he had never been a reliable party man, that without him there would be more offices for the friends of DeWitt Clinton and the Livingstons, and that his fall would leave the vice presidency vacant in 1805, must have been weighty considerations. His shrewdness in snatching the vice presidential nomination in 1800 had not been forgotten and, in spite of his

[2] S. H. Wandell and Meade Minnigerode, *Aaron Burr* (2 vols., New York, 1925), I, 240; Levermore, "Rise of Metropolitan Journalism," *American Historical Review*, VI, 448.
[3] *American Citizen and General Advertiser*, March 11, 1800; *Dictionary of American Biography*, IV, 47. The *American Citizen* was a daily.
[4] *New-York Herald*, December 19, 1807.

support of George Clinton's ticket in 1801, it was decided to have his scalp.[5]

The inky battle was fought in New York City which was the chief and almost the only citadel of Burrism in the entire state.[6] The assault began in 1802 when Cheetham in his "Narrative of the Suppression by Colonel Burr of the History of the Administration of John Adams" accused Burr of persuading too vehemently Republican John Wood to moderate his history of the Adams administration in order not to offend the Federalists. To Wood's defense of Burr, Cheetham replied with "An Antidote to John Wood's Poison." The Manhattan Company, created by Burr, now ousted Burr and his friend Swartwout from their directorships, an incident that led to a duel between Swartwout and DeWitt Clinton. The administration's organ, the *Albany Register*, turned against Burr. And in July Denniston and Cheetham published Cheetham's full statement of the case against Burr, a pamphlet that he called, "A View of the Political Conduct of Aaron Burr, Esquire." [7] The principal accusations against Burr were that he had not always supported the orthodox candidates for office and that he had sometimes sought office for himself.[8]

The friends of Burr struck back. John Wood wrote "A Full Exposition of the Clintonian Faction" in which he pointed out that although George Clinton's Revolutionary services had given him certain claims upon the gratitude of the state, DeWitt Clinton, now the party leader, had no such claims. DeWitt's attempt to succeed Governor Clinton was "one of those instances, where vice is descended from virtue, and vicious inconsistency from prudent resolution"—a politic tribute to the governor. Wood suggested that it was perhaps the great temperamental gulf between George Clinton and Aaron Burr that had produced a mutual dislike. Certainly, he declared, the Clintons tried to have Langdon of New Hampshire made vice president in 1800 instead of Burr; and George Clinton had even remarked to his friends

---

[5] R. R. Livingston, Minister to France since October, 1801, took little or no part in the assault on Burr, but he nevertheless incurred Burr's hostility. R. R. Livingston to DeWitt Clinton, Paris, February 5, 1803, DeWitt Clinton Papers.

[6] John Armstrong to DeWitt Clinton, Clermont, June 24, 1802; DeWitt Clinton Papers.

[7] For sale on July 19. *Watch Tower*, July 17, 1802.

[8] Davis, *Burr*, II, 205–09; Fox, *Aristocracy*, 59–61; Hammond, *New York*, I, 185–90.

that he himself would have run to keep Burr out of the vice presidency. The Clintons were accused of trying to foment trouble between Jefferson and Burr and of employing that "jacobin infidel," Cheetham, to attack the innocent Burr.

The crowning efforts of the Burrites to discredit the Clintons was "Aristides'" famous pamphlet that was entitled, "An Examination of the Various Charges exhibited against Aaron Burr." [9] It was some months before it was discovered that "Aristides" was William P. Van Ness, an intimate of Burr's. Van Ness's outspoken malignity and convincing plausibility made "Aristides" perhaps the most effective tract of its generation. Certainly its awkward truths and its equally embarrassing misrepresentations made the political fur fly. Although in the earlier Burrite pamphlets Governor Clinton had been generally spared at his nephew's expense, "Aristides" launched a ferocious attack at the governor himself. George Clinton's popularity, he wrote, had declined steadily since 1788; "he has never been the idol of the party, which his unblushing eulogists wish the world to believe"; and he has now "dwindled into the mere instrument of an ambitious relative, and his mercenary adherents; that a paltry and contemptible faction, alike destitute of talents and of worth, are sheltering themselves under his name, availing themselves of the imbecility of his age, and converting him into a convenient tool, through whom they may dispose of the honors and offices of the state for their own profit and aggrandizement." His adherents, who had always "deemed his right to the chief magistracy so divine and indefeasible, that every man who had the audacity to refuse him his suffrage . . . was branded with every odious epithet," had never forgiven Burr for his opposition to Clinton's reelection in 1789. In 1800 Burr was the first choice of his party and Clinton was given an opportunity of refusing the nomination only out of respect for the feelings of an old man. And "Aristides" added the startling observation that George Clinton had called Jefferson "an accommodating trimmer, who would change with times and bend to circumstances for the purposes of personal promotion."

Cheetham sent a copy of "Aristides" to George Clinton who declared it "worse than Billingsgate." [10] The attack was too telling to be borne

[9] Published in December, 1803.
[10] George Clinton to DeWitt Clinton, December 13, 1803, DeWitt Clinton Papers.

in silence. Governor Clinton wrote to DeWitt, explaining "Aristides" away in seven indignant pages. Other explanations followed and even the publishers of "Aristides" were hunted down and prosecuted. By July 1804, both the author and the publishers promised DeWitt Clinton a "complete denial of the calumnies which have been published against you; provided you withdraw the suits."[11] The governor's suggestion that Commodore James Nicholson, Gallatin's emissary of 1800 who had offered him the vice presidential nomination, be asked to tell the truth about his mission of 1800 was at once adopted by DeWitt Clinton. Nicholson responded promptly, and although the governor approved of his nephew's plan to print the Nicholson narrative if it could be made more temperate than "Aristides," it seems never to have appeared in print.[12] The governor thought it placed too little emphasis upon the fact that in 1800 Burr was only a second choice for the vice presidency.[13]

Meanwhile the troublesome "accommodating trimmer" statement had to be explained away. About a week after he first saw "Aristides," Clinton wrote Jefferson, denying that he had made such statements and expressing a wish that Jefferson would not allow the misrepresentations of "Aristides" to come between them. Jefferson's reply was a most generous one. He wrote Clinton from Washington on the 31st of December:

I received last night your favor of the twenty-second, written on the occasion of the libellous pamphlet lately published with you. I began to read it, but the dulness of the first page made me give up the reading for a dip into here and there a passage, till I came to what respected myself. The falsehood of that gave me a test for the rest of the work, and considering it always useless to read lies, I threw it by. As to yourself, be assured no contradiction was necessary. The uniform tenor of a man's life furnishes better evidence of what he has said or done on any particular occasion than the word of an enemy ... Little squibs in certain papers had long ago apprized me of a design to sow tares between particular republican characters, but to divide those by lying tales whom truths cannot divide, is the hackneyed policy of the gossips of every society.[14]

[11] M. Ward and L. Gould to D. Clinton, New York, July 30, 1804; DeWitt Clinton Papers.
[12] A copy of the narrative dated December 26, 1803, is in DeWitt Clinton Papers. It was printed in *American Historical Review*, VIII, 512f.
[13] George Clinton to DeWitt Clinton, January 2, 1804, DeWitt Clinton Papers.
[14] Jefferson, *Writings*, H. A. Washington, ed. (Washington, 1854), IV, 520.

A year later in a letter to DeWitt Clinton the President referred to "so atrocious a libel as the pamphlet Aristides." [15] If it was the intention of the Burrites, as it undoubtedly was, to alienate the Virginia dynasty from the Clintons so decisively and irremediably that George Clinton could not possibly become Burr's successor in the vice presidency, Jefferson's good temper or political sagacity frustrated Van Ness's attempt. "Aristides" did indeed create consternation in the Clintonian camp but it did not save Burr from political annihilation nor keep George Clinton from Washington. The inky battle of 1802 and 1803 resulted in a decisive victory for the Clinton faction. It eliminated Burr politically almost as effectively as Burr was eliminated by his tragic duel with Hamilton.

During the three years of George Clinton's last governorship the Republicans of New York were as secure in their ascendancy as were the Republicans at Washington. "I believe we may consider the mass of the States south and west of Connecticut and Massachusetts as now a consolidated body of Republicanism," Jefferson wrote to Governor McKean on February 19, 1803. [16] The Federalist opposition was reduced to a pitiful minority. Such measures as the reduction of taxation and the simultaneous reduction of the national debt, strenuous action against the Barbary pirates, repeal of the Naturalization Act, and the acquisition of Louisiana, brought the Jefferson administration to the zenith of its popularity. Naturally enough the Republican regime in New York profited by the triumph of Republicanism at Washington. When Jefferson's foreign policy was put to a test vote in the New York Assembly on February 2, 1803, only 19 out of 89 assemblymen refused to give their approval. It was apparent that there was serious opposition in only a few counties in the entire state. Significantly three of these, Albany County, its neighbor Columbia, and Oneida County to the westward in the Mohawk Valley, were thoroughly saturated with Federalist immigrants from Massachusetts and Connecticut. Thanks to its commercial and landed interests Albany had long been Federalist in policy. On the other hand, the New York City area, which had been

---

[15] Letter of October 6, 1804, DeWitt Clinton Papers.
[16] Henry Adams, *United States*, II, 811.

so predominantly Tory and Federalist in the decade and a half after the Revolution, was by 1802 staunchly Jeffersonian.[17]

Governor Clinton occasionally consulted on questions of patronage with such administration leaders as Gallatin and Robert Smith as well as with the President.[18] On several occasions in his messages to the legislature he expressed his hearty approval of the administration at Washington. In his first message on January 26, 1802, the governor congratulated the legislature on the flourishing condition of the United States "under an administration extensively possessing and highly meriting the public confidence."[19] This was, it may be noted, before "Aristides" accused Clinton of disloyalty to Jefferson. A year later Clinton came to the support of the administration in its protests to Spain against the termination of the right of deposit at New Orleans. According to DeWitt Clinton this virtual closing of the Mississippi would be a severe blow to New York which had in the past enjoyed the greatest part of the Mississippi trade. The governor thereupon came to the defense of the right of deposit in his annual message although he had, he declared, "always avoided interfering with affairs appertaining exclusively to the General Government."[20]

The Republican administrations at Albany and at Washington, if the vice president may be excepted, seem to have been almost completely in harmony.

Very naturally the sections of the state that were Jeffersonian were also Clintonian. About half of the meager band of Federalist survivors in the state legislature came from Albany County and neighboring Columbia, and the western counties of Chenango, Oneida and Ontario and Genesee supplied most of the others. The Federalists might control a vote or two in the Richmond, Queens, and Ulster delegations; but the great majority of the delegates from such well-represented

[17] *New York Assembly Journal*, February 2, 1803. Other divisions on both state and federal issues (February 2, 3, and 18) show a striking correlation. Richmond County was still Federalist.
[18] See, for instance, Gallatin to Clinton, August 11, 1802, George Clinton Papers, vol. XXVII.
[19] Lincoln, *Messages*, II, 506.
[20] George to DeWitt Clinton, January 26, George Clinton Papers; DeWitt to George Clinton, January 11, DeWitt Clinton Papers.

counties as New York, Westchester, Dutchess, Washington, Montgomery and, even, Rensselaer Counties were politically loyal to the Clintons.[21] There was now and again evidence that tenants were renouncing the political apron strings of their Federalist landlords and voting the Republican ticket.[22] When they did not quarrel among themselves the Republicans had a tremendous—a steam roller—majority.

Consequently the Republicans did about as they wished. They chartered a New York State Bank that was to be Republican in its control. They redistricted the state in 1802 in the hope of increasing their representation, and a year later they "equalized" the senatorial districts by transferring Montgomery County from the Western to the Eastern District—a piece of gerrymandering the efficacy of which Governor Clinton seriously doubted.[23] They very properly turned out Robert M'Clallen, the state treasurer appointed during Jay's administration, who was found to have defaulted to the extent of some $3,000. When General John Armstrong resigned from the United States Senate in February 1802, DeWitt Clinton was named to succeed him. But as the young senator did not relish the isolation of Washington nor the expense of maintaining two households, he persuaded his uncle in the fall of 1803 to make him mayor of New York. "Clinton is appointed mayor of the city of New York," wrote Senator Plumer of New Hampshire, "an office worth from eight to ten thousand dollars pr. annum, which he has accepted, & resigned his seat in the Senate. His absence will not be the subject of regret to a single member of the Senate. He is a man of violent passions, of a bitter vindictive spirit,—unfeeling—insolent—haughty—& rough in his manners." [24] The New York Republicans were able to make and replace United States senators at will; five men, all Republicans, represented New York at various times in the Senate of the eighth Congress.

No doubt the governor was glad to have DeWitt back in New York. That he was occasionally leaning heavily upon his capable nephew for

[21] *New York Assembly Journal*, January 25, February 2, 18, 1803; February 7, 1804.
[22] See a "Letter from Lansingburgh" in *American Citizen*, May 4, 1803.
[23] H. W. Tillotson to DeWitt Clinton, April 14, 1802 and George Clinton to DeWitt Clinton, February 25, 1803; DeWitt Clinton Papers.
[24] E. S. Brown, *William Plumer's Memorandum of Proceedings in the United States Senate* (New York, 1923), 26.

advice and guidance is evidenced by a letter that he wrote to DeWitt on the third of September, 1803: [25]

> You will have some Leisure before your departure for Congress. Will you employ a part of it in drafting a communication to the Legislature for the next session. Your knowledge of the present Situation of our Affairs will fournish you with Materials and from my former Communications you will be able to collect my sentiments on the different Subjects. I have been so long dealing in Speeches that I found it extremely difficult to draft one for the last session without committing Plagiarism. This I shall be able to avoid by getting outlines from you. It will be easy for me to make such Additions & Alterations as Circumstances may require.

The aging governor must have regretted that he had no son of his own with DeWitt's abilities and fondness for politics. His only son, George Washington Clinton, was the black sheep of the family—an ailing, bad-tempered ne'er-do-well. Discontented in Albany where his father had perforce moved after his election to the governorship, young Washington returned to New York City, visited at Philadelphia, returned to New York, and there planned a voyage to the East Indies. To the despair of his entire family he neglected his profession and his books, and made associations of the worst kind. After Washington's return from Philadelphia in 1802 John McKesson wrote of him to Genêt that, "Least some of his father's friends should attempt to impede his disgraceful carreer he has purchased a pair of Pistols which he threatens to use in defense of that Independence . . ." of which he is so tenacious. In referring to DeWitt's brother George Clinton Jr., John Wood paid his respects to both cousins by writing that "perhaps a greater simpleton is not to be found in the whole city of New York, if his cousin, the Governor's son, be excepted . . ." Dysentery and consumption notwithstanding he outlived his father and quarreled with the other heirs of the governor's estate.[26]

In spite of the factional quarrels of the last Clinton administration a few measures of a decided Republican character were carried out. In

[25] DeWitt Clinton Papers.
[26] John McKesson to E. C. Genêt, July 17, 1802, and Pierre Van Cortlandt, Jr. to Genêt, October 15, 1802, Genêt Papers; George to DeWitt Clinton, December 14, 1801, DeWitt Clinton Papers; John Wood, *Full Exposition of the Clintonian Faction,* 15; Genêt to M. B. Tallmadge, August 20, 1812, George Clinton Papers.

1804, for instance, the legislature passed over the veto of the council of revision a bill extending the elective franchise, a bill which the governor approved of in the main and which DeWitt Clinton favored whole-heartedly.[27] State finance became more conservative. The governor complained in his first message that the Federalists' resort to general taxation was unfortunate and unnecessary. By 1804 the so-called "state tax," introduced by the Federalists, had been virtually abandoned; expenditures had been sharply reduced; the state debt had been reduced by two or three hundred thousand dollars; and a few thousand dollars had been invested to the state's credit.[28] This rigorous financial policy was strikingly similar to that of Clinton's own administration of fifteen years earlier and also to the more recent measures of Secretary of the Treasury Gallatin at Washington. By and large, however, the New York Republicans showed but few evidences of constructive statesman-ship. The democratic idealism of George Clinton's earlier years had somehow been engulfed and lost in the muddy sea of political bickering and bartering.

By 1804 the state Republicans were even more firmly entrenched than they had been in 1801 when Clinton took office. Albany, Oneida, and Ontario and Genesee Counties were still represented by anti-Clinton delegations in the Assembly, but virtually all of the other counties, now including Columbia, were Republican. If the Assembly vote of February 1804 on the new council of revision is any indication, the administration forces outnumbered their opponents by more than five to one! [29] As far as New York was concerned the governor had every reason to be content. But there were other worlds to conquer. Clinton could not quite forget Washington.

[27] John Broome to DeWitt Clinton, Mar. 12, 1804; DeWitt Clinton Papers.
[28] Lincoln, *Messages*, II, 506; D. C. Sowers, *Financial History of New York*, 302–06, 324.
[29] Vote of February 7, 1804.

CHAPTER XXII

POUGHKEEPSIE AND WASHINGTON

GOVERNOR CLINTON did not want an eighth term. His health was poor; he was approaching sixty-five, and the governorship was too strenuous for a man of his years. Furthermore, he felt that his party, now at the zenith of its power, did not need his name on the ballot in order to carry the state. In arriving at his decision not to offer himself for renomination, however, he was ignoring the pleadings of his nephew who felt that no other candidate could be counted upon to keep the state out of the clutches of Burr. The governor warned DeWitt Clinton of his decision as early as November 1803,[1] pointing out that the cause of Republicanism was well established and that his health and comfort required his retirement. To persuade his uncle, DeWitt turned to the President of the United States. He wrote twice to Jefferson, mentioning the machinations of Burr, the certainty of his uncle's carrying the state by "an immense majority," and the possible disintegration of the party in New York should the old governor refuse a nomination. In spite of DeWitt Clinton's appeals, Jefferson refused

---

[1] Letter of November 16 in DeWitt Clinton Papers.

to interfere in the politics of the state and George Clinton stood obdurate.[2]

After three years' residence in Albany, Clinton was planning to return to Poughkeepsie to lead the life of a country gentleman—at least until something more alluring than another term as governor should offer itself. Poughkeepsie was the home of Gilbert Livingston, James Tallmadge Jr., and a number of other close friends of the Clintons; there the Clintons had lived from 1778 to 1783; and there or in neighboring communities the governor had from time to time invested in good mortgages and properties in land. In the fall of 1804 he was to subscribe rather generously toward the purchase of Baldwin's Hotel at Poughkeepsie so that it might be used as Republican headquarters.[3]

It was probably in the winter of 1804 that he purchased the house and property on the Hudson at the mouth of Jan Casper's Kill at Poughkeepsie, an estate that was to be his home for the rest of his life. The old stone house on the Casper's Kill estate, which the Clintons used from 1804 to 1806, was too small; and the governor wrote his son-in-law, Pierre Van Cortlandt Jr., in May 1804, that he intended to build a brick house about fifty feet long by forty-five wide. As soon as he was free of the governorship he joined his family at Casper's Kill and by midsummer the work was under way. In October he wrote the Genêts that although there was a lack of good "mechanicks," he hoped to finish the "works" that fall and commence the brickwork early in the spring. He needed especially a good laborer who could be trusted to drive his horses. He wished in 1805 to plant some fruit trees and build some sadly needed fences. There were delays in the building—the Vice President had a way of elaborating on his own plans as he got into the spirit of the project—and it was not until 1806 that the impatient family moved into the new house while the plastering was still under way.[4] Although the brick house has been described as a small one, George

[2] Henry Adams, *History of the United States* (9 vols., New York, 1891–1901), II, 173.
[3] Platt, *History of Poughkeepsie*, 83, 306.
[4] Several useful articles on Clinton's homes and properties in Poughkeepsie by Helen Wilkinson Reynolds appear in Dutchess County Historical Society *Year Book*, 1922, 1926, 1929. Clinton's letter of Oct. 19, 1804 to Genêt is in the Genêt Papers. See also Clinton to M. B. Tallmadge, Aug. 2, 1804, in New York Historical Society and Aug. 6, 1804, in Historical Society of Pennsylvania.

CLINTON POINT AT POUGHKEEPSIE

Home of George Clinton, 1805–1812

Washington Clinton told his father in 1811 that "our tax" of thirty-two dollars was the highest paid by anyone in Poughkeepsie. The place, which was made over before Clinton's death to his son Washington, was valued by the family at $20,000.[5]

When they came to Poughkeepsie the Clintons left Cornelia and Edmond Genêt at their home at Greenbush near Albany. George Clinton had bought the Greenbush house—built by Kiliaen Van Rensselaer about 1742 on the east bank of the Hudson some four miles below Albany—and had persuaded the Genêts to take it off his hands and move to Albany in 1802 to be near them at the new state capital. The house was a modest one; the estate comprised about six hundred acres. A few years later, but before Clinton's death, the Genêts left the Greenbush place and settled at Prospect Hill, a new home on the ridge to the eastward.[6] But when the old gentleman died in 1812, the Genêts still owed him $12,500 on the Greenbush farm.

The Clintons also left the Tallmadge family behind them at Albany. Matthias B. Tallmadge, the governor's son-in-law and man-of-affairs, made a tremendous hit with the old gentleman in 1804 by naming his new-born son after him. The governor was much concerned over the health of the mother, Betsy Tallmadge, and sent to Albany currant jelly, pickles, walnuts, and medicinal herbs for Betsy's use.[7] He constantly urged her to come to Caspar's Kill to visit and promised to supply her with a reliable pair of riding horses and to let her use his safe new boat. He wrote to her frequently during those autumnal years after Cornelia's death with a tenderness and a solicitude that he seldom revealed, even to his wife and children, in earlier periods of his life.

He also found time to write to "My dear good Boys," George Clinton Tallmadge and Charles William his younger brother. Sometimes the letters were in a playful vein as when the fond grandfather wrote from Washington to "Captain George Clinton Tallmadge," then four years old:

[5] Letter of December 1811 in George Clinton Papers, vol. XXXI; Memorandum of papers examined by the family of the late Vice President . . . July 17, 1812, in New York Historical Society.

[6] Helen W. Reynolds, *Dutch Houses in the Hudson Valley* (New York, 1929), 117–18, 166. See also Genêt Papers, Box 1802–1843.

[7] Letters of July 25, 28, and August 4, 1804, and April 15, 1805, Clinton to Tallmadge, Historical Society of Pennsylvania.

"My dear Sir,

Being informed by your aunt Maria that your Papa is gone to Pough-keepsie and consequently that the care of the Family has devolved upon you I cannot refrain expressing the confidence I feel in you, and that your Mama and every other member of it will find themselves safe and happy under your protection and patronage. Your Mama's delicate Health and the Tender age of your little Brother render them objects of your peculiar care and Tenderness. I need not remind a young Gentleman of your prudence of the necessity there is of having the Door shut and bolted, and the Fires well covered before you go to bed or at least to give directions to have these Things done.

Give my Love to your Mama and Aunt Maria kiss them and your little Brother for me—remember me also to your good Mamy

Yours very affectionately,

Geo. Clinton." [8]

Although George Clinton might see in 1804 that New York was most unlikely to revert to Federalism or Burrism, there were those in New York and out who hoped that a combination of those two factions might bring about the triumph of both. Federalist New England, impatient of Jefferson's ascendancy, was turning decisively and unmistakably toward secession. Scores of New England's leading statesmen approved and many more accepted the amazing project as inevitable. But New England was a small section. Its Federalist leaders felt that New York should be invited to join the new confederation and that that state, which had so little in common with the Virginia dynasty, might respond if properly approached. There was in New York only one outstanding political figure who might be counted upon to defeat a Clinton-Livingston candidate for governor and who might also be receptive to Federalist overtures. Burr's friends had for some months been supporting Federalist candidates [9] and Burr himself had been repudiated by the dominant wing of the Republicans. New England Federalists like Pickering and Griswold therefore looked to Burr as a rallying post for the forces of defection and consequently urged the New York Federalists to give him their ballots. In spite of the outspoken opposition of Hamilton, Burr was nominated both at Albany and at New York City

[8] Letter of Feb. 25, 1808; New York Historical Society.

[9] E.g., John Randolph to Monroe, June 15, 1803, James Monroe Papers, Library of Congress.

late in February and with the exception of a few leaders the New York Federalists gave him their support, "at the same time admitting to [their] own Honor and that of the Party that they considered him a man wholly Destitute of principle." [10] Hamilton told Rufus King that he feared Governor Clinton's decision to retire gave Burr a real chance of success.[11]

Hamilton would have preferred to nominate a thoroughgoing Federalist like King in the hope that the united Federalists could defeat the hopelessly divided Republican factions. Failing that, Hamilton was willing to throw his support to the first nominee of the Republicans, Chancellor Lansing, a conservative gentleman whose nomination aroused no real opposition from the Federalists and no enthusiasm from the Republicans. But a few days after the nomination, the Chancellor reconsidered and declined to stand. Three years later Lansing explained that shortly after he was nominated during an interview with Governor Clinton "an attempt was made by them [the Republicans] to induce me to pledge myself for a particular course of conduct in the administration of the government of the state," and that he had declined to make any pledges. He had been given to understand that he would be expected to defer to the political advice of DeWitt Clinton, Ambrose Spencer, and their associates. When this was denied in 1807 by the two Clintons and Spencer, Lansing added that George Clinton had suggested he make DeWitt chancellor of the state, a proposition which he was compelled to reject. DeWitt Clinton countered with the statement that the disposition of the chancellorship had never been mentioned during the Clinton-Lansing conversations.[12] However that may have been, Lansing withdrew and DeWitt Clinton speedily secured the nomination for Chief Justice Morgan Lewis, a son-in-law of Robert R. Livingston, who seemed likely to prove amenable to the Clintonian whips. This easy-going, respectable, but vain and scarcely distinguished individual, had been appointed attorney general by Governor Clinton in 1791; he had been elevated to the supreme court two years later and made chief justice in the Republican year,

[10] Morgan Lewis to DeWitt Clinton, April 4, 1804, DeWitt Clinton Papers.
[11] Letter of February 24, 1804, Hamilton, *Works*, Lodge, ed., VIII, 609; McMaster, *United States*, III, 51.
[12] Hammond, *New York*, I, 241-43.

1801. In 1803 he had been disappointed of the mayoralty of New York when DeWitt Clinton, choosing to doubt Lewis's good faith, had himself volunteered to assume the burdens of that office. Both of the Clintons distrusted the Livingstons and feared their approaching defection from Republicanism, but no better candidate than Morgan Lewis offered himself in 1804.[13]

The retiring governor at Albany watched the elections with much interest and with entire confidence. He did not agree with Hamilton that Burr could be elected. He first predicted Lewis would win by 4600 votes; late in April he told DeWitt that he would alter his opinion only to increase the majority; and early in May he suggested DeWitt inform his friends, particularly the President, that Lewis would be elected by a majority of about 8000 ballots. The actual margin of Aaron Burr's defeat was nearer to nine than to eight thousand, the most decisive defeat administered to any major contender for the New York governorship in its entire history up to that time. Traditionally strong in New York City, Burr carried that metropolis by a fair margin and the city of Albany by a few votes. Elsewhere there was no great enthusiasm for the anomalous Federalist-Burrite ticket.[14]

In view of Morgan Lewis's impressive majority, it is most unlikely that Hamilton's guarded and under-cover opposition to candidate Burr was responsible for his defeat. Hamilton's opposition to the adoption of Burr by the Federalists in 1804 brought on the famous duel at Weehawken, not because it kept Burr from the governorship, but simply because it was one more in the now considerable series of grievances between the two men. Burr shot Hamilton on July 11, 1804, about two months after the spring elections, and his victim died on July 12. "The malignant federalists or tories," wrote Burr, "and the imbittered Clintonians, unite in endeavoring to excite public sympathy in his favour and indignation against his antagonist." "Our most unprincipled Jacobins are the loudest in their lamentations for the death of General Hamilton . . ."[15]

[13] C. W. Spencer, "Morgan Lewis," *Dictionary of American Biography;* Bobbé, *DeWitt Clinton,* 97–99; George Clinton to DeWitt Clinton, September 17, 1803, DeWitt Clinton Papers.

[14] George Clinton to DeWitt Clinton, April 27, 1804, DeWitt Clinton Papers.

[15] Davis, *Burr,* II, 327.

Some time after the duel George Clinton told a United States Senator that New Yorkers "in the habit of approving duels" considered Hamilton to have been under no obligation to accept the challenge since (1) Burr did not name the exact time, place, or particular word of offense in his challenge, and since (2) so much time had elapsed between the time of the offending remarks and the challenge. Furthermore, the circumstance that Burr's intention to challenge Hamilton was known to others "induced many to consider it more an assassination than a duel." In this conversation with Senator Plumer, Clinton had no redeeming comments for Burr. He told Plumer, however, "that Hamilton was a great man—a great lawyer—a man of integrity—very ambitious—& was very anxious to effect that ruinous measure, *a consolidation of the States.*" [16] Clinton was still an Antifederalist.

Well might Clinton congratulate himself and his party on the unity of the "Republican interest" in state and nation. The Weehawken duel not only eliminated the most capable Federalist leader in the nation, but it also completed the political downfall of that equally troublesome free-lance, Aaron Burr. Opposition in New York to Republican domination seemed in 1804 to have melted away. At Washington Jefferson's reëlection was a certainty, and, to the great satisfaction of the Clintons, Burr would not attempt to stand for a second term as vice president.[17]

The adoption of the Twelfth Amendment to the Constitution of the United States early in 1804 changed the entire nature of the vice presidency. For by providing that the electors vote separately for candidates for president and for vice president, the Twelfth Amendment made the vice presidency a thing for politicians to barter. It would through the rest of its history be awarded by astute politicians to wavering states or to sections in return for votes. Although this lowering of the prestige of the office was most unfortunate, it was of course necessary in order to prevent a recurrence of the disgraceful Jefferson-Burr contest of 1800.

Generally speaking, the Twelfth Amendment was supported by the

[16] E. S. Brown ed., *William Plumer's Memorandum of Proceedings in the Senate,* 451–52.
[17] Burr mentioned his approaching retirement to Jefferson January 26, 1804; F. B. Sawvel, *Complete Anas of Thomas Jefferson* (New York, 1903), 224–25.

Republicans and opposed by the Federalists. DeWitt Clinton championed the measure in the United States Senate and quarreled violently with Senator Dayton's proposal that, to achieve the same end, the vice presidency itself be abolished. After passage by the United States Senate and House on December 2 and 8, 1803, only three states, Massachusetts, Connecticut, and Delaware, all notoriously Federalist, failed to ratify. In New York Governor Clinton called for ratification in his January message and the legislature responded in less than two weeks. Only fourteen assemblymen, most of whom represented the Federalist counties of Albany and Oneida, opposed ratification.[18]

George Clinton had one more reason than other men to favor the Twelfth Amendment. There was under the system of 1789 some danger that a Federalist who had the united support of his own party might snatch the vice presidency away from a somewhat divided Republican field, much as Jefferson had become vice president to the Federalist Adams in 1797. This Clinton did not wish to see happen for the practical reason that he himself expected to be the Republican candidate for vice president. He was now an old man—"the venerable Clinton"—and if the prize should this time slip through his fingers, it was clear that he would spend the rest of his days at Casper's Kill.

Through the medium of DeWitt Clinton a letter was obtained from the governor expressing his willingness to be nominated for vice president. The letter was read before the caucus of 108 Republican senators and representatives—excepting Burrites—who met at the Capitol in Washington on February 25; and the caucus gave the governor the hitherto elusive nomination by the convincing vote of 67 to 20 for the western candidate who was Breckenridge of Kentucky, and 21 for the remainder of the field.[19] Burr, who was reported as "intreaguing," received no votes. Jefferson was of course nominated by acclaim. A national Republican campaign committee was named consisting of one member from each state.

On only one front was there disharmony. Apparently the New

[18] *New York Assembly Journal*, February 9, 1804; Hatch, *Vice Presidency*, 5–9; Brown ed., *Plumer's Memorandum, passim*. DeWitt Clinton and Hamilton both advocated amending the Constitution as early as 1802; *American Citizen*, February 6, 1802; Hamilton, *Works*, Lodge, ed., VIII, 595.

[19] Levi Lincoln 9; Langdon 7; Gideon Granger 4; Senator Mackay, 1.

AARON BURR

From a painting by John Vanderlyn

England representatives felt that the Clinton nomination was being crammed down their throats and they attempted to adjourn the caucus. They finally gave way, however, and in March Granger was able to write to DeWitt Clinton that all New England was entirely agreed upon the vice presidential nominee. Indeed, he added, "I believe there is not an eastern man who did not consider his pretensions superior to those of any citizen in New England." [20]

The only doubt about the outcome of the election was the size of the Republican majority. That majority was as a matter of fact overwhelming, allowing the Federalists only 14 electoral votes, all in their old strongholds, Connecticut, Delaware, and Maryland, against 162 for the Jefferson-Clinton ticket. George Clinton must have felt that such a triumph had been indeed worth waiting for. It was a dramatic scene when the votes of the electors were opened in the old Senate chamber before crowded galleries on February 13 by an aspirant for their favors who was to find amid the parchments and seals not one vote cast in his favor. The vice president was indeed a pathetic figure. Generally neglected after the Weehawken duel by men of all parties he was, however, by the last weeks of his term of office more noticed than formerly, "whether from commiseration or from hatred to H——," George Clinton Junior would not attempt to say.[21] With striking "regularity and composure," Burr supervised the opening and counting of the ballots and then proclaimed Jefferson and Clinton to be duly chosen president and vice president of the United States.

Two weeks later, on March 2, this remarkable man made his final adieux to high public office. "This day I have witnessed one of the most affecting scenes of my life," Senator Samuel L. Mitchill wrote to his wife from Washington. At two o'clock the vice president rose unexpectedly to pronounce his farewell address. "He did not speak to them, perhaps, longer than twenty minutes or half an hour, but he did it with so much tenderness, knowledge, and concern that it wrought upon the sympathy of the Senators in a very uncommon manner . . . When Mr. Burr had concluded he descended from the chair, and in

[20] Granger to Clinton, March 27, DeWitt Clinton Papers. Hatch, *Vice Presidency*, 137–38; McMaster, *United States*, III, 187–88.
[21] Letter to DeWitt Clinton, February 20, 1805, DeWitt Clinton Papers. Cf. American Antiquarian Society, *Proceedings*, 1923 (Worcester, 1924), 134.

a dignified manner walked to the door, which resounded as he with some force shut it after him. On this the firmness and resolution of many of the Senators gave way, and they burst into tears. There was a solemn and silent weeping for perhaps five minutes. . . . Burr is one of the best officers that ever presided over a deliberative assembly." [22]

[22] "Dr. Mitchill's Letters from Washington: 1801–1813," in *Harper's Magazine,* vol. LVIII, 749–50.

CHAPTER XXIII

THE ELUSIVE PRESIDENCY

THE United States Senate of 1805, over which Vice President Clinton presided, was a tiny assemblage of thirty-four mediocrities. It had neither the distinguished membership, the prestige, nor the size of the House of Representatives. Its chamber was "much less superb" than that of the House. And although its presiding officer was the second in rank at Washington, he received what John Adams thought the much too modest sum of $5000 each year. The Senate was distinctly the second, or lower-ranking house, of the federal Congress.

It was unfortunate both for the venerable vice president and for the Senate itself, which needed an infusion of vitality, that the dashing Burr, with his outstanding abilities as a presiding officer, should have been succeeded by the prematurely aged Clinton. Clinton's seven years in the vice presidency did considerably less than nothing to enhance the old warrior's reputation, for by 1805 in his late sixties, he could make no claims to constructive statesmanship of a national variety or even to ordinary ability as a presiding officer.

Strangers found the president of the Senate of "a most grave, dignified and venerable appearance."[1] but they were not enthusiastic about his abilities as a chairman. A month after George Clinton first assumed the gavel Senator John Quincy Adams wrote his father that "we find great reason to regret the loss of our late President."[2] Some days later after having been crossed by the vice president on a point of order, he explained Clinton's deficiencies in more detail:[3]

Mr. Clinton is totally ignorant of all the most common forms of proceeding in Senate, and yet by the rules he is to decide every question of order without debate and without appeal. His judgment is neither quick nor strong: so there is no more dependence upon the correctness of his determinations from his understanding than from his experience. As the only duty of a Vice-President, under our Constitution, is to preside in Senate, it ought to be considered what his qualifications for that office are at his election. In this respect a worse choice than Mr. Clinton could scarcely have been made.

Giles told Adams that if Clinton's friends had sent him to Washington with a view to pushing him for the presidency, their expedient had been a most unfortunate one.[4]

Senator Plumer of New Hampshire was even more severe upon the vice president. "He is old, feeble & altogether uncapable of the duty of presiding in the Senate. He has no mind—no intellect—no memory—He forgets the question—mistakes it—& not infrequently declares a vote before its taken—& often forgets to do it after it is taken—Takes up new business while a question is depending."[5] Yet this same Plumer could also write of Clinton that:

". . . the more I see & know of this man the more highly he rises in my estimation. He is an old man—time has impaired his mental faculties as much as it has the powers of his body. He is too old for the office he now holds; little as are its duties. . . . And he assured me that the sitting three hours in the Chair at the time was extremely fatiguing to him. But there is something venerable in his appearance—There is that pleasing cheerful-

[1] American Historical Association, *Annual Report*, 1896, I, 928.
[2] J. Q. Adams, *Writings*, W. C. Ford ed., III, 133.
[3] J. Q. Adams, *Memoirs*, C. F. Adams ed. (12 vols., Philadelphia, 1874–77), I, 385.
[4] *Ibid.*, 449.
[5] Plumer, *Memorandum*, E. S. Brown ed., 634.

ness—that easy access—that flow of good humor—& docile manners, that are so seldom found in men of his age—& which renders him, to me, a very interesting companion. He appears honest." [6]

This genial old widower came always to Washington in his own carriage accompanied by one of his daughters and a servant. He took room and board "like a common member," maintaining no establishment of his own and attempting no entertaining. Never fond of Washington, he was always eager for the return to Poughkeepsie. He was frank to say that he preferred the landscape, manners, and institutions of New York and New England to those of Washington and the South.[7] All in all, it is difficult to understand why the old patriot should have been so ready to leave Casper's Kill for the Potomac. And even yet the Clinton family was not satisfied with the honors it had received.

George Clinton of course went to Washington for the inauguration. He left New York City on February 19,[8] and, arriving in Washington, put up at Stelle's Hotel close by the Capitol, joined the inaugural throng in the stuffy little Senate chamber, and listened to Jefferson mumble his second inaugural address. Aaron Burr was among the gallery crowd that watched Jefferson and his new vice president take the oath of office.[9] Although the first session of the Ninth Congress met on December 2, 1805, Clinton was not yet in Washington and Samuel Smith of Maryland was chosen president *pro tempore*. The vice president arrived in town a few days later, on the 11th, but seems not to have attended the sessions of the Senate until Monday, the 16th.[10]

It was not to be expected that he would play any very active part in the work of the session. By his casting vote the Senate postponed for about a year consideration of the bill to prohibit the slave trade after January, 1808.[11] When General Armstrong's nomination to conduct the Florida negotiation with Spain encountered anti-administration

[6] *Ibid.*, 450.

[7] J. Q. Adams, *Memoirs*, C. F. Adams ed., I, 373; Plumer, *Memorandum*, 348.

[8] Clinton to M. B. Tallmadge, New York, February 18, 1805; Historical Society of Pennsylvania.

[9] Adams, *loc. cit.*; *National Intelligencer*, March 6, 1805. For Stelle's Hotel see the *Records* of the Columbia Historical Society, vol. VII (Washington, D.C., 1904), 86–92.

[10] Plumer, *loc. cit.*; *Annals of Congress*, December 2, 16.

[11] There were varied alternative proposals before the Senate.

snags in the Senate, Clinton's casting vote saved Armstrong from rejection and the administration from some humiliation.[12] But once that vote had been given, the vice president informed the Senate he would soon leave Washington, not to return again during the session. He had not wished to take his seat at all during the term and although he had yielded, he felt by early March that he could be of no particular service at Washington. He wanted to get back to the new brick house on Casper's Kill. "My health is impairing for want of Exercise," he wrote to DeWitt Clinton in March.[18] Although he was in Washington for the opening of the second session of the Ninth Congress on December 1, 1806, we may well imagine that he begrudged the Senate every hour it kept him from the Hudson Valley.

It was during the winter of 1806–1807 that the vice president's youngest daughter, Maria, then twenty-one years old, became dangerously ill at Washington. For many weeks her condition was critical and for a time Clinton watched over her bedside day and night. This bedside duty must have been exhausting work for on one day at least, February 16, Clinton could not attend the Senate; whereupon that sympathetic body adjourned until the morrow. Maria Clinton was still ill and very weak in May.[14]

Clinton took only an occasional part in the bewildering politics of his state. The nearly fifteen-year-old alliance between Clintons and Livingstons was approaching a violent termination through the patronage quarrels of Governor Lewis and his council and through the governor's advocacy of the bill chartering the Merchants' Bank of New York, a Federalist bank that the Clinton Republicans were fighting tooth and nail. By 1807 the alliance of Federalists and of Livingston Republicans, known to the Clintons as "Quids," had swept the state and was tumbling the Clintonians, including Mayor DeWitt Clinton, out of their jobs. The years that followed saw a curious but scarcely significant see-sawing of Clinton and Livingston interests.

[12] American Historical Association, *Report*, 1913, II, 168; Henry Adams, *United States,* III, 153.
[18] DeWitt Clinton Papers. Date of letter is uncertain.
[14] J. Q. Adams, *Memoirs*, I, 457; letters of February 10, April 8 and May 12, George Clinton to DeWitt Clinton, DeWitt Clinton Papers.

To save the Clintonian faction from the possibly fatal consequences of the break in Republican ranks, some Clinton leader or leaders hit upon the questionable but plausible scheme for a reunion with the Burrites. According to Matthew L. Davis, Burr's friend and one of the chief participants in the skirmish, the author of the plan was none other than DeWitt Clinton, who nevertheless kept himself in the background ready for a strategic retreat.[15] The pipe of peace was first smoked at a famous meeting at Dyde's in New York on February 18, 1806, where postmaster Theodorus Bailey presided and represented the Clintonians. Seldom had a political meeting created so much interest and protest. The intent of the move was interpreted as designed to overthrow Governor Lewis, to rehabilitate Aaron Burr, or to make one of the Clintons president of the United States. Cheetham, who had roundly abused Burr for four years now spoke of "a union of honest men." If the meeting was a trial balloon, it soon showed that most of the Clintonians heartily regretted the move and they told DeWitt Clinton so in no uncertain terms. Even the old vice president wrote DeWitt from Washington a word of warning: "I am happy to hear of the predominance of the republican Interest, though I cannot say that it would add to my Pleasure if it resulted from the accession of the Burrites to the Party."[16]

It was promptly arranged to have the rapprochement with the Burrites repudiated. This was effectively done by a large Clintonian meeting on February 25 in Martling's Long Room and by an emphatic public letter of DeWitt Clinton's written on March 3. Meanwhile the vice president had explained at Washington that the meeting at Dyde's had been entirely accidental as far as Bailey had been concerned. It had, however, been carefully prepared by the Burrite chiefs "& while they were at their cups they pressed the good & unsuspecting Bayley to take the chair." Later Bailey had apologized for his attendance and acknowledged that he had been imposed upon.[17] Clinton was a long distance from the political intrigues of his native state

[15] M. L. Davis, *Letters of Marcus* (1806), 1–3.
[16] DeWitt Clinton Papers, Letters to, III, 60.
[17] Plumer, *Memorandum,* 450–51.

and not wishing to believe that his own faction had been so weak as to offer to compromise with Burr, he accepted the first explanation that came to hand, however lame.

Without allies the Clinton Republicans were badly routed in the elections of 1806. It was necessary for them to rebuild their political fences and recapture the governorship in 1807. It was not, however, easy to find a strong and at the same time reliable candidate for that office. DeWitt Clinton and Ambrose Spencer were too much involved in sordid practical politics to make acceptable candidates and this time they wanted no Livingston candidate. So, as in 1804, they turned to George Clinton, sounding him out as early as January 1807. We may imagine that they stressed, as they did in 1800 and 1801, the vital importance of his standing for the office in order to save the Republican cause. The old vice president, however, replied to DeWitt Clinton that he could not consider it. He had made a sacrifice in 1801; he had exercised the arduous duties of the office for three years although he had accepted it on the understanding that he might resign; and he wanted no part of the governorship in 1807.[18] In this Clinton was undoubtedly a better judge of his capacities than were his friends and nephew. He seems to have then used his influence to bring order out of the Republican chaos,[19] and to have persuaded the bewildered Clintonians to unite on the former Burrite, Judge Daniel D. Tompkins of the Supreme Court. Tompkins, "the farmer's son," who had no high family connections to his political discredit, won over Morgan Lewis, much to Clinton's delight. He wrote of the election from Washington that, "It is perfectly understood here as a struggle between the Old sound (whig) republican Party and the Federalists."[20]

The vice president watched Burr's activities in the West with indignant concern. Burr's charms had never ensnared Clinton. He did not doubt in late December of 1806 that Burr's plans were criminal in character although his reasons were vague enough. He could only suggest that Burr's preparations were too extensive for a land

[18] Letter of January 17, 1807, DeWitt Clinton Papers.
[19] "An Address to the People of the American States" (Washington, 1808), 6; [Baltimore] *Weekly Register,* H. Niles ed., August 8, 1812.
[20] To DeWitt Clinton, May 12, 1807, DeWitt Clinton Papers.

expedition. He approved emphatically of Jefferson's measures to check Burr and made every effort to coöperate with General Dearborn and the administration in getting intelligence of Burr's sources of men and money in New York. Both Federalism and "Quiddism" would, he felt, suffer through the failure of the Burr project.[21] Clinton had not seen Burr for over four years—since about the time the Clintonians undertook to drive him out of the party—but he seems to have cherished a rancor toward Burr more bitter than any similar relationship in his entire career. He told Plumer that he considered Burr "as having great talents—but as a designing, intriguing, dangerous man."[22]

Before his elevation to the vice presidency George Clinton had exerted himself on a number of occasions to avoid any semblance of a break with Jefferson. He had written certain of his messages to the legislature largely for Republican consumption at Washington; he had corresponded now and then with the President on such subjects as appointments and the safety of the port of New York; and he had, as we have seen, carefully countered the attempt of "Aristides" to sow discord between himself and Jefferson. But as the elections of 1808 approached, the vice president threw off all restraint and, in his personal correspondence at least, showed no hesitation in criticizing Jefferson and his administration. He complained of the appointment without his knowledge of a new naval agent at New York and he fumed over Jefferson's indiscreet suggestion that there was being agitated a plan to divide New York into two states—a plan that Clinton believed would be most welcome to Virginia as a means of lessening the importance of New York.[23] Clinton was also offended that, when Governor Morgan Lewis visited Washington, he received as much attention at the "Palace" as ever he himself had done. And he accused the executive of deliberately attempting to expose him to derision when he, overlooking the "confidential" tabs on certain messages sent to the Senate by the President, allowed them to be read before open galleries.[24] Most significant, however, was the vice president's attitude toward the Jeffersonian foreign policy.

When Jefferson retaliated for the outrageous attack on the frigate *Chesapeake* in 1807 by requiring all British warships to leave American waters, Clinton wrote him enthusiastically that Republicans and Federalists alike approved of his measures.[25] But the vice president wished the federal government to prepare definitely for war. Congress had consistently refused to fortify New York and Jefferson's only response in 1805 to Mayor DeWitt Clinton's appeal was a promise of a consignment of new gunboats for the defense of the port.[26] The vice president had no great faith in Jefferson's gunboats. "The Truth is that a Ship or any thing above a Gunboat is irksome to the Administration," Clinton wrote, "& yet the Gun Boat system will be useless indeed impracticable without some larger Vessels to act with & train Officers & others for them."[27] The drastic embargo act of December 1807 bore heavily upon New York's grain producers as well as on its great commercial interests, and it was perhaps to be expected that Clinton should privately condemn the measure. "The Embargo must bear hard on your City," he wrote to his nephew. "I regret it and was in hopes that the Bill for preserving the Peace and authority of Government within our Ports and harbours which long since passed the Senate would ere this have found its way through the other House. This Bill authorized fitting out all our Frigates & Vessells of War & would have afforded an Asylum for our Seamen who are thrown out of Employ by the Embargo & are now a Burthen to our Cities & Dupes to Federal Iintrigue . . ."[28] A month later he wrote indignantly of a pitiful appropriation of one million dollars to defend the entire coast. To add to his indignation, he was not consulted on matters of foreign policy.

He now thought war inevitable and negotiation of value only for

[24] J. Q. Adams, *Memoirs*, C. F. Adams ed., I, 516, 529.
[25] Letter of July 9, Jefferson Papers, Library of Congress.
[26] Jefferson to DeWitt Clinton, January 29, 1805, DeWitt Clinton Papers.
[27] George Clinton to DeWitt Clinton, January 12, 1808, DeWitt Clinton Papers.
[28] *Ibid*. Cf. Virginia D. Harrington, "New York and the Embargo," *Quarterly Journal of the New York State Historical Association*, April, 1927.

purposes of proscrastination until the country should be prepared.[29] To the despair of the Clintons, however, little or nothing was done to prepare. "It is in my opinion impossible," the vice president wrote on April 10, "that the Cause of republicanism can exist much longer under the present visionary Feeble and I might add corrupt Management of our National Affairs."[30] It is not difficult to understand why Jefferson felt that his old friend Clinton was estranging himself.

Although the anti-administration press, including the ubiquitous James Cheetham, continued its attack on the embargo, Governor Tompkins declared in its favor and by early summer even DeWitt Clinton had seen fit to abandon his opposition. There is no reason, however, to believe that the vice president ever gave the measure his outspoken approval and it was, on the other hand, generally understood that he was the presidential candidate of those who were hostile to it and to the other pacific features of the Jefferson-Madison foreign policy.

The presidential situation in 1808 was complicated by divisions among the Virginia Republicans themselves. Madison, the heir apparent of Jefferson, found a rival in Monroe whose British treaty, negotiated in 1805–06, had never been thought worthy by Secretary of State Madison of being sent to the Senate; and Monroe apparently had no objections to being groomed by such friends as John Randolph, L. W. Tazewell, and John Taylor.[31] Jefferson took pains, however, to declare his neutrality in the contest as between Madison and Monroe as well as between George Clinton and the two Virginians.[32]

In general the supporters of Monroe, who disliked the Madisonian policies, were also Clinton men.[33] Many of them proposed placing Clinton at the head of the ticket. As vice president, Clinton was in line for the elevation; his promotion would answer the petulant New Yorkers who accused Virginia of wanting to monopolize the presidency; and, again, Clinton was a very elderly man who might not

[29] DeWitt Clinton, February 23, DeWitt Clinton Papers.
[30] DeWitt Clinton Papers.
[31] Dictionary of American Biography, XIII, 89.
[32] Jefferson, Writings, P. L. Ford, ed., IX, 177.
[33] John Taylor was not a Clinton man. See his letter to Monroe, March 20, 1808, Library of Congress.

survive the term of office. Tazewell, for instance, favored putting Clinton at the head of the ticket to preserve party harmony among the states.[34] John Randolph came out for Clinton as early as 1807 but this, Dr. Mitchill observed to J. Q. Adams, was only another point against the vice president for "Randolph was so completely down that his support was enough to insure the old gentleman's defeat." [35] Possibly, as Henry Adams points out, Randolph was only using Clinton and Monroe as tools to defeat Madison, favoring each one in the sections where he was strong; but Randolph offered no other candidate.

In New York George Clinton's candidacy was openly discussed as early as June, 1807.[36] DeWitt Clinton made every effort to capitalize anti-administration sentiment for his uncle and a large group of New York congressmen including Mitchill, Josiah Masters, and George Clinton Jr., were urging his cause. Clinton had strength in certain other states including Pennsylvania, Maryland, and, of course, Virginia. Congressman Lyon of Vermont preferred a real democrat from New York to either of the Virginia country gentlemen. The Quaker congressman, Slocum of New Jersey, predicted in March that Clinton and Monroe would sweep the nation. Congressman Masters of New York told Genêt at about the same time that Monroe was gaining ground in Virginia and that it was well understood that he was to stand only for the vice presidency. There were, he thought, about fifty Republican congressmen and a few more Senators who wished to see Clinton and Monroe elected. Clinton should by all means be formally and quickly nominated.[37] He had considerable newspaper support, for not only did Cheetham's *Republican Watch-Tower* and *American Citizen* and the Clintonian *Albany Register* back him, but his candidacy was urged by the *Democratic Press* of Philadelphia and the *Washington Expositor*.[38] Citizen Genêt was among the most able of the pamphleteers who came to his assistance.

Naturally Virginia did not wish to relinquish the presidency. Legis-

[34] Tazewell to Monroe, October 8, 1808, Library of Congress.
[35] J. Q. Adams, *Memoirs*, I, 478.
[36] Randolph to Monroe, May 30, 1807, Library of Congress.
[37] Letter of March 29, 1808, Genêt Papers, Library of Congress.
[38] S. E. Morison, "First National Nominating Convention," *American Historical Review*, XVII, 746.

lative caucuses in Virginia met and nominated first Madison and then Monroe.[39] The Madison men, fully realizing their candidate's strength in the federal Congress, called a Republican caucus at the Capitol in Washington on January 23 which was attended by 89 members. This rump caucus, which was studiously ignored by about fifty Republicans of the Randolph school, placed Stephen Roe Bradley in the chair and promptly nominated Madison by 83 votes to 3 for Monroe and 3 for Clinton. Pope then recommended unanimity in the choice of a candidate for vice president, and the caucus responded half-heartedly with one vote for John Quincy Adams, 3 for Langdon, 5 for Dearborn, and 79 for Clinton. Madison and Clinton made a geographically logical but otherwise incongruous ticket.

The engineers of the caucus of January 23 had for good and sufficient reasons failed to consult the vice president or even to ask his consent to nominate him.[40] The absentees had included not only a number of anti-Madison Southerners but also most of the New York delegation that feared to offend the Clintons. Among the absentee New Yorkers was Dr. Mitchill, who admitted two days after the caucus that,[41]

I do not know what harm I could have done, either to him [Clinton] or the cause by going. But apprehending from the temper of some of the New-Yorkers that I should be blamed for having anything to do with the business at this time, I thought it prudent to stay at home. . . . Last evening I called to see Governor Clinton, and I am sensible he considers himself treated with great disrespect and cruelty by the gentlemen of his own party who acted at the caucus. But so it is, and it may be owing to his own self-complacency that he has been unable to discern what was as plain as daylight to every body else. I told him frankly he was the man of my preference. But really there does not appear the remotest probability of his success as President . . .

The situation was amusing. The indignant vice president would have none of the caucus or its work. On February 13 he wrote DeWitt that none of the members of the late caucus had called on him to ask whether he would consent to stand for the vice presidency. "They

[39] The Randolph "Quids" nominated Monroe on January 21.
[40] George Clinton to DeWitt Clinton, February 18, DeWitt Clinton Papers.
[41] "Dr. Mitchill's Letters from Washington: 1801–13," Harper's Magazine, LVIII, 752.

dare not speak to me on the subject; they find themselves much embarrassed & they shall remain so as long as I can be silent on the subject with propriety." [42] He apparently gave his full approval to the vitriolic attack on the caucus that was issued by Representative Joseph Clay and some other Congressmen under the suggestive title, "George Clinton's Legacy: The Pope vs. King Caucus." [43] The congressional caucus was to survive until the famous Adams-Clay-Crawford-Jackson scramble of 1825, which brought its short career as a method of nominating presidents to an abrupt end; but the performance of 1808 started the caucus on its downward path.

Finally Clinton made public a letter stating that he had never been consulted by the caucus either before or after the nomination, [44] and this forced the caucus to make advances. Its committee called on the vice president late in March and "received from him a tart, severe and puzzling reply to the message they delivered. They and their associates," Mitchill wrote, "are as much in a quandary as ever what to do with their nomination of him; . . . It is an awkward affair at this time." [45] By March Clinton's candidacy for the first office was generally known.

Whether or not Clinton's friends had any confidence that he would be elected president, they continued to agitate in his favor. They attacked the caucus itself as an unconstitutional measure that had no right to assume to name candidates for high office. Congressman Masters of New York had denied the right of Bradley of Vermont to call the caucus even before it met and Gray of Virginia supported Masters by denouncing midnight meetings designed to usurp the right of nomination. [46]

The Clinton men attempted to capitalize northern jealousies of Virginian domination of the presidency. Virginia naturally takes pride, they contended, in having given the nation a Washington and a Jefferson, but "this pride has stimulated the people of that state to believe

[42] DeWitt Clinton Papers.
[43] Dated February 27, 1808. A printed copy is in the New York Historical Society.
[44] Letter of March 5 in E. C. Genêt, *Communications on the Next Election*, 35, and in [Philadelphia] *United States Gazette*, March 8, 1808.
[45] "Dr. Mitchill's Letters," 753.
[46] McMaster, *United States*, III, 314-15.

that Virginia geese are all swans."[47] It was pointed out that in spite of his years Clinton had been regular in his attendance in the Senate and that his age had given him a wealth of experience. New York had a right to expect that the presidency would fall to Clinton as it had to Vice Presidents Adams and Jefferson.

That Clinton was not associated with the embargo was a decided element of strength in his candidacy. His son-in-law Genêt contributed letters to the *Albany Register* offering Clinton's candidacy as an escape from the "vain theories and suspicious schemes" that characterized the administration's foreign policy; for, according to Genêt, "the embargo is the undisputed property of a few southern systematic politicians."[48] Again, it was urged that Clinton was a thoroughgoing democrat whose views were those of the mass of the American yeomanry.[49] Matthew Lyon wrote enthusiastically of "the Vice-president, whose generosity is as it were proverbial, whose heart never fails to feel for the distressed, and whose hand never fails to extend relief to proper objects, [who] has not excelled in splendid dinners, balls, card parties, or squeeses at his house: he has lived in the same plain republican stile, which our beloved President did during his Vice-presidency."[50]

There were on the other hand a number of convincing reasons that, even his closest friends must have realized, put the presidency out of his reach. He was too old. It was clear that his powers were declining, that he was approaching "the imbecility of second childhood."[51] Even Cheetham called him the "venerable sage" and his enemies spoke of him as an "aged barque" who was "querulous, weak, and indecisive." He had had no experience with diplomacy and the times demanded a skilled diplomat at the helm of the state. He had few of the social assets that the presidency demanded. Dr. Mitchill summed up the objections to Clinton even before the caucus when he wrote to Mrs. Mitchill that,[52]

[47] "Nestor," *An Address to the People of the United States* (Washington, 1808), 5.
[48] The letters were subsequently printed in Genêt's pamphlet, *Communications on the Next Election for the President of the United States* (1808).
[49] *Ibid.*, 34.
[50] *An Address to the People of the American States* (Washington, 1808), 23.
[51] J. T. Danvers, *A Picture of a Republican Magistrate* (New York, 1808), 83.
[52] "Dr. Mitchill's Letters from Washington," 752.

Mr. Madison and Mr. Clinton are the two prominent characters talked
of to succeed [Jefferson]. The former gives dinners and makes generous
displays to the members. The latter lives snug at his lodgings, and keeps
aloof from such captivating exhibitions. The Secretary of State has a wife
to aid his pretensions. The Vice-President has nothing of female succor on
his side. In these two respects Mr. M. is going greatly ahead of him. Besides, people object to Mr. Clinton, his advanced age, and his want of
diplomatic knowledge and of the foreign relations of the country. Notwithstanding all his integrity, worth, and decision, I do not at present see
how we can assure his election to the Presidency.

Even more important than these considerations, George Clinton had
neither the support of the administration nor the combined support
of all of the anti-Madison factions. Some of Monroe's friends would
not consider Clinton for the head of the ticket; New England, which
heartily disliked Madison and his embargo, had no love for Clinton;[53] and, finally, Clinton failed to bag the Federalist nomination
which would have made him at least a major candidate.

It is not easy to imagine George Clinton running for office on a
Federalist ticket, but it nearly came to pass in 1808. In spite of the
increased strength that the embargo had given the Federalists, they
remained a hopeless minority in most of the states. Some of them had
proposed an alliance with the Monroe forces, but by April that project had been abandoned.[54] It was then only natural that they should
look to the Clintons. Among the Federalists George Cabot and Harrison Gray Otis of Massachusetts were enthusiastic over the plan for
an alliance with Clinton and were more than willing to make the
first move when early in June the prominent Philadelphia Federalist
Charles W. Hare wrote to Otis that it was essential Massachusetts and
Pennsylvania act together.[55] A Federalist legislative caucus promptly
suggested a meeting in New York and named a committee to correspond
with Federalists in other states. The result was what Professor Morison
has called the first national nominating convention in American history, a meeting of 25 to 30 Federalists from New Hampshire, Vermont,
Massachusetts, Connecticut, New York, Pennsylvania, Maryland, and

---

[53] Clinton's friends in April seem to have offered J. Q. Adams the post of Secretary of
State in return for his support. J. Q. Adams, *Memoirs*, I, 533.

[54] Morison, "First National Nominating Convention," 748.

[55] *Ibid.*, 748, 755.

South Carolina in New York during the latter half of August. The purpose of the meeting was to determine,

> Whether it shall be advisable for Us to have federal Candidates for President and Vice-President? If so, Who shall they be? If not, then, Shall the federal Electors, wherever they may happen to be chosen, vote for Clinton or for Madison? and lastly, Shall the Removal of the Seat of Government back to Philadelphia, be attempted? [56]

There were two principal reasons why the convention did not nominate George Clinton. First, the New York Federalists would have none of him. They knew too well that at heart George Clinton was no Federalist and they feared he would repudiate the alliance as his partisans repudiated Burr after the famous conciliation dinner at Dyde's.[57] Secondly, the Pennsylvania Republicans about August 1 came out strongly for Madison, making it evident that Clinton could not carry that state. Without Pennsylvania no coalition candidate could win. Faced, therefore, with inevitable defeat, the Federalists determined to nominate two staunch Federalists, C. C. Pinckney and Rufus King. A number of them, including Otis and, probably, Theophilus Parsons in Connecticut, worked on for Clinton, hoping that he would show unexpected strength before the electors cast their ballots.[58]

In New York the Livingstons, Lewisites and Burrites were supporting Madison, thus isolating the Clintons. Governor Tompkins, loyal as he was to the Clintons, saw no reason why New York should throw away its electoral vote in a lost cause, alienating the new federal administration. Apparently DeWitt Clinton's insistence finally won a compromise by which New York's electors gave thirteen votes to Madison and six to Clinton, the only presidential ballots that the vice president received. Madison's victory was decisive for he won 122 votes to 47 for the Federalist Pinckney.

Although certain Republicans such as John C. Calhoun warned that Clinton in the vice presidency would provide a dangerous rallying point for the malcontents of the party,[59] he made almost as clean a

[56] *Ibid.*, 751.
[57] Ibid., 757–58; Danvers, *Republican Magistrate*, 87; Fox, *Aristocracy*, 100.
[58] Morison, *loc. cit.*, 762.
[59] American Historical Association, *Annual Report*, 1899, II, 86–87.

sweep of the second office as Madison did of the first. The Federalist Rufus King received 47 votes, Langdon 3, Madison 3, Monroe 3, and Clinton 113, all of them from states west or south of New England.[60] This triumph, however, gave the vice president but little satisfaction.

[60] New York 13, New Jersey 8, Pennsylvania 20, Maryland 9, Virginia 24, North Carolina 11, South Carolina 10, Georgia 6, Kentucky 7, Tennessee 5. *Annals of Congress, Tenth Congress, Second Session, February 8, 1809, p. 1425.*

CHAPTER XXIV

THE SENATE MOURNS

CLINTON SNUBS PRESIDENT MADISON
THE VICE PRESIDENT IN THE OPPOSITION
HE FINISHES OFF THE UNITED STATES BANK
HE GIVES HIS REASONS
ENCROACHMENTS OF AGE
A FANCY FOR PEGGY O'NEALE
DEATH AT WASHINGTON
FAINT PRAISE FROM GOUVERNEUR MORRIS
GEORGE CLINTON RETURNS TO KINGSTON

CLINTON was in no haste to take the oath of office. Probably he preferred not to be present on March 4 when the man his friends had for months been busy vilifying took the president's oath from Chief Justice Marshall. Instead it was John Milledge of Georgia, the president *pro tempore* of the Senate since Clinton's "retirement" at the end of January, who led the Senators into the hall of the Representatives where James Madison, dressed patriotically in a suit of American-grown merino wool, took the oath and harangued the assembled notables, including his great patron of Monticello.[1] The vice president was still absent when the Senate adjourned without day three days later, but he was present and took his oath of office when the Senate convened on May 22. Procrastination in taking the oath seems to have characterized the early history of the vice presidency for in this regard Clin-

[1] *National Intelligencer,* March 6, 1809; *Annals of Congress,* Senate, January 30, March 4, 1809.

ton may be classed with his predecessor John Adams and with his successors, Elbridge Gerry, Daniel D. Tompkins, Martin Van Buren, William R. King, and Andrew Johnson.[2]

Stirring as were the times and significant as were the debates in those critical years when the nation was balancing on the brink of war, the stodgy little Senate of the eleventh and twelfth Congresses was not an inspiring one. Its personnel and influence were still much inferior to those of the House and there is no evidence that the aging New Yorker enjoyed his task of presiding over its labors. His health was poor and he was often absent from its sessions and from Washington. In 1809 he was troubled with an inflammation of the eyes that made letter writing, a favorite occupation, difficult. He was seriously ill in the winter of 1810,[3] absent during several periods that winter, and absent again for over a week at the end of the session in February and March a year later. Later in 1810 he was greatly affected by the loss of his daughter, Cornelia Genêt, who had been very dear to him.

In spite of his reticence and of an increasing indifference towards politics, the vice president seems to have been a rallying point for the opposition as Calhoun had predicted. Some years later Gallatin, always a critic of Clinton, wrote that he had known "the effect of having had . . . Mr. Clinton, then a decided opponent of the Administration, in 1808 to his death."[4] "From my experience both when Mr. Jefferson was made Vice-President and when, in 1808, Mr. Clinton was reëlected to the same office, I know that nothing can be more injurious to an Administration than to have in that office a man in hostility with that Administration . . ."[5] When Gallatin analyzed the "navy coalition," which early in 1809 supported a bill for enlarging the neglected navy, he found it included six of George Clinton's followers. Henry Adams pointed out that the Senate had an anti-administration cabal led by Giles of Virginia, which, if it could act with the Federalists, could control the Senate; and that to this group belonged the vice president, openly hostile, possessed of "strong quali-

---

[2] Robert W. Winston, *Andrew Johnson* (New York, 1928), 262.
[3] Draft letters in George Clinton Papers, Vol. XXX.
[4] Albert Gallatin, *Writings*, Henry Adams, ed. II, 298.
[5] *Ibid.*, 296.

ties," but, fortunately for the administration, too old for serious effort.[6]

Clinton felt that the party had repudiated him in denying him the presidency, and he believed himself free from all responsibility to that party. "They have wedded the Cause of Republicanism to the Measures of the Administration particularly the Embargo," he wrote to Anthony Lamb soon after the electors had cast their ballots, "and they [will sink] or swim together."[7] After Madison's election had become inevitable the not always charitable John Quincy Adams commented that:

If the Vice President and his *particular* friends have wavered a little more than they could justify to the sternest principles of patriotism upon the recent system of the present administration, the successful candidate and his friends should recollect the *peculiar* situation in which Mr. C. has been placed, and make allowances for the feelings of human nature.[8]

While the charitable historian may point out that Clinton's opposition was based upon sincere differences of policy as well as upon thwarted ambition, it is not easy to understand why, in the circumstances, he allowed himself to be reëlected to the vice presidency.

Vice presidents seldom have opportunities to make history. Perhaps the only stroke of prime importance for which Clinton was responsible in the seven years of his vice presidency was the *coup de grâce* that he dealt to the first United States Bank. Always distrustful of banks and bankers he was able in 1811 to destroy the nation's first national banking system which he believed to have been unconstitutionally created for the benefit of the privileged minority.

Clinton's views on banks were a strange mixture of convictions on the dangers of concentrated wealth with practical politics. He distrusted all of New York's first three incorporated banks, the Bank of New York, the Bank of Albany, and the Bank of Columbia at Hudson. But all three of those banks were controlled by the Federalists. On the other hand, when Aaron Burr established his Man-

[6] *United States*, IV, 428.
[7] Letter of January 8, 1809; George Clinton Papers. The words given above in brackets are illegible in the MS.
[8] Adams, *Writings*, W. C. Ford ed., III, 261.

hattan Company under Republican auspices in 1799, Clinton was quick
to see the need for such an institution which would extend credit to
loyal members of his own party. He even invested in a block of its
stock.[9] But he never whole-heartedly supported any other bank. He
threw all his influence against Swartwout's attempt to get a charter
for a new bank in New York City in 1803, informing that gentleman of his "uniform opposition to Banks as Great Evils in a Republic." At the same time he confided to DeWitt Clinton that he
would consider the granting of such a charter "as the death Warrant
of Republicanism in this State." And he could muster no enthusiasm
for the establishment by his Republican friends of a new state bank
at Albany in 1803—a stock jobbing project that succeeded.[10]

In casting his decisive ballot in the Senate against the United States
Bank it may possibly have occurred to him that the institution he was
destroying had been the creation of his once great rival, the first Secretary of the Treasury. But that vote was entirely consistent with his
convictions on the subject of banks.

Unless its charter should be renewed, the bank would expire in 1811.
It had operated successfully since 1791, but powerful interests were opposed to it. This was due in part to the rivalry of the now numerous
state banks, to the belief that its stock was held largely in England,
and to the personal unpopularity of its outstanding champion, Secretary of the Treasury Gallatin. It was perhaps not to be expected that
any measure championed by Gallatin would receive Clinton's approval,
and it was widely known that he did not approve.[11]

The votes which rejected the bill for the renewal of the bank charter
in the House of Representatives in January 1811 were chiefly Republican.[12] The proponents then renewed the attack by introducing a
similar bill in the Senate. The Federalists would support it as well
as a few Republicans led by William H. Crawford of Georgia. If
enough Republican apostates could be found, it would pass the Senate and the House might reconsider. But it was vigorously attacked

---

[9] Account book in George Clinton Papers.
[10] Correspondence between George and DeWitt Clinton in George Clinton Papers
and DeWitt Clinton Papers.
[11] Henry Adams, *United States*, V, 337.
[12] J. A. Stevens, *Albert Gallatin* (Boston, 1884), 263. The vote was 65 to 64.

by Henry Clay and even by such friends of the President as Giles of Virginia, Samuel Smith of Maryland, and Leib of Pennsylvania. When the decisive vote was taken on February 20, it was found that seven Federalists and ten Republicans favored it and seventeen Republicans opposed. The resulting tie gave Clinton an opportunity to exercise one of the eleven casting votes of his vice presidency.[13] Clinton not only gave his vote against the bank but he justified it in a brief address to the Senate, a course that only one vice president, John Adams, had previously followed and that on only one occasion.[14]

Sixteen years later Henry Clay stated that he had assisted the white-haired vice president in drafting the funeral oration of the bank that he delivered in the Senate on that twentieth day of February 1811. The Kentuckian did not, however, maintain that the speech was his own, and if the sentiments it contained were Clay's, they were also Clinton's own. "Mr. Clay," wrote J. Q. Adams in 1825, "said that he wrote the speech of Vice-President George Clinton which he delivered in Senate upon giving the casting vote against the renewal of the old Bank of the United States. He said it was perhaps the thing that had gained the old man more credit than anything else he ever did. He had written it, but under Mr. Clinton's dictation, and he never should think of claiming it as his composition."[15]

The reasons given by Clinton for his veto of the bank bill were those of a strict constructionist. Throughout his life he had opposed centralization in government whether at London or the provincial capital at New York or at Washington; and in his reiteration of his convictions on that subject he ran true to form. He admitted, however, that Congress might under certain conditions have power to establish a bank, but he did not believe that the Congress could constitutionally "create a body politic and corporate [as contemplated by this bill], not constituting a part of the Government, nor otherwise responsible to it by forfeiture of charter, and bestow on its members privileges, immunities and exemptions not recognized by the laws of the States,

---

[13] The casting vote had been used by Vice President Adams 29 times; by Jefferson 3 and by Burr 3. *American Historical Review*, April, 1915, 571.

[14] *Ibid.* There were only two other cases to 1915.

[15] J. Q. Adams, *Memoirs*, VII, 64. Cf. Hammond, *New York*, I, 290,n.

nor enjoyed by the citizens generally." He did not doubt that Congress could "pass all necessary and proper laws for carrying into execution the powers specifically granted to the Government . . . ; but in doing so, the means must be suited and subordinate to the end." The power of creating corporations, he contended, was not generally granted and was "not accessorial or derivative by implication, but primary and independent." He could not believe that this construction of the Constitution would to any degree defeat its purposes. "On the contrary," he stated, "it does appear to me, that the opposite exposition has an inevitable tendency to consolidation, and affords just and serious cause of alarm. In the course of a long life I have found that Government is not to be strengthened by an assumption of doubtful powers, but by a wise and energetic execution of those which are incontestable; the former never fails to produce suspicion and distrust, while the latter inspires respect and confidence." If greater powers are needed for the attainment of the objects of government, the Constitution may be amended.[16] Here was an excellent statement of the position Jefferson had taken in 1791 in refuting Hamilton's contention that the bank could be properly established upon the doctrine of implied powers.

Gallatin, resenting his defeat on the bank issue and urging his resignation upon the President, attributed the fall of the bank in a large measure to the dissatisfaction of "the Clinton party" at Madison's elevation over Clinton in 1809.[17] Clinton's action on the bank received other unflattering comments. His ancient enemy in politics, Rufus King, announced that since the bank was doomed, he was not sorry that the vice president had "given it its Death blow—it has brought him out & shewn him such as we know him to be." Trumbull wrote indignantly from London: "Since the death of the United States Bank, how many must join with us in admiring the name of Clinton!!! *by their works ye shall know them.*"[18] The defeat of the bank did not increase the popularity of either of the Clintons in the Federalist camp. Yet among the Republicans there was an outburst of approval.

[16] *Annals of Congress,* Eleventh Congress, Third Session, February 20, 1811, p. 346.
[17] Gallatin, *Writings,* Henry Adams, ed. II, 441.
[18] Rufus King, *Life and Correspondence,* C. R. King, ed. V, 241, 245.

George Clinton had been true to the time-honored principles of Republicanism. He had not forgotten in his age the democratic impulses of his youth. Van Buren felt that "a large majority of the people" fully approved of the vice president's course and he rejoiced that the bank "received its *quietus* by the glorious casting vote of a Northern man." [19]

However much acclaim his vote on the bank may have brought the old patriot, it became more and more evident that his political career was nearly over and that his nephew was the only Clinton who might expect to be president. In spite of the opposition of the Martling men, who heartily disliked both Clintons,[20] DeWitt Clinton captured the lieutenant governorship in 1811, filled the state hierarchy with his followers, and was generally considered the outstanding anti-Madisonian candidate for the presidency. With enough Federalist support he might indeed be president. But neither the Madison Republicans nor the opposition seriously considered nominating the gouty old vice president for the highest office or renominating him for the second.[21] On the contrary, the politicians were busily wrangling over the vice presidency months before the electors were to meet and even, according to Mrs. Dolly Madison, while its neglected incumbent was on his death bed. "The Vice-President," she wrote on March 27, "lies dangerously ill, and electioneering for his office goes on beyond description—the world seems to be running mad, what with one thing or another." [22]

Clinton must have realized that, entirely aside from political considerations, his age alone prevented his aspiring to more political honors. He did not carry his seventy years any too gracefully. He found the labor of traveling back and forth between Casper's Kill and Washington most fatiguing, although he attributed it "to the extreme badness of the Road between this and Washington." [23] And he showed

[19] Martin Van Buren, *Autobiography*, John C. Fitzpatrick, ed. (Washington, 1920), 411, 631. See also P. B. Porter to DeWitt Clinton, Washington, February 23, 1811; DeWitt Clinton Papers.
[20] Fox, *Aristocracy*, 175.
[21] American Antiquarian Society, *Proceedings 1923* (Worcester, 1924), 370; G. Mumford to George Clinton, January 1812, George Clinton Papers.
[22] Allen C. Clark, *Life and Letters of Dolly Madison* (Washington, D.C., 1914), 130.
[23] To Genêt, March 3, 1811, Genêt Papers, Box 1802–43.

signs of that second childhood which may invite consideration and affection in private life but which received little sympathy in public. Jefferson told Rush in 1811 that, "It is wonderful to me that old men should not be sensible that their minds keep pace with their bodies in the progress of decay. Our old revolutionary friend Clinton, for example, who was a hero, but never a man of mind, is wonderfully jealous on this head. He tells eternally the stories of his younger days to prove his memory, as if memory and reason were the same faculty." [24] The loquacious old vice president must have cut a pathetic figure in Dolly Madison's gay Washington.

Clinton arrived at Washington in time for the opening of the session on November 4, 1811. He found comfortable lodgings at Mr. O'Neale's,[25] where he took a grandfather's fancy to the landlord's little daughter Peggy, a charming girl whose marriage to Secretary Eaton of Jackson's cabinet was later to make history. He informed his son, the ailing Washington, to whom he wrote frequently, that his health was good. But the session bored him. He told Betsy that he grew "very Tired of Confinement and Fatigue," and since he could see no end to the Congress, he would soon leave Washington. As was his custom when he was actually in Washington, he attended the Senate's sessions with conscientious regularity during the winter months and it was not until March 23 that his health kept him away. "The Vice President being indisposed, the Senate adjourned." [26] The next day the vice president was still absent and William H. Crawford was made president *pro tempore*.

It was soon known that the old New Yorker was critically ill. He was in his seventy-third year and not likely to withstand "the general decay of Nature" and the ravages of pneumonia. His son-in-law, Pierre Van Cortlandt,[27] the son of General Van Cortlandt who had been so long Clinton's lieutenant governor, was fortunately at the time in Washington as a member of the House; and this Van Cortlandt seems to have attended the old man faithfully and unremittingly during

[24] Jefferson, *Writings*, P. L. Ford ed. (New York, 1898), IX, 327.
[25] *National Intelligencer*, April 21, 1812. O'Neale's hotel was near the present corner of Twentieth and H streets N.W.
[26] *Annals of Congress.*
[27] Husband of Clinton's eldest daughter, Catharine.

the last weeks.[28] The governor's long years of public service ended at nine on the morning of Monday, April 20, 1812.[29]

The old patriot received the highest honors from the state and nation that he had served so long. Senator Crawford in announcing his death to the Senate declared that, "by this afflictive dispensation of Divine Providence the Senate is deprived of a President rendered dear to each of its members by the dignity and impartiality with which he has so long presided over their deliberations; and the nation bereaved of one of the brightest luminaries of its glorious Revolution." [30] The Senate met on Tuesday only to arrange for the funeral.[31] It was determined that the chair of the president of the Senate should be shrouded in black for the remainder of the session and that each Senator should wear crepe on his left arm for thirty days. On the same day at half past two a body of cavalry escorted the remains of the late vice president from Mr. O'Neale's to the Capitol. At four the funeral procession, which included cavalry, the marine corps, the Congressional chaplains, the family, the President of the United States, the members of Congress, the Cabinet and other officers of government, moved slowly to the Congressional Cemetery on the east side of Washington where the burial took place in the presence of more people than had ever before assembled in the capital city.[32] Men had always been attracted by George Clinton's fine masculinity and rugged integrity, and there were probably few in the little city of Washington, whatever their politics, who did not feel that they were witnessing the passing of a heroic figure.

New York paid its respects to its late governor on May 19 when an imposing military and civil procession wended its way from the City Hall to the Presbyterian Church in Wall Street. Suitable as was the Calvinist environment, most inappropriate was the selection of the orator for the occasion, Gouverneur Morris. Morris, who had never shared Clinton's sturdy democratic faith, himself admitted that his

[28] The Clinton Papers show that he paid the expenses of the illness.
[29] National Intelligencer, April 21, 1812.
[30] Annals of Congress, Senate, April 20.
[31] April 30 the Senate resolved to pay the expenses of the funeral from its contingent fund. Annals of Congress.
[32] National Intelligencer, April 21, 23, 1812; [Baltimore] Weekly Register, April 25, 1812.

oration was but coldly and indifferently delivered.[33] It was unsuitable
enough that the man whose chief loyalties and endeavors had been
for his state should be buried in far-away Washington; it was pathetic
that his eulogy should be delivered by a man who had no desire to
eulogize him.

Ninety-six years later, in 1908, New York again paid its respects to
its first governor. The leaden casket and the modest monument with
its quaint medallion were removed from the Congressional Cemetery
on the Potomac and moved slowly in triumphal progress to New
York City and up Clinton's beloved Hudson to Kingston where General Clinton first took his oath of office as governor of the state. There
in the quaint old churchyard of the Dutch Church the monument still
stands, bearing the inscription

To the Memory of George Clinton
He was Born in the State of New York on the
26th July, 1739, and Died at the City of
Washington on the 20th April, 1812,
In the 73d Year of his Age.
He was a Soldier and Statesman of the
Revolution, Eminent in Council, Distinguished
In War. He Filled with unexampled Usefulness,
Purity and Ability, Among Many other High
Offices, those of Governor of his
Native State, and Vice President
of the United States.
While He lived, His Virtue, Wisdom, and Valor
Were the Pride, the Ornament and Security
Of his Country, and when He Died, He
Left an Illustrious Example of a
Well Spent Life, Worthy of all
Imitation.
This Monument is Affectionately
Dedicated by his Children.

[33] Gouverneur Morris, *Diary and Letters,* A. C. Morris, ed. (2 vols., New York, 1888),
II, 541.

BIBLIOGRAPHICAL NOTE

MANUSCRIPT SOURCES

Original letters to and from George Clinton and other manuscript material regarding his career are to be found in most of the larger manuscript collections in the United States. The greatest collection of George Clinton Papers is in the New York State Library at Albany. Because of the tragic State Library fire of 1911 which destroyed all but 10 volumes and some fragments out of an original total of 52 volumes, this collection is of infinitely less value than it might otherwise have been. Of the papers that have survived many are military and state papers already printed in the *Public Papers of George Clinton* and literally thousands are charred fragments legible only in the center of the page. Some of the papers have been restored. The destruction of so many of the papers in this collection has enhanced the value of the George Bancroft Calendar of Clinton Papers in the New York State Library, which is in the possession of the New York Public Library.

The New York Public Library also has some George Clinton letters scattered through several collections. Its Abraham Yates Jr. papers are invaluable to students of Antifederalism. Its copies of Gilbert Livingston's reports of the Poughkeepsie Convention supplement admirably the reporting of Francis Childs.

Some important George Clinton letters are in the New York Historical Society Library. This Library also has very valuable collections of papers of James Duane, John Jay, John Lamb, John McKesson and Robert G. Livingston, all of which proved useful in this study.

Among the collections of the Library of Congress that have been consulted are the extensive Continental Congress, Washington, Hamilton, Monroe, James Kent, Philip Schuyler and Genêt Papers, as well as a few letters of George Clinton and members of his family.

The Library of Columbia University has the great and very useful collection of DeWitt Clinton Papers.

The State Museum at Newburgh, New York, has a small collection of interesting Clinton letters.

A number of useful Clinton letters will be found in the Library of the Historical Society of Pennsylvania.

George Clinton papers and letters, or manuscript copies thereof, are also to be consulted in the Buffalo Historical Society, the Huntington Library at San Marino, California, the Massachusetts Historical Society, the William L. Clements Library at Ann Arbor, Michigan, and the Wisconsin Historical Society at Madison.

Clinton stated in 1799 that he had "had all his Papers destroyed at the Conflagration of the Town of Kingston whither they had been sent for safety . . ." ("Answer to Mr. Schoffield's Inquiries . . . respecting the Estate belonging to the late Sir Henry Clinton in the State of New York," William L. Clements Library). Clinton probably referred to the burning of Kingston by the British in 1777.

NEWSPAPERS

Very little information bearing directly upon George Clinton's career is to be found in the newspapers published before the end of the Revolution. From 1783 on, however, newspapers, especially in New York State, are essential to any study of Clinton's public career. Of the papers published in New York City most use has probably been made of the *American Citizen, Daily Advertiser, Evening Post, Herald, Independent Journal, Journal, Packet* and *Republican Watch-Tower.* Other useful papers in New York State include the Albany *Gazette,* the Hudson *Weekly Gazette,* and the Poughkeepsie *Country Journal.* Mention should also be made of the *Maryland Journal* and of the *Weekly Register* published at Baltimore, the *Independent Chronicle* published at Boston, the *Gazette of the United States* published both at New York and Philadelphia, and the *National Intelligencer* published at Washington.

OTHER PRINTED SOURCES

References to George Clinton will be found in a great many of the general and local histories and of the other sources covering the period from the outbreak of the Revolution to 1812. In compiling the following list of printed sources most useful for a study of Clinton's career I have omitted, because of limitations of space, such obvious ones as the

Journals of the Continental Congress, the Annals of Congress, civil lists, the journals or proceedings of the several New York provincial and state assemblies, conventions, congresses, and legislature, and, in general, statesmen's works, as well as many other primary and secondary sources, some of which contain more than passing references to George Clinton. It will be noted that many authorities mentioned in the footnotes are not listed here.

Anonymous. *Revolutionary Relics or Clinton Correspondence* (New York, 1842).

Beatty, Joseph M., Jr. "The English Ancestry of the Clintons of New York," *New York Genealogical and Biographical Record,* October 1935, Vol. 66 (1935), pp. 330–35.

Beatty, Joseph M., Jr. "Notes on the English Ancestry of George Clinton, First Governor of New York," *New York Genealogical and Biographical Record,* Vol. 52 (1920), pp. 360–62.

Bobbé, Dorothie. *DeWitt Clinton* (New York, 1933).

Brink, Benjamin Myer. "Governor George Clinton," a series of 20 articles on Clinton's life through the Revolution in *Olde Ulster,* vols. 4 and 5, 1908–09.

Burnett, Edmund C., ed. *Letters of Members of the Continental Congress* (8 vols., Washington, D.C., 1921–36).

Campbell, W. W. *Life and Writings of DeWitt Clinton* (New York, 1849).

Childs, Francis, printer. *Debates and Proceedings of the Constitutional Convention of New York, Poughkeepsie, June 17, 1788* (reprint, Poughkeepsie, 1905).

Clinton, Charles A. Article on the Clinton family in A. C. Niven, ed., *The Centennial Memorial: Hundredth Anniversary of the A. R. Presbyterian Church of Little Britain* (New York, 1859).

Clinton, George. *Public Papers of George Clinton, First Governor of New York . . . , published by the State of New York* (10 vols., New York and Albany, 1899–1914). [The introductory sketch of Clinton's life by Hugh Hastings, the then State Historian, is inaccurate.]

Cochran, Thomas C. *New York in the Confederation: An Economic Study* (University of Pennsylvania Press, 1932).

Corning, A. Elwood. *Washington at Temple Hill* (Newburgh, New York, 1932).

Danvers, J. T. *A Picture of a Republican Magistrate* (New York, 1808).

"Epaminondas" [pseud.]. "George Clinton," [Baltimore] *Weekly Register*, August 8, 1812.

Flick, Alexander C., ed. *History of the State of New York* (10 vols., New York, 1933–37).

Force, Peter, compiler. *American Archives* (9 vols., Washington, 1837–53).

Ford, Paul Leicester, ed. *Essays on the Constitution of the United States* (Brooklyn, 1892).

Fox, Dixon Ryan. *The Decline of Aristocracy in the Politics of New York* (New York, 1919).

Genêt, Edmond Charles. *Communications on the Next Election for the President of the United States* (1808).

Hamilton, Alexander, The Works of. Henry Cabot Lodge, ed. (12 vols., New York, 1904).

Hammond, Jabez Delano. *The History of Political Parties in the State of New York* (2 vols., Cooperstown, 1846).

Hasbrouck, Gilbert D. B. "Governor George Clinton," *Quarterly Journal of the New York State Historical Association*, July 1920, pp. 143–64.

Herring, Elbert. An Oration on the Death of George Clinton late Vice President of the United States of America delivered before the George Clinton Society on the 20th of May, 1812 (New York).

Hosack, David. *Memoir of DeWitt Clinton* (New York, 1829).

Jay, John. *Correspondence and Public Papers*, H. P. Johnston, ed. (4 vols., New York and London, 1890–93).

Jenkins, John Stilwell. *Lives of the Governors of the State of New York* (Auburn, New York, 1851).

Lincoln, Charles Zebina. *Messages from the Governors*, Volume II, 1777–1822 (Albany, 1909).

McBain, Howard Lee. *DeWitt Clinton and the Origin of the Spoils System in New York* (New York, 1907).

Miner, Clarence E. *The Ratification of the Federal Constitution by the State of New York* (New York, 1921).

Monaghan, Frank. "George Clinton," *Dictionary of American Biography* (20 vols., New York, 1928–36), IV, p. 226.

Monaghan, Frank. *John Jay: Defender of Liberty* (New York and Indianapolis, 1935).

Moore, Charles B. "Sketch of the Clinton Family," *New York*

Genealogical and Biographical Record, XII, pp. 195–98; XIII, pp. 5–10, 139, 173–80.

Nevins, Allan. *The American States during and after the Revolution 1775–1789* (New York, 1927).

Nickerson, Hoffman. *The Turning Point of the Revolution* (Boston, 1928).

Pound, Arthur. *Native Stock* (New York, 1931).

Prime, Ralph Earl. *George Clinton: some of his Colonial, Revolutionary and Post-Revolutionary Services*—An Address delivered before the Historical Society of Newburgh Bay and the Highlands, March 24, 1903.

Reynolds, Helen Wilkinson. Articles in Dutchess County Historical Society Year Book, Vol. VII (1922), pp. 37–79; Vol. X (1925), pp. 49–59; Vol. XI (1926), pp. 28–34; Vol. XVII (1932), pp. 70–79.

Ruttenber, Edward M. *History of the Town of New Windsor, Orange County, New York* (Newburgh, New York, 1911).

Ruttenber, Edward M. *Obstructions to the Navigation of Hudson's River* (Albany, 1860).

Spaulding, Ernest Wilder. *New York in the Critical Period 1783–1789* (New York, 1932).

Stone, William L. "George Clinton," *Magazine of American History,* June 1879, pp. 329–54.

Washington, George, *Writings.* John C. Fitzpatrick, ed. (vols., Washington, 1931–   ).

Weaks, Mabel C., and Victor H. Paltsits, compilers. *Calendar of Messages and Proclamations of General George Clinton, first Governor of the State of New York, August 1777 to September 1781* (New York Public Library, 1927).

Wood, John. *A Full Exposition of the Clintonian Faction* (1802).

INDEX

leaves Verplanck's Point, 78; Putnam and George Clinton retreat before, 81; message to Burgoyne, 82; in Hudson Valley, 83–84; fleet ascends Hudson, 128; estates of, 231

Clinton, James (grandfather of George Clinton), 4

Clinton, James (brother of George Clinton), 11; career and family, 7–8; owns slaves, 10; campaigns in French and Indian War, 15; becomes colonel, 45; aids in construction work, 57; in command at Fort Montgomery, 76; commands Fort Clinton, 77; wounded, 79; command under Sullivan, 127; on Sullivan's expedition, 129; refused commission, 137; sons of, 161; in Convention, 177; buys lands, 234

Clinton, Mrs. James, 132

Clinton, Maria (daughter of George Clinton), birth, 101; illness of, 282

Clinton, Martha Washington (daughter of George Clinton), born, 101

Clinton, Mary (daughter of James Clinton), 8

Clinton, William, 2–14

Clinton, as place name, 149

Clinton County, vote rejected, 203

Clinton family, ancestry, 1–6; lands in Ulster, 10; includes no Tories or Federalists, 109; moves to New York City, 160; friends placed in office, 258

Clinton, Fort, 58; taken by British, 79

Clinton Museum, 100

Clintonians, support Burr for Senate, 199; oppose Jay Treaty, 214; counties loyal to, 266; distrust Livingstons, 274; end of alliance with Livingstons, 282; proposed union with Burrites, 283; routed in 1806, 284; see also Antifederalists

"Clinton's Purchase," 152

Colden, Caldwallader, and Charles Clinton, 6, 14; acts as governor, 26–27; New York boundary, 143

Colden, Caldwallader Jr., rejected for Assembly, 21

Colden family, 25

Coleman, William, 259

Columbia College, 194

Columbia County, election of 1792, 204; Federalist, 265

Committee of Correspondence, 36; 40

Committee of Mechanics, 50

Committee of Safety, Clinton's resignation, 65; approves Polopel's Island plan, 66; plan for New Jersey expedition, 67

Committees, in New York, 44; 45

Conditional amendments, proposed for Constitution, 179–80

Confiscation Act, 110; 112

Congress (U.S.), welcomed to New York, 191; leaves New York, 196; in 1805, 279; caucus nominates Madison, 289

Congress (ship), 81

Constitution of New York, framing of, 87; proclaimed, 88; characterization of, 94

Constitution (Federal), 173; result of bad times, 162; depression makes possible, 167; Clinton's objections, 174–75; amendments, 174; Clinton criticizes, 179–80; ratified by New York, 181; forces favoring, 222; Twelfth Amendment, 275–76

Constitution, Fort, 66; burning of, 80; boom at, 105

Constitution Island, works at, 70

Continental Congress, 37, 43; delegates to, 38; delegates chosen for, 40–41; meets, 42; Clinton in, 48; asks appointment of officer, 52; approves Clinton's conduct, 85; requests Clinton fortify Highlands, 105; advances money, 115; deficient representation, 116–17; powers of, 119–20; Hartford Convention, 120; refuses James Clinton commission, 137; inactive regarding New Hampshire grants, 144–45; plan for New Hampshire Grants, 145; favors Vermont, 147; Indian Commissioners, 150–51; president visits Clinton, 161; invited to Kingston, 168; Clinton dislikes, 169

Continental money, depreciation of, 114

Convention (state), chooses delegates, 41; Clinton writes to, 55; calls out militia, 58; records of, 60; Clinton writes to, 63; and Clinton's resignation, 71; Clinton in, 86; chooses officers for state, 88; new state government, 93, 99; called to amend constitution, 256

Convention at Philadelphia, 171

Convention at Poughkeepsie, delay in calling, 175–76; chooses Clinton president, 178

Morris, General Lewis, 190; congratulates Clinton, 132
Morris, Richard, 186–87
Morris, Robert, appeals, 117
Morristown, mutiny near, 136
Mount Vernon, planting at, 160
Murderers' Creek, 66
Mutiny, in Pennsylvania line, 136

"Narrative of the Suppression . . . of the History . . . of John Adams," 261
Naval engagement, George Clinton in, 16–17
Negroes, 138
New England, supplies for, 122; defeats Clinton, 208; strengthens New York Federalism, 225; immigrants to New York, 245; politics of, 272; on Clinton nomination, 277; no love for Clinton, 292
New Hampshire, ratifies Federal Constitution, 181
New Hampshire Grants, 143ff.; claimants under New York titles, 143–44; Clinton offers New York titles, 144
New Hartford, 232
New Jersey, expedition into, 66–68
New Jersey Plan, 172
New Orleans, 265
New Rochelle, 61
New Windsor, 67; Clinton surveyor of, 19; Clinton's farm at, 32; Clinton returns to, 36; committee of observation, 47; Clinton's troops return to, 84; Clintons leave, 99; farm sold, 116; Clinton's mills at, 230
New York City, Clinton studies law in, 18–19; British enter, 62; Putnam wishes to attack, 103; Clinton advises against attack, 107; supplies for, 122; evacuation promised, 139; Clinton enters, 140; Clintons move to, 160; gives Clinton freedom of city, 160; doctors' riots, 164; cheers Federalist delegates, 177; celebrates Federal Constitution, 182–83; Clinton in 1789–90, 194–95; harbor fortifications, 213; revolt against Federalist rule, 219–20; dooms Federalism, 225; center of Burrism, 261; DeWitt Clinton mayor, 266
New York County, Committee, 37; Republicans carry in 1797, 219; in 1800, election, 237; carried by Republicans 1800, 239
New York Genesee Company, 152
New York State, conservative in 1775, 43; delays action on independence, 50–51; contribution to Washington's army, 60; Loyalists in, 110; condition of, 118; cedes western lands, 121; evacuation by British, 138–39; recognizes Vermont statehood, 148; ratification of Constitution, 176ff.; governorship of, 184; finances, 202; carries 1800 elections, 237; nadir of politics in, 250; captured from Federalists, 259; politics in, 282; plan to divide, 285; Congress refuses to fortify, 286; right to presidency, 291
New York State Bank, 266
Newburgh, headquarters of Washington, 139; Washington at, 231
Nicholson, Commodore James, 241, 263
Non-importation, 37
North Castle, 68
North, Lord, peace proposal, 130

Officers, system of choosing, 56
O'Neale, Peggy, 302
O'Neale's, at Washington, 302–03
Oneidas, 151
Otis, Harrison Gray, 292
Otsego County, vote rejected, 202; lands in, 234

Paine, Thomas, 260
Paper money in New York, 163–64
Parker, James, 27
Parsons, Samuel H., in New Jersey, 67; comments on fall of Fort Montgomery, 80; in the Highlands, 105
Parties, political, 222ff.; in 1792, 207; remain the same, 223
Patronage, federal, turned against Clinton, 253
Pawling, Levi, 41
Pearl Street, New York, 193
Peck, Jedediah, 222
Peekskill, militia at, 58; Clinton visits, 65; retreat from, 70
Pennsylvania, fails Clinton, 293
Phillips, Moses, 54
Phoenix (British ship), 58
Phoenix Fire Company, 230
Pickering, Colonel, 153, 272

Wyllys, John P., 80
Wynkoop, Dirck, 31
Wynkoop family, 31

Yates, Abraham, 65; and state constitution, 94
Yates, Peter W., 252

Yates, Robert, plan, 87; at Philadelphia, 171–172; letter to Clinton, 172; candidate for governor, 187; considered for governor, 199; candidate for governor 1795, 217
Yeomanry, supports Clinton, 188, 245
Yorktown, Battle of, 137
Young, Dr., 240